D0712714

GLEANINGS

OF

VIRGINIA HISTORY.

AN HISTORICAL AND GENEALOGICAL COLLECTION,
LARGELY FROM ORIGINAL SOURCES.

COMPILED AND PUBLISHED

BY

WILLIAM FLETCHER BOOGHER.

GENEALOGICAL PUBLISHING CO., INC.
BALTIMORE   1976

Originally Published
Washington, 1903

Reprinted
Genealogical Publishing Co., Inc.
Baltimore, 1965
Baltimore, 1976

Library of Congress Catalogue Card Number 64-20825
International Standard Book Number 0-8063-0048-5

Made in the United States of America

PREFACE.

DURING the course of researches into the family history of many individuals, extending over a period of several years, there was discovered by the compiler much original material relating to two most interesting periods of Virginia's history —the French and Indian War and the War of the Revolution. Little of this material has ever appeared in print, and the compiler feels it a duty to preserve to history the names of those who participated in the two wars mentioned.

The part played by the Colony and State of Virginia in both of these conflicts need not be detailed here. It is sufficient to say that many of her gallant sons were at Braddock's defeat and helped to save the remnant of the British regulars on their retreat; while in the Revolution they were at the front until the triumph of the American arms at Yorktown, in the siege of which there participated fully six thousand Virginia troops, both of the continental line and the militia, being over one-third of the troops engaged.

Two of the most useful documents in this book, for the student of family history, are the Poll Lists for the election of members to the House of Burgesses from Prince William county, in the year 1741, and from Fairfax county in 1744. The first of these counties, at the date named, comprised the territory embraced in the present Prince William county, together with the counties of Fairfax, Loudoun, and Fauquier. It was the first halting place in the march of emigration from lower Virginia westward to the Shenandoah Valley, and thus formed the gateway to what was then the western frontier. From 1744 to 1757 Fairfax county comprised the present county of that name and also the county of Loudoun.

The Rosters of Troops in the French and Indian Wars are taken from Hening's *Statutes of Virginia*, a work generally well known to the legal profession, but one with which the average person in search of family history is unacquainted. For this reason it is desirable that the lists referred to should be made readily accessible.

The original Muster and Pay Rolls of officers and men of the Revolution are in possession of the compiler and furnish the names of many persons not to be found elsewhere. Where matter previously printed is inserted in this work, special reference to the source will be found.

More or less complete genealogies of various Virginia families are also included, and it is hoped that they may be found useful to their thousands of descendants who are interested in their family histories.

Virginia has done and is still doing much to preserve the history of her people, but during his researches, the compiler has been impressed with the fact that not enough attention has been given to the rank and file of her pioneers, many of whose descendants to-day occupy the front ranks of American professional and business life. If this work shall be regarded as in any degree valuable in preserving to posterity the almost forgotten names of many of those whose loyalty and self-sacrifice made our Republic possible, the compiler shall feel repaid for his labor.

"The history of a nation is the history of its people."

WILLIAM F. BOOGHER.

Washington, D. C., April, 1903.

CONTENTS.

PART I.

HISTORICAL. FROM 1607 TO 1744.

PART II.

REVOLUTIONARY WAR RECORDS, 1775–1791.

PART III.

FAMILY HISTORY AND GENEALOGY.

EARLY TIMES IN VIRGINIA.

Settlement. The first settlement in Virginia was made at Jamestown, May 14th (May 24th, N. S.), 1607, by a party of 105* colonists sent out by the London Virginia Company. This company owned the territory until 1624–5, when it was dissolved, and the colony reverted to the crown.

Original Grant. In the Second Charter granted by King James, May 23, 1609, the limits and extent of the colony are pointed out. Section 6 provides: "We do also . . give, grant and confirm, unto the said treasurer and company . . all those lands, countries and territories . . . in that part of America called Virginia . . from Point Comfort, all along the Sea coast to the Northward two hundred miles, and from said Cape Comfort all along the Sea coast to the Southward two hundred miles, and all that space and circuit of land . . from Sea to sea, west and northwest; and also all the islands lying within one hundred miles along the coast of both seas."

Even after limits were more clearly defined, Virginia included all the territory now embraced within Virginia proper, West Virginia, a portion of Pennsylvania, all of Kentucky, Ohio, Indiana, Michigan, Illinois, Wisconsin, and a portion of Minnesota.

From this vast realm were detached in 1784 the Northwest

---

* Authorities differ as to this number. Howe, in Historical Collections of Va., says: "In the whole company there were but four carpenters, twelve laborers and fifty-four gentlemen," or 70 in all. Tyler, in "The Cradle of the Republic," copies names from Captain John Smith's History, viz: 6 members of council, 48 gentlemen, 4 carpenters, and 24 laborers; total, 82, with the remark, "with divers others to the number of one hundred." He says further: "The total number left at the Island on June 22, 1607, was 104." Howe says: "Newport sailed on the 15th of June [1607], leaving one hundred men in Virginia." We leave these disagreements to the doctors to harmonize.

territory; in 1792, Kentucky, and in 1863 what is now West
Virginia, leaving but 42,450 square miles as the present area
of the State.

Original Subdivisions into Shires or Counties. In 1634 the
country was divided into eight shires, which were to be gov-
erned as the shires in England. Names: James City, Henrico, Charles City, Elizabeth City, Warwick River, Warrosquyoake, Charles River, and Accawmack.

Of this number the names James City, Henrico, Charles
City, Elizabeth City, Warwick, and Accomack have been retained. In 1642–3, by Act 13 of the Assembly, the name
Accawmack was changed to Northampton. In 1672 the
limits were reduced by the formation of Accomack county
of the present time. By the same act the name of Charles
River was changed to York and Warwick River to county
of Warwick. Warrosquyoake was changed to Isle of Wight
in 1637.

Original Officers. In 1634 it was decreed that Lieutenants
were to be appointed the same as in England, who were to
take care in special manner of the war against the Indians.
Sheriffs were elected with same powers as in England; and
where need was, sergeants and bailiffs were chosen.

First Assembly. The first assembly held in Virginia convened on July 30, 1619, under orders from Sir George Yeardley, then governor, at Jamestown, called "James City." No
definite acts were made.

Early Records. Perhaps the most authentic record of these
early acts of legislation is the compilation known as "Hening's Statutes at Large," published from original sources in
1823. This compilation is a mine of legal and historic information respecting those early days. The orthography, com-
position and subject-matter reveal fully the body and spirit
of the times. We give a few specimens:

Primitive Acts and Regulations. The following extracts are
taken from laws passed at different times during colonial
days:

1. There shall be in every plantation, where the people use to meete for the worship of God, a house or roome sequestered for that purpose, and not to be for any temporal use whatsoever, and a place empaled in, sequested only to the buryal of the dead.

2. Whosoever shall absent himself from divine service any Sunday without an allowable excuse shall forfeite a pound of tobacco, and he that absenteth himself a month shall forfeit 50 lbs. of tobacco. . . .

3. That there be an uniformity in our Church as neere as may be to the canons in England, both in substance and circumstance, and that all persons yield redie obedience unto them under paine of Censure.

.   .   .   .

23. Every dwelling house shall be pallizaded in for defence against the Indians. [This act and the subsequent ones grew out of the condition of the country from the terrible massacre of March 22, 1622,* in which 347 men, women and children were slaughtered. The Indians came unarmed, "with fruits, fish, turkeys and venison to sell." But for the friendly act of a converted Indian, the slaughter would have been more extensive. . . .]

24. That no man go or send abroad without a sufficient party well armed.

25. That men go not to work in the ground without their arms (and a centinell upon them).

26. That the inhabitants go not aboard ships or upon any other occasions in such numbers as thereby to weaken and endanger the plantation.

27. That the commander of every plantation take care that there be sufficient of powder and ammunition within the plantation under his command, and their pieces fixt and their arms compleate.

28. That there be dew watch kept by night.

29. That no commander of any plantation do either himself

---

* Hening's Statutes give the date of this massacre as 1621 instead of 1622.

or suffer others to spend powder unnecessarily in drinking or entertainments, &c. (Passed March 1623–4.)

. . . . . .

A very wise regulation looking to the good of posterity was that contained in—

Act. 10. In every parrish Church within this colony shall be kept by the mynister a booke wherein shall be written the day and yeare of every christeninge, weddings and buriall. [Had this prudent and far-seeing enactment been observed by the churches of Virginia and the books preserved, the records of the State would to-day be the envy of the nation. They would, in fact, be a mine of inexpressible value.]

Act 11. Mynisters shall not give themselves to excesse in drinkinge, or riott, spendinge theire tyme idellye by day or night, playinge at dice, cards, or any other unlawfull game, but at all tymes convenient they shall heare or reade somewhat of the holy scriptures, or shall occupie themselves with some other honest study or exercise, alwayes doinge the things which shall apperteyne to honesty, and endeavour to profitt the church of God, alwayes havinge in mynd that they ought to excell all others in puritie of life, and should be examples to the people to live well and christianlie.

["Speak thou the things which become sound doctrine."— Paul to Titus. This act of the legislature of Virginia, while not so orthodox, perhaps, as the advice of the Apostle, contains much food for reflection. Portions of it might, with propriety, be commended to the churches of the present day. For this reason it is well, perhaps, to stir up their pure minds by way of remembrance.]

. . . . . .

Act. 51. All men that are fittinge to beare armes shall bring their pieces to the church; uppon payne of every offence, yf the mayster allow not thereof, to pay 2 lb. of tobacco, to be disposed by the church-wardens, who shall levy it by distresse, and the servants to be punished. . . .

Act 67. *It is ordered,* That the 22d. day of March be yearelie kept Holyday in commemoration of our deliverance

from the Indians at the bloodie massaker which happened
uppon the 22d. of March, 1621. [Passed February, 1631–2.]

Under laws passed in 1666, a fine of one hundred pounds
of tobacco was imposed upon any person who, without lawful
reason, neglected or refused to appear "upon the days of exercise and other times when required to attend upon the public
service." These "days of exercise" were occasions known
later as "muster days."

In 1682, the forts having been dismantled in the counties
of Henrico, New Kent, Rappahannock and Stafford, Companies of militia of 20 men each were organized under the
command of a captain and a corporal, whose duties were "to
command, lead, traine, conduct and exercise the said twenty
soldiers." The captain furnished his own supplies and was
allowed an annual salary of 8,000 pounds of tobacco, and the
corporal 3,000. Each soldier under similar conditions was
allowed 2,000 pounds.

The fine for neglect of an officer to attend muster was 500
pounds of tobacco; to go out on "range or scout," 1,000
pounds. The soldier was fined 100 pounds for not attending
muster, and 2,000 pounds for not going out on a scouting expedition.

Early Governors. As a matter of reference and a means
of fixing events, a list of the various governors to the close
of the 18th century is appended:

1st. UNDER THE VIRGINIA COMPANY.

Edw. M. Wingfield, President,	1607.
John Ratcliffe, "	1607–8.
Capt. John Smith, "	1608–09.
Sir George Percy, "	1609.
Thomas West, Lord de la Warr, Gov.,	1609–11.
Thomas Dale, High Marshall,	1611–16.
George Yeardley, Lieut.-Gov.,	1616–17.
Capt. Saml. Argall, Lieut.-Gov.,	1617–19.
Sir George Yeardley, Governor,	1619–21.
Francis Wyatt,	1621–25.

1st. UNDER THE CROWN.

Sir George Yeardley, Governor, 1626–27.
Francis West,   "   1627–28.
John Potts,   "   1628–29.
John Hervey,   "   1629–35.
John West,   "   1635.
John Hervey,   "   1635–39.
Francis Wyatt,   "   1639 41.
Sir Wm. Berkeley,   "   1641–45.
Richard Kemp, Lieut.-Gov.,   1645.
Sir Wm. Berkeley, Governor,   1645 52.

3d. UNDER COMMONWEALTH.

Richard Bennett, Governor,   1652–56.
Edward Digges,   "   1656–58.
Samuel Matthews   "   1658–60.

4th. UNDER THE CROWN.

Sir Wm. Berkeley, Governor,   1660–77.
Herbert Jeffries, Lieut.-Gov.,   1677.
Herbert Jeffries, Governor,   1677–78.
Henry Chicheley,   "   1678–79.
Lord Culpeper,   "   1679–80.
Henry Chicheley,   "   1680–84.
Lord Howard, Governor,   1684–89.
Nathaniel Bacon, Lieut.-Gov.,   1689 90.
Francis Nicholson, Lieut.-Gov., 1690–92.
Sir Edmond Andros, Governor, 1692–98.
Fran. Nicholson,   "   1698–1704.
The Earl of Orkney,   "   1704–05.
Edward Nott, Lieut.-Gov.,   1705–06.
Edward Jennings, Lieut.-Gov., 1706–10.
Robert Hunter,   "   1710.
Alex. Spotswood,   "   1710–22.

Hugh Drysdale, Lieut.-Governor, 1722–26.
Robert Carter,   "   1726–27.
William Gooch,   "   1727–49.
John Robinson, Sr.,   "   1749.
Lord Albemarle, Governor, 1749–50.
Louis Burwell, Lieut.-Governor, 1750–52.
Robert Dinwiddie,   "   1752–58.
John Blair,   "   1758.
Francis Fauquier, Governor, 1758–68.
John Blair, Lieut.-Governor, 1768.
Norborne Berkeley, Governor, 1768–70.
William Nelson, Lieut.-Governor, 1770–72.
Lord Dunmore, Governor, 1772–76.

5TH. IN THE REVOLUTION.

Patrick Henry, Governor, 1776–79.
Thomas Jefferson, " 1779–81.
Thomas Nelson, " 1781.
Benjamin Harrison, 1781–84.
Patrick Henry, { Under articles of } 1784–86.
Edmund Randolph, { Confederation. } 1786–88.

6TH. UNDER THE U. S. CONSTITUTION.

Beverly Randolph, Governor, 1788–91.
Henry Lee,   "   1791–94.
Robert Brooke,   "   1794–96.
James Wood,   "   1796–99.
James Munroe,   "   1799 1802.

IMMIGRANT LIST, 1707.

THE following persons shipped at Bristol, England, with James Gaugh, captain and owner of the ship Joseph and Thomas, and received their wages as boat hands (Liber Z, folio 422, Aug. 2, 1707, Stafford County):

Abraham Loyd,	John Wall,
James Ginning,	Arthor Marly,
Thomas Jones,	Thomas Calmers,
Robert Goalfold,	William Johnson,
William Shough,	Ellis Giles,
David Vaughn,	William Roach,
William Harmous,	William Adams,
William Price,	Thomas Parris,
Lewis Johns,	George Paines.

From the records it is not certain that any of these persons remained in Virginia, but from the similarity of names found in the western portion of Stafford county, and after 1730 in Prince William, it is believed a good portion of them settled in Virginia, whose descendants are now scattered throughout the South and West.

FRENCH AND INDIAN WAR—LORD DUNMORE'S WAR.

Interesting Study in American History. One of the subjects of thrilling interest in American history is the struggle between the French and the English for possession of the great valley connecting the Great Lakes and the mouth of the Mississippi river.

English Claims. The English discoveries and occupations embraced belts of territory along the Atlantic coast, and were supposed to include all territory between certain parallels from the Atlantic to the Pacific.

French Settlements and Claims. The French had not been successful in securing footholds along the Atlantic, within the bounds of the present United States, but had secured possessions farther north around the mouth of the St. Lawrence. French Catholics, too, had discovered the mouth of the Mississippi river, and ascended that stream, laying claim, under the law of nations, to all the territory drained by it and its tributaries.

This claim, if acknowledged, would cut the vast continent into two unequal divisions, giving to the English the string of a bow along the Atlantic, while the French took the bow from one end, at the mouth of the Mississippi, up that stream to the mouth of the Ohio, and thence up that stream, with its tributaries, the Alleghany and French creeks, to Lake Erie, and finally across the lakes to the mouth of the St. Lawrence, the other end of the bow.

If this theory of national rights could be maintained, it would plainly secure, as subsequent events have developed, not only the great bow already described, but the rich game in front, together with all the wealth to be developed in the path along which civilization has since spread.

Line of Forts between the Lakes and the Mississippi. The manifest policy of the French, then, was to secure possession of these rich territorial tracts by a line of forts and other means of protection from the Great Lakes to the Mississippi. Accordingly, these preliminary steps were taken, and then began the game of chess between two mighty European rival nations for the rich prize at stake. Of Napoleon, at a later date, Byron wrote—

> "Whose game was empires and whose stakes were thrones;
> Whose table earth; whose dice were human bones."

We repeat, this problem is one of the most interesting studies to the intelligent reader, and presents the key-note to the proper and easy understanding of those gigantic struggles which, for a time, involved the stability and supremacy of European governments, as well as the growth and prosperity of American settlements.

Origin of the War. As a result of three years' controversy between commissioners appointed under the Treaty of Aix-la-Chapelle (1748) to settle the question of boundaries in America between France and England, what is known in America as the "French and Indian War"—in Europe as the "Seven Years' War"—was waged.

Conflicting Territorial Claims. From 1750 to 1753 these commissioners at Paris wrangled over the matter. By the Treaty of Utrecht (April 11, 1713) Acadia was an English possession. But what did Acadia embrace? According to the English commissioners, it included not only the peninsula of Nova Scotia, but the entire tract between the St. Lawrence river on the north, the gulf of the same name on the east, the Atlantic on the south, and New England on the west.

The French conceded only about one-twentieth of this territory, viz., not even all the Acadian peninsula, but only a part of its southern coast and an adjacent belt of barren wilderness. Formerly the French claim was quite as extensive as that now made by the English; but conditions having changed, their contention was changed.

Bienville's Expedition in 1749. Nor was Acadia the only ground of contention. In the prosecution of the deep-laid scheme of the French, Celeron de Bienville had been sent in 1749 by Galissoniere, the governor of Canada, into the Ohio valley with "a suitable escort of whites and savages to take formal possession of the valley in the name of the King of France, to propitiate the Indians, and in all ways short of actual warfare to thwart the English plans." Bienville made a detailed report at Montreal, whither he had returned, but it was not favorable to his lordship. The English were swarming in the valley and had succeeded in securing the Indians as allies.

Marquis Duquesne Succeeds Galissoniere. Within a few years

Galissoniere was succeeded by the Marquis Duquesne. The latter, discovering the trend of events and being a man of action, decided to take immediate steps. Early in 1753 he sent a strong force by Lake Ontario and Niagara to seize and hold the northeastern branches of the Ohio river. Passing over the portage between Presque Isle and French creek, it constructed Forts Le Boeuf and Venango.

Washington's Mission under Gov. Dinwiddie in 1753. Late in the same year (11th of December) a messenger from Governor Dinwiddie * arrived. This messenger was Major George Washington, Adjutant-General of the Virginia militia, then in the 22d year of his age. His guide was Christopher Gist, who was well acquainted with the route and thoroughly competent to perform his task. The burden of this embassy was to inform the French commander at Le Boeuf that he was building his fort on English territory and to suggest that he would do well to depart. After three days, which Washington employed usefully in making observations, he received a reply. This he returned to Gov. Dinwiddie, reaching Williamsburg on the 16th of January, 1754, after a journey of nearly 600 miles over "lofty and rugged mountains and through the heart of a wilderness."

Washington to Build a Fort at Forks of the Ohio. Gov. Dinwiddie drafted 200 men from the Virginia militia and placed them under the direction of Washington, with instructions to build a fort at the forks of the Ohio. The Virginia Assembly,

* Robert Dinwiddie was born in Scotland, 1690, and died in Clifton, England, Aug. 1, 1770. While clerking in the customs department, he detected his principal in the perpetration of gross frauds on the government. For his services in this exposure he was made surveyor of customs for the Colonies, and shortly thereafter lieutenant-governor of Virginia.

He reached Virginia in 1752, and in the following December he submitted to the Board of Trade an elaborate report favoring the annexation of the Ohio Valley; hence his sending of Washington to Fort Le Boeuf. Subsequent to Washington's defeat at Fort Necessity, an alienation between the governor and his field marshal existed.

He was recalled to England in 1758, leaving in dispute an unsettled account of £20,000.

forgetting temporarily its controversy with the governor, voted
£10,000 to be expended for the purpose, but only under the
direction of a committee of its own members.

Want of Co-operation with Dinwiddie.   Dinwiddie found
difficulty in securing co-operation from the other colonies in
this enterprise.   The attitude of the Quaker element in Pennsylvania prevented that colony from giving the aid it might
have furnished.   Some backwoodsmen finally pushed across
the mountains and began the construction of the projected
work.   These, however, were driven away by a superior
French force, and the latter immediately began the construction of Fort Duquesne on the site now occupied by Pittsburg
at the confluence of the Allegheny and the Monongahela
rivers.

*Military Expedition to Forks of Ohio in 1754—Great Meadows
and Death of French Commander.*   Gov. Dinwiddie was engaged, meanwhile, in organizing a regiment of militia, under
Colonel Joshua Fry, with Washington second in command,
to support the backwoodsmen in their work.   Washington
had advanced with a portion of the command to Will's Creek,
now Cumberland, Md.; and later, with 150 men, he reached
Great Meadows, where he learned that the French had been
reinforced and were sending out a party against him.   Through
the assistance of an Indian, Half-King, who had the previous
year been with him on the expedition to Fort Le Boeuf,
Washington learned that the French, under Jumonville,
were in lurking for him.   With this assistance the French
were defeated and their leader killed.

Fort Necessity Built—Washington's Surrender.   While wait-
ing for reinforcements under Colonel Fry, Washington threw
up imperfect intrenchments at Great Meadows and called
them Fort Necessity.   Finally, Fry's men, some 300, arrived
without their leader, he having died on the journey.   With
this force, increased later by a company of South Carolina
troops, Washington was attacked, July 3, 1754, by a greatly
superior body.   From eleven in the morning to eight at night

he held his ground. Then surrendering with the honors of war, he led his troops back to Will's Creek and abandoned the Ohio Valley to the French.

A roster of the troops commanded by Washington in the Battle of the Big Meadows, in 1754, including 263 men, wounded 43 and killed 12, can be found in the Virginia Magazine of History, Vol. I, pp. 278–284. The original rolls are on file in the War Department in Washington.

English Resist Encroachments. Notwithstanding peace by treaty existed between France and England, every precaution was taken by the latter country to repel encroachments on the frontier, but not to invade Canada. Accordingly, all movements were made with these purposes in view.

Arrival of General Braddock in America. On the 20th of February, 1755, there landed at Hampton, Va., for co-operation with the colonies against the French in a war soon to break out in all its fierceness, two regiments of British regulars, under command of General Braddock,* the newly-chosen commander-in-chief of English forces in America. These troops were then transferred to Alexandria, Va., to which point all the Virginia levies were directed to repair.

Conference at Alexandria. On the 14th of April he held, at Alexandria, with Commodore Keppel, a conference, at which

---

* Edward Braddock was born in Perthshire, Scotland, in 1695 and died near what is now Pittsburg, Pa., July 13, 1755.

He had had forty years' experience in military operations and had attained the rank of Major-General.

He was thoroughly skilled in the science of war, as developed in the text-books and practiced among civilized nations. He was "proud, prejudiced and conceited;" or, as Walpole puts it, "a very Iroquois in disposition."

He resented all suggestions that might have aided him in his great expedition. To Benjamin Franklin's intimation that if he could reach Fort Duquesne he could doubtless capture it without much difficulty, but that the long, slender line his army would have to make "would be cut like thread into several pieces" by the hostile Indians, his reply was a "smile at his ignorance." He declared further that "these savages may indeed be a formidable enemy to raw American military, but upon the king's regular and disciplined troops, sir, it is impossible they should make an impression."

were present the following governors: William Shirley,* of Massachusetts, Delancey,† of New York, Morris,‡ of Pennsylvania, Sharpe,§ of Maryland, and Dinwiddie, of Virginia.

Four Expeditions Planned. To accomplish the purpose for which he was sent to America, Braddock projected four dis-

---

* William Shirley was born in Preston, England, in 1693. Having become a lawyer, he settled in Boston in 1734. He was royal governor of Massachusetts 1741–5; planned a successful expedition against Cape Breton in 1745; lived in England 1745–53; returned to Massachusetts, as governor, in 1753; treated with Indians, 1754; was commander-in-chief of British forces in North America at commencement of French and Indian War; appointed lieutenant-general in 1759; became subsequently governor of Bahama Islands; died at his residence in Roxbury, Mass., in March, 1771.

† James De Lancey was born in New York City, Nov. 27, 1703, and died there July 30, 1760. He was graduated at Cambridge, England, and subsequently studied law in the Inner Temple, London. He returned to New York in 1725 and soon became prominent in public life. He drafted, in 1730, a new charter for New York City, and in recognition was granted the freedom of the city, this being the first bestowment of such an honor. In 1733 he was appointed chief-justice of New York, and retained the position during the remainder of his life.

He convened and presided over, June 19, 1754, the first Congress ever held, in Augusta. At its session Benjamin Franklin proposed a plan for the union of all the colonies, by act of Parliament, against the Indians.

He, as governor, granted the charter of King's (now Columbia) College, Oct. 31, 1754. The next spring he attended the conference of colonial governors at Alexandria.

He was a man of great learning and unusual personal influence.

‡ Robert Hunter Morris was lieutenant-governor of Pennsylvania from October, 1754, to August, 1756. For twenty-six years he acted as one of the council of New Jersey, and for a period served as chief-justice, resigning in 1757, seven years prior to his death, which occurred February 20, 1764.

He responded to General Braddock's invitation to the Alexandria Conference.

§ Horatio Sharpe, whose position as proprietory governor of Maryland from 1753 to 1769 made him a conspicuous figure in colonial times, came from London in the ship *Molly*, commanded by Captain Nicholas Coxen, and arrived at Annapolis on the 11th of August, 1753.

On February 4, 1754, he visited Baltimore town to study his people, and was received by the citizens with wild demonstrations of satisfaction.

In July of the same year he was commissioned lieutenant-colonel in the British army. He was one of the counsellors with Braddock at the conference in Alexandria.

tinct expeditions: Lawrence,* lieutenant-governor of Nova Scotia, was to secure the right of England in that region; Johnson, of New York, was to enroll the Mohawk Indians and lead them against Crown Point; Shirley agreed to drive the French from Niagara; and Braddock, commander-in-chief, reserved the honor of recovering the Ohio Valley.

Expedition against Acadia. In the execution of this program Lawrence, with the advice and consent of his counsellors, decided to remove and disperse the entire French population of Acadia (or Nova Scotia) among the English colonies of North America. Colonel John Winslow, commander of the New England forces, known for the firmness, but humaneness of his character, was intrusted with the practical execution of this project. The purpose was to take those of the same neighborhood and, without severing family ties, plant them in a new station. In the execution of the scheme some 6,000 persons, men, women and children, were deported. The first embarkation occurred October 8, 1755.

Story of Evangeline. In the story of Evangeline, Longfellow represents these Acadians as a peaceful, simple-hearted people, and their houses as picturesque, vine-clad, strongly-built cottages—the embodiment of all that would be classified as ideal homes. Instead, however, the people are said to have been contentious and quarrelsome among themselves, and grossly superstitious under the priests who dominated them.

Expedition against Crown Point. General William Johnson,†

---

* Charles Lawrence was a British general of distinction. He died in Halifax, Nova Scotia, October 19, 1760.

In 1750 he built Fort Lawrence at the head of the Bay of Fundy. He was appointed lieutenant-governor in 1754, and governor in 1756. He was made a colonel in September, 1757, and a brigadier-general the 31st of the following December. He was present at the siege of Louisburg.

† Sir William Johnson was born in Smithtown, Ireland, 1715; died in Johnstown, N. Y., July 11, 1774. Was educated for mercantile life, but, disappointed in love negotiation, he finally located on a tract of land on the Mohawk river, N. Y., and became a trader with the Indians.

His courtesy, honesty and adaptability to circumstances gave him great power over the Indians, who made him a sachem.

At the council in Alexandria, April 14, 1755, he was commissioned by Brad-

of New York, was intrusted with the expedition against Crown
Point, on Lake Champlain.   His forces came mainly from
Massachusetts and Connecticut, New Hampshire also supply-
ing one regiment which joined him at Albany.

At the head of navigation on the Hudson there had been
established a fort, which, in honor of a boat commander, had
been called Fort Lyman.

Fort Lyman Changed to Fort Edwards.   The name was
changed by Johnson to that of Fort Edwards.   A garrison
being left, Johnson, with some 5,000 men, including Hendrick,
the noted Mohawk chief and his warriors, and such noted
men as Israel Putnam and John Stark, started for the head
of Lake George, and thence to Lake Champlain.

Attack on Fort Edwards and Death of Col. Williams.   The
French made every effort to check this advance.   Baron
Dieskau, collecting 200 regulars and 1,200 Indians and Cana-
dians from the region of Montreal, determined to attack Fort
Edward.   Johnson detached 1000 men, under Ephraim Williams, of Massachusetts, and 200 Mohawks, under Hendrick,
to relieve the post.   Advised of their approach, the French
assumed a position in ambush.   Presently the English were
entrapped, and on the 5th of September (1755) were defeated,
both Williams and Hendrick losing their lives.   As they re-
treated they were assisted by the cannon and forces in camp,
and finally, after a five hours' contest, the enemy were compelled to retreat.   In the rout the French and Indians were
also assailed by the New Hampshire regiment on its way from
Fort Edwards, and thrown into a panic-stricken condition,
the commander, Baron Dieskau, being captured.

Though the success of the day was due largely to the efforts
of General Lyman, the honors were assumed by General
Johnson.   He was subsequently made a baronet and given a
bonus of £5,000.

dock "sole superintendent of the affairs of the six United Nations, their allies
and dependents."   He was also made a major-general and assigned to the leader-
ship against Crown Point.

Expedition against Niagara. According to the Alexandria arrangement Shirley was to march against Niagara. Colonel Philip Schuyler had command of the first regiment in this expedition.

At Oswego boats were constructed to carry 600 men by lake. Shirley, by way of the Mohawk, reached Oswego on the 21st of August. Delays of various kinds occurred. Finally, in October, a council of war decided that the attack on Niagara should be deferred one year.

Shirley's Failure. Shirley's great project proved abortive, and terminated ultimately in simply strengthening the defenses of Oswego, and leaving them in command of Colonel Hugh Mercer with 700 men.

Braddock's Expedition. Braddock's part in this grand movement now needs attention. His forces, designed to capture Fort Duquesne and clear the Ohio Valley, left Alexandria on the 20th of April. They crept along at the rate of three or four miles per day, stopping, as Washington said, "to level every mole-hill; to erect a bridge over every creek."

Finally, on the 9th of July, with about one-half his army, Braddock reached the vicinity of the fort. No scout had been employed. The march was along a road twelve feet wide. Drums and fifes furnished martial music for the occasion.

Battle in Ambush. Suddenly the Indian war-whoop was heard. His columns were attacked, but no enemy was visible. Not heeding the advice of his subordinates, he directed his men to maintain organized form and fire in platoons. The result of this order was that many of his men were shot by their comrades.

Braddock's Defeat and Death. About half the force engaged —viz., 800 men—were killed and wounded. Sixty-four of the eighty-five officers were lost. Braddock was finally wounded and the command devolved on Washington. The latter covered the retreat to Great Meadows, where Braddock died.

Thus ended, in supreme disaster, the leading one of the

2

various campaigns planned by the general-in-chief of the English army.

Formal Declarations of War. Though war had actually existed between France and England, thus involving their respective colonies in the New World, the formal declaration by England was not made until the 18th of May, 1756, and by France on the 9th of June following.

Montcalm—New French Commander. Marquis de Montcalm became the leader of the French in America. He was furnished with two battalions (1200) of men for operations in Canada. His entire command was about 4,000 men. The militia strength of the province was 10,000 to 15,000, but this was hardly reliable. Meanwhile, Montcalm strengthened the outlying forts, and endeavored to ascertain from Indian scouts the strength of the British in opposition. These scouts seemed to be open to negotiations, and hence were somewhat unreliable.

Shirley Commander-in-Chief. After the death of Braddock, Shirley became commander of the British forces in America. His military training was inadequate, and his plans, though gigantic, were not successful. In his proposed operations against Crown Point, Lake Ontario, Fort Duquesne, and up the Kennebec river, he was anticipated and checked by Montcalm, who easily took a number of the English forts and destroyed them.

Earl of Loudoun Succeeds Shirley. Shirley was succeeded by John Campbell, Earl of Loudoun, noted later for his "masterly inactivity and indecision." As a result, the year 1757 was not distinguished by any military movement of much importance to the English. In fact, it was to them the darkest period of the war.

Capture of Fort George by Montcalm. Montcalm took the initiative, and with 7,606 men penetrated the country and invested Fort George. On the 9th of August the fort was compelled to surrender, with 2,264 men. By this victory the French acquired complete control of Lakes Champlain and

George.   The destruction of Oswego gave them control of the Great Lakes, and the retention of Fort Duquesne held control of the Mississippi Valley.

William Pitt, Head of English Ministry.   A change in English administration now began.   William Pitt was placed at the head of affairs, and his letters assured all the colonies of a new order of things and inspired full confidence.   He assured them of complete co-operation in the war against the French, and called for volunteers.   Massachusetts agreed to furnish 7,000 men ; Connecticut, 5,000 ; New Hampshire, 3,000.

THREE EXPEDITIONS PROJECTED—LOUISBURG CAPTURED BY ABERCROMBIE.

Under the new regime three expeditions were proposed :

The first was against Louisburg.   An army of 14,000 men, under command of Major-General Jeffery Amherst, captured the place July 26, 1758.

Attack on Ticonderoga.   The second was that under Lieutenant-General James Abercrombie, successor, as commander-in-chief, of Loudoun in America, against Ticonderoga and Crown Point.   The attack on Ticonderoga occurred on the 8th of July, 1758, and was quite disastrous, the English loss in killed and wounded being 2,000 men.

Forbes' Expedition against Duquesne.   The third was the second expedition against Fort Duquesne.   It began in October, 1758, under the direction of Brigadier-General John Forbes.   His command consisted of 1,200 Highlanders, 350 royal Americans, and about 5,000 provincials.   In the latter number were 2,000 Virginians, under command of Colonel Washington.

Fort Captured and Name Changed to Fort Pitt.   Though Forbes started from Philadelphia in July, he did not reach Raystown (now Somerset, Pa.) until September.   He did not leave Raystown until October, and, owing to obstructions to his march, he did not arrive at Fort Duquesne until the 25th of November.   " The garrison, being deserted by the Indians,

and too weak to maintain the place against the formidable
army which was approaching, abandoned the fort the evening
before the arrival of the British and escaped down the Ohio in
boats." An English garrison was placed, and the fortification
had its name changed to Fort Pitt, in compliment to the new
and popular minister of state.

General Amherst Succeeds Abercrombie. In the meantime
General Amherst was appointed (Sept. 30, 1758) commander-
in-chief of the English forces, his victory at Louisburg having
led to the same.

Campaigns of 1759. The campaigns of 1759 were more
favorable to the English. Under the skillful operations
of Major-General James Wolfe, consummated by General
Townshend, his successor, Quebec was captured in September.
On the 25th of July Fort Niagara, under the command
of Ponchot, was forced to capitulate.

Presque Isle, Venango and Le Boeuf were, in consequence
of lack of support, easily taken by Colonel Bouquet, who had
been sent to summon them to surrender.

Ticonderoga and Crown Point were taken with comparative
ease ; and the only point of importance uncaptured was Montreal. Finally, after concentrating at that place the various
armies which had operated in Canada, the city capitulated
and the English flag was hoisted on the 8th of September,
1760. The conquest was complete. It was the end of " New
France."

Treaty of Peace. The end of the French and Indian War
was fixed by the Treaty of Paris, February 10, 1763, by which
the French king lost his entire possessions in the New World.

Pontiac's Conspiracy. Though the war had nominally
ended, Indian depredations did not cease. Pontiac, chief of
the Ottowas, who is supposed to have been present at Braddock's defeat, endeavored to form a union of the Indians
against the English. In May, 1763, nine garrisons, ranging
in position from western Pennsylvania to Mackinaw, were
either destroyed or dispersed. From May 12th to the 12th

of the succeeding October in the same year, Pontiac personally conducted an attack on Detroit.

Depredations against settlers in Maryland, Virginia and Pennsylvania were frequent. These were the result of a jealousy felt by Pontiac because he did not receive from the English the recognition which he considered due him. This feeling allied him to the French, and finally alienated his followers from him. In 1766 he made terms with the English.

Col. Bouquet's Expedition. Colonel Henry Bouquet was a British soldier of courage and ability. He co-operated with Forbes in the expedition which captured Duquesne in 1758. In 1763 he was ordered to go from Philadelphia with 500 Highlanders to the relief of Fort Pitt. At Bushy Run, on the 5th of August, he encountered a force of Indians, which he defeated with the loss, on his side, of 8 officers and 115 men. Two days later he relieved the fort.

Expeditions against Ohio Indians. In October, 1764, he conducted an expedition against the Ohio Indians and compelled them to make peace at Tuscarawas.

Lord Dunmore's War. Lord Dunmore, governor of Virginia from 1772 to 1776, was suspected of playing double. While efforts were being made by the General Congress, in 1774, to resist the encroachments of Great Britain against the colonies, and while the Indians were committing depredations along the western frontiers, the indignation of the people compelled their reluctant governor to take up arms and march against the very Indians whom he was suspected of having incited by intrigues to hostility.

Colonel Lewis' Victory at Point Pleasant. Lord Dunmore marched his army in two columns; the one under Colonel Andrew Lewis he sent to the junction of the Great Kanawha with the Ohio, while the other he led to a point higher up on the Ohio, with the alleged purpose of destroying certain Indian towns and then joining Lewis at Point Pleasant. The real purpose, however, is suspected to have been the concentrating of the entire Indian force upon Lewis and thus weakening and humiliating Virginia. If such were his purpose, he was thoroughly disappointed; for Lewis, with inferior numbers, but unusual skill and gallantry, met the Indians at Point Pleasant October 10, 1774, and after a day's hard fighting and the loss of nearly all his officers, completely defeated them.

The immediate effect was visible in the migration which at once began to seek homes in Kentucky, eastern Tennessee, and the more remote regions of the Northwest. It developed the pioneer movements of Boone in Kentucky, Robertson and Sevier in East Tennessee, and George Rodgers Clark in the Northwest. With this theory coincides the view that Lewis was a patriot and Lord Dunmore a traitor to the best interests of Virginia and the whole country.

We need not express surprise, therefore, that the name of Dunmore county was changed to Shenandoah in 1777, one of the delegates to the Assembly saying: "My constituents no longer wish to live in, nor do I desire to represent, a county bearing the name of such a Tory. I therefore move to call it Shenandoah, after the beautiful stream which passes through it." His motion prevailed.

LEGISLATIVE ENACTMENTS

THAT CONNECT THE PRECEDING HISTORIC SKETCH WITH THE ADJUDICATION OF THE RESULTING ACCOUNTS WHICH FOLLOW.

ACT OF ASSEMBLY STATE OF VA., MARCH, 1756,

For making provision against invasions and insurrections, &c., and for raising the sum of twenty-five thousand pounds, for the better protection of the inhabitants on the frontiers of this Colony, and for other purposes therein mentioned. Hening's Statutes, Vol. 7, page 26.

Section 3. And be it further enacted that there shall be raised and paid by the public to the officers and soldiers drawn out into actual service by virtue of this and the before-recited acts, and to the look-outs, after the rates following, to wit:

To the county-lieutenant, or commander-in-chief, ten shillings per day.

Horses.

A Colonel, ten shillings.
Lieutenant-Colonel, ten shillings.
Major, ten shillings.
Captain, ten shillings.
Lieutenant, five shillings.
Cornet, four shillings.
Quarter-Master, two shillings.
Corporal, one shilling and four pence.
Trumpeter, one shilling and four pence.
Trooper, one shilling and three pence.

} Per day.

Foot.

A Colonel, ten shillings.
Lieutenant-Colonel, ten shillings.
Major, ten shillings.
Captain, ten shillings.
Lieutenant, five shillings.
Ensign, four shillings.
Serjeant, one shilling and four pence.
Corporal, one shilling and four pence.
Drummer, one shilling and two pence.
Soldier, one shilling.

} Per day.

A look-out, after the rate of twenty shillings per month.

Section 4. That every smith, wheelwright, carpenter, or other artificer, and all watermen employed in the service, as by this and the said recited acts is directed, shall be paid and allowed by the public, after the rates following, to wit:

Every smith, five shillings.
Wheelwright, three shillings.
Carpenter, three shillings.
Waterman, one shilling and six pence.

} Per day.
Vol, 7, page 28.

Act thirteen, General Assembly of Virginia, April 14, 1757, 3d Session.

Commissioners appointed to examine, state and settle accounts of the several charges and expenses of the officers and men as shall from time to time be referred to them, &c., &c. Be it therefore enacted, etc., etc., That William Prentice, James Coke and Thomas Everard, gentlemen, shall be, and they are hereby appointed. Vol. 7, page 75.

Act fifteen. Committee appointed to direct the pay of present officers and soldiers now in the pay of this colony, to the rangers formerly employed, and for the expense of building a fort in the Cherokee country, and to the militia that have been drawn out into actual service, and also for provisions for the said soldiers, rangers and militia, or persons as shall be from time to time directed by John Robinson, Peyton Randolph and Charles Carter, esquires, Benjamin Waller, John

Chiswell, Richard Bland, James Power, William Diggs, Dudley Diggs, John Page, John Norton, William Harwood, George Wythe, Landon Carter, Edmund Pendleton, and Robert Carter Nicholas, gentlemen, or any five of them, with the consent and approbation of the government or commander-in-chief of this dominion, for the time being.

THE SCHEDULE TO WHICH THIS ACT REFERS.

To the Militia of the County of Accomack, and for Provisions furnished by sundry Inhabitants of the said county, Hening's Statutes, Vol. 7, page 200, Sept., 1758 :

	£	s.	d.
To Major Thomas Custis, for his pay and the pay of the Guards conducting drafted Soldiers to Fredericksburg,	12	18	00
To James Rogers, Sheriff, for maintaining drafted soldiers in Goal,	9	17	6
To Major John Wise, his account for carrying drafted Soldiers to Fredericksburg in 1756,	23	13	
	£46	13	6

Albemarle County.

Hening's Statutes, Vol. 7, page 202–4.

	£	s.	d.
To Charles Ellis, for provisions to Indians,	4	6	
To William Floyd, for provisions to Indians,	4	9	4
To William Pryor, do.	3	13	6
John Buckner, do.	3	4	11
Ambrose Lee, do.	7	9	
James Nevil, do.	1	12	
William Woods, do.		16	
Henry Key, do.		8	
Richard Murray, do. for & ferriages,	1	13	2
John Lewis, do.	7	4	
George Taylor, for provisions,	1	14	5

	£	s.	d.
To Mr. Allen Howard and William Cabell, jun., to pay a company of militia of his county, under the command of Captain James Nevil, according to his muster-roll, to the eighth day of Sept., 1758, inclusive,	298	17	6
To Charles Ellis, for provisions,	2	8	1
John Daily, do.		4	2
Elizabeth Birk, do.	1	10	5
Robert Davis, jun., do.	7	9	8
Nicholas Davis, do.	1	16	6
William Cabell, do.		17	8
Edward Spalden, do.		19	2
Francis Ellison, do.	2	18	10
To David Lewis, paid for carrying ammunition,		15	
To William Gallaway, for salt,		3	
Gideon Thomas, for horse hire,		8	9
Captain Charles Ellis,	3	18	
Cornelius Thomas, lieutenant,	1	19	
Charles Tuly, ensign,	1	6	
John Freeman, serjeant,		9	4
Jacob Brown, corporal,		13	4
Thomas Cotrell, do.		17	6
To Edward Weir and Thomas Powell, 7s. each,		14	
To Malcolm Allen, Richard Powell, Ashcroft Roach, Benjamin Hensley, William Henson, John Powell, Edward Spolden, Benjamin Stinnett, Benjamin Stinnett, jun., Henry Guffey, William Williams, Solomon Carter, Joshua Fowler, John Hix, George Adam Salling, John Bryan, David Davis, Mark Lively, Henry Fuller, William Bratchy, John Burk Lane, Stephen Cash, Philip Henson, William Becknel, James White, James Randel, Nicholas Pryor, Caleb Burton, and Isham Davis, 13s. each,	18	4	

	£	s.	d.
To Jacob Smith,		7	
To William Shoemaker and William Pryor, 10s. each,	1		
To John Woods, as lieutenant,	1	19	
William Woods, as ensign,	1	6	
Andrew Greer, serjeant,		17	4

To Samuel Stockton, Thomas Jameson, Hugh Alexander, Robert Pogece, John Wallace, Adam Gaudilock, Michael Woods, jun., Bartholomew Ramsey, Henry Randolph, William Stockton, James Kinkade, Thomas Harbet, Henry Brenton, Joshua Woods, Alexander Jameson, Daniel Maupin, John Maupin, William Maupin, Matthew Mullins, Samuel Woods, William Whiteside, David Gass, Abraham Howard, Thomas Grubs, John Cowen, George Brackenridge, and William Pogue, 13s. each,   17 11

To William Woods, lieutenant,   2   8
David Martin, ensign,   1   6
To Charles Wakefield and William Martin, serjeants, 17s. 4d. each,   1 14   8
To William Wakefield, Henry Wakefield, Charles Hughes, Langsdon Depriest, Aaron Hughes, John Depriest, James Glen, James Robertson, Charles Crawford, John Bigs, John M'Anally, Robert M'Whorter, and Richard Prior, 13s. each,   8   9
To James Martin, Michael Morrison, James Morrison, and Adam Lackie, 10s. each,   2
To Alexander M'Mulen, Lawrence Smith, Matthias Hughes, Michael Israel, and William Cartie, 16s. each,   4 00 00
To Robert Barnet, for horse hire,   1

	£	s.	d.
John Rucker, for provisions,		2	
Charles Ellis, for do.		5	8
To David Lewis, for conducting soldiers to Fredericksburg and maintenance of one do.	3		
To John Been, for provisions.	2	18	9
To Captain John Hunter, for his pay and the pay of the guards conducting drafted soldiers to Fredericksburg,	6	16	
To Obadiah Woodson, the balance of his account for provisions, a horse, sundry necessaries, and paid to several soldiers,	80	4	9
To Samuel Ridgway, jun., for a horse lost in the Shawnese expedition,	3		
	£516	8	9

Amelia County.

Hening's Statutes, Vol. 7, page 201–2.

	£	s.	d.
To Richard Booker, for Provisions to Indians,	2	17	6
To Captain Henry Anderson,	31	16	
Lieutenant Branch Tanner	15	18	
Ensign George Farley,	10	12	
To Richard Craddock, John Cox, Serjeants 7£ 2s. each,	14	4	00
To John Chumley, Abel Man, John Baldwin, James Harris, John Dier, Robert Blanchet, John Culpeper, Richard Hooff, William Forster, Francis Smith, Bryan Farguson, 5£ 6s. each,	58	6	
To Humphrey Hendrick,	4	11	

To William Jackson, Robert Hinton, Peter Burton, John Appling, Charles Harrison, John Hendrick, Frederick Reams, Samuel Mann, John Cooke. Shem Cooke, William Cannon, Thomas Farguson, Peter Web-

	£	s.	d.

ster, Richard Farguson, John Wilson, James Arnold, William Childre, James Lockett, William Abney, William Hill, Joseph Burgess, Charles Smith, William Wood, William Hudson, Christopher Hinton, George Hasting, 5£ 6s. each,   **137   16**

To James Cheatham,   **4   8**

To Stephen Howell, William Ray, John Hamton, William Haynes, John Hammock, John Minear, Robert Steady, John Githings, Abram West, John James Farley, 5£ 6s. each,   **53   00   00**

To Captain John Winne,   **31   16**

Lieutenant James Clark,   **15   18**

Ensign John Fitzpatrick,   **10   12**

Serjeant Robert Hall,   **2   16**

To William Ford and William Whitworth, serjeants, 7£ 1s. 4d. each,   **14   2   8**

Bowling Hall,   **1   2**

To Herman Thompson, serjeant, instead of Hall,   **4   5   4**

To Herman Thompson, a soldier,   **2   2**

To Moses Estis, John Estis, Benjamin Meadows, William Person, Ralph Shelton, William Harris, Robert Hamm, William Estis, John Avery, William Hamm, James Campbell, William Farguson, Joseph Goodman, John Brassfield, Richard Fauster, Robert Fauster, Edward Farguson, John Hermon, Charles Man, Daniel Prisnall, Thomas Wright, Ambrose Cumpton, Thomas Jones, Joel Hurt, James Hurt, William Hurt, John Fauster, George Ridley, James Rice, Uriah Hawks, George Moore, Richard Hawks, Bell Hulm, John Moore, Thomas Hulm,

	£	s.	d.
Henry Clay, James Hurt, jun., John Loving, William Hutcherson, Thomas Gunn, John Harris, Edmond Ballard, and Nimrod Herron, 5£ 6s. each,	227	18	
To James Hallis,	3	4	
To Henry Paulin and Benjamin Parrot, 5£ 6s. each,	10	12	
To Richard Condrow,		13	
William Burgh,		10	
John Harris, jun.,	5	6	
To Major Wood Jones, for carrying drafted soldiers to Fredericksburg in 1756,	6	14	
	£670	19	6

Augusta County.

Hening's Statutes, Vol. 7, page 179–200.

	£	s.	d.
To Captain Alexander Sayers, for his pay and the pay of his officers and company of militia to the last day of Aug., 1758, inclusive, as per muster-roll,	246	14	8
To Captain Abraham Smith,	5	8	
Sampson Archer, lieutenant,	2	5	
James Henderson, ensign,	1	18	
Benjamin Kinley, serjeant,	1		
Jonas Friend, corporal,	1	1	4
Robert Tremble, do.	1	2	8
To Robert Mitchell, William Blackwood, John Black, Richard Yedley, and John Lawn, 19 shillings each,	4	15	00
Adam Dunlop,		18	
John Crosby, Robert M'Coy, Andrew Little, and George Lewis, 17 shillings each,	3	8	00
Henry Benningar,		13	

	£	s.	d.
To Adam Harper and Woolrey Coonrod, 16 shillings each,	1	12	
To William Minter, William Cunningham, Robert M'Carney, Daniel M'Night, John Cunningham, Andrew Cunningham, jun., John Cunningham, Edward Watts, Charles Driver, James Anderson, James Young, William Rolestone, Matthew Rolestone, John Peterson, Darby Conway, Martin Cornet, Thomas M'Namar, Thomas Peterson, James Fowler, and Samuel Semple, 15 shil. each,	15	00	00
To Michael Mallow,		11	
John Stevenson,		14	
To John Shill,		11	
Matthew Patten,		9	
To Richard Wilson, Hugh Diver, Daniel Henderson, James Ramsay, and John Johnson, 12 shillings each,	3	00	00
To Alexander Craig, John Melcum, and Joseph Melcum, 6 shillings each,		18	
To Michael Props and Adam Props, 3 shillings each,		6	
To Robert Minice,		4	
William Gragg,		12	
To David Cloyd, for provisions,	27	3	10
Rhoda Evans, for do.	24	2	9
To Benjamin Kinley, carpenter, 6 days rebuilding Fort Syvers, at 2 shillings and six pence,		15	
To Jonas Friend and William Minter, carpenters, 1£ 2s. 6d. each,	2	5	00
To Robert Mitchell, Robert Tremble, William Blackwood, Richard Yadley, John Lawn, Adam Dunlop, John Black, John Crosby,			

	£	s.	d.

Woolry Coonrod, Andrew Little, George
Lewis, Adam Harper, William Cunning-
ham, Robert M'Kay, Daniel M'Night,
John Cunningham, Andrew Cunningham,
and John Cunningham, jun., George
Watts, John Stevenson, James Anderson,
James Young, William Rolestone, Mat-
thew Rolestone, James Patterson, Derby
Conway, Martin Cornet, Thomas M'Na-
mare, Thomas Patterson, Samuel Semple,
for 9 days' work at 9s. each,   13 10 00
To Henry Peninger, William Gragg, James
Fowler, Richard Wilson, Hugh Diver,
Daniel Henderson, James Ramsay, and
John Johnston, for five days' work, at 5s.
each,   2 00 00
To Charles Diver, for six days' work at one shil-
ling,   6
To Alexander Craig, John Melcum, Joseph Mel-
cum, Michael Props, and Adam Props, for
two days' work at two shillings each,   10
To Abraham Smith, as lieutenant,   9
William Cravens, serjeant,   4
To Sampson Archer, John M'Kay, Robert Min-
nis, Henry Smith, John Smith, Adam
Stephenson, William M'Gill, jun., Robert
Boyd, William M'Gill, sen., Matthew Pat-
ton, Moses Hall, Peter Veneman, John
Young, Michael Erhart, William Minter,
Richard Wilson, John Shanklin, Edward
Megary, Paul Shever, James M'Clure,
James Fowler, Joseph Shidmore, Nicholas
Huffman, Henry Peninger, and Robert
Megary, three shillings each,   3 15 00
To Abraham Smith, for provisions,   17

	£	s.	d.
To Abraham Smith, as lieutenant,		12	
John M'Coy, serjeant,		5	4
To Benjamin Kinley, John Malcum, William Cunningham, Larkin Pearpoint, James Gray, Robert Gragg, Robert Cunningham, David Smith, Robert Minnis, William Bratton, Josiah Shipman, William Rolestone, Robert Trimble, John Stephenson, Adam Stephenson, and John Gum, 4 shillings each,	3	4	00
To Jacob Sivers, for provisions,		10	
Abraham Smith, for horse-hire,		5	
Christian Avey, for provisions,	4	13	9
Michael Maller, for do.	1	5	8
Captain Abraham Smith,	3		
Lieutenant William Cunningham,	1	16	
Ensign John Hopkins,		14	
William Clark, serjeant,		10	8
John Jameson, corporal,		10	8
To John Walker, Christian Clement, and Robert Gibson, twelve shillings each,	1	16	
To John M'Clure, James Bell, John Long, William M'Farlin, John Peary, William Black, David Scott, James Steel, Gilbert Christian, James Meteer, James Lockart, John Shields, and John Woods, eight shillings each,	5	4	00
To John M'Kay, serjeant,		9	4

To Arthur Trader, Robert Patterson, Robert M'Geary, Matthew Black, Jonas Friend, Nathan Harrison, Robert Minnis, Leonard Herron, Cornelius Sullivant, Edward Shanklin, John Skidmore, Hugh Campbell, James Skidmore, Samuel Briggs, Michael Dickie, John Davis, Robert Cun-

3

	£	s.	d.
ningham, Thomas Nichols, James Fowler, Archibald Gilkison, John Malcom, William Elliot, and Thomas Spencer, seven shillings each,	8	1	00
To John Jordan, William Makenry, Joseph Jenkins, Daniel Evans, Richard Shanklin, and William Hooks, five shillings each,	1	10	00
To Abraham Smith, for provisions,	8	1	1
Matthew Patton, for do.	1	5	
Joseph Skidmore, for do.	1	17	
Lodowick Folk, for do.		7	
George Mouse, for do.	5	16	3
Peter Moses, for do.	2	15	5
Philip Harper, for do.	1	13	6
George Hamener, for do.	3	2	6
Nicholas Huffman, for do.	2	8	11
Henry Penninger, for do.	1	18	9
Peter Veneman, for do.	1	17	7
Michael Erhart, for do.	1	6	4
Nicholas Frank, for do.		7	
Henry Laurel, for do.	2	3	4
John Wilson, for do.	16	4	8
Nicholas Haven, for do.	4	16	10
Michael Freeze, for do.	1	8	7
Roger Dyer, for do.	2	9	4
Michael Props, for do.	3	9	8
Adam Weese, for do.		12	4
Jacob Peterson, for do.		7	
Leonard Hire, for do.		10	
Henry Carr, for do.		13	
Jacob Harper, for do.		2	3
Valentine Kyle, for do.		15	
Jacob Goodman, for do.		15	1
Woolry Coonrod, for do.		9	6
George Coplinger, for do.		2	

	£	s.	d.
John Dunkel, for do.		4	6
William Dyer, for do.		10	10
Matthias Tyce, for do.		11	3
Michael Mallow, for do.		11	6
Jacob Sivers, for do.	2	11	4
Abraham Smith, for do. and horse-hire,	2	8	9
To John Buchanan, as captain, pay to himself, his officers and company, from the 13th day of Apr., 1758, till the first day of Sept. following,	292	3	8
To Captain John Dickenson, for pay to sundry persons employed in building a fort at Craig's Creek and for horse hire,	22	16	
To Rhoda Evans, for provisions,	3		9
James Boreland, for do.	10		
John Dean, for do.	10		
David Cloyd, for do. to Indians,	8	16	7
William Stevison, for do. to do.		19	6
To John Gum, for horse hire,		3	9
To John Moore, for a sorrel mare impressed for the Shawnese expedition, and not returned, appraised to	6	00	00
To John Gisens, for the use of his horse in the same expedition,	3	17	6
To Walter Cunningham, for conducting Indians,	2	15	
To Robert Bratton, for horse hire,	3	17	
To Alexander Sayers, for a horse impressed and killed, appraised to	14	10	
To John Smith, for do. and for hire of another horse,	9	12	6
To Captain Abraham Smith,	44	8	
Lieutenant Sampson Archer,	3	15	00
John M'Cay, serjeant,	8	16	
William Cravens, do.	6	2	8
Robert Minice,	2	6	

	£	s.	d.
James Camble,		18	
James Alexander,	1	3	
John Johnson,	2	5	
Thomas Lawrence,		17	
James Stephenson,	2	5	
Daniel Remi,	2	12	
To John Farrell and William Kite, 45s. each,	4	10	00
Adam M'Cormick,	2	2	
John Leonard,	8		
Benjiman Kinly, corporal,	3	8	
Martin Philips,	7	13	
William Woods,	4	3	
James Burke,	1	4	
Thomas Prichard, corporal,	3	9	4
Abraham Earhart,	7	18	
John Blor,	7	15	
George Watts,	7	11	
Gasper Smith,		10	
Michael Earhart,	7	9	
To Nicholas Hufman, Philip Harper, Valentine Castle, Jacob Harper, and George Hamer, £7 8s. each,	37		
To Jacob Hornbery,	6	9	
Nicholas Frank,	7	9	
Thomas Boyne,	1	3	
Peter Moses,	5	17	
George Moses,	6	17	
Adam Harper,	6	16	
To George Mouse and Paul Shaver, £7 8s. each,	14	16	
To Loudwig Folk,	7	9	
Michael Frees,	4	12	
Peter Vanimon,	7	3	
Philip Hufman,	7	8	
William Wilson,		18	
Henry Benigar,	7	3	

	£	s.	d.
John Cunrod,	6	16	
John Malcomb,		16	
James M'Clure,		14	
John Cunningham,		16	
William Minter,	1	11	
Isaiah Shipman,		6	
To Jacob Peterson, Jacob Wiece, Joseph Wiece, Benjamin Hagler, John Hagler, John Wizer, Postine Hagler, Henry Carr, Jacob Hagler, Martin Peterson, Jeremiah Cooper, 16s. each,	8	16	00
To Robert Trimble,	1	19	
Jacob Goodman,	2	7	
Gabriel Pickins,		15	
William Shaw,	6	15	
John Young,	1	12	
Michael Earhart, junior,	1	8	
To Mathias Tice, Gasper Smith, Nicholas Sivers, Nicholas Havener, Jacob Aberman, William Dyer, Andrew Full, John Still, Michael Malow, Michael Eberman, Adam Little, and John Aberman, 14s. each,	8	8	00
To William Wilson,	1	11	
To Robert Homes, Daniel Evans, David Lard, 30s. each,	4	10	
To Jacob Rolman and Thomas Bowens, 27s. each,	2	14	00
To John Fhares, corporal,	4	4	
Matthew Black,	1	10	
Larkin Pearpoint,		16	
William Minter, corporal,	2		
George Malcomb, do.	5	12	
John Crosby, junior,	1	14	
Robert Trimble,	1	8	
Thomas Lawrence,	2	8	

	£	s.	d.
George Goodman,	4	17	
George Capliner,	1	5	
John Malcomb,		12	
Henry Smith,		9	
To Michael Hogshead,	0	10	00
John Crosby, senior,		19	
William Cunningham,		13	
John Young,	1	6	
William Flemin,		13	
Robert Cunningham,	2		
Thomas M'Comb,		10	
Richard Wilson,	1	6	
William Gragg,		19	
Thomas Paterson,	1	16	
Robert Magery,	1	1	
Joseph Dikton,	1	16	
To William Woods and Daniel Reme, 54s. each,	5	8	
To George Hedrick, John Seller, John Miller, Charles Man, Jacob Pence, Jacob Grub, Charles Rush, Conrod Kinsel, 51s. each,	20	8	
To William Blair,	1	16	
To Michael Eberman, John Reiger and Nicholas Sivers, 46s. each,	6	18	
To James Camble,	1	1	
To Michael Malow, John Stilt, John Eberman, Adam Little, John Colley, William Dyer, and Jacob Eberman, 46s. each,	16	2	00
To John Dunkle,	1	19	
Gasper Smith,		15	
Christopher Colley,	1	9	
To Roger Dyer, George Malow, George Fults, Mathias Tice, Walter Cunrod, Gabriel Kite, Jacob Kite, Valentine Kite, George Kite, Jacob Havener, 46s. each,	23	00	00
To Nicholas Havener, George Dunkle, 39s. each,	3	18	

	£	s.	d.
To Thomas Barrow,	1	15	
George Anderson,	1	18	
William Ralston,	1	15	
James Bradshaw,	1		
John Davis,	1	18	
To Robert Minice and Robert M'Cay, 35s. each,	3	10	
To Daniel Long,		13	
Andrew Little,	1	2	
John Cunningham, junior,	1		
James Alexander,	1	1	
Andrew Full,	1		
To Captain Francis Kirtley, 17s. 6d. deducted for hides received by him,	15	12	6
To Lieutenant Christian Bingaman,	7	10	
Benjamin Kindly, serjeant,	1	6	8
John Ozban, serjeant,	1	14	8
John Bingaman,	1	2	00
Daniel Price,		9	
John Massey,	1	8	
George Man,	1	11	
Peter Miller,	1	12	
Tetrarch Couch,		18	
Jacob Moyers,		12	
Stephen Hanburgher,	1	3	
Jacob Fudge,	1	9	
Adam Hedrick,	1	18	
Nicholas Mildebarler,	1	11	
Henry Long,	1	12	
James Fowler,	1	18	
John Fraizer,	1	10	
Robert Belche,	1	14	
Hugh Wilson,		13	
James Lawrence,		8	
William Hook,	1	14	
Mogis Algier,	2	13	00

	£	s.	d.
Thomas Wilmouth,	1	11	
Adam Miller,	1	10	
Jacob Miller,		13	
Jacob Man,	1	13	
Thomas Powell,		16	
George Kite,	1	10	
Gunrod Umble,	2	2	
William Kinsey,	2		
Cornous White,	1	16	
To Nicholas Null, Charles Fie, John Early, 11s. each,	1	13	
To John Ferrel,	1	2	
To Gunrod Peterfish,	1	11	
Jacob Runkle,		9	
To Peter Trusler, George Shillinger, 31s. each,	3	2	
To Arthur Trader,		12	
To Nathaniel Harrison, Robert Black, 17s. each,	1	14	
To Matthew Black,	1	10	
William Shannon,		9	
Thomas Pointer,	1	13	
Moses Sample,		7	
Henry Coler,	1	11	
To Jacob Richards, John Richards, 35s. each,	3	10	
To Ury Umble, Daniel Cloud, 30s. each,	3	00	00
To Christopher Armontrout, Jacob Kindler, 32s. each,	3	4	
To Isaac South,	1	7	
John Fulse, Poston Nosler, 19s. each,	1	18	
To Holerick Hushman,		17	
William Shaw,		14	
Martin Umble,	1	2	
Lieutenant Daniel Smith,		15	

To Matthew Patton, William Cravens, William
      Wilson, James M'Clure, James Thomson,
      Edward M'Gary, Michael Mallow, Honicle

	£	s.	d.
Hufman, Henry Peniger, Willry Cunrod, John King, Robert Patterson, James Patterson, George Moffett, John Reburn, James Robertson, Alexander Craig, Samuel Kerre, John Armstrong, Thomas Patterson, Adam Reburn, Robert Anderson, Edward Ervin, Frederick Eister, Samuel Patterson, Matthias Dice, John Dunkle, Lodowick Wagoner, Thomas Baskine, John Baskine, David Bell, Michael Hogshead, Robert Trimble, James Campbell, George Dunkle, James Hamilton, William Ervin, James Young, John Young, James Anderson, George King, James Stephenson, Thomas Stephenson, John Stephenson, Gaun Leeper, Arthur Greer, Adam Miller, 5s. each,	11	15	00
To Captain Ephraim Love,	7	16	
William Craven, serjeant,	2	12	
Adam Stevenson, corporal,	1	10	8
Thomas McCome, do.	1	6	8
To John Campbell, Andrew Little, James Young, 20s. each,	3		
To Edward Ervin,	1	2	
John Stevenson, James Stevenson, 23s. each,	2	6	
Thomas M'Namar,	1		
Robert Minnis,	1	3	
William Blair,	1		
Archibald Huston,	1	5	
To Thomas Wilson,	1	10	00
Thomas Bowen,	2	5	
Joseph Jenkins,	1	18	
William Hooks,	1	9	
To Daniel Evins, Richard Shanklin, 32s. each,	3	4	
To James Hooks,	1	11	

	£	s.	d.
John Reburn,		16	
To Archibald Hopkins, John Shanklin, 35s. each,	3	10	
To James Fowler,		12	
John Harrison,	1	9	
John Shanklin,		15	
John Gordon,	1	15	
To Hugh M'Garey, Samuel Peterson, 25s. each,	2	10	
To Leonard Herren,		18	
Cornelius Sulivan,	1	6	
Nathaniel Harrison,		12	
To James Thomson, Jacob Roleman, 36s. each,	3	12	
To David Smith,	1	12	
To Robert M'Garey, Henry Downs, 26s. each,	2	12	
To Joseph Dicton,	1	15	
To William Rolestone, William Ross, 22s. each,	2	4	
To Robert M'Comey,	1		
William Shanon,	1	17	
Lieutenant John Hopkins,	2	14	
John M'Cay, serjeant,	1	2	8
Jonas Friend, do.	1	4	
Gideon Harrison,		18	
Leonard Harring,		13	
To John Harrison, Nathaniel Harrison, Thomas Peterson, 18s. each,	2	14	
To Jacob Roleman,		16	
To John Gordon, John Shanklin, 18s. each,	1	16	
To James Young, James Anderson, Alexander Craig, and James Alexander, 17s. each,	3	8	
To James Thomson,		10	
To Adam Stevenson, George Watts, Thomas Macklemare, and Robert Trimble, 17s. each,	3	8	
To Robert M'Garey,		16	
Robert Minnis,		15	

	£	s.	d.
Robert Cunningham,		9	
To Robert M'Comey, John Stevenson, James Stevenson, 14s. each,	2	2	
To Thomas Spence,		9	
John Crevens,		11	
Joseph Dictom,		16	
To Robert Black, Samuel Hemphill, 8s. each,		16	
To John Skidmore,		17	
James Skidmore,		16	
To Archibald Hopkins, Samuel Patterson, Cornelius Sullivan, 12s. each,	1	16	
To the executors of James Patton, deceased, for Oznabrigs, for Indians,	4	14	6
To John Caryle, for a horse impressed, on the Shawnese expedition, and not returned,	5	10	
To James Caryle, for do.	5	2	6
Elizabeth Preston, for provisions,	1	2	8
Robert M'Clanahan, for do.	1	14	
George Robinson, for do.		13	4
To Peter Wallace, for two mares lost on the Shawnese expedition, appraised to	14	10	
To Edward Kenny, for one mare, do.	7	10	
To Bryan M'Donnell, assignee of Joshua M'Cormick, for a mare, a horse, and a pack saddle, do.	8	2	
To James Greenlee, for a horse and halter, do.	6	10	00
To do., for five pack saddles, do.	1		
To Joseph Lapsley, for one do., do.		5	
To do., for four do., do.		16	
To Nathaniel Evans, for a horse lost on the Shawnese expedition, appraised to	5		
To William Moore, for a horse, do.	6	10	
John Guy, for a horse, do.	5	10	
Robert Gwin, for a horse, do.	7		
To Bryan M'Donell, assignee of Joshua M'Cormack, for a horse and a mare, do.	9		

	£	s.	d.
To Robert Young, for a mare, do.	3	15	
To do., assignee of Thomas Branner, for a mare, saddle, bridle, and bell, do.	10		
To John Crockett, for provisions, do.	5	1	
To John Buchanan, for work, horse hire, and a blanket, do.	2		
To John Smith, horse driver, do.		9	6
To Alexander Hamilton, hire for his mare, do.	3	17	6
To Captain William Preston, for his pay, and the pay of company of militia, from the first day of May to the seventh day of June, 1757, inclusive, as per muster-roll,	134	16	4
To Loftus Pulton, for a horse,	6	10	
Adam Stephenson, for provisions,	1	15	8
William Armstrong, for do.	12	5	
William Burnett, for do.		10	10
John Kinkade, do.		7	6
To Matthew Patton, assignee of George Mous, for do.		10	
To Alexander Hering, for do.	6	12	9
To Matthew Patton, assignee of Michael Earhart, for do.		15	6
To William Garvin, for do.		3	
Robert Rennick, for do.		2	8
To William M'Cutchison, assignee of Patrick Savage, for do.	1	12	9
To John Miller, for do.	6	4	7
Robert Gibson, for do.		12	9
David Moor, for do.	2	16	6
William Wilson, for do.	10	15	6
Stephen Wilson, for do.	4	12	2
John Ramsay, for do.		10	
Robert Looney, for do.	3	14	8
Michael Doughterty, for do.		14	8
John Carlyle, for do.	1	15	9

	£	s.	d.
Robert Carlyle, for do.	1	1	7
Daniel Deniston, for horse hire,		13	9
John Trimble, for do.		15	
George Skillern, for expresses,	2	7	6
Robert Young, for provisions,	1	13	3
John Robinson, for do.		13	
James Clark, for do.		16	6
Samuel Wilson, for do.	2	9	10
Thomas Armstrong, for do.		19	4
To Elizabeth Preston, for do. and horse hire,	1	14	8
To John Bell, for provision and express,		11	6
To Elijah M'Clanahan, for horse hire,	6	7	6
To James Bell, an express,		11	
Thomas Black, horse hire,		5	
Joseph Mais, do.		16	4
Loftus Pullon, do. and provisions,	2	10	7
Captain William Christian,	2		
Lieutenant James Henderson,	1		
Michael Henderson, serjeant,		10	8
To Francis Alexander, William Long, William Anderson, George Robinson, Hugh Allen, James Robertson, William Blackwood, Nathaniel Donlap, James Turk, Robert Thomson, Anthony Black, John Black, Robert Gibson, John Finley, John Finley, jun., John Patrick, James Steel, James Patterson, 8s. each,	7	4	00
To John Brown, James Allen, Alexander Thompson, 21s. each,	3	3	
To Samuel Henderson, James Allen, jun., 14s. each,	1	8	
To John Thomson, John Young, John Vance, George Wilson, Robert Gibson, 7s. each,	1	15	
To Dimnick Beret,		6	
To Henry Hecks, James Lockart, John Black,			

	£	s.	d.

Moses Thompson, Robert Thompson, George Robertson, John Hutcheson, John Finley, John Finley, jun., Jas. Gillaspey, Jas. Steel, John Davison, Charles Patrick, William Hutchison, John Long, James Bell, James Gifins, William Cunningham, John Camble, Jonathan Jones, Hugh Allen, Hugh Mackclure, Alexander Steuart, 7s. each, — 8 1

To Major John Brown, for provisions, — 8 11 9

James Cull, — 1

To Thomas Robinson, James Bryans, Abraham Keeny, Abraham Duncklebery, Robert Brown, Thomas Ford, Samuel Ford, James Caghey, Thomas Cashaday, Jacob Graham, John Davison, 7s. each, — 3 17

To Samuel Norwood, captain, — 15

Charles Wilson, lieutenant, — 7 6

Ensign Cunningham, — 6

To John Willey, William Hambleton, Robert Hambleton, John Gilmore, Thomas Gilmore, Jacob Cunningham, James Simpson, James Moor, George Croford, Halbart M'Clurr, John Willey, Robert Willey, James Davis, Eldad Reed, George Gibson, 3s. each, — 2 5 00

To Robert Young, Edward Farses, 10s. each, — 1

To Robert Tolford, David Tolford, 8s. each, — 16

To Adam Dickinson, for provisions, — 2 12 9

John Smith, major, — 13

To Peter Looney, serjeant, Benjamin Hansley, do., 32s. each, — 3 4

To John M'Alhaney, Benjamin Davies, Timothy Stoten, John Putt, Joseph Clerk, John Bell, John Crockett, Daniel M'Bridge,

	£	s.	d.
James Anon, Gardner Adkins, John Hughs, John Medley, 24s. each,	14	8	
To John Montgomery, George Rowland, 7s. each,		14	
To Jacob Graham, John M'Neal, Henry Long, William Kerr, 9s. each,	1	16	
To Robert Armstrong, serjeant,		9	4
To Sampson Sayers, Samuel Bell, William Hog, William Elliot, Archibald Gilkson, 7s. each,	1	15	
To William Bell,		6	
John Trimble,		4	
John Graham,		6	8
Joseph Vauhob,		4	
To Robert Armstrong, William Mar, John Clark, John Wilson, James Risk, 5s. each,	1	5	
To William Christian, captain,	9		
John Davice, serjeant,	3	4	00
To George Marchel, William Currey, Caleb Hermon, James Tobit, Christopher Finney, 48s. each,	12		
To Robert Carlile,		11	
To Edward M'Donald, for provisions and waggonage,	5	7	6
To John M'Gown, for provisions,	1	5	
John Boyens, for do.		12	
Robert Young, for do.		3	
John Mieles, for do.		17	6
James Boreland, for Salt,	2		
John Maxwell, for Provisions,	1	4	
James Wilson, for Horse Hire,		6	3
Andrew Hays, for Provisions,	2	14	3
John Boyer, do.		18	9
Robert Campbell, do.	1	2	6
John Bowen, do.	4	6	5

	£	s.	d.
John Gilmore, do.	3	16	10
Michael Swadley, do.		17	5
John Buchanan, do.		7	3
Michael Prepest, do.		10	10
James Clark, do.	1	6	
Mary Car, do.		2	6
John Maxwell, do.		14	6
Benjamin Davis, do.	7	3	9
John Moore, for Horse Hire,	3	17	6
To Sampson Matthews, Executor of John Matthews, for Provisions,	1	7	4
To William Graham, for Provisions,		7	6
Mark Taled, for do.	5	4	1
Samuel Davidson, for Horse Hire,		10	
Alexander M'Clure, for Provisions,	2	1	
Thomas Hicklins, for do.		9	4
James Cowan, for do.		15	
John Ward, for do.	2	11	
John Crafurd, for do.		16	6
John Ward, for do.		12	
To William Ledgwood, for provisions,		11	4
Samuel Steele, for do.	2	15	3
John Ramsay, for do.		14	10
William Lewis, for do.	1	5	
Robert Hustan, for do.		12	3
Robert Steel, for do.	2	4	
John Paxton, for do.	1	16	
Adam Dean, for horse hire,		6	3
John Williams, for twenty days' service,	1		
John Hamilton, for eight days' do.		8	
John Crocker, for provisions,	1	9	
To Sampson and George Matthews, assignees of John Bradley, for driving pack horses,	4	14	3
To Walter Cunningham, for a mare lost, appraised to	9		

	£	s.	d.
To Moses M'Clure, for one horse, two pack-saddles, do.	5	11	
Robert Young, for one horse, do.	6	10	
To William Ward, for an horse lost, and appraised to	11		
To John Lowry, do.	3	10	
Thomas Wilson, do.	5		
Thomas Weems, do.	5	10	
Robert Guy, do.	12		
James Guy, jun., do.	6		
James M'Cay, do.	8		
Samuel Hodge, do.	8		
James Lockridge, do.	5		
Samuel Sprowle, for horse hire,	3	17	6
John Cartmill, for do.	3	17	6
Raph Laferty, for do.	3	17	6
Henry Guy, for do.		6	3
John Buchanan, for flour,	27	14	
To John Campbell, for provisions to Indians,		12	
To Thomas Stinson, for do.	2	7	9
Jacob Campbell, do.	1		8
Evan Evans, do.	4	10	
To Moses M'Clure, do.	2	10	00
John Ward, do.		10	
James Wallace, do.	2	2	4
Alexander Walker, do.		10	3
Henry Reburn, do.	2	1	10
John Stevenson, do.	2	7	4
William Beard, do.	1	5	2
To John Arrentrot, do.	2	14	4
Patrick Frazier, do.	6	15	10
John Matthews, do.	1	19	1
John Stevenson, do.	1	10	8
Samson Archer, do.		19	7
William Gregg, do.		10	8

4

	£	s.	d.
Samson Archer, do.	8	6	1
Archibald Huston, do.		5	8
William Christian, do.		6	3
William M'Gee, do.	10	19	2
James Simpson, do.	1	16	3
John Holmes, do.	3	17	10
Archibald Huston, do.	1	11	6
James Bruister, do.		11	4
Thomas Bradshaw, do.	1	5	
Patrick Campbell, do.	3	1	
Thomas Lorimore,	3	3	
To Andrew Hamilton and James Givens, do.	3		9
To John Ree, do.	2	15	
Thomas Millsaps, do.	3	15	8
To John Buchanan, for paid William Henderson, Abraham Brown, and David Looney, for carriage of provisions, &c.,	9	8	
To do., for Alexander Mackie,	1	7	2
To Ruben Harrison, for provisions for Indians,	1	1	8
To Samson Archer, do.	1	9	8
Jonathan Douglass, do.	4	11	10
John Anderson, do.	2	2	1
John Davis, do.	21	10	7
David Moor, do.	14	9	10
Edward M'Donald, do.	3	2	8
Andrew Leeper, do.	1	14	2
William Thompson, do.	1	13	5
Elijah M'Clanahan, do.		6	8
Joseph Crocket, do.	1	7	6
Joseph Love, do.	2	14	7
Robert Looney, do.	2	1	
James Huston, do.		15	9
John Matthews, sen., do.		5	9
James Arbuckle, do.		12	
William Graham, do.		11	9

	£	s.	d.
William Beard, for waggonage,	2		
William Whiteside, for work,		11	8
John Maxwell, captain, as lieutenant,	2	8	
To John Matthews, Matthew Campbell, 16s. each,	1	12	
To John Bowin, serjeant,	1	1	4
To John Bowin, jun., Henry Bowin, Moses Bowin, Reice Bowin, George Matthews, John Campbell, Robert Dew, Richard Matthews, Michael Kelly, 16s. each,	7	4	
To Daniel Goodwin, William Matthews, 8s. each,		16	
To Joshua Matthews, William M'Kinney, 19s. each,	1		
To William Bowin,		8	
Sampson Matthews,		10	
John Matthews, as ensign,		10	
Matthew Campbell, as serjeant,		6	8
To James Wilson, James Magavock, 5s. each,		10	
To John Armstrong, John Bowen, jun., Moses Bowen, James Gilmore, Jonathan Whitley, James Hughston, Andrew Hall, William Buyers, Patrick Porter, William Lapesley, Arthur M'Clure, Samuel Todd, 4s. each,	2	8	
To David Steuart, colonel, as captain,	2	2	
William Lewis, as Lieutenant,	1	1	
John Henderson, as ensign,		14	

To Robert Brackenridge, Robert Craig, Samuel Carr, Robert Patterson, Thomas M'Come, George Moffet, Samuel Patterson, Going Leeper, James Blair, James Young, James Patterson, Robert Willey, Alexander Craig, John Blair, George Anderson, William Polog, George King, James Stewart, Arthur Greir, John King, Robert Finley,

	£	s.	d.
Henry Murry, Walter Cunningham, William Tencher, John Robinson, Audly Hamilton, William Anderson, George Roger, Alexander M'Clanahan, William Reed, Adam Dunlop, James Stevenson, Robert Hunter, William Purzins, 7s. each,	11	18	00
To James M'Dowell, lieutenant,	1	7	
To John Wardlaw, James Couden, serjeants, 12s. each,	1	4	
To James Kenaday, William Kenaday, James Wardlaw, James Logan, Samuel Huston, David Moore, Nathaniel Evans, James M'Clong, John M'Clong, Henry M'Collom, Robert Steel, John Sproul, Moses Whiteside, John Lyle, jun., Robert Lusk, John Montgomery, John Hawl, John Thompson, Archibald Alexander, Patrick Lowry, John Lowry, Thomas Seirl, Charles Allison, Thomas Paxton, James Huston, 9s. each,	11	5	
To Alexander Thompson, as lieutenant,	1	4	
Audley Paul, as ensign,		12	
Matthew Camble, as serjeant,		8	
To Robert Henry, James Wilson, John Mayers, 6s. each,		18	
To George Davison, Thomas Hamilton, 7s. each,		14	
To John Plunkett, James Ward, sen., William Ward, Joseph Ward, 6s. each,	1	4	
To Alexander M'Mullan,		8	
To Robert Allen, jun., James Ward, jun., 6s. each,		12	
To James Davison, Richard Pryar, 7s. each,		14	
To Patrick Savage, Robert Allen, sen., Phelty Cogh, Jacob Botters, 6s. each,	1	4	
To Robert Thompson,		8	

	£	s.	d.
Patrick M'Closkey,		6	
Andrew Hays, captain,	1	4	
Archibald Buchanan, lieutenant,		16	
To Alexander Buchanan, Thomas Hudson, serjeants, 5s. 4d. each,	10	8	
To Edward Cenney,	3		
To John Mitchell, John Tinley, Charles M'Anally, Samuel Davice, Andrew Fitzpatrick, Andrew Miscampbell, Filey Yacome, Samuel M'Dowell, Samuel Lyle, Patrick Lowry, John Lowry, Daniel Lyle, John Putt, William Crurothers, William Taylor, Francis Randols, James M'Clung, David Bryans, David Gray, James Colter, Moses Edmiston, Alexander Walker, John Hays, David M'Croskey, John Dunlop, Andrew Buchanan, David Sayer, John Porter, David Guin, James Buchanan, James Gulton, Matthew Lindsey, John Snodgrass, 4s. each,	6	12	00
To Andrew Hay, captain,	2	8	
Archibald Buchanan, lieutenant,	1	4	
To Henry M'Cullon, Alexander Buchanan, 10s. 8d. each,	1	1	4
To William Buchanan, William Reah, Robert Rheah, Archibald Rheah, James Colter, Alexander Walker, Matthew Linsey, Thomas Gilmore, John Moore, David M'Croskey, Moses Edmistone, David Edmiston, John Robinson, 8s. each,	5	4	
To James Borlane,		5	
To David Sayers, Robert Stevenson, 8s. each,		16	
To Samuel M'Cutchison, John Kilpatrick, William Ward, John Clerk, William M'Cutchison, James Rusk, James M'Cutchison, Walter Trimble, John Wilson, 9s. each,	4	1	

	£	s.	d.
To John Woitlaw, James Woitlaw, 8s. each,		16	
To Hugh Martin, for provisions,		4	
To Colonel John Buchanan, charges of building Fort Fauquier,	11	9	
To do., for paid sundry persons for provisions for Indians,	7	5	1
To do., for provisions to Indians,	1	11	3
James Camble, for provisions,	1	4	1
Sarah Cunningham, do.	2	1	9
James Camble, do.	4	10	5
do. do.	6	13	2
Colonel John Buchanan, do.		3	9
To David Stewart, for horses, horse hire, and drivers, on the Shawnese expedition,	31	13	6
To John Buchanan, Miller, for provisions,	2	9	
To William Long, do.	7	6	6
To David Stewart, for paid sundry persons for provisions,	17	9	5
To Peter Cochan, for a mare killed in the Shawnese expedition,	5		
To James Dunlop, captain,	51	10	
Alexander Hamilton, Lieutenant,	25	15	
Thomas Cadon, corporal,	6	17	4
John Gay, do.	6	10	4
Alexander Legat,	4	8	
Robert Stevenson,	3	13	
James Stevenson,	2	3	
Josiah Wilson, ensign,	20		
David Galloway, serjeant,	6	13	4
John Low,	4	14	
William Elate,	4	5	
Andrew Jameson,	3	15	
Alexander Sutherland,	4	16	
William Hamilton,	3	10	
Patrick Cargon,	4	12	

	£	s.	d.
To Thomas Smith, Ralph Laferty, and James Hugart, sen., £4 9s. each,	13	7	
To James Cartmill and Robert Steuart, £4 5s. each,	8	10	
To George Jameson,	3	3	
To John Cartmill,	4	2	
John Hamilton,	3	11	
To James Miligan, Richard Mase, and Arsbel Clendinin, £3 19s. each,	11	17	
To James Steenson, James Hugart, Jun., and James M'Henry, £3 18s. each,	11	14	
To James Burnsides,	3	14	
Edward Howard, Serjeant,	4	18	8
John Salley,	2	16	
To Matthias Cleeke & James Stuart, £3 14s. each,	7	8	
To Robert Lusk, Corporal,	4	13	4
To David Gallaw, Jun., and Samuel M'Murray, £3 3s. each,	6	6	
To Thomas Hugart, Serjeant,	3	16	
William Edemston, do.	3	12	8
To John Cantley, James Bunton, and Samuel Edemston, £2 14s. each,	8	2	
To John Cain and John Clendinin, £2 10s. each,	5		
To Andrew Buchanan,	2	12	
To John Sprout and Robert Campbell, £2 7s. each,	4	14	
To Thomas Vance,	2	3	
William Matthis,	2		
To John Withlaw, James Cowdown, James Steele, £1 16s. each,	5	8	
To James Gay and Andrew Sitolentown, £1 15s. each,	3	10	
To Dennis M'Nely,	1	3	
To Lawrence Murphy and George Barkley, £1 13s. each,	3	6	

	£	s.	d.
To Robert Grimes and James Grimes, £1 11s.,	3	2	
To William Moore,	1	10	
John Hudson,	1	4	
John M'Coy,	1	10	
Christian Tuley,		15	
Edward Crump,	1	3	
Benjamin Kinsey,	1	8	
To John M'Culley and John Stuart, £1 7s. each,	2	14	
To Alexander M'Elvan,	1	6	
To John Davis and John Hardin, £1 4s. each,	2	8	
To John Williams,		17	
Hugh Gilespy,	1	3	
Hendrey M'Collam,		18	
To Thomas M'Clunge and Joseph M'Clunge, 16s. each,	1	12	
To John Maxwell, Captain,	2	10	
Robert Rennick, Lieutenant,	1	5	
To Robert Montgomery, Samuel Montgomery, James Montgomery, John Montgomery, Joseph Montgomery, James Montgomery, Jun., Thomas M'Ferrin, John M'Ferrin, James M'Ferrin, James Gatlive, Dennis Getty, and Samuel M'Ferrin, 10s. each,	6	00	00
To Francis Reity,		9	
To George Robinson, Captain,	4	16	
To Moses Hambleton, Matthew Shaddin, John Armstrong, John Carr, Richard Carr, William Carvin, George Gunn, William M'Mullin, Jeremiah Green, William Walker, Michael Cloyd, James Lee, and Jones Wabreaner, £1 4s. each,	15	12	
To George Robinson, Captain,	50		
Edwin Peterson, Lieutenant,	3	17	6
Joshua M'Cormack,	10		
Matthew Sheddin,	2	3	

	£	s.	d.
James Cloyd,	9	16	
David Mitchell,	1	15	
Bryan M'Donnall,	7	15	
David Miller,	1	4	
James Snodgrass,	5	1	00
George Clark,	9	17	
Abraham Bist,	5		
Matthew Rollin,	4	19	
Thomas Wilson,	4	16	
Abraham Thompson,	9	9	
James Moore,	9	7	
William Armstrong,	7		
Dennis Getty,	7	17	
To Lodowick Slodser and Christopher Stoder,			
£3 17s. each,	7	14	
To Samuel Rolston,	1	19	
William Garvin,	6	8	
Hugh Martin, for provisions,	5	6	5
Stephen Wilson, for do.		7	6
Felix Gilbert, for do.		15	
James Boreland, for do.	9	9	8
William Meas, for do.	1	8	6
Robert Allen, for do.	8	6	8
William M'Murray, for do.	6	5	8
Joseph Waughub, for do.		12	
To Samuel M'Murrey, for do.	1	12	
Lawrence Contsman, for do.	1	11	9
John Wilson, for do.	2	3	4
William Doughterty, for do.		8	
John Gay, for do.	1	4	
William M'Cutchin,	2	8	4
Alexander Legat, for two beef casks,		10	
To Robert Read, for 9 lbs. powder, £1 13s. 9d.;			
for 9 lbs. lead, 6s. 9d.,	2		6
To Gabriel Jones and Thomas Walker, to pay a			

	£	s.	d.
company under the command of John Smith, according to his muster-roll, ending the 25th day of June, 1756,	576	13	
To Captain John Smith, the balance of his, and his son's pay as lieutenant in the said company,	20	15	
To do., his account paid to sundry persons for provisions and horse hire, and for inlisting soldiers,	199		2
To James Campbell, for provisions,		6	
Ephraim Voss, for do.	4	3	
William Graham, for do.	3		
John M'Farlin, for do.	7	10	
Jacob Rent, for do.	11	18	
Adam Harmon, for do.	1		
Samuel Jackson, for do.	1	17	6
William Thompson, for do.	3	19	5
Conrad Carlock, for do.	1	5	7
William Graham, for do.	8	13	
Thomas Campbell, for cooper's work,	3	12	9
	£3866	3	5

Augusta County was formed from Orange County in 1738. " Previously all that part of Virginia west of the Blue Ridge was included in Orange, but in the fall session of this year it was divided into the counties of Frederick and Augusta." Even after this division it included, in addition to forty counties in Western Virginia, the territory embracing a portion of Pennsylvania, and all of Ohio, Indiana, Michigan, Illinois, and Wisconsin.

Bedford County.

To the Militia of the County of Bedford, and Provisions furnished by sundry Inhabitants of the said County, viz.:

	£	s.	d.
To John Phelps, as captain,	2	8	
Richard Callaway, lieutenant,	1	4	
Samuel Hairston, ensign,		16	
To John Hunter, William Edwards, Ambrose Bryant, serjeants, 10s. 8d. each,	1	12	
To James Callaway, John Talbot, James M'Ronolds, Joseph Looney, Robert Hairston, Nicholas Hays, Thomas Cooper, William Bumpass, David Rosser, Richard Tiths, Nathaniel Patterson, John Alstan, John Martin, John Lawson, George Coldwell, William Hinton, Jonathan Jennings, John Brown, Archibald Campbell, Francis Siver, Amhus Bramlet, Robert Martin, William Chalmore, John Spurlock, Bartlet Henson, John Robertson, William Manley, William Twiddy, Isaac Buterworth, Joseph Ryon, James M'Murtry, Richard Philips, John Lawson, Samuel Gilbert, Daniel Gilbert, Pharaoh Ryley, William Fuqua, John Jackson, John Robertson, jun., Jacob Anderson, Patrick M'Dade, Christopher Sitton, John Hardman, and Charles Talbot, 8s. each,	17	12	
To Captain Matthew Talbot,	38	14	
Thomas Prather, ensign,	10	16	
To William Simmons, serjeant,	8	9	4
To Gross Scruggs and Meshach Haile, serjeants, £7 5s. 4d. each,	14	10	8
To George Haynes,	5	4	
John Richardson,	4	6	
Joshua Richardson,	5	1	
Evan Morgan,	4	5	
John Morgan,	5	5	
John Mackey, jun.,	5	9	

	£	s.	d.
To James Mackey,	4	13	
William Haynes,	4	15	
To John Richardson and William Morgan, £3			
8s. each,	6	16	
To Thomas Morgan,	3	9	
William Yates,	2	18	
To Joseph Benning, John Benning, Samuel			
Arrenton, John Thomas, Richard Taylor,			
John Moore, and Zachariah Roberson,			
£1 14s. each,	11	18	
To Jonathan Richardson,	3	8	
John Grymes,	3	3	
John Pyburn,	3	13	
Thomas Hunt,	3	1	
Jeremiah Pate,		18	
John Pate,	3	7	
Matthew Pate,	1	3	
Anthony Pate,	1	8	
Jacob Pate,		7	
John Macky,		19	
John Casey,	2	3	
To John Loson, David Loson, William Lucks,			
Samuel Gilbert, James Bryan, William			
Layne, and Abraham Chandler, 15s. each,	5	5	
To William Morgan, Jesse Bryan, Barnabas			
Arthur, George Hackworth, Merry Carter,			
and Daniel Richardson, 8s. each,	2	8	
To Robert Martin,	1	14	
Stephen Runnals,	1	9	
Stephen Towns,	1	7	
Barnabas Arthur, jun.,	1		
To John Talbot, James Talbot, Augustine Left-			
wick, John Hall, and Christopher Mun-			
day, 10s. each,	2	10	
To James Millwood,	2		

	£	s.	d.
To John Snow,		12	
Abraham Smith,		18	
To James Spencer, Archelus M'Neale, and John Vardeman, 17s. each,	2	11	
To William Arthur,	4	2	
Thomas Sexton,	2	10	
Moses Preston,	2	11	
Matthew Talbot, for provisions,	27	18	11
Charles Talbot, as lieutenant,	2	14	
Thomas Gilbert, ensign,		16	
To Daniel Gilbert, Benjamin Gilbert, John Hardiman, Richard Edwards, Elliot Lacey, Charles Harris, George Caldwell, and Head Lynch, 8s. each,	3	4	
To William Edwards, Jeremiah Pate, Jacob Pate, and John Pate, 16s. each,	3	4	
To Thomas Reade, John Brown, Acquiller Gilbert, Isaac Butterworth, Thomas Murry, Peter Rawlins, Robert Shipley, Robert Shipley, jun., Anthony Rawlins, and Patrick M'David, 10s. each,	5		
To William Simmons,	1		
Zachariah Burnley,		4	
John Anthony, as lieutenant,	9		
Benjamin Hatcher, ensign,	6		
To Richard Andrews, serjeant,	4		
Richard Ragsdale, do.	3	1	4
To Isaac Brown, John London, John Mattox, Josiah Gibson, Peter Jones, Peter Ragsdale, George Abbott, Nathan Tate, William Tate, William Haynes, and James Mackie, £3 each,	33		
To Robert Oglesby,	2	13	
To George Smith and Sandiver Cashiah, £2 6s. each,	4	12	

	£	s.	d.
To William Whiteside and Henry Prunk, 39s. each,	3	18	
To Joseph Ray,	2	17	
William Arthur,	1	17	
James Callaway, for provisions,	8	17	
John Anthony, do.	9	9	
Richard Woodward,	7	3	7
Stephen English, do.	7	3	
James Neely, do.	1	2	6
Thomas Morgan,	1		
Ralph Fuqua, do.	1	4	
Daniel Morris, do.		10	
William Mead, do.		6	8
William Boyd, do.		6	8
To Edward M'Daniel, assignee of Henry Ferguson, for horse hire,		7	6
To Joseph M'Daniel, assignee of William Crawford, for provisions,	1	3	6
To Thomas Tharman, for provisions, and 13 days' service,		15	
To Adam Beard, for provisions,	7	1	3
Richard Callaway, as serjeant,		5	4
To Jeremiah Early, Jacob Henderson, Ambrose Bryan, Samuel Brown, James Fair, Charles Bright, John Watts, and John Handy, 4s. each,	1	12	
To Richard Callaway, for provisions,	11	6	9
Edward Bright, for do.	5	16	
Charles Bright, for do.	1	18	
James Turner, do.	4	11	8
William Meade, as lieutenant,	1	19	
Jeremiah Yarborough, ensign,		6	
Joseph Rentfroe, serjeant,		6	8
Thomas Prather, do.		4	
To Matthew Talbot, William Morgan, jun.,			

	£	s.	d.
James Board, John Morgan, David Preston, Evan Morgan, John Pyburn, John Wright, and George Grundy, 3s. each,	1	7	
To Moses Rentfro, Joseph Richardson, and William Fuqua, 6s. each,		18	
To Edward Choat,		9	
To Augustine Choat, Robert Pepper, Samuel Pepper, Philip Preston, John Yates, John Robertson, Pharoah Royley, Samuel Robertson, and George Thomas, 7s. each,	3	3	
To Daniel Richardson, George Adams, and James Moore, 5s. each,		15	
To Joseph M'Daniel,		10	
To Nathan Richardson and Thomas Overstreet, 4s. each,		8	
To William Handy,		5	
William Meade, for provisions,	1	13	
Joseph Rentfroe, as lieutenant,	15	15	
To Robert Jones, William Carson, Stephen Rentfroe, John Anderson, William Davis, Edward Davis, Charles Cox, John Riley, William Puttect, James Puttect, James Rentfroe, Nathan Pottlet, Thomas Jones, and William Crabtree, £5 5s. each,	73	10	
To John Davis,	5	1	
James Corser,	3	7	
David Morse,		12	
To Rueben Keef, William Dilenham, Samuel Woodward, and Nathan Richardson, 3s. each,		12	
To Joseph Rentfroe, for provisions,	46	3	6
Robert Hairston, for do.	2	5	4
William Crawford, for do.		4	6
Robert Ewing, for do.		12	
Joseph Crocket, for do.		10	

	£	s.	d.
To Nicholas Welch, for do.	5	2	4
Samuel Hairston, as lieutenant,	2	17	
Robert Hairston, ensign,	1	4	
James Patterson, Serjeant,	1	2	8
To Joseph M'Murty, Abraham M'Clelan, and Thomas Oglesby, 12s. each,	1	16	
To Andrew Hairston and Patrick Hensey, 5s. each,		10	
To Nathaniel Patterson, Serjeant,		9	4
To William Manley, William Twedey, John Galloway, David Rosser, and James Carson, 7s. each,	1	15	
To Archibald Campbell, Edward Ohair, William Chalmor, James M'Runnals, John Thompson, Abraham Mitchell, Nicholas Hays, and John Pratt, 6s. each,	2	8	
To Luke Murphy, George Adams, and James Johnston, 7s. each,	1	1	
To Samuel Hairston, as ensign,	2	14	
John Hunter, serjeant,	1	16	
James Patterson,	1	4	
To Thomas Oglesby and John Neilson, £1 each,	2		
To James Morris, James Murphy, Luke Murphy, and Charles Simmons, 8s. each,	1	12	
To John Daunn and John Galloway, 13s. each,	1	6	
To John Dixton, Joseph Murty, and Israel Young, 9s. each,	1	7	
To William Manly, William Tweedy, and George Adams, 12s. each,	1	16	
To Abraham Thompson,		11	
Henry Ferguson, for provisions,		7	10
Captain John Quarles,	42	6	
William Irvine, ensign,	4	6	
Ambrose Bramlett, serjeant,	2	17	4
John Robinson,	7		

	£	s.	d.
William Bramlitt,	5	19	
William Nix,	6	12	
John Abston,	6	3	
William Anderson,	6	2	
Jesse Paty,	6	1	
Patrick Vance,	6	11	
Thomas Overstreet,	4	19	
William Stone,	2	5	
John Spurlock,	4	18	
George Smith,	4	2	
William Wooddie,	4	6	
Jonathan Ginnings,	2	8	
Thomas —right,	2	16	
To William Ragsdale, Nathan Tate, William Tate, Peter Ragsdale, Isaac Brown, John Mattocks, Peter Jones, and Sandesur Kesier, £4 19s. each,	39	12	
To George Abet and Benjamin Hatcher, £2 15s. each,	5	10	
To John Mitchum,	6	11	
John Tinker,	2	5	
John Martin,	2	3	
Jonathan Jones,	2	12	
Thomas Daws,	1	17	
To William Morgan,	1	4	00
To James Board and William Board, £2 14s. each,	5	8	
To John Morgan,	2	10	
Patrick Halloguan,	1	13	
John Mead and Abel Mead, 32s. each,	3	4	
John Robinson,	1	5	
William Irvine, lieutenant,	14	14	
Ambrose Bramlett, ensign,	7	18	
To Josias Gipson and Richard Andrews, serjeants, £6 12s. each,	13	4	

5

	£	s.	d.
To James Alcorn,	1	17	
James Moore,	1	5	
John Haynes,		15	
To Daniel M'Foll and James M'Fall, 14s. each,	1	8	
To James Jones and Josiah Ramsey, 11s. each,	1	2	
To John Pate,	1	10	
To Anthony Pate and Jacob Pate, 20s. each,	2		
To Matthew Pate,		17	
David Irvine,	1	2	
Thomas Owens,		14	
To Patrick Johnson, John Patrick Burks, and Robert Jones,	1	10	
To James Galloway, Samuel Robinson, Hugh Crocket, and Thomas Baker, 12s. each,	2	8	
To John Orrack and John Ward, 9s. each,		18	
To Jonathan Prather and James Presnal, 8s. each,		16	
To William Walker,		7	
To William Phelps and William Montgomery, 5s. each,		10	
To Jeremiah Earley, lieutenant,	8	2	
To George Watts and Edmund Fair, serjeants, £3 12s. each,	7	4	
To James Fair, Samuel Brown, James Galloway, Richard Woodard, sen., Charles Bright, Edward Bright, Richard Maples, John Jones, Richard Woodard, Richard Burks, Boling Burks, William Woodard, John Woodard, James Orchard, and Edward Watts, £2 14s. each,	43	4	
To Richard Pritchard,	2	4	
John House,	1	17	
To Thomas Duly, James Duly, and Thomas Maclin, 31s. each,	4	13	
To James Wine,		16	

	£	s.	d.
John Watts,		14	
Jeremiah Early, lieutenant,	8	11	
To George Watts and Jacob Anderson, serjeants, £3 16s. each,	7	12	
To Edmund Fair, James Galloway, Samuel Brown, Richard Woodard, Charles Bright, James Fair, Edward Bright, Richard Maples, John Jones, Thomas Thirman, Richard Woodard, sen., and John Hughs, £2 17s. each,	34	4	
To James Bromlet,	2	14	
To Richard Burks, jun., William Burks, Boling Burks, Edward Watts, and James Orchard, £2 11s. each,	12	15	
To William Woodward, John Bush, John Woodward, Isaac Woodward, Michael Poore, and Richard Pritchard, £2 6s. each,	13	16	
To Andrew Poore,	1	16	
Jeremiah Early, for provisions,	7	17	3
To William Galloway, for provisions to militia and Indians,	61	2	6
To James Galloway, for provisions to Indians,	7	9	00
To Leonard Hall, for conducting Indians,	1	10	
To James Standerfield, for provisions for do.	4	8	6
To John Hues, for conducting Indians,	2		
To Charles Bright, for provisions for do.	1	13	
To Jeremiah Yarborough, for do.	1	10	
Henry Tate, for do.	1	15	
Joseph Rentfro, for do. to militia,	7	12	4
Thomas Dooley, for do.		14	
William Galloway, for do.	3	3	2
John Reade, for do.	5	3	10
	£1101	12	9

Brunswick County.

To the Militia of the County of Brunswick, and for provisions furnished by sundry inhabitants of the said County, viz.:

	£	s.	d.
To Captain Edward Goodrich,	30	00	00
To Frederick Maclin and John Parish, lieutenants, £15 each,	30		
To Vines Collier and Jeptha Arthington, ensigns, £10 each,	20		
To Thomas Briggs, William Rose, Nathaniel Tatum, and John Tilman, serjeants, at £6 13s. 4d. each,	26	13	4
To James Scott, drummer,	4	14	6

To Richard Gower, William Parsons, Isham
Harris, William Bryan, James Hargrove,
Robert Wall, Charles Wall, Peter Jackson,
Frederick Glover, Thomas Mannim, Mark
Jackson, Daniel Wall, Robert Peebles,
William Foster, Zebulon Lewis, Jesse
Brown, William Parham, Nicholas Fennell, Abram Martin, William Martin, John
Ramsey, John Calton, Richard Ramsey,
Benjamin Simpson, Thomas Connally,
Thomas Haulcom, Edward Tatum, Moses
Tomerlin, Samuel Jackson, Peter Freeman, Edward Freeman, Henry Jackson,
Charles Guntur, John Carlile, William
Edwards, Elias Fowler, John Barnet,
Richard Dobbins, Joel Smith, Daniel Collier, Samuel Russell, Robert Gee, jun.,
William Cooke, William Gaultney, Sampson Mosely, George Walton, jun., William
Randolph, William Ledbetter, Samuel
Sexton, William Ledbetter, jun., Nathan
Harris, Robert Gaultney, Thomas Walton,

	£	s.	d.
John Moore, Robert Lanier, Thomas Denton, William Denton, Nathaniel Steed, Edmonds Barker, Lewis Barker, David Moss, James Linch, David Adam, Roger Tilman, William Upchurch, Thomas Nance, Thomas Ravenscrop, Michael Upchurch, John Upchurch, George Wall, Thomas Nance, John Hailes, Francis Mitchell, Tobias Moore, and Robert Nance, at £5 each,	375		
To David Kelly and John Ray, 15s. each,	1	10	00
To John Tilman, sen.,	4	00	00
Joseph Parish,	4	10	
To John Wooley and Peter Sinclair, £1 10s. each,	3		
To George Brewer,		7	
John Hix,	1	13	
Druary Sims,	4		
Mark Rollins,	2	5	
To Captain Edward Goodrich, for provisions and cart hire,	17	4	5
To do., for his pay and the pay of the guards conducting drafted soldiers to Fredericksburg,	8	11	
	£533	38	3

Caroline County.

	£	s.	d.
To George Muse, the balance of his pay as lieutenant-colonel of the first Virginia Regiment,	6	10	00
To Benjamin Philips, for an horse lost on the Shawnee expedition,	6		
	£12	10	00

Chesterfield County.

	£	s.	d.
To Mr. Archibald Gary, for provisions,	27	16	00
To Robert Kennon, for his pay, and the pay of the guards conducting drafted soldiers to Fredericksburg, and for their subsistence,	14	5	
	£42	1	00

Cumberland County.

	£	s.	d.
To Captain Poindexter Mosby, for his pay and the pay of the guards conducting drafted soldiers to Fredericksburg,	5	5	9

Culpeper County.

	£	s.	d.
To Valentine Sevear, for provisions,	3	10	8
Benjamin Davis, do.'	2	12	4
John Strother, do.	1	8	
Joseph James, do. for Indians,	2	1	4
David Johnston, do.		15	
Valentine Sevear, for horse hire,		15	
Michael Lawler, for provisions,	2		10
Richard Covington, for horse hire,	1	17	6
To William Slaughter and Reuben Long, for do.		11	3
To John Parker, by Colonel Martin's certificate,	18		
To William Lightfoot, for carrying drafts to Winchester, as by account proved, and command of a company nine days,	10	16	3
To William Slaughter, lieutenant, 54 days, at 3s.,	8	2	
To John Payton, serjeant, Richard Doggett, do., £3 12s. each,	7	4	

To John Ballenger, John Field, Thomas Slaughter, Francis Brown, Anthony Strother, Francis Strother, John Peyton, William Baker, William Edwards, Robert Scott, James Browning, Henry Stonsafer, Wil-

	£	s.	d.

liam Wall, John Yancy, William Tutt,
George Goggins, Nathaniel Parker, John
Shingleton, Charles M'Queen, John Cox,
John Powell, John Berry, Thomas Ray,
Joshua Sherrill, 54s. each, — 64 | 16 | 00

To Henry Bowen, for provisions, — 00 | 11 | 1½

James Crumley, do. — | 5 | 4½

Nathaniel Bell, do. — | 15 | 1

James Cunningham, do. — 3 | 6 | 5½

David Booth, do. — 1 | 3 | 4½

Jacob Hite, do. — 2 | 1 | 3

Robert Cunningham, do. — 2 | 4 | 2

To Reuben Long, William Underwood, Thomas
Yeates, Jun., John Morgan, Hankinson
Read, Richard Parker, Alexander Frazier,
French Strother, Edward Bush, John Care,
William Thornhill, James Story, William
Poe, Oliver Towles, Samuel Pannell, John
Banger, William Day, Peter Rucker, Wil-
liam Hopper, John Pabley, James Corder,
John Chisum, Christopher Ziglar, Mark
Hardin, Samuel Hensley, John Bradley,
Richard Parks, Allen Wiley, John Wither-
head, Edward Brown, Thomas Baker,
Joseph Duncan, John Anderson, John
Faver, Jun., William Collin, Francis
Jacoby, William Robertson, John Duncan,
William Nalle, Jun., John Cox, James
Garrett, James Green, Peter Fleshman,
Jacob Broil, 9s. each, — 19 | 16

To Lieutenant William Slaughter, from the 15th
of May to the last of August, 1758, inclu-
sive, being 109 days, at 3s., — 16 | 7

To Ensign Charles Yancy, the same time, at 2s., — 10 | 18

To Serjeant Hankinson Read, the same time, at
1s. 4d., — 7 | 5 | 4

	£	s.	d.
To Serjeant John Payton, do.	7	5	4
To Colonel Robert Slaughter, the pay of 40 men sent by order of Mr. President Blair, to Garison Patersen's Fort, the same time,	218		
To Richard Parks, going express to Winchester,	1	1	6
	£415	10	1

To the Militia of the county of Culpepper, viz.:

	Lbs. tob.
To William Russell, Lieutenant-Colonel,	640
To William Brown, Captain,	2700
To John Field, Lieutenant,	2375
To do., for two horses impressed and employed in the service,	2700
To George Weatherall, serjeant,	1710
To Roger Dixon, assignee of William Nalle, junior,	1656
To William Nalle, the elder,	1710
To Charles Yancy, Ensign,	1900
To John Strother, Captain,	2850
To Francis Strother, Lieutenant,	2375
To William Roberds, Ensign,	1900
To Stephen Rogers, Serjeant,	1710
To John Gambill, do.	1710
To Henry Gambill, do.	1710
To Sallis Hansford, do.	1710
To do., for a horse impressed and employed in the service,	230
To eight foot soldiers, viz.: Francis Cooper, William M'Daniel, John Thomas, Miles Murfee, John Hayes, John Graham, assigned to John Strother, Joshua Sherald, assigned to do., and William Wall, assigned of William Green, 1385 each,	11080

To nineteen foot soldiers, viz.: Jocob Browning, Wil-

Lbs. tob.

liam Boworn, John Laton, Richard Burk, Richard Parks, Nicholas Yager, Cornelius Mitchell, John Browning, William Tapp, Samuel Moore, John Willhoit, John Strother, assignee of James Gillison, Benjamin Morgan, John Shropshire, David Bridges, Roger Dixon, assignee of John Younger, John Bowman, George Goggan, Martin Nalle, assignee of Mordock Mackenzie, and William Eastham, assignee of Jacob Wall, 1425 each,   28500

To William Russell, for his servant, John Dixon Wright, a foot soldier,   180

To Roger Dixon, assignee of Daniel Delaney and Alexander Baxter, foot soldiers,   2760

To John Cave, James Nash, William Twiman, and Joel Yarborough, foot soldiers, 1380 each,   5520

To Francis Grant, foot soldier,   1245

To Adam Maland, Adam Barler, John Greson, John Relsback, Andrew Carpenter, Lewis Fisher, John Gloor, Matthias Weaver, Christopher Barlor, Timothy Swindele, John Plunketpeter, Matthias Rouce, and William Yager, foot soldiers, 105 each,   1365

To John Grim, Jacob Harroback, and Harmer Young, foot soldiers, 150 each,   450

To Henry Gaines, a foot soldier,   120

To Henry Stringfellow,   260

To William Roberts, for one horse impressed and employed,   270

To Francis Strother, for do.   270

To John Strother, assignee of William Shropshire, for do.   270

To do., assignee of James Gillson, for do.   270

To do., assignee of Benjamin Morgan, for do.   270

To do., assignee of Robert M'Clanham, for one cow for the militia,   500

Lbs. tob.

To William Brown, assignee of John Hite, for one
    sheep and two shoats for do.   300

To do., assignee of do., for 591 lbs. of flour and two
    bags for do.   1382

To John Strother, assignee of Robert M'Coy, for
    bread for do.   100

To do., assignee of Sarah Chester, for one sheep for do.   150

To John Strother, assignee of John Hite, for meal
    for do.   80

To do., assignee of Robert M'Coy, for one steer for do.   350

To do., assignee of Charles Perkins, for waggon hire,   375

To George Weatherall, for bread,   40

To Samuel Moore, for corn,   100

To William Roberts, for meat and braed,   160

To William Johnson, for do.   310

To William Duncan, for beef,   300

To John Strother, for beef, bread, salt, & three bags,   510

To John Rosin, assignee of William Judd, for one
    horse impressed and employed,   120

To William Green, assignee of Charles Lewis, for
    one cow,   700

To the clerk, for certifying 84 allowed claims,   200

Elizabeth City County.

Wilson Cary, county Lieutenant, return of Field officers for said county Nov. 22, 1751. (Calendar Virginia State Papers, Vol. I, page 247.)

    John Hunter, Col.
    John Tabb   "
    Robert Armstead, Maj. of Foot.
    Cary Selden, Capt. of 100 militia.
    Charles King, Capt. of 66 troopers.
    Westward Armstead, Capt. of 60 troopers.
        Names of men not given.

Essex County.

A list of Officers and Common Soldiers in Essex County, April 9th, 1753, under the Command of the Hon. Richard Corbin, Esq. (Calendar Virginia State Papers, Vol. I, page 247.)

JOHN CORBIN, Col. of militia.
Thomas Waring, Col. of Horse.
Wm. Dangerfield, Col. of Foot.
Fran. Smith, Major of Horse.
Wm. Roan, Major of Foot.

Capts.	No. of men.	
Forest Upshaw,	65	Essex Militia.
James Jones,	59	
Wm. Covington,	43	
Fra. Waring,	70	
Richard Tyler,	59	
Thos. Edmundson,	51	
Wm. Garrett,	69	
Saml. Hipkins,	73	
Simon Miller,	70	
	559	

R. CORBIN.

Sept., 1758, Hening's Statutes, Vol. 7, page 214.

	£	s.	d.
To Captain Forest Upshaw, for his pay and the the pay of the guards conducting drafted soldiers to Fredericksburg,	9		
To James Emerson, maintaining drafted soldiers in prison,	6		
	£15	00	00

ACT OF ASSEMBLY FOR THE STATE OF VIRGINIA, MAR., 1756.

Hening's Statutes, Vol. 7, Pages 21 & 22.

And whereas divers companies of the militia of the several counties of Prince William, Fairfax, and Culpepper, were lately drawn out into actual service for the defence and protection of the frontiers of this colony against the incursions and depredations of the French and their Indian allies, whose names, and the time they respectively continued in the said service, are contained in a certain schedule to this act annexed, and it is just and necessary that they should be paid for such their service.

To the Militia of the County of Fairfax, Va., Hening's Statutes, Vol. 7, pages 21–22 :

	Lbs. tob.
To Lewis Ellzey, Captain,	1500
Sampson Turley, Lieutenant,	1250
Samuel Tillett, Corporal,	1100
James Tillett, do.	1100
Sampson Demovil, do.	1100
To Jeremiah Hutchinson, Corporal,	1100
Joseph Stevens, do.	1100
Philip Grymes, do.	330
Gilbert Simson, jun., do.	660
To sixteen Troopers, viz., George Shortridge, Benjamin Ladd, Nathan Williamson, Vincent Boggess, Joseph Fry, Daniel Thomas, Benjamin Hutchison, George Simson, Helland Middleton, Thomas Shore, William Southard, Robert Watson, servant to Lewis Ellzey, Thomas Simmonds, John Berkley, junior, Francis Eaton, and William Pickett, 1000 each,	16000
To nine Troopers, with impressed horses, viz., Jesse Martin, Charles Newland, Thomas West, John Price, Richard Newall, James Chamberlayne, Thomas Cartwright, David Thanas, junior, and Edward Davis, 750 each,	6750

Lbs. tob.

To seven horses impressed for the above Troopers, belonging to William Crump, John Williams, Thomas Wyatt, Charles Broadwater, Henry Taylor, Barnaby Curry, and John Summers, 250 each,   1750

To twenty Troopers, viz., William Peake, junior, William Trammell, Gilbert Simson, junior, William Scutt, William Musgrove, William Hayes, Edward Masterson, Mark Chilton, Thomas Triplett, William Morris, William Smith, John Stephens, Thomas Osborn, George Saunders, Daniel Shoemaker, Joseph Burson, Simon Shoemaker, Edward Hardin, Nicholas Grymes, and Michael Regan, junior, 300 each,   6000

To eight Troopers, with impressed horses, viz., William Owsley, Joseph Jones, Joseph Martin, William Stackhouse, John Sinclare, David Smith, Clement Gamer, and John Dawson, 225 each,   1800

To eight impressed horses, for the above Troopers, belonging to Daniel French, Benjamin Satterfield, William Palmer, John Hough, Benjamin Pool, John Pultney, and Jacob Morris, 150 each,   1050

	Current money.		
To Thomas Coulthard, for a horse impressed and lost,	£6	—	—
To Benjamin Vanlandingham, an express,	1	5	—
To Edward Seed, do.		5	—
To Thomas Graffert, do.	1	3	4
To Garrett Bolin, do.		5	
To William Sewell, for an express, and a cart and horses,	2	8	
To William West, for necessaries and expresses,	5	10	10

                         £   s.   d.

To John Gladin, for necessaries for the soldiers,   2 18 —

To Richard Moxley, do.   16 3

To Carlyle and Dalton, for powder, lead, flints, and for an express,   6 10 7½

To the Clerk, for certifying ten claims,   200

Fairfax County.

(*Continued from pages 217–218.*)

                         £   s.   d.

To Nicholas Minor, captain,   15 12 00

Josiah Clapham, lieutenant,   7 16

William Trammell, ensign,   5 4

To Charles Martin, Francis Summers, Jesse Martin, Serjeants, £3 9s. 4d. each,   10 8

To Edward Hardin, John Donalson, William Calvin, Samuel Philips, James Thomas, William Darns, Joshua Meaks, John Wren, William Shortridge, Samuel Jenkins, Samuel More, Richard Pell, William Bowling, Philip Merchant, George Valendingham, Robert Bowling, Isaac Hussey, Benjamin Williams, Moses Howard, James Robinson, John Davis, Thomas Jenkins, Abraham Stiff, Joseph Adams, Joseph Bradley, Thomas Cartwright, Francis Awbrey, Joshua Claypole, William O'Daniel, Thomas Saunders, Edward Rice, William Cottrill, John Car, Simon Shoemaker, John Shore, Joseph Martin, Peter Wilson, William Jackson, William M'Coy, Henry Townsend, Thomas Morgan, Thomas Ray, William Massey, Franklin Perry, George Shoemaker, £2 12s. each,   117 00 00

	£	s.	d.
To Captain James Hamilton, his pay and guards' subsistence carrying soldiers to Winchester,	10	4	1
	£166	4	1

Frederick County.

	£	s.	d.
To Archibald Ruddall, lieutenant,	3	6	
Henry Selser, serjeant,	1	9	4
John Jones,	1	1	
To Jeremiah Odle, Moses Job, Reudy Mank, George Bennet, Jonathan Odle, and James Thruston, 17s. each,	5	2	
To Patrick M'Kenny,	1	2	
To Richard Mank, Henry Mank, and Daniel Mank, 17s. each,	2	11	
To Henry M'Kenney,	1	2	
To Nathaniel Baily, Peter Baily, and William Cross, 15s. each,	2	5	
To Richard Murphy,		17	
Thomas Speak, as ensign,		8	
Charles Littleton, serjeant,		5	4
To Daniel Johnston, Stephen Suthard, Edward Linsey, Josiah Springer, Jacob Pricket, Stephen Stradler, Charles Colson, John Hampton, Samuel Mason, Peter Petanger, Francis M'Cormick, Thomas Alfort, Richard Stearman, and Thomas Linsey, 4s. each,	2	16	00
To Robert Pearis,	12		
Thomas Speake, lieutenant,	6		
John Horden, ensign,	4		
To William Matthew and John Stephenson, £2 13s. 4d. each,	5	6	
To John Vance, James Meamack, James Morris,			

	£	s.	d.
William Hall, William Miller, Benjamin Foolam, William Locard, Thomas Linsey, Levi Jones, Edward Martin, Josiah Springer, Mark Hardin, Solomon Burkem, Samuel Stubbs, Gilbert Gorden, George Bell, Charles Colson, James Grigson, George Rice, John Miller, William Jacobs, Joshua Ewings, and Thomas Conaly, £2 each,	46		
To Isaac Lindsey, David James, and Edward Trummens, 39s. each,	5	17	
To Owen Wingfield,	1	5	
Walter Shirley,	1	14	
Robert Goosberry,	1	16	
Jarvis Shirley,	1	14	
To John Parks and Isaac Thomas, £2 each,	4		
To James Jack and Hugh Johnston, 33s. each,	3	6	
To James Jones,	1	3	
Francis Maginis,	1	5	
Joseph Lyon,		11	
Joseph M'Dowell, as lieutenant,	1	7	
John Allen, ensign,		18	
James Ireson, serjeant,		12	
To Thomas Allen, Andrew Blackburn, William Stephenson, John M'Gill, Benjamin Blackburn, Isaac White, Matthew Harbison, William Blackburn, Bryan Money, James Hughes, Joseph Fleming, William White, John Young, Joseph Taucett, John Capper, David Williams, Leonard Cooper, Joseph Carroll, John Cook, William Wilson, Samuel Vance, Andrew Vance, James Huston, William Hughes, and John Cooper, 9s. each,	11	5	
To Thomas Speak, captain,	2	14	

	£	s.	d.
John Hardin, lieutenant,	1	4	
Magnus Tate, ensign,		14	
Charles Littleton, serjeant,		12	
John Champain, do.		9	4

To Daniel Johnson, Stephen Suthard, James Lindsey, Thomas Lindsey, Jacob Pricket, Thomas Price, Robert Stewart, Stephen Johnson, Isaac Lindsey, John Regan, Edward Timons, John Hampton, John Colston, Solomon Littleton, Thomas Robinson, Edward Degell, 9s. each, — 7 4

To Francis M'Crimar, Gasper Bewtoole, Hugh Stephenson, Edward Haven, John Hudson, Benjamin Fullom, John Vance, John Stephenson, Josiah Coombs, James Morris, 8s. each, — 4 00 00

To John Laman, James Legat, John Dickson, Holaway Perry, Joseph Pierce, Henry Vanmetar, Lawrence Lender, Edward Mergee, Joseph Vanmeter, Jacob Mergee, Remembrance Williams, Joseph Polson, William Fiell, Nicholas M'Intire, Edward Lucas, Robert Buckus, Benjamin Sweet, John Taylor, and Anthony Turner, 7s. each, — 6 13 00

To Robert Cropper, for a horse for Indians, 4

To John Allen, lieutenant, 1 4

James Iresen, ensign, 6

George Wright, serjeant, 10 8

To William Hughs, Bryan Money, John Magill, James Hugh, James Huston, John Cooper, 8s. each, — 2 8

To James Camp, 7

To Richard Hankins, John Cook, Andrew Vance, Samuel Vance, John Duckworth,

6

	£	s.	d.
Joseph Greenway, Joseph Wattbroke, Anthony Dunlevy, 8s.	3	4	
To William Wilson,		3	
John Vance,		7	
Will Elimus Ghink, Doctor,		4	
Jesse Jackson,		7	
To Samuel and Anthony Blackburn, administrators of John Blackburn, for provisions,	2		
To John Mendenhall, for do.	2	4	8½
James Jack, for do.	4	6	
John Shearer, for do.	1	7	10
James Magill, for do.		19	6
Edward Sningers, for do.	2	5	9
Robert Stockdale, for do.	3	8	4½
Van Swearingen, for do.	5	3	
Isaac Pearce, for do.		13	8
To James Magill, for the estate of William Nealy, for do.	7	8	8
To Edward Stroud, for do.	2	16	8½
To Lewis Stephens, for horse hire and provisions,	7		10
To Isaac Perkins, for do.	7	5	7
Evans Watkins, for do.	1	10	
John Philips, for do.	1	15	
	£218	17	6½

Gloucester County.

	£	s.	d.
To John Wyatt, for carrying drafted soldiers to Fredericksburg, in 1756,	11	5	6

Goochland County.

	£	s.	d.
To Mr. John Payne, for provisions to Indians,	3	8	00
To William Pryor, do.		3	8
Walter Lake, for horse hire,		2	6

	£	s.	d.
William Rutherford, for provisions,		12	4
To Colonel Charles Lewis, for do. to Indians,	3	19	
	£8	5	6

Halifax County.

	£	s.	d.
To colonel Abraham Maury, for pay to lieutenant Thomas Green, and a party of militia under the command of the said Green, in Halifax, as by muster-roll,	42	1	
To do., for pay to Thomas Spragin, as a lieutenant, and a party of the militia of the said county under the command of the said Spragin, as by muster-roll,	5	10	
To do., for pay to captain Robert Wooding and a company of militia of the said county, under the command of the said Wooding, as by muster-roll,	82	19	
To do., for pay to James Dillard, as a lieutenant, and a party of militia of the said county, under the command of the said Dillard, as by muster-roll,	102	4	8
To do., for pay to captain Peter Wilson and a company of militia of the said county, under the command of the said Wilson, as per muster-roll,	33	3	4
To Thomas Callaway, as ensign,		16	
To Thomas Edwards, Edward Peregoy, John Lewis, Peter Manin, John Childers, William Simmons, Huncrest Scarlock, and John Wade, 7s. each,	2	16	
To John Hickie, for provisions to Indians,	17	11	5
To do., for a horse for do.	5	10	
To John M'Grigger, for provisions for do.	18	13	3

To colonel Abraham Maury, for 28 dars' ser-

	£	s.	d.
vice in riding to the forts and settling townships,	14		
To do., for riding from Williamsburg to Halifax with Mr. President's instructions, 150 miles,	2	10	
To do., for 10 days' riding to Williamsburg and attending on the committee to settle militia accounts,	5	00	00
To captain Robert Wade, jun., for pay to himself, officers, and a company of militia of the said county under his command, as by muster-roll,	475	8	6
To do. for provisions,	99	2	5
do. for horse hire,	7	10	
To William Griffith, for provisions,	1	1	6
To colonel Abraham Maury, for pay to captain James Dillard and a company of militia of the said county, under command of the said James Dillard, as by muster-roll,	414	11	4
To captain James Dillard, for horse hire, &c.,	2	8	
To John Frederick Miller, for provisions,	12	9	7
To Hamon Crite, for do.	12	13	8
To captain Thomas Callaway,	6	18	
William Edwards, lieutenant,	3	9	
Hugh Harris, ensign,	2	6	
To James Elkin and John Edwards, serjeants, 30s. 8d. each,	3	4	1
To John Harris, John Rice, Thomas Norton, Thomas Fern, John Harris, Jun., John Wade, Benjamin Croley, Richard Moore, Archibald Thompson, John Blevins, Clement Lee, Weels Ward, Nathaniel Hendley, John Sturd, James Sturd, William Blevins, Jun., Josiah Cox, Ningum Prator, Nehemiah Praier, John Blevins, Sen., William Asher, and John Garcer, 23s. each,	25	6	

	£	s.	d.
To William Rickle,		1	5
To Joseph Morton, John Lindsey, William Murfee, and George Young, 4s.		16	
To John Sillivant and William Seales, 7s. each,		14	
To Daniel Durbin, Edward Peregoy, William Ratcliff, Silas Ratcliff, and William Satterwhite, 12s. each,	3		
To John Frederick Pikcle and Daniel Newman, 6s. each,		12	
To James Blevins,		15	
To John Talbot, Thomas Wollin, and Pearce Gwin, 8s. each,	1	4	
To William Cox and William Blevins, Sen., 9s. each,		18	
To John Williams,		14	
To Nathaniel Terry, the balance of his pay for attending militia and building three Forts,	29	10	
To do., assignee of William Fuqua, for provisions to Indians,	3	8	
To William M'Daniel, do.	3	18	8
John Cook, do.	1	13	2
William Dillingham, do.	1	10	6
Adam Lovin,	2	5	9
John Confey, do. and for horse hire,	5	13	
	£1456	17	9

The following claims from the County of Hampshire, Hening's Statutes, Vol. 7, page 25, viz.:

	Lbs. tob.
To George Parker, for two hogs,	510
John Decker, for one barrel of Corn,	120
John Kirkendale, for corn and wheat,	175
Sarah Decker, for corn,	72
John Forman, for wheat,	180

	Lbs. tob.
William Buffington, for one cow,	450
Do. for corn and wheat,	601
Do. for wheat and flour,	124
Margaret Sinder, for corn,	45
To Mary Sinder, for one hog and one shoat,	200
Nathaniel Kirkendale, for two steers,	1300
Do. for corn,	60
Do. for one hog and corn,	402
Henry Vanmeter, for three Beeves,	1080
Do. for salt,	360
Thomas M'Guire, for corn,	72
Benjamin Kirkendale, for corn,	120

	£	s.	d.
To David Gummery, for corn,	4		
To William Buffinton, for wheat,		16	6
To do., for four steers and one mutton,	8	12	
To do., for two steers,	5	8	
To George Parker, assignee of James Fowler, for one cow,	1	16	3
To Benjamin Kirkendale, for pork and flour,	1	16	3
To Henry Vanmeter, for beef, pork, flour, & corn,	11	2	2
To Abraham Hite, for corn,	1	18	
To John Kirkendale, for beef, flour, pork, & salt,	5	12	1
To Job Pearsal, for one hog and salt,	1	6	4
To Joseph Edwards, for flour and bread,	7	18	1½
To do., for cheese and salt,		8	7½
To do., for pasturage of horses,	1	1	6
To David Edwards, for one cow,	2		

Hanover County.

	£	s.	d.
To Captain Christopher Hudson, for pay to him, his officers and company, to the last day of August, 1758, inclusive, from the time of enlistment,	302	10	2

	£	s.	d.
To do., for provisions,	17	1	6
To William Huson, for cart hire,	10	10	
To Christopher Hudson, paid for a guide,		18	
To David Henderson, for digging a well at fort Dunlop,		15	
To captain George Pitt, for his pay and the pay of his Guards conducting drafted soldiers to Fredericksburg,	7		
	£338	14	8

Henrico County.

	£	s.	d.
To Thomas Mosely, for provisions,	3	16	1
To do., for his pay and the pay of the guards conducting drafted soldiers to Fredericksburg,	6	10	
To Messieurs Coutts and Crosse, assignees of James Hollis, for two horses lost in the Shawnee expedition, appraised to	9		
	£19	6	1

James City County.

	£	s.	d.
To captain William Vaughan, for his pay and the pay of the guards conducting drafted soldiers of this county and Williamsburg to Fredericksburg,	6	14	
To John Grainger, for maintaining soldiers in gaol,	1		
To Josiah Chowning, for horse impressed,		2	6
To John Valentine, for provisions, &c., to Indians,		7	
To George Holmes, for ferriages of Indians,	1	5	9
	£9	9	3

King George County.

	£	s.	d.
To captain William Rowley, for his pay, the pay of the guards, and for substance, conducting drafted soldiers to Winchester,	15	5	6
To William Lightfoot, for provisions and ferriages,	9	11	10
To Moses Hopwood, for provisions,		4	4
To colonel Charles Carter, for arms, &c., bought of Mr. William Cunninghame, for the use of the militia, and left in the service of the country,	38	18	10
	£64	00	6

Louisa County.

	£	s.	d.
To captain Samuel Waddy, his pay, and the guards', and for subsistence, conducting drafted soldiers to Fredericksburg,	12	7	3
To James Overton, as ensign,		10	
To Henry Dickenson, Clifton Rhodes, Jeduthon Harper, James Robinson, Zenus Tate, Thomas Jones, Nicholas Meriwether, and Humphry Bickley, 5s. each,	2		
To William Howard, for provisions to Indians,	1	12	8
To Mr. Thomas Walker, contractor for victualing the rangers and militia in Agusta,	349	12	9
	£366	2	8

Loudon County.

	£	s.	d.
To captain Nicholas Minor,	1	00	00
Aeneas Campbell, lieutenant,		7	6
Francis Wilks,	1	17	
James Willock,	1	15	

	£	s.	d.
To John Owsley and William Stephens, 15s. each,	1	10	
To Robert Thomas,		10	
John Moss, Jun.,		4	
John Thomas, for provisions,		5	
John Moss, do.		2	8
William Ross, do.		2	
	£7	13	2

Lunenburg County.

	£	s.	d.
To captain John Cargill,	12	00	00
Cornelius Cargill, Jun., lieut.,		6	
William Hunt, ensign,		4	
Bryan Coker, serjeant,	2	13	4
John Flin, do.	2	12	
Joseph Coker,	2		
John Ashworth,		11	
M'Kerness Goode,	1	5	
Samuel Ashworth,	1	19	
Isaac Ashworth,	1	14	
James Bardin,	2		
William Blanks,	1	19	
Daniel Cargill,	2		
To Joel Elam, James Flin, and Philip Goode, 39s. each,	5	17	
To John Hight,	1	14	
William Hudson,	2		
To James Hudson, Richard Hudson, Francis Linsey, and Henry Prewitt, 39s. each,	7	16	
To Alexander Strange,	1	14	
John Ragsdale,	1	19	
Augustine Rowland,	1	14	
To John Thompson and William Tibbs, 39s. each,	3	18	

	£	s.	d.
To Henry Wade,	2		
Aaron Williams,	1	14	
Thomas Dandy,	1	1	
John Cargill, Jun.,	2		
To Edward Darby, John Lucas, and Joseph Huse, 39s. each,	5	17	
To William Caldwell, major, as captain,	5	2	
To Richard Dudgeon, lieutenant,	2	2	
John M'Ness, ensign,	1	8	
William Dudgeon, serjeant,		18	
Andrew Rogers, do.	1	2	
To Thomas Daugherty, John M'Connal, Talton East, and Leonard Keeling, 17s. each,	3	8	
To James Vernon,		14	
To Thomas Howle, Barned Roberson, and David Logan, Jun., 17s. each,	2	11	
To John East,		14	
To William East, William Cunningham, James Ross, Robert Sanders, John Ward, Thomas Keasy, Thomas Moore, and William Dixon, 17s. each,	6	16	
To Thomas Pollett, John Caldwell, Mathew Watson, Robert Caldwell, and Hezekiah Jarrott, 14s. each,	3	10	
To John Orr, Robert Martin, James Caldwell, John Vernor, Richard Berry, Richard Adams, James Martin, Daniel Slayton, William Anderson, George Levil, and Tarrance M'Daniel, 12s. each,	6	12	
To William Philby, Edward Shipley, and John Gregory, 5s. each,		15	
To James Doherty,		17	
Thomas Boldin, as lieutenant,		12	
Jacob Womack, as ensign,		8	
Samuel Mortou, serjeant,		5	4

	£	s.	d.
To Abraham Vaughn, Peter Young, David Maddox, Thomas Jones, Francis Moore, John Hankins, James Fauster, Gabriel Ferrill, John Acuff, John Hall, Thomas Smith, Peter Hamlin, Thomas Hamlin, Nathan Adams, David Perryman, John Perrin, Thomas Williams, John Williams, Daniel Handcock, Thomas Hall, Isaac Munday, Richard Hicks, jun., John Worsham, and William Skelton, 4s. each,	4	16	00
To Abraham Martin,	33	6	
William Stokes, lieutenant,	16	1	
James Guillum, ensign,	2	14	
Thomas Jones, do.	1	16	
Thomas Jones, serjeant,	1	16	
Joshua Wharton, ensign,	6	10	
Peter Hamblin, serjeant,	5	12	
William Poole, do.	4	6	8
James Letts, do. in Poole's stead,	2	8	
Peter Hamlin,	1	7	
James Lett,	3	11	
To Gabriel Ferrill, James Fauster, James Worshborne, John Williams, John Perrin, Nathan Adams, Thomas Smith, and John Davis, £5 11s. each,	44	8	
To James Cooper, James Norrell, and Thomas Hill, £5 7s. each,	16	1	
To William Eastis,	4	2	
To Robert Lark, John Abraham Degranch, John Mannin, Aaron Drummon, Frass Atkins, Edward Atkins, Henry Stokes, Richard Ward, Bennett Hallaway, Thomas Bell, James Spead, William Ashley, and Francis Norrell, £5 7s. each,	69	11	
To John Ather,	4	8	

	£	s.	d.
To Thomas Leftwich and Merry Carter, £4 7s. each,	8	14	
To Henry Snow, William Leftwitch, and John Hall, £4 6s. each,	12	18	
To Hezekiah Hall and Aquilla Hall, £4 5s. each,	8	10	
To Jacob Matthews,	5	7	
John Hains,	4	3	
Thomas Pate,	2	7	
James Daulton,	3	10	
John Lett,	2	4	
Micajah Scoggins,	2	3	
Richard Jones,	2	1	
Stephen Hatchill,	3	6	
To John Pollert and William Parsons, 17s. each,	1	14	
To Alexander Richey and William Harvey, 22s. each,	2	4	
To David Parish,	1	4	
Thomas M'Cormack,	1	3	
James Thweat,	1	6	
Nance Hitchcock,		19	
Zachariah Dodd,		8	
To Clement Read, for paid lieutenant Hunt his wages,	5	15	
To do., for paid James Taylor,	20		
To do., for 29 days in purchasing provisions for the Forts in Halifax and Agustia, at 10s.,	14	10	
To do., for his account of expenses in said service,	6	5	3
To do., for 9 days to Bedford and Halifax, at 10s.,	4	10	
To do., for his expenses in said service,	15	10	
To do., for paid James Roberts for necessaries for soldiers,	1	12	10
To do., for paid David Cloyd for beef,	1		
To do., for paid John Austin's wages, one year,	18	5	

	£	s.	d.
To do., for dieting do. one year, at 6d. per day,	9	2	6
To do., for 10 days in settling accounts with commissioners, &c.,	5		
To Pinkithman Hawkins, captain,	39	12	
William Mitchell, lieutenant,	19	16	
John Colson, ensign,	13	4	
Jacob Gunson, serjeant,	8	16	
To William Farrar and Charles Knight, serjeants,	8	13	4
To John Hammons and John Mitchell, do.	6	13	4
To William White, Edmund Hames, John Trusty Matthews, Samuel Glass, Adam Thomson, William Townsend, £6 12s. each,	39	12	
To Lawrence Matthews and Nathan Richeson,	6	12	
Henry Sage,	6	12	
Henry Talley, Jun.,	3	2	
John Hammons,	1	12	
To John Coleman and Charles Allen, Jun.,	5	3	
To Charles Knight,	2	4	
To Peter Knight, William Monroe, Richard Hamblet, Samuel Wilson, James Henderson, John Bray, John M'Neal, John Warren, Richard Ragsdale, James Vaughan, and William Comer, £6 8s. each,	70	8	
To William Parham and Vachel Dillingham,	5	6	
To William Howard, Ephraim Hudson, and James Kidd, £5 6s. each,	15	18	
To Nathan Ellis and Reuben Keith,	5	6	
To James Ellis and William Dillinham,	5	6	
To George Benn, Arthur Matthews, and John Fann, £5 6s.,	15	18	
To captain Pinkithman Hawkins, for his pay, and the pay of the guards, and for subsistance, conducting drafted soldiers to Winchester,	60	9	9

	£	s.	d.
To Thomas Williams, for horse hire,	1	6	3
To Thomas Waller, for provisions,		4	6
To Liddal Bacon, for horse hire,	1		
To Benjamin Dixon, for provisions,		4	8
David Caldwell, for waggonage,	10	7	
Robert Caldwell, do.	13	4	6
Erwin Paterson, do.	39	13	6
Richard Dudgeon, do.	10	7	
John Rodgers, do.	13	4	6
Andrew Martin, do.	10	7	
Thomas Joyce, do.	13	4	6
John Caldwell, do.	9	15	6
John Dudgeon, do.	13	4	6
John Murfy, for horse hire,		14	
To Benjamin Clement, for taking care of a wounded soldier,	3		
To Joshua Chafin, for damage done to an horse impressed,		12	6
To David Caldwell, do.		18	
To Clement Reads, for corn for the use of the Cherokees,	1	5	
To David Gwinn, for do. for soldiers,		8	
To Richard Ward, for damage done a mare impressed,	3	5	
To Joel Towns, for do.		4	
Richard Stith, do.		10	
Thomas Covington, do.	1	1	6
Robert Caldwell, for waggonage,	8		
To David Caldwell, for waggonage, provisions, and a guard,	10	6	6
To John Logan, for shoeing horses for Catawbas and provisions for do.		11	6
To James Roberts, for provisions for Cherokees,	1	11	9
To John Camp, for do.	10		
To Pinkithman Hawkins, for bounty money paid a Volunteer Soldier,	5		

	£	s.	d.
To John Cargill, for damage done to his horse on an express,	1	2	6
To Joseph Austin, for Waggonage,	6	18	
To John Cargill, for attending 5 days to guard a township in Halifax,	1	10	
To Clement Reade, for provisions,	38		10
To do., for necessaries furnished to militia,	4	17	10
To Jacob Womack, serjeant,	1		
To John Worsham, John Hankins, John Hall, Robert Hall, William Russell, Francis Moore, and Abraham Womack, 15s. each,	5	5	
To John Mitchell,		13	
	£1074	5	11

Middlesex County.

	£	s.	d.
To captain Christopher Curtis, for his pay and the pay of the guards conducting drafted soldiers to Fredericksburg, and for their subsistance,	6	17	
To William Molson, for maintaining drafted soldiers in prison,	1	14	4
	£8	11	4

Nansemond County.

	£	s.	d.
To captain Edward Wright, for his pay and the pay of the guards conducting drafted soldiers to Fredericksburg, and for their subsistance,	34	13	4

Northampton County.

	£	s.	d.
To captain John Waggoman, for his pay and pay of the guards conducting drafted soldiers to Fredericksburg,	8	5	

	£	s.	d.
To Michael Dixon and John Pigot, for their pay as lookouts, from the 14th day of June, 1757, till the 12th day of September, 1758, £14 17s. each,	29	14	
	£37	19	00

Northumberland County.

	£	s.	d.
To John Heath, for his pay and the pay of the guards conducting drafted soldiers to Fredericksburg,	7	3	6
To major William Tate, for conducting drafted soldiers to Fredericksburg, in 1756,	4	2	6
	£11	6	00

New Kent County.

	£	s.	d.
To captain Charles Crump, for his pay and the pay of the guards conducting drafted soldiers to Fredericksburg,	2	14	
To Thomas Morton, for an horse lost in the Shawnese expedition,	7		
	£9	14	00

Princess Anne County.

	£	s.	d.
To captain Christopher Wright, for his pay and the pay of the guards conducting drafted soldiers to Fredericksburg, and for soldiers maintenance in prison,	19	12	00

Prince Edward County.

	£	s.	d.
To Henry Watkins, ensign, for pay to himself, two serjeants, and 16 men, militia of the said county, as by muster-roll,	80	13	

	£	s.	d.
To do., for horse hire for expresses,	1	17	
To do., for salt,	1	15	
To Charles Gilliam, for horse hire,		13	9
John Cloyd, for provisions,		9	
Samuel Ewings, for do. to Indians,		16	4
James Wimbish, for do. to do.	1	5	4
To captain Philemon Halcomb, pay for himself and guards carrying drafted soldiers to Fredericksburg,	6	9	4
To Mr. John Nash, for provisions,	20	7	8
To captain John Nash, jun., for the pay of his company from the 8th of June, 1757, till the 8th day of July following,	82	8	
	£196	14	5

Prince George County.

	£	s.	d.
To colonel Richard Bland, paid for provisions to Indians and ferriages,	4	1	4
To captain Richard Bland, jun., for his pay and the pay of the guards conducting drafted soldiers to Fredericksburg,	8	3	
	£12	4	4

Prince William County.

(*Hening's Statutes, Vol. 7, page 24.*)

To the Militia of the County of Prince William :

	Lbs. tob.
To John Frogg, Major,	920
William Baylis, Captain,	2400
Richard Taylor, Lieutenant of Horse,	2790
William Splane, do.	2790
William Farrow, Cornet,	2325

7

	Lbs. tob.
Samuel Porter, Corporal,	2046
Jacob Spilman, do.	2046
William Whaley, do.	2046
Lewis Reno, do.	2046
William Buchanan, Corporal,	1452
Thomas Ford, do.	1452
George Kenner, do.	1452
Henry Floyd, Serjeant,	1188
Foushee Tebbs, Captain,	390
John Baylis, do.	780
James Seaton, Lieutenant of Foot,	650
Richard Hampton, do.	550

To fifteen Troopers, viz., John Neville, Richard Matthews, Benjamin Wilson, Stephen Maurice, Thomas Marshall, Richard Marshall, John Luttrell, Thomas Doyle, Joshua Welch, Nathaniel Freeman, Standley Singleton, Samuel Batson, John Murray, William Fielder, & Andrew Cannaird, 1860 each, 　　27900

To twenty-one Troopers, viz., John M'Millon, Henry Kemper, John Fishback, Clement Norman, Joseph Martin, Richard Byrne, Peter Pierce, Michael Lynn, John Cornwell, John Dowell, William Key, Robert Nevill, Thomas Gardner, Charles Smith, Isaac Gibson, Benjamin Edwards, John Coreham, Griffin Matthews, John Bland, junior, William Peake, and William Berry, 1320 each, 　　27720

To Gilbert Crupper, a Trooper,	180
William Barr, do.	160
Nathaniel Overal, do.	260
Samuel Grigsby, do.	180

To fifteen foot soldiers, viz., Nicholas Hill, John

Lbs. tob.

Bolling, Edward Oneal, Joseph Neal, John
Carter, Thomas Shirley, Lewis Oden, John
Green, Martin Suttle, David Parsons,
George Rose, John Low, James Crocket,
William Suttle, and William Bolling,
1395 each,   20925

To six foot soldiers, viz., Isaac Settle, William
Jennings, Valentine Barton, William
Crouch, Moses Coppage, and John Rice,
990 each,   5940

To William Baylis, for paid John Edwards,   12s.
To George Calvert, junior, for an express,   6s. 8d.
To the clerk for certifying two allowed claims,   40

Prince William County.

(*Continued from pages 229–30.*)

	£	s.	d.
To colonel Henry Lee, for the pay of captain William Tebbs' and captain Thomas M'Clanahan's companys of militia, to the 30th day of August, 1758, inclusive, as by muster-roll,	479	6	4
To captain Thomas M'Clanahan, for his pay and the pay of the guards conducting drafted soldiers to Winchester,	2	4	
To do., for an horse killed upon an express,		12	
To Thomas Atwell, for provisions,	1		
To Thomas Blakemore, for do. to Indians,	1	7	4
To Charles Morgan, for do.		4	
John Duncan, for do.	1		4
Catherine Hollzclaw, for do.		10	
Tilman Weaver, for horse hire,	1		
John Embers, for provisions,		6	
Robert Montgomery, for do.		2	
Richard Coventon, for provisions,	1	1	10

	£	s.	d.
To John Markham, corporal, for 66 days' service,	4	2	6
To Francis Braunough, an express,		16	8
	£565	1	00

Richmond County.

	£	s.	d.
To the executors of Moore Fantleroy, deceased, for carrying drafted soldiers to Fredericksburg, in 1756,	3	3	8

Southampton County.

	£	s.	d.
To captain Peter Butts, for his pay and the pay of Guards conducting drafted soldiers to Fredericksburg,		8	8
To Mr. Benjamin Simmons, for victualling drafted soldiers in gaol, and for the bounty paid to two Volunteers,	13	18	1
	£22	6	1

Spottsylvania County.

Militia officers appointed by Governor Dinwiddie, October, 1757, for Spottsylvania County (Calendar Virginia State Papers, Vol. 1, page 252):

John Spottswood, county lieutenant.
John Thorton, Col.
Richard Tutt,   "
Rice Curtis,   "
William Linn, Major.
Benjamin Pentleton, Major.
Charles Lewis, Major.
John Craine, Capt.
William Muller, Capt.

Aaron Bledsoe, Capt.

Thos. Estis, Capt.

—— Allen, Capt.

NOTE: The commissions of Capt. Bledsoe and Estis were opposed by Col. Thorton as improper persons. (See his letter to Gov. Dinwiddie, Oct. 29, 1757, Vol. 1, page 252, Virginia State Papers.)

(*Hening's Statutes, Vol. 7, page 231.*)	£	s.	d.
To Captain Thomas Estis, for his pay and the pay of the guards conducting drafted soldiers to Fredericksburg,	3	8	00

Surry County.

	£	s.	d.
To Captain William Seward, jun., for the balance of his pay and the pay of the guards conducting drafted soldiers to Fredericksburg,	2	3	6
To Robert Gray, for provisions to Indians,	3	17	4
To William Cocke, for do.		15	4
	£6	16	2

Sussex County.

	£	s.	d.
To captain James Wyche, for his pay and the pay of the guards conducting drafted soldiers to Fredericksburg,	7	9	00

Stafford County.

Officers appointed for the county of Stafford Aug. 19, 1751: William Fitzhugh, county lieutenant; Henry Fitzhugh, Jr., Col. of Militia; Francis Thorton, Lieutenant-Col.; Wm. Fitzhugh, Maj. of Horse; Banj. Strother, Maj. of Foot; Gerrard

Fowkes, 1st Capt., &c.   (Calendar of Va. State Papers, Vol. 1, page 247.)

	£	s.	d.
To captain Withers Conway, for his pay and the pay of the guards conducting drafted soldiers to Winchester, and for subsistance,	17	2	6

(Hening's Statutes, Vol. 7, page 231.)

Westmoreland County.

	£	s.	d.
To captain John Newton, for his pay and the pay of the guards conducting drafted soldiers to Fredericksburg,	8	1	
To major John Martin, for carrying drafted soldiers to Fredericksburg, in 1756,	4	13	
	£12	14	00

York County.

	£	s.	d.
To captain Robert Shield, for his pay and the pay of the guards conducting the drafted soldiers of this county and of Warwick county to Fredericksburg,	9	1	
To doctor James Carter, for cutting off and curing a soldier's arm,	10		
To major John Prentis, for carrying drafted soldiers to Fredericksburg, in 1756,	18	3	6
	£37	4	6

General assembly of Virginia, Jan. 14, 1762. An act for giving recompense to the officers of the Virginia regiment—one full year's pay, over and above what shall be due to them until the disbanding of the said regiment, viz.: Colonel Wil-

liam Byrd, Lieutenant-colonel Adam Stephen, Major Andrew
Lewis, Captains Robert Stewart, John McNeil, Henry Wood-
ard, Robert McKenzie, Thomas Bullett, John Blagg, Nathaniel
Gist, Mordecai Buckner, Captain-lieutenant William Danger-
field, lieutenants William Fleming, Leonard Price, Charles
Smith, George Wooden, Jethro Summer, John Lawson, Wil-
liam Woodford, Joseph Fent, John Sallard, Thomas Gist,
Alexander Boyd, William Hughes, David Kennedy, Robert
Johnson, Walter Cunningham, William Cocke, Alexander
Menzie, Larkin Chew, Reuben Vass, and John Cameron,
ensigns Henry Timberlake, Philip Love, John Sears, Burton
Lucas, David Long, Alexander M'Laugham, George M'Night,
and Surgeon John Stewart. (Hening's Statutes, page 493.)

On page 378 to 390 of Volume 1, Virginia Magazine of History, are found the names of several companies in the French
and Indian Wars. The roster gives rank, name, age, size,
place of enlistment, nativity and trade of each man, and
shows that the troops were secured from every part of the
colony of Virginia.

Oct., 1765. An Act for appointing commissioners to examine and state the accounts of the militia lately ordered out
into actual service, and for other purposes therein mentioned.
(Hening's Statutes, Vol. 8, page 124.)

By this act Archibald Cary, Thomas Walker, John Fleming, William Cabell, George Carrington, Thomas Lewis, and
Peter Hog, gentlemen, were appointed commissioners for the
counties of Augusta, Bedford, Halifax, and Amherst, and
James Hamilton, Richard Lee, Thomas Rutherford, Thomas
Marshall, William Green, and James Wood, gentlemen, for
the counties of Frederick, Hampshire, Culpeper, Loudoun,
Fauquier, and Prince William; or any three of them to examine, state and settle the accounts of such pay, provision,
arms, and etc., of the counties of which they are appointed,
and all arrears whatsoever relating to the militia.

Section 3, folio 126. And be it further enacted, by the
authority aforesaid, That the said commissioners shall also

settle and allow any claims that shall be produced to them
for provisions furnished the volunteers and captives on their
return from Pittsburg to this colony.

SCHEDULE to which this Bill refers:

Albemarle.

		£	s.	d.
1756. To William Fuqua, for his pay,		1	18	0
Thomas Walker,		87	10	6

Amherst.

		£	s.	d.
1756	John Tarrant, for horse hire,	0	3	0
	Benjamin Denny, for do. and provisions,		14	
	Aaron Higginbottom, for provisions,		5	
	Peter Carter, for horse hire,	0	5	0
	William Fowler, for do.		4	
	Jacob Brown, for provisions,		10	8

Augusta.

		£	s.	d.
1759. To Israel Christian, administrator, &c., of Alexander Sayers, deceased, for his pay as a captain of Militia,		12	6	0
Audley Paul, lieutenant,		6	3	
Joseph Ray, sergeant,		2	14	9

Robert Steel, James Haynes, Charles
Ramsey, John Greenlee, James
Greenlee, Charles Slinker, Samuel
Newbery, William M'Donald, John
Robertson, Henry Filbrick, Joseph
M'Clellan, Abraham Thomson,
James Stewart, James Berry, James
Amox, James Dooley, Henry Dooley, Daniel Young, Edmund Young,
Abraham Dooley, Thomas Caldwell, Humphrey Baker, James

	£	s.	d.
Hay, Charles Lockart, Samuel Vance, Alexander Collier, John Cox, David Cox, James Arbuckle, Matthew Arbuckle, John Arbuckle, Gilbert Christian, and John Gregory, £2 1s. each,	67	13	

To be paid to Israel Christian for the use of the lieutenant and men, and accounted for by him to the treasurer, if the claimants do not apply for the same.

	£	s.	d.
Arthur Campbell, his pay while a prisoner,	41		
Capt. John Smith, do.	83	13	9
1763. To William Matthews, for Provisions,	10	10	0
Joseph Carpenter, for do.	4	6	10
Zopher Carpenter, for do.	7	12	8
Matthias Teas, for horse hire,		4	6
Samuel Campbell, for provisions,		10	
Joseph Mayes, for do.	10	8	6
do. for horse hire,		10	
Francis Ivy, for provisions,		12	5
Joseph Skidmore, for do.	11	10	6
Nicholas Hofman, for do.	5	3	6
Philip Harper, for do.	1	10	
Thomas Maller, for do.		13	6
George Harmond, for do.	12	5	7½
Jacob Harper, for do.	2	17	6
Jonas Friend, for do.	14	0	9
George Coplinger, for do.	13	3	4
Nicholas Havener, for do.		12	6
Henry Stone, for do.	2	2	9
James Gemmel, for do.	3	15	
John Young, for do.	1	18	
Robert Carlyle, for do.	1	8	5

	£	s.	d.
Robert Dunlop, for do.	2		
Posteon Hover, for do.		13	1½
Peter Smith, for do.	1	3	8
Jacob Rolman, for do.		7	
Wallis Estile, for do.	3	6	4½
George Coyle, for do.	1	14	6
Robert Hall, for do.	4	15	7½
John Mann, for do.	1	19	3
Daniel Harrison, for do.	2	18	8
John Gum, for do.	1	13	6
Josiah Hamilton, for do.	2	13	6
Frederick Stern, for do.	11	16	5
William Fitzjarrel, for horse hire,	3	4	6
Joseph Carpenter, jun., for provisions,	3	15	5
Philip Petro, for do.	2	15	
William Shannon, for horse hire,	3		
Benjamin Harrison, capt., for pay of himself and company, as per roll,	176	9	4
Benjamin Harrison, for provisions,	1	00	5
do. for ammunition,	8	10	6
Thomas Walker, for 4 days' attendance as commissioner,	2		
Thomas Lewis, for do.	2		
Peter Hog, for do.	2		
Andrew Lewis, for his pay as colonel 219 days, at 10s.,	109	10	
William Preston, for do. as major 213 days, at do.	106	10	
John Hawkins, as clerk to the commissioners,	30		
The above settled by Commissioners.			
George Moffet, for provisions,	11	12	8
Anthony Bledsoe, for do.	6	17	9
James Ewing, for salt,		1	3

1763.

		£	s.	d.
1761.	Alexander Sawyers, for waggonage and provisions,	281	9	6
1758.	William Carvin, for horse hire and provisions,	8	10	6
	Robert Brackenridge, for himself and company,	46	2	10
	Edward Carvin,	5		
	James Hughes,	10	9	8½
	John Crawford,	8		
	Michael Teibolt,	10		
	John Armstrong,	30		
	Lantey Armstrong,	30		
1758.	John Donnelly,	10		
	James Bryan,	9	10	
	John Smith,	75		
	Samuel Meredith,	3	1	
	Robert Kirkum and Joseph Bates, 14s. each,	1	8	
	To sundry persons for damages, provisions, &c., as per account settled by commissioners at Staunton,	111	16	1¼

Bedford.

		£	s.	d.
1758.	To Joseph Rentfro, for provisions,	56	0	11
	Henry Haynes, for amunition,		13	6
	Joseph Rentfro, for a horse,	7	0	0
	William Irvine,	5		

Chesterfield.

		£	s.	d.
1760.	To George Farrar, for the balance of Abel Farrar's pay as Lieutenant,	19	15	0
	Stephen Blankenship, his pay while a prisoner,	75		

	£	s.	d.
Culpeper.			
1763. To Francis Browning, for provisions, &c.,	0	16	0
John Corbin, for provisions,	2	15	10
William Roberts, for do.		14	3
Sundry inhabitants of this county, Hampshire and Frederick, for guns, provisions, etc., impressed, as per commissioners report with the Governour's warrant,	157	16	7
Fauquier.			
1759. To Francis Moore, for prison fees paid for a deserter of the Virginia regiment,	1	18	0
Frederick.			
1759. To Richard Pearis,	81	18	
The administratrix of William Staunton,	10		
Captain Luke Collins, for 10 days' pay, at 6 shillings,	3		
Halifax.			
1758. To Peter Vanbever, for provisions,	1	16	6
Sarah Davis, for do.	6	12	10
James Rentfro, for do.	3	14	
Elizabeth Carson, for do.	3	17	8
Peter Vanbever, jun., for do.	1	12	5
Rebekah Stalker, for do.	1	7	9
Joseph Willis, for do.	5	2	8
Charles Witts, for do.	2	18	
William Satterwhite, for salt,		15	
1759. Benjamin Dickson, for an express,	2	10	
1760. George Boyd, lieutenant, his pay for himself and company, as per roll, and for some necessaries found,	22	6	10½

		£	s.	d.
	George Yates, for provisions,	1	00	00
1759.	Joshua Powell, for his roll settled by commissioners with governour's warrant,	41	16	
1763.	James Roberts, jun., assignee of Preston Hampton, for provisions,	7	9	6
	Hamon Crite, for do.		14	
	William Wright, for do.		7	4
	Theophilus Lacey, for do.	1	3	4½
	William Wright, for do.		9	8
	John Weldrick Bender, for do.		10	6
	John Talbot, for do.	1	0	6
	George Young, for do.		6	8
	Bethany Hanes, for do.		4	
	John Lynk, for do.	1	1	4
	Hamon Crite, for do.	2	18	6
	George Young, for do.		3	4
	Thomas Billing, for do.		3	4
	James Roberts, jun., assignee of Patrick Shields, for do.		11	8
	Bethany Hanes, for do.		3	
	Moses Airs, for an express,	1		
	John Dean, for his pay in the service,		10	6
	Stephen Terry, for do.		10	6
	Richard Murfey, for do.		10	6
	Thomas Jones, for provisions,	1	4	7
	Peter Rogers, for a horse lost,	8	10	
	Robert Wade, capt., his pay,	23	8	
	Peter Rogers, lieut., do.	13	3	
	James Lyon, ensign, do.	9	15	
1763.	To Henry Scrugs and John Link, sergeants, £7 3 0 each,	14	6	
	Joshua Jones and Jonathan Jones, £3 16 6 each,	7	13	
	John Bently, Thomas Hix, William			

	£	s.	d.
Falling, John Hampton, Bryan Nowling, Frederick Edwards, Edward Morgan, Jacob Bouyiis, William Follas, Richard Griffin, jun., William Robinson, William Bell, John Smith, and William Rosebury, £5 17 0 each,	81	18	
The executors of Robert Wade, jun., deceased, for Richard Condron and James Symms, 20s. each,	2		
John Ray,	3	12	
John Dyer,	4	7	
Abraham Whitter, Joshua Smith, Elias Brock, Elisha Pierce, and John Goff, £4 10 0 each,	22	10	
Jacob Shepard,	2	8	
Edward Cason, Larkin Cason, David Bolling, Frederick Farmer, David Hamby, Jonathan Hamby, and John Jennings, £2 5 0 each,	15	15	
Robert Wade, for horse hire,	3	18	
Peter Rogers, for do.	7	16	
do. for provisions,		17	7
Walter Dunn, for ammunition, &c.,	6	9	7
Robert Wade, for a horse,	8	10	
William Satterwhite, for salt, bags, &c.,	2	5	
Peter Rogers, lieutenant, his pay,	1	7	
do. for a horse,	8	10	
John Link, Barton Link, John Salmon, Edward Cason, Larkin Cason, Richard Turner, William Follas, John Login, and James Page, 7s. each,	3	3	
Walter Dunn, for sundries,	3	10	10

	£	s.	d.

Hanover.

	£	s.	d.
1763. To John Boswell, for provisions,	0	18	8
William Winston, damage done, &c.,	25	0	0

James City.

	£	s.	d.
1763. To John Chriswell and company, for lead and provisions,	110	6	4

King George.

	£	s.	d.
1763. To John Terrier, for damage done by Virginia regiment,	20	0	0
Charles Carter, for do.	45		

King and Queen.

	£	s.	d.
1757. To John Richards, for guarding draughted soldiers to Fredericksburg,	4	16	0

Loudoun.

	£	s.	d.
1757. To Robert Adams, assignee of Stephen Thatcher, for his pay,	5	12	6
Do., do of Thomas Bond, for do.	4	10	
Thomas Gore, for a rifle gun impressed,	4	10	
Stephen Emorie, for dressing guns for militia,		13	
James Clemons, for a gun impressed,	4	10	
1763. Captain Moss, for 60 days' pay at 6s.,	18		
Lieutenant Gore, for do. at 3s. 6d.,	10	10	

Louisa.

	£	s.	d.
1763. To Susannah Wash,	30	0	0

	£	s.	d.

Lunenburg.

		£	s.	d.
1758.	To David Gwin, for corn for militia,		10	
	John Ashworth, for waggonage,	32	5	6
	Bryan Lester,	4		

Nansemond.

		£	s.	d.
1758.	To Jethro Summer, for a horse,	9	0	0

Norfolk.

		£	s.	d.
1758.	To Henry Darnell,	37	14	0

Orange.

		£	s.	d.
1758.	To William Johnson, for provisions, &c.,	2	9	2
	William Kendall, for do.		11	4
	William Johnson, for do.		12	8

Prince William.

		£	s.	d.
1763.	To William Baylis and company, per roll,	35	10	8

Spotsylvania.

		£	s.	d.
1758.	To John M'Nelly, for repairing arms for Virginia regiment,	15	9	9

THE SCOTCH-IRISH OF AUGUSTA COUNTY, VIRGINIA.

So much has been written concerning that sturdy race who called themselves Scotch-Irish, and who were the pioneer settlers of the upper Valley of the Shenandoah, and beyond, that any extended notice of them and their characteristics would be mere repetition of many abler writers. However, as this work contains the names of so many people of that race who constituted the skirmish line of civilization, a few words here concerning them may not be out of place.

All authorities concede that John Lewis led the van of this heroic race when he settled, in 1732, near the present city of Staunton. But there soon gathered around him many of his own race, who bore their parts manfully in the development of a new country, and whose descendants, now scattered through many states of the West, South, and Southwest, still preserve the characteristics which made their forefathers conspicuous in earlier times.

These pioneer settlers of Augusta were men of deep religious convictions, and their churches were the centres from which radiated the influence of the various communities as a whole. The Augusta, or Old Stone Church, was the first to be established, ih 1740, and this venerable structure, erected more than a century and a half ago, still stands as a monument to the heroic men and women by whom it was built in days of difficulty and trial. Tinkling Spring Church, also established in 1740, was perhaps stronger in numbers and wealth than the Augusta Church, but three or four church structures have been erected there since the establishment of the congregation, and therefore it is not so interesting historically as the other.

During the period of the French and Indian War the Scotch-Irish of Augusta, which then comprised an immense

8

territory to the west and southwest, stood as a bulwark against Indian incursions east of the Blue Ridge, and so valuable were the services rendered by these people that colonial laws asserting the supremacy of the Episcopal, or Established Church, were not enforced against these Dissenting Presbyterians.

When the prelude of the Revolution began, the Scotch-Irish of the upper valley marched to Point Pleasant, and there, under the command of General Andrew Lewis, son of the pioneer settler of Augusta, fought one of the bloodiest battles with the Indians to be found in the annals of our colonial history. In this engagement it is stated that 650 men from Augusta County alone participated, and by that time the limits of the county had been very much reduced. When the Revolution opened, the sons and grandsons of the original settlers were almost unanimously in favor of American independence, and Scotch-Irish officers and men were found on every field of the Revolution, from Saratoga to Yorktown.

It would be impossible, within the limits of this brief sketch, to give the names of all officers worthy of mention who entered the service from Augusta County; but Andrew Lewis, who commanded at Point Pleasant, was a Brigadier-General of the Virginia Continental Line, and was chiefly instrumental in driving Lord Dunmore, the last of the Virginia colonial governors, from her borders. Three of his brothers were officers of rank during the Revolution, and Robert and Alexander Breckenridge were captains of the line in the same struggle. Stout George Mathews, colonel of the 9th Virginia Line, entered the service from Augusta, and was captured with his regiment at the battle of Germantown, Pa., because he dared to press too far against the British centre without proper support. Col. George Moffett, county lieutenant of Augusta, marched with his militia to South Carolina, and aided Morgan in winning the brilliant victory of the Cowpens. Robert, James, Andrew, and William, sons of John Anderson, who was one of the first elders of the Old Stone Church, were brave and efficient officers in the Revolutionary army, the first serving in South Carolina as colonel under General Pickens, and the other three as captains. Robert Gamble, a captain of the line, led the forlorn hope at the capture of Stony Point, and his younger brother John also served as an officer in the American army. James Tate, a captain of the Augusta militia, gave up his life at Guilford Court House, and many other names might be added to this list.

During the invasion of Virginia, in 1781, the militia of Augusta were almost constantly on the march, and many of them were at Yorktown, where the final act in the drama was played.

When the Revolution ended, these brave and enterprising men began the march of civilization westward, and the first settlers of Kentucky were almost entirely from the upper portion of the Virginia Valley. The Prestons, Breckenridges, Logans, Allens, Trimbles, Andersons, McDowells, and many others, sought their fortunes in the new lands west of the Allegheny Mountains, and from these pioneer settlers has descended a race of people unsurpassed by any in the world for chivalry, courage, eloquence, and statesmanship. They have been found in every station of life, filling well the place which destiny has assigned to them, and the highest tribute which could be paid to the Scotch-Irish pioneers of Augusta County would be the roster of distinguished men who trace their ancestry to this section of the Valley of Virginia.

THE POLL FOR THE ELECTION OF BURGESSES FOR THE COUNTY OF PRINCE WILLIAM, A. D. 1741.

Candidate.	*Candidate.*	*Candidate.*	*Candidate.*	*Candidate.*
WM. FAIRFAX.	**COL. JNO. COLVILLE.**	**MAJ. BLACKBURN.**	**VAL. PEYTON.**	**THOS. HARRISON.**
Thos Davis	Jno Roberts	Thos Davis	Jno Ambrose	Jno Ambrose
Chas Sneed	Jos Dixson	Chas Sneed	Francis Watts	Francis Watts
Henry Bromlet	Richd Roberts	Darby Callahan	Jno Roberts	Henry Bromlet
Jos Dixson	Waugh Darnell	Thos Coleson	Henry Taylor	Henry Taylor
Richard Roberts	Jno Darnold	John Owen	Wm Hall	Benj Stone
Darby Callahan	J Darnold	Marshall Duncan	Jno Owen	Thos Leachman
Edw Barry	Benj Newell	John Bush	Benj Stone	Joseph Wright
Ferd Bronough	Jno Alexander	Wm Teague	Thos Leachman	Cinc Garner
Wm Hall	Jno Hopper	Richd Wright	Vincent Garner	C W Carr
Thos Colson	Jno Blackwell	John Allen	C W Carr	Jno Hendon
Marshall Duncan	Jno Crump	John Carfey	Jno Hendron	Jno Bush
Jos Wright	Jno Grautmus	Jno Jones	Wm Teague	Waugh Darnel
Jno Allen	E W Cors	Wm Davis	Richd Wright	Alex Morgan
Jno Carfey	Jno Duncomb	Geo Rogers	Alex Morgan	John Darnel
John Jones	Richd Abell	Ebenezer Mors	French Mason	Ferd Darnel
Alex Clements	James Spurr	Jno Lattimore	Wm Thorn	Alex Clements
Jno Alexander	Wm Gunnel	Peter Cornwell	Richd Grubbs	Jno Hopper
Wm Davis	Thos Darnes	Thos Atwell	Charles Garner	Wm Thorn
Geo Rogers	David Thomas	Nich Anderson	Thos Dowell	Jos Blackwell
Jas Spurr	Jno Mead	Fra Wright	Jno Overall	Jno Crump
Wm Gunnel	Nathan Nabus	Snowden Kirkland	Jas Holmes	Jno Grantam
Thos Darnes	Wm Harld	Jos Mintor	Wm Whitledge	Jno Duncan
Wm Harld	Henry Gunnel	James Keith	Matt Moss	Richd Abrell
Henry Gunnel	Wm Boyleston	Wm Tassey	Henry Harding	David Thomas
Wm Boilston	Jas Roberts	Jno Oldham	Peter Cornwell	Jno Mead
Jas Roberts	Jno Roberts	Simon Gosling	Thos Hart	Nath Nabus
Jno Roberts	Jas Young	Chas Holmes	Jno Peyton	Richd Grubbs
Jas Dowel	Jno Brown	Wm Low	Thos Conway	Jno Lattimore
Nich Anderson	Jno Bradford	Phil Waters	Wm Corbam	Chas Garner
Fras Wright	Peter Camper		Thos Witledge	Jas Young
Wm Gladdin	(Kemper)	In all, 29	Thos Atwell	Jno Overhall
Jno Musgrove	Wm Gladdin		Geo Crosbey	Jas Homes
Robt Stephens	Jno Musgrove		Thos Hooper	Wm Whitledge
Jas Keith	Robt Stephens		Henry Floyd	Matt Moss
Danl McDaniel	Lewis Elzey		Jas McGlarhan	John Brown
John Frogg	Peter Dyer (swore)		Thos Duncan	Henry Harding
Lewis Elzey	Amos Janney		Snod Kirkland	Jno Bradford
Wm Tassey	David Davis		John Wood	Thos Hart
Simon Carnel	Jos Clapham		Dennis Couniers	John Peyton
Amos Janney	Richd Carpenter		Jos Minter	Thos Conway
Josiah Clapham	Richd Brown		Simon Counel	Wm Coreham
Owen Williams	Lovell Jackson		Jno Oldham	Thos Whitledge
Richd Brown	Jno Summers		Owen Williams	George Crosby
Lovel Jackson	Soloman Organ		Ferd Branaugh	Thos Hooper
Ferd Branaugh	Robert Bates		Saml Stone	Henry Floyd
Jno Warner	John Ball		Thos Stone	Jas McGlaham
Benj Hawley	Abram Lay		David Darnell	Peter Camper
Wm Shortridge	Wm Grimes		Edw Kirkland	(Kemper)

Candidate. WM. FAIRFAX.	Candidate. COL. JNO. COLVILLE.	Candidate. MAJ. BLACKBURN.	Candidate. VAL. PEYTON.	Candidate. THOS. HARRISON.
Howson Kenner	Jno Warner		Richd Simpson	Jos Duncan
Simon Gosling	Benj Hawley		James Keen	John Wood
Kelly Jennings	Wm Shortridge		Edw Graham	Dennis Couniers
Saml Stone	Thos West		Wm Barker	Daniel McDaniel
William Low	Walter Williams		Philemon Waters	John Frogg
John Gess	Moses Ball		Morgan Darnell	Peter Dyer (sworn)
Thos Scandall	George Ball		John McMillon	David Davis
Wm Nichols	Jno Withers Harper		Jon Wright	Richd Carpenter
Saml Conner	Bryan Breeding		John Orear	Jno Summers
Wm Thomas	Edw Homes		Wm Foster	Soloman Organ
Elias Hoar	Jas Robinson		Burr Harris	Robt Bates
John Melton	Edw Vilet		Lewis Reno Jr	John Ball
Richd Simpson	Thos Stone		John Tacket	Abram Lay
James Keen	John Guess		Jos Reid	Wm Grimes
James Vyat	Thos Scandel		Owen Gilmore	Howson Kenner
Edward Graham	Wm Nichols		Richd Crupper	Kelly Jennings
Wm Barker	Saml Conner		Jonas Williamas	Thos West
Richard Stephens	Wm Thomas		Baxter Simpson	Walter Williams
James Cullems	Jno Melton		Chas Hugget	Moses Ball
Garret Trammel	James Wyatt		Jno Robinson	Geo Ball
John Gladden	Richd Stephens		Wm Stut	Jno Withers Harper
Benj Bulley	Garret Trammel		Cinc Lewis	Bryan Breeding
Jas Cork	Jno Gladdin		Thos Furr	Chas Homes
Lewis Sanders	Lewis Sanders		Jno Hampton	Edwd Homes
Luke Cannon	Edwd Hues		Morris Veale	Jas Robinson
Jas Fletcher	Thos Washington		Geo Reeves	Edwd Vylet
Edw Hughes	Jno Washington		Saml Jackson	David Darnel
Thos Washington	Chatwin Crutcher		Richd Kirkland	Edwd Kirkland
Chattin Crutcher	William Davy		Bond Veale	Elias Hoar
Chas Griffith	C Griffith		James Key	French Mason
John Washington	Robert King		Wm Sampson	James Cullens
Henry Norman	Amos Sinkler		Jacob Ramey	Benj Bullitt
Robart King	James Curry		Wm Smith	Morgan Darnel
Amos Sinkler	Edw Barry		John Bland	Jno McMilion
Geo Harrison	Thos Winsor		Geo Pemberton	John Wright
James Murry	Wm Winsor		John Brown	Jas Cork
Mich Regan	Richd A Green		John Taylor	John Orear
John Brown	Wm West		Job Carter	Luke Cannon
Edw Feagan	John Murphey		Benj Brown	Jas Fletcher
Aaron Fletcher	Wm Ashford		Thos Reno	Wm Foster
Owin Gilmore	Wm Scut		Wm Furr	Wm Davey
Joseph Read	Wm Williams		Thos Smith	Henry Norman
Richd Crupper	James Whaley		Chas Morris	Burr Harris
Baxter Simpson	Tho Lewis Jr		Mich Dermond	Lewis Reno Jr
Thos Winsor	Richd Ricksey		Wm Hall Jr	John Tacket
Wm Winsor	Wm Trammel		Henry Murphet	Geo Harrison
Chs Hugget	Jno Kincheloe		Peter Glascock	Mich Reagan
Richd C Green	John Keen		Richd Litteral	Jno Brown
Wm West	Wm Thompson		Jos Furr	Edwd Feagan
Thos Lewis	Henry Hawley		Wm Williams	Aaron Fletcher
Lohn Robinson	Edwd Lawrence		Jno Glascock	Jonas Williams
Wm Williams	Richd Jervice		Wm Bland	Thos Lewis
C Lewis	Patrick Hamricks		Jas Bland	Jno Murphey
Wm Roberts	Mich Ashford		Jno Nevile	Wm Ashford
Jno Hampton	Elias Guess		Jno Reeves	Wm Roberts

Candidate. WM. FAIRFAX.	Candidate. COL. JNO. COLVILLE.	Candidate. MAJ. BLACKBURN.	Candidate. VAL. PEYTON.	Candidate. THOS. HARRISON.
Jno Kimble	Richd Kirkland		Jas Bland	Jas Whaley
Morris Veale	Isaac Simmons		Geo Calvert	Thos Lewis Jr
Geo Reeves	Mal Cummins		Jno Garner	Richd Ricksey
Richd Kirkland	Thos Martin		Blag Hopper	Wm Crammel
Henry Tyler	Jno Holtsclaw		Richd Kirkland	Thos Furr
Bond Veale	Henry Otterback		Isaac Simmons	Saml Jackson
Jas Hey	Eben Floyd		Thos Ford	Henry Tyler
Wm Simpson	Peter Hitt		George Nevile	Wm Thompson
Jacob Ramey	Jonas Williams Jr		Geo Foster	Jno Canterberry
John Keen	Peter Hedgman		Jno Lasswell	Jos Dulany
Wm Smith	Col Fitzhugh		Townsd Dade	Tobe Carter
Jno Canterbury	Aug Jennings		Jno Peak	Henry Hawley
Jno Bland	David Jones		Jas Smith	Benj Brown
Geo Pemberton	Gerd Alezander		Jno Bronough	Thos Reno
Jno Brown	Richd Osborn		Wm Kirkland	Wm Furr
Jno Taylor	Robt Baugess		Jno Morehead	Jas Hawley
Thos Smith	Wm Terrett		John Syas	Edw Lawrence
Alex Morris	Henry Watson		Geo Harper	Richd Jarvis
Jas Hawley	Geo Brent		Gabl Murphey	Henry Murphet
Wm Hall	Guy Broadwater		Wm Melton	Peter Glascock
Wm Williams	Danl French		Jno Fergerson	Pat Hamrick
Wm Hogan	Jacob Holtsclaw		Robt Bland	Richd Litteral
Wm Bland	Thos Davis		Thos Hicks	Jos Furr
James Bland	Fra Triplett		Peter Leland	Jno Glascock
Wm Bennit	Thomas Wren		Wm Spiller	Wm Hogan
Jno Bennit	Jno Askford		Andrew Dalton	Wm Bennit
James Bland	Jno Martin		Geo Simpson	Jno Bennit
Mason Bennit	Jno Morehead		Val Digs	Jno Nevile
Alexr Beach	John Hartley		Thos Morley	Jno Reeves
Michl Ashford	Jno Husk		Isaac Farguson	Mason Bennit
Elias Guess	Jno Jenkins		Jos Davis	Alexr Beach
Jno Northcut	Col Chas Carter		Wm Shadburn	Geo Calvert
Benj Grayson	Col Thos Turner		Fre Ash	Jno Garner
Jno Gregg	John Doe		Parish Garner	Blag Hopper
Moses Linton	Harry Turner		Jas Norris	Thomas Ford
George Neville	Jas Jenkins		Jno Gibson	Jno Northcut
Geo Foster	Jno Lucas		Jno Carr	Mal Cummins
Wm Bailiss	Michl Scandling			Benj Grayson
Jno Lasswell	Ezekl Jenkins		141	John Gregg
James Mews	Jno Sinkler			Moses Linton
Eben Floyd	Stephen Lewis			Jno Holtsclaw
Col Fitzhugh	Wm Brooks			Wm Bailiss
David Jones	Jno Camper			Peter Hitt
Thos Sudden	(Kemper)			Henry Otterback
Garrot Alexander	Thos Hicke			Jas Mews
Richd Osborn	Wm Champneys			Jas Williams
Robert Boggess	Jno Gordon			Peter Hedgman
Thos Pearson	Jno Carr			Aug Jennings
Wm Cornwell	Thos Moxley			Thos Sudden
Wm Butler	Wm Blachwell			Wm Deury Terrett
John James	Jas Robinson			Thos Pearson
Henry Watson	Wm Jenkins			Thos Pearson
Geo Brent	Rhodham Tullos			Jno Peake
Guy Broadwater	Auth Seale			Chas Cornwell
Danl French	Richd Blackburn			Wm Butler

Candidate. WM. FAIRFAX.	*Candidate.* COL. JNO. COLVILLE.	*Candidate.* MAJ. BLACKBURN.	*Candidate.* VAL. PEYTON.	*Candidate.* THOS. HARRISON.
James Smith	Jno Grant			Jno James
John Short	Aug Washington			Jacob Holtsclaw
Robt Hedges	John Snowden			Jno Short
Wm Kirkland	Jno Sturman			Robt Hedges
Wm Kirns	Wm Bekley			Wm Kirns
John Cofer	Nimrod Hot (Hitt?)			John Cofer
Fras Triplet	Geo Burn			Jno Dartley
Thos Wren	Jere Sparks			John Syas
Jno Ashford	Burr Harrison			Jno Savage
Cine Wyat	Edwd Hans			Jno Florence
John Martin	Thos Stribling			George Darper
John Husk	Jacob Lasswell			Jacob Spilman
Jno Jenkins	Dennis McCarty			Gabrl Murphey
Col Alex Carter	Ferd Bronough			Jas Heryford
Col Thos Turner	John Dawkins			Fr Cofer
John Doe	John Johnson			Henry Watkins
Wm Florence				Benj Newell
Harry Turner				Richd Melton
John Lucas				Richd Foote
Jacob Spillman				F Jackson
Henry Watkins				George Foote
Richd Melton				Richd Melton
Mich Scanlon				Thos Stone
Richd Foote				John Sinclair
Ezekl Jenkins				John Catlett
John Dagg				Lewis Tacket
Wm Peake				Wm Brooks
Fra Jackson				John Camper
Geo Foote				(Kemper)
Jno Heryford				Peter Lehue
Wm Godfrey				Martin Harding
Thos Stone				Isaac Kent
Stephen Lewis				Wm Spiller
John Catlet				Andrew Dalton
Lewis Tacket				Thos Jordan
John Ferguson				Peter Newport
Richd Bland				Tilman Weaver
Martin Hardin				John Carr
Isaac Kent				Cal Higgs
Wm Champnys				Isaac Ferguson
Geo Simpson				Thos Bosman
John Gordan				Wm Blackwell
Thos Gordan				Wm Shadburn
Peter Newport				John Madden
Tilman Weaver				Fra Ash
Jos Davis				Rodam Tullos
Thos Bosman				Geo Fent
John Madden				Parish Garner
Jas Robinson				John Young
Wm Jenkins				Wm Fletcher
George Jent				Richd Higgins
John Young				John Graham
Wm Fletcher				Thos Arrington
Richd Diggins				Burr Darrison
Richd Blackburn				Thos Darrison

Candidate.	Candidate.	Candidate.	Candidate.	Candidate.
WM. FAIRFAX.	COL. JNO. COLVILLE.	MAJ. BLACKBURN.	VAL. PEYTON.	THOS. HARRISON.
John Grant				Edwd Hems
Aug Washington				Thos Stribling
John Graham				John Waugh
John Snowden				Leo Barker
Jos Wade				Wm Farrow
John Sturman				Thos Welsh
Wm Berkley				Danl Marr
Nimrod Hot (Hitt?)				Benj Strother
Chas Ewell				John Gibson
Geo Burn				John Carr
Ferd Sparks				John Mercer
Thos Arrington				Thos Dent
Thos Harrison				Jno Johnson
James Norris				Benj Sebastin
John Waugh				John Diskin
Leo Barker				
Wm Farrow				234
Thos Welsh				
Danl Marr				
Jacob Laswell				
Benj Strother				
Dennis McCarty				
Calvert Peyton				
John Mercer				
John Dawkins				
Thos Dent				
Benj Sebastin				
John Diskim				
249				

A Copy Test,   EDWIN NELSON,

Clerk County Court, Prince William County, Va.

This register includes the names of persons who, in the election of Burgesses, in 1741, polled 828 votes for the candidates indicated. Many of the voters' names are repetitions, several candidates having received the votes of the same person. The territory covered the limits of the present county of Prince William, together with that now included within the counties of Fairfax, Loudoun, and Fauquier. In other words, it extended along the Potomac to the Blue Ridge.

FAIRFAX COUNTY, VIRGINIA.

THE POLL LIST FOR THE ELECTION OF BURGESSES FOR FAIRFAX COUNTY IN THE YEAR 1744.

THIS county was entitled to two members in the House of Burgesses. The names of the candidates were Col. John Colville, Capt. Lawrence Washington, Capt. Lewis Ellzey, and John Sturman. Two candidates only were to be voted for by the same person. The names of the voters are recorded under the names of the candidates for whom they voted.

Col. John Colville.	Capt. Law. Washington.	Capt. Lewis Ellzey.	Jno. Sturman.
Esq Fairfax	Esquire Fairfax	Magr Cock	Daniel Deskins
Catesby Cocke	John Grant	Chas Green	Thos Bosman
John Grant	James Scott	Daniel Deskins	Richard Carpenter
James Scott	James Keith	Jas Dixon	James Lane
James Keith	John Graham	Saml Harris Sr	Jno Hartley
John Graham	Thos John	Edw Norton	Edw Graham
Thos John	Col Blackson	Jno Hampton	Jas Roberts
			Thos Brown
Col Blackburn	Daniel Hart	James Lane	Jno Allen
Daniel Hart	John Hamilton	Amos Jenney	Moses Linton
Charles Green	Nimrod Hitt	Wm Kitchem	Geo Dunbarr
John Hamilton	Thos Beach	Jno Hartley	Thos Willis
	Thomas Lewis		
Nimrod Hitt	William Dodd	Abel Jenney	Wm Simpson
Thomas Bosman	Amos Jenney	Saml Stone	Jno Hatshorn
Thomas Beach	John Shaddedin	Francis Hange	Jno Roberts
James Dickson	Abel Jenney	Edmond Sands	Andrew Hutchinson
Thomas Lewis	Samuel Stone	Jacob Jenney	Rich'd Simpson
Samuel Harris Sr	Daniel French	Jerh Fairhurst	Wm Harle
Edward Norton	Geo Harrison	Thos Brown	John Roberts
William Dodd	John West	Geo Simpson	Jno Keen
Richard Carpenter	Rich'd Sanford	Fredr Wilks	Jno Canady
Jno Shadedin	Thos Marshall	James Roberts	Jno Guest
Daniel French Jr	Balwin Dade	Henry Netherton	Jas Wyatt
George Harrison	Henry Peyton	Jno Allen	Thos Lewis Jr
John West	Zeph Wade	Geo Dunbar	James Grimsley
Richard Sanford	Jerh Bronaugh	Jno Grantham	Jno Trammell
Thomas Marshall	Francis Hage	Wm Simpson	Amithl Ashford
Balwin Dade	Edmond Sands	Ger'd Trammell	Wm Roberts
Henry Peyton	Jacob Janney	Danl Young	Thos Windsor

Col. John Colville.	Capt. Law. Washington.	Capt. Lewis Ellzey.	Jno. Sturman.
Zeph Wade	Edw'd Grymes	Jno Roberts	Wm Peake
Jereh Bronaugh	Col Eltinger	Vincent Lewis	Jno Ferguson
Cornelus Ellengee	Jerh Fairhurst	Jac Sanders	Wm Barae
Robert Sanford	Robert Sanford	Andw Hutchinson	Wm Smith
Thos Monteith	Thomas Monteith	Lewis Sanders	James Keen
Robert Baker	Jas Jacobs	Richd Simpson Sr	Thos Kicks
Nathaniel Chapman	Francis Wilks	Jas Smith	Christo Pritchett
Vall Peyton	Robert Bates	Abram Lay	Thos Owsley
Benjamin Adams	Nathaniel Chapman	Wm Harle	Wm Moore
Nathaniel Popejoy	Val Pelton	Jno Roberts Sr	Wm Buckley
Stephen Lewis	Nathaniel Popejoy	Jno Canady	Wm Hawling
W K Terrett	Stephen Lewis	Wm Barkley	Fielding Turner
Townsend Dade	W H Terrett	Fielding Turner	Philip Noland
William Clifton	Townsend Dade	Jacob Reny	Rich Coleman
John Turley	Wm Clifton	Rich Ornshandro	Wm Ashford
William Bartlett	Moses Linton	Thos Penson	Wm Meckley
John Grantum	John Turley	David Richardson	Thos Smith
Owen Williams	Wm Stribling	Job Carter	Jno Martin
William Stribling	Henry Watson	Samuel W Tillet	Jno Cockrell
Henry Watson	Garret Trammell	Baxter Simpson	Jno Robinson
John Mede	Author Neale	Jno Trammell	Wm Trammell
Cenths Neale	Daniel Young	James Jeffery	Abraham Lindsy
William Gunnel	Jno Hartshorn	Richard Wheeler	Jacob Smith
Moses Ball	Wm Gunnell	Henry Gunnell	Francis Summers
	Moses Ball	Wm Grimes	Jno Melton
William Gunnell Jr	Wm Gunnell Jr	Wm Boydston	Henry Baggers
James Daniel	Jas Daniel	Thos Wren	Robt Foster
	Gilbert Simpson	Wm Roberts	Jas Ried
			Thos Standall
		Thos Winsor	Jas Murray
Jas Sanders	William Williams Sr	Rich Kirkland	Sml Conner
Gilbert Simpson	Henry Brent	Bland Dunran	Chas Griffin
Wm Williams Jr	Thos Carney	Daniel Trammell	
Henry Brent	Gabriel Adams	Jno Higgerson	
Thos Carney	Wm Saunders	Wm Barton	
	Jno Jenkins	Wm Wright	
Abraham Lay	Benj Adams	James Spurr	
Gabriel Adams	Owen Gilmore	Wm Barker	
Wm Saunders	Jacob Romey	Wm Smith	
Bryant Allison	Rich Malumdro	Jno Bronaugh	
Jno Jenkins	Jno Ashford	Thos Hall	
Jno Keen	Daniel Thomas	Thos Ford	
Jno Musgrave	Charles Broadwater	Rich'd Kirkland	
Wm Davis	Saml Conner	Benj Sebastian	
David Thomas	Wm Windsor	James Keen	

Col. John Colville.	Capt. Law. Washington.	Capt. Lewis Ellzey.	Jno. Sturman.
Ezekiel Jenkins	Thos Moxley	James Turley	
Jno Guss	James Waugh	Thos Hicks	
Gabriel Adams Jr	Charles Griffin	Wm Moore	
David Richardson	Jas Robinson	Jno Lucas	
William Hall Jr	Robert King	Wm Shortridge	
Jno Ellett	Thos Whitford	Wm Buckley	
Jno Manly	Jno Minor	Jno Hurst	
Thomas Lewis Jr	Wm Champneys	Edward Ennus	
George Taylor	Jno Masgrove	Wm Halling	
Richard Wheeler	Wm Davis	Philip Noland	
Henry Gunnell	David Thomas	Wm Roirdon	
Wm Grymes	Ezekiel Jenkins	Joseph Garrett	
Wm Perkins	Gabriel Adams Jr	Thos Smith	
Wm Bailston	James Wyatt	Jno Martin	
Wm Bowling	Saml Tillett	Owen Williams	
Samuel Warner	Jno Aylatt	Robert Thomas	
Michael Ashford	Jas Grymsley	James Halley	
Wm Jenkins	George Taylor	Wm Kirkland	
Bland Durran	James Jeffery	Wm Scutt	Wm Boundreal
Robert Baggess	Wm Perkin	Jacob Smith	Jno Hampton
Francis Triplet	Thos Wrenn	Jno Gorham	Wm Kitchen
Jno Taylor	Wm Bowling	Francis Summers	Jos Jacob
Owen Gilmore	Samuel Warner	Jno Melton	Geo Simpson
Wm Peake	Wm Jenkins	Josiah Clapham	Henry Netherton
Jno Farguson Sr	Daniel Trammell	Geo Adams	Vincent Lewis
Guy Broadwater	John Hiskerson	Geo Foster	Lewis Saunders
James Spurr	Wm Barton	Daniel Thomas	James Smith
Daniel French Sr	Robert Boggess	Jno Ball	Thos Penson
James Jenkins	Francis Triplet	James Waugh	Job Carter
John Bronaugh	Wm Wright		Baxter Simpson
Jno Baxter	John Taylor		Rich S I Kirkland
Jacob Lucas	John Manley		Thos Hall
Thos Hord	Guy Broadwater		Sam Turley
Richard Kirkland	Daniel French Sr		Isaac Simmonds
Sampson Darrell	James Jenkins		Robert Thomas
Levell Jackson	John Baxter		John Robinson
John Lucas	Jacob Lucas		John Goram
Wm Shortridge	Benj Sebastian		Geo Adams
Hugh West	Christopher Pritchett		Geo Foster
John Husk	Thos Owsley		
Garrett Alexander	Sampson Darrel		
Isaac Simmons	Lovell Jackson		
John Summers	Garrat Alexander		
Thos Falkner	Hugh West		
Wichard Coleman	Edward Ennus		

Col. John Colville.   Capt. Law. Washington.   Capt. Lewis Ellzey.   Jno. Sturman.

William Ashford
Wm Reardon
Francis Aubrey
Walter Williams
William McBee
Thos Darris
Wm Trammell

Thos West
Michael Valandigam
    [Valandingham]
Capt Chas Ewel
Jno Cockerill
Wm Gladding
Wm Kirkland
Jno Gladding
Thomas Ellet
Bertram Ewell
John Straham
William Stutt
John Diskins
Robert Diskins
Christopher Neale
Jadwin Crutcher
Jacob Lawful
Jas Reid
Thos Scandall
Wm Hall Sr
James Murray
John Ashford
Chas Broadwater
Wm Winsor
Thomas Moxley
John Ball
James Robinson
Robert King
George Platt
Thos Whitford
John Junior
Wm Champneys

Jno Summers
Thos Faulkner
Francis Aubrey
Walter Williams
Thomas Dams
Josiah Garrett
Thomas West
Michael Valandigam
    [Valandingham]
Chas Ewet
Wm Gladding

John Gladding
Thos Ellett
Bartram Ewell
John Straham
John Meade
John Diskins
Abraham Lindsey
Josias Clapham
Henry Baugus
Christo Neale
George Plat
Robert Foster
Jadwin Crutcher
Bryant Allison
Jacob Lawful

A copy Poll List for the House of Burgesses, recorded Liber A, No. 6, page 237, and examined.

Truly Recorded,

A copy, Test,   Test,   CATESBY COCKE, *Cl. Cur.*
    F. W. RICHARDSON, *Clerk.*

Fairfax county was formed in 1742 from Prince William. At the date of this poll, in 1744, it still included what is now Loudoun county. The latter, however, was detached in 1757. The voters whose names are given in the foregoing list were included, therefore, in the inhabitants then living within what are now Fairfax and Loudoun counties.*

* It may be of interest to note the fact that in the year 1769 the House of Burgesses of Virginia passed an act concerning the manner in which members of this body should be elected. Section 7 of said act provides as follows: "And be it further enacted, by the authority aforesaid, That after publication of such writs, and at the day and place of election, every freeholder actually resident within his county shall personally appear, and give his vote, upon penalty of forfeiting two hundred pounds of tobacco to any person or persons who will inform or sue for the same, recoverable, with costs, by action of debt or information, in any court of this dominion." Hening's Statutes, vol. 8, page 308.

VIRGINIA IN THE REVOLUTION.

THE part which Virginia took in the Revolutionary War cannot be detailed in this work. We can give only a few items to show that as a state she performed her full duty, though complete credit has not been given to her in the past.

By virtue of her location she was a battlefield during the Revolution, especially during the closing period. The services of her militia were not taken into account, and hence by comparison with other states she appears to have furnished a smaller number of troops than were her quota.

She had, however, a goodly number of militia, or minutemen, whose services were confined to state territory. The Virginia Historical Magazine began, in 1898, the publication of the lists of these men, commencing with 1777. The information furnished is exceedingly valuable and is heartily commended to our readers.

A very interesting list of the Continental Line during the Revolution, including the general-in-chief, major-generals, colonels, lieutenant-colonels, majors, captains, lieutenants, etc., may be seen in Vol. 2, pp. 243 to 258 of the Virginia Magazine of History and Biography; and a corresponding list of the State Line of the same period on pages 357 to 370 of the same publication.

The total contribution by Virginia of troops of all kinds, including continental and state forces, militia, riflemen, rangers, minutemen, etc., may not be correctly stated. At the opening of the war, and also during its progress, men enlisted for a year at a time. Some of them enlisted several times in succession.

In making up the total service, these repetitions need to be considered. The State's contribution to the Continental army is given, however, as 26,678; to which are to be added some 30,000 members of State forces, making a total of 56,678 men. The only state which claims to have approximated Virginia's forces was the state of Massachusetts, with 87,907 men. This number, for reasons stated elsewhere, must be accepted with a grain of allowance.

Virginia had originally fifteen regiments in the Continental service.

In a letter to General Washington, in 1776, Richard Peters, Secretary of the Board of War, transmits the following list of Field Officers in the Service of Virginia. See American Archives, 5 series, vol. 2, page 320.

BATTALIONS.	COLONELS.	DATE OF COMMISSION.	REMARKS.
1st	William Christian		Declined to serve.
2d	William Woodford	Feb. 13, 1776	Resigned.
3d	Hugh Mercer	" "	Appointed Brig.-Gen.
4th	Adam Stephen	" "	Appointed Major-Gen.
5th	William Peachy	" "	Resigned.
6th	Mordecai Buckner	" "	Cashiered.
7th	William Dangerfield	Feb. 29, 1776	Resigned.
8th	Peter Muhlenberg	Mar. 1, 1776	Brig.-Genl.
9th	Thomas Fleming	Mar. 2, 1776	Died Aug., 1776.

October 18, 1776, it was resolved by the House of Delegates that six new battalions of Infantry be raised and employed in the Continental Service; and that provision be made for completing the nine battalions formerly raised, and extending the additional bounty to such of them as shall be willing to enlist on like terms. (See Am. Arch., 5 series, vol. 2, page 1112.) Under this order the following men were appointed colonels on the 15th of November: Edward Stevens, Daniel Morgan, James Wood, Samuel Meredith, Charles Lewis, and David Mason. (See Am. Arch., 5 series, vol. 3, page 695.)

HISTORICAL NOTES.

As showing the changes and difficulties in mobilizing her forces, we have examined the original archives and made note of some things which will tend to throw light upon this period. So far as possible, the chronological order is observed.

By the Continental Congress it was decreed, August 13th, 1776, that the 8th Virginia should have pay from May 27th, and the 7th from 17th of the same month.

The first Virginia regiment marched from Williamsburg for New York the 16th of August, 1776.

On the 21st of August, 1776, the captains and subalterns of the 1st and 2d regiments presented a petition to the governor and council of the State to have their relative ranks properly adjusted as compared with the forces of North Carolina.

At the October session of the General Assembly, held in Williamsburg, it was announced that six additional battalions of infantry were to be raised. The reward was: "To every non-commissioned officer and private soldier a present bounty of twenty dollars, an annual bounty of a suit of clothes—to consist for the present year of two linen hunting shirts, two pair of overalls, a leathern or woolen waistcoat with sleeves, one pair of breeches, a hat or leathern cap, two shirts, two pair of hose, and two pair of shoes, amounting in the whole to the value of twenty dollars, or that sum to be paid to each soldier who shall procure those articles for himself—and to provide the following portions of land, to be given at the close of the war, or whensoever discharged, to the officers and soldiers who shall engage in the said service, or their representatives, if slain by the enemy, to wit: To every non-commissioned officer or soldier, one hundred acres; to every ensign, one hundred and fifty acres; to every lieutenant, two hundred acres; to every captain, three hundred acres; to every major, four hundred acres; to every lieutenant-colonel, four hundred and fifty acres; and to every colonel, five hundred acres."

On the 1st of November, 1776, four companies of the Virginia Battalion on the eastern shore were directed to march, under command of a field officer, to Dover, Del., and await further orders.

On the 1st of November, 1776, it was ordered by Congress that commissions be granted to fill vacancies in the 4th, 5th and 6th Virginia Battalions; and on the 6th, Brigadier-General Stephens was directed to fill in dates and deliver the commissions.

November 4, 1776, Capt. George Gibson, of the 1st regiment, sent by the governor to New Orleans on a special expedition, was provided by Caesar Rodney, at Dover, Del., with a number of horses and £6 for expenses.

On the 5th of November, 1776, the returns of the 1st regiment, under command of Col. John Fleming, showed present a total strength of 486 officers and men.

On the same date the 3d regiment, under command of Col. George Weeden, at Camp John Fushee's, had 603 rank and file.

November 20th, 1776, Col. Wm. Crawford, of the 7th regiment, severed his relation with the command, and, in reply to a testimonial of confidence by his subordinates, expressed his purpose to devote himself "to the utmost defense of American liberty, justice, and the rights of humanity."

On the 26th of November, 1776, it was directed that a regiment of artillery, to be armed with muskets and bayonets, should be raised in Virginia, to include two companies already formed.

At Williamsburg, on the 6th of December, 1776, Col. Thomas Fleming, of the 9th regiment, issued an order calling for the return of all officers and soldiers absent with leave and the joining of the regiment at Philadelphia on its march to reinforce Washington.

On the 27th of December, 1776, it was decreed by Congress that the Virginia militia marching to the aid of Washington should receive a pair of shoes and stockings, and the same rations and monthly pay as were given to other continental troops.

9

On the same day, the 2d and 7th Virginia regiments, with all convalescents from other commands left in the State, were ordered to march at once to join Washington.

On the same day, too, owing to the necessity of reinforcing Washington at once, Virginia was " empowered to call into service, at the continental expense, three regiments of militia, or minutemen, if such measure shall by that state be judged necessary."

These troops were enlisted "to serve during the continuance of the present war, unless sooner discharged."

By the session of the Assembly, which began May 5th, 1777, was authorized the forming of militia companies of males over 15 and less than 50 years of age. These companies were to be not less than 32 nor more than 58 in number, and were to meet for muster once per month, at 11 o'clock, accoutred as follows: County lieutenants, colonels, lieutenant-colonels, and major, with sword; captains and lieutenants, with firelock and bayonets, cartouch-box, sword, and three charges of powder and balls; every ensign with sword; every non-commissioned officer and private with rifle and tomahawk, good firelock and bayonet, with pouch and horn, or cartouch or cartridge-box, and with three charges of powder and ball.

At the October session it was enacted, that to assimilate the Virginia with those from other states, fourteen of the said regiments be reduced to eight companies each, and then be completed by volunteers or drafts. It was also suggested that the officers of the fourteen regiments, including those of the 9th captured at Germantown, co-operate in this work. In the draft Mennonites and Quakers were to be exempt. Enlistments were for three years or during the war.

The following letter from Governor Henry to John Lawrence, aide-de-camp on the staff of General Washington, indicates the difficulty of securing recruits from Virginia in the year 1778.

Accordingly, in September, 1778, the fifteen regiments from Virginia were reduced to eleven in number and reorganized as follows : The 9th was joined with the 1st; the 6th with the 2d; the 5th with the 3d ; the 8th with the 4th ; the 7th was called the 5th ; the 10th the 6th ; the 11th the 7th ; the 12th the 8th ; the 13th the 9th ; the 4th the 10th ; and the 15th the 11th.

WILLIAMSBURG, *June* 18, 1778.

Sir : General Washington sent me an account of the Drafted Soldiers that have joined the army from this state; and it appears that not one-half of the number voted by the Assembly have got to camp.   Truth obliges me to add that very few more of the Drafts will ever be got into the service.

I lament this capital deficiency in our Quota of troops; but no efforts of the Executive have been sufficient to prevent it.

The Assembly, at their late sitting, have directed three hundred and fifty cavalry and two thousand infantry to be forthwith raised and to join the grand army. Some of the former will be raised, but from every appearance I am sorry to say there is little reason to expect any success in getting the infantry.   I can only assure you, sir, that I shall pay due regard to the Requisition you are pleased to make for compleating our quota of men by exerting myself to the utmost, altho' I fear it will be in vain.

. . . .

With highest regard, I have the honor to be, sir,
Your most obedient and humble servant,
PATRICK HENRY.
The Honorable Mr. Lawrence.

Names of colonels in command of Virginia regiments in 1779–1780, with date of commission :

1st Regiment, Richard Parker, Feb. 10, 1778.
2d   "   Christ. Fibiger, Sept. 26, 1777.
3d   "   Will. Heath,   April 30, 1778.
4th   "   John Neville   Dec. 11, 1777.
5th   "   Will. Russell,   Dec. 19, 1776.
6th   "   John Greene,   Jan. 26, 1778.
7th   "   Dan. Morgan,   Nov. 12, 1776.
8th   "   James Wood,   Nov. 12, 1776.
9th   "   John Gibson,   Oct. 25, 1777.
10th   "   Will. Davis,   Mar. 20, 1778.
11th   "   Abrh. Buford,   May 16, 1778.

In March, 1781, an act was passed to raise two legions for

defense of the State. The preamble, which is quite historic, provides: "Whereas, at this critical juncture, when the enemy have made this state the object of their vengeance, it is necessary to provide a standing force for the immediate defense thereof. It is therefore enacted that two legions, to consist of six companies of infantry and one troop of cavalry, of one hundred men each, be forthwith raised to serve during the war, but not to take the field or to do duty except in cases of actual or threatened invasion."

On the 7th of May, 1781, the Assembly began its sessions in Richmond, and continued them, by adjournment, to Staunton, in Augusta county. This transfer, made necessary by military conditions, was authorized under a general law of the Assembly.

At this session the governor was authorized to appoint recruiting officers to enlist, by persuasion, three thousand soldiers for two years, or during war—each to be 5 ft. 4 in. high, not a deserter, not subject to fits, of able body and sound mind.

Virginia in the navy during the Revolution was not so conspicuous as in her land service. Her work was meritorious, and her officers occupied honorable positions. On this subject valuable information and authentic lists of names, with relative ranks, may be found in the Virginia Magazine of History and Biography, vol. 1, pp. 64–75.

It may be proper to say, that conspicuous among these naval heroes was Commodore James Barron, who, with his brother Richard, commanded "The Liberty" and "The Patriot," two important vessels during this period. Commodore Barron participated in twenty different actions, in all of which he was very successful. He died in 1787. His sons, James and Samuel, were also conspicuous in naval affairs during and subsequent to the Revolution. Descendants of the Barrons subsequently located in Maryland, concerning whom it may be well to consult Genealogical Manuscript, by the author of this volume.

Virginia had a good representation in the artillery branch

of the service. Companies were commanded by Captains Nathaniel Burwell, Thomas Baytop, Samuel Booker, John C. Carter, Whitehead Coleman, John Dandridge, Samuel Eddens, John Gregory, John Henry, Valentine Peyton, James Pendleton, William Pierce, George Rice, Drury Ragsdale, and Anthony Singleton.

Nine of these companies, viz., Nos. 1, 2, 3, 4, 5, 6, 8, 9, and 10, commanded respectively by Captains Pierce, Burwell, Singleton, Ragsdale, Pendleton, Dandridge, Eddens, Baytop, and Henry, were attached to Col. Charles Harrison's Virginia and Maryland Regiment of Artillery, from Nov. 30, 1776, to April, 1782. They were stationed at Valley Forge, Smith's Clove, Pluckemin, and camp near Chester at various times.

Captain Burwell was commissioned an aide to Brig.-Gen. Robt. Howe, Nov. 30, 1776, and served to the end of the war.

The scope of this volume will not permit the tracing in detail of the changes through which the various organizations passed from first to last. As battalions became depleted they were consolidated, and this resulted in many supernumerary officers, who had either to be retired from the service or assigned to other commands.

Great interest will attach to the accompanying final pay-roll of officers at the close of the Revolution.

Estimate of the Balance of Specie Due the Officers of the Virginia Line, on Account of Three Months Specie Pay in 1782, and Four Months in 1783.

	Pay rec^d.	What entitled to.	Am° due.	Am° overpaid.
Cap. James Armstrong. *Lees corps,* 2 m°s pay in 1782 & 4 m° in 1783......		300		
deduct: Rec^d of John Pierce......	100			
" of John S. Dart......	50			
" Gen. Greenes Bills......	100			
" John Pierce......	50	300		
L^t & Adj^t Robert Breckenridge. 3 mo. in 1782 & 4 mo's in 1783......	106.60	267.6		{To be paid in certificates.
This officer having rec^d as much or more specie than he was intitled to receive, is to be paid the bal. left due to him by Mr. Dunscombs settlement in certificates. deduct: Rec^d of Chas Stockley......	79.30			
" John S. Dart......				
" Gen. Greene's Bills......	79.30	265.30	1.66	
Cap. Lt Ambrose Bohannan. 3 mo. pay in 1782 & 4 mo. 1783......	33.30	233.30		
deduct: rec^d of John Pierce......	50			
" John Pierce......	100			
" Charles Stockley......	100			
" Charles Stockley......		283.30		50
Cap. Lt Lewis Booker. 3 mos. pay in 1782 & 4 mo. 1783......	66.60	233.30		
deduct: rec^d of John S. Dart......	100			
" Charles Stockley......		166.60	66.60	
Lt John Brooke. 3 m° pay in 1782 & 4 m° in 1783......	33.30	232		
deduct: rec^d of John Pierce......	33.30			
" John S. Dart......	98.60			
" Gen. Greenes Bills......	100			
" Charles Stockley......		265.30		33.30

Entry	Deductions	Amount		
Lt Francis Brooke. 3 mo 1782 & 4 mos pay in 1783		316.60		10.60
deduct: recd of John Pierce	33.30			
" " Gen. Greens	66.60			
" " Charles Stockley	100.60			
" "	126.60	327.30		
Cap. William Barret. 2 mo pay in 1782 & 4 mo pay 1783		300		
deduct: recd of John Pierce	150			
" " Charles Stockley	150	300		
Lt Henry Bowyer. 3 mo pay in 1782 & 4 mo in 1783		226.60		
deduct: recd of John S. Dart	33.30			
" clothing rec'd of Hamilton	54.70			
" John S. Dart	33.30			
" Gen. Greens Bills	66.60		11.80	
" Charles Stockley	26.60	214.70		
Cap. Samuel Booker. 2 mos pay in 1782 & 4 mo. pay in 1783		240.00		
deduct: recd of John S. Pierce	40			
" Charles Stockley	200	240		
Colo George Baylor. 2 mo pay in 1782 & 4 mo in 1783		562.45		
deduct: recd of John Pierce	187.45		354.17	
" John Hamilton	20.73	208.28		
Lt & Q. M. Jacob Brown. 2 mo pay in 1782 & 4 mo in 1783		277.60		
deduct: recd of Chs Stockley		224	53.60	
Surg: Cornelius Baldwin. 2 mo pay in 1782 & 4 mo 1783		366		
deduct: recd of John Pierce	59			18
" " Charles Stockley	325	384		
Mate John Bull. Lees corps. 2 mo pay 1782 & 4 mo in 1783		258		
deduct: recd of John S. Dart	40			
" Genl Greenes Bills	90		63.64	
" Col. Carrington, for a horse	64.26	194.26		
Carried forward				

	Pay rec'd.	What entitled to.	Am'e due.	Am'e overpaid.
Amount brought forward				
Cap. Patrick Carnes.　2 M° pay in 1782 & 4 M° in 1783.		300		
Lees corps,　deduct: rec'd of John Pierce	100			
〃　Hen Lee.........	50			
〃　John S. Dart.........	50			
〃　Gen. Greenes Bills.........	100	300		
L' George Carrington.　3 M° pay in 1782 & 4 M° in 1783.		233.30		
Lees corps,　deduct: rec'd of John Pierce.........	100			
〃　Col. H. Lee.........	66.60			
〃　Gen. Greenes Bills.........	66.60	233.30		
Ens. Clement Carrington.　2 M° pay in 1782 & 4 M° in 1783		160		
Lees corps,　deduct: rec'd of John Pierce.........	80			
〃　Col. H. Lee.........	53.30			
〃　Gen. Greenes Bills.........	53.30	186.60		26.60
L' Joseph Conway.　3 M° pay in 1782 & 4 M° 1783		186.60		
deduct: rec'd of John S. Dart	53.30			
〃　Gen. Greenes Bills.........	53.30			
〃　Charles Stockley.........	106.60	213.30		26.60
L' Richard Claiborne.　3 M° pay in 1782 & 4 M° 1783		233.30		
deduct: rec'd of John Pierce	33.30			
〃　Cha° Stockley	200	233.30		
L' Archibald Campbell.　3 M° pay 1782 & 4 M° 1783.		186.60		
deduct: rec'd of John Pierce.........	26.60			
〃　Charles Stockley.........	160	186.60		
L' Thomas Coverly.　3 M° pay 1782 & 4 M° in 1783		186.60		
ded': rec'd of John Pierce	26.60			
〃　Cha° Stockley.........	160	186.60		

Description	Deduct	Amount	Net	Certificates
L.ᵗ Edmund Clarke. 3 Mᵒ pay in 1782 & 4 Mᵒ in 1783		186.60		
dedᵗ: recᵈ of John Pierce	26.60			
" Chaˢ Stockley	160	186.60		
Surgeon Thomas Christie. 2 Mᵒ pay 1782 & 4 Mᵒ 1783		502		
dedᵗ: recᵈ of John Pierce	307			
" Goods recᵈ of Col. Carrington	31.72		33	
This officer having recᵈ already more specie than he was entitled to, is to receive the balance found due to him in Wm. Dunscomb's settᵗ in certificates.				{18 To be paid to him in certificates. 129.31
" Gen. Greenes Bills	130	468.72		
L.ᵗ Nathaniel Darby. 3 Mᵒ pay in 1782 & 4 in '83		186.60		
dedᵗ: recᵈ of John S. Dart	53.30			
" Clothing of Hamilton	40.31			
" Gen. Greenes Bills	53.30			
" Charles Stockley	160	316		
L.ᵗ John Drew. 3 Mᵒ pay in 1782 & 4 Mᵒ 1783		233.30		
dedᵗ: recᵈ of Jnᵒ Pierce	33.30			
" Charles Stockley	200	233.30		
Majʳ Joseph Eccleston. 2 Mᵒ pay in 1782 & 4 Mᵒ '83		340		
Lees corps, dedᵗ: recᵈ of John Pierce	100			
" Henʸ Lee	80			
" John S. Dart	60			
" Gen. Greenes Bills.	100	340		
L.ᵗ & Adjᵗ William Eskridge. 3 Mᵒ pay 1782 & 4 Mᵒ 1783		238.60		
dedᵗ: recᵈ of John Pierce	26.60		13	
" Charles Stockley	199	225.60		
Cap. Thomas Edmunds. 2 Mᵒ pay in 1782 & 4 Mᵒ 1783		240		
dedᵗ: recᵈ of John Pierce	80			
" Goods of Carrington	38.71		81.19	
" John Pierce	40	158.71		
Amount carried forward				

	Pay recd.	What entitled to.	Amo due.	Amo overpaid.
Amount brought forward				
Ens. John Eustace. 3 mo pay in 1782 & 4 mo 1783.........		140	80	
deduct: recd of Chs Stockly............		60		
Maj. Samuel Finley. 2 mo pay in 1782 & 4 mo 1783		300		
deduct: recd of John S. Dart	50			
" Gen. Greenes Bills	100			
" Charles Stockley	250	400		100
Lt William Fitzhugh. 3 mo pay in 1782 & 4 mo 1783........		233.30		
deduct: recd of John S. Dart........	66.60			
" Gen. Greenes Bills........	100			
" final settlt certificate........	66.60	233.30		
Colo Nathaniel Gist. 2 mo pay in 1782 & 4 mo in 1783		525	75	
deduct: recd of Maj. Wm Lewis........	225			
" John Pierce.........	225	450		{ To be paid in certificates.
Col. Gist having recd all the specie he was intitled to, is to receive this bal. in certificates.				
Lt John Gordon. 3 mo pay in 1782 & 4 mo in 1783		278.30	133.30	
Lees corps. deduct: recd of John Pierce.........	145	145		
Ens. A. D. C. Alexr Garden. 3 mo pay in 1782 & 4 mo in 1783........		332	1.18	
Lees corps. deduct: recd of John Pierce.......	180			
ditto.	26.60			
" Gen. Greenes Bills	53.30			
" John Hamilton	70.72	330.72		
Lt & Adjt Ambrose Gordon. 3 mo pay 1782 & 4 mo 1783		285.60	145	
deduct: recd of John S. Dart	48.30			
" Gen. Greenes Bills.......	92.30	140.60		

Ens. William B. Harrison. 3 m° pay 1782 & 4 m° 1783		186.60		
Lees corps. deduct: rec^d of John Pierce	186.60	244.46		
" Hamilton clothes	57.76			57.76
Lt George Hite. 3 m° pay in 1782 & 4 m° in 1783		233.30		
deduct: rec^d of John S. Dart	33.30			
" John Pierce	133.30			
" John Hamilton	19.40	186.10	47.20	
Cap. John Hughes. 2 m°s pay 1782 & 4 m°s in 1783		300		
deduct: rec^d of John S. Dart	50			
" Gen. Greenes Bills	100			
" Charles Stockley	150	300		
Lt John Harris. 3 m° pay in 1782 & 4 m° in 1783		233.30		
deduct: rec^d of John S. Dart	33.30			
" Gen. Greenes Bills	66.60	100	133.30	
Cap. James Heard. 2 m° pay in 1782 & 4 m° in 1783		300		
dedc^t: Rec^d of John Pierce		300		
Lt John Heth. 3 m° pay in 1782 & 4 m° in 1783		186.60		
deduct: rec^d of Thos Bradford	60			
" John Pierce	26.60			
" Charles Stockly	80	166.60	20	
Cap. George Handy. 2 m° pay in 1782 & 4 m° 1783		300		
P. 3909. *Lees corps.* deduct: rec^d of John Pierce	100			
" Hen: Lee	50			
" John S. Dart	50			
" Goods; rec^d of Col. Carrington	15.16			
" Gen. Greenes Bills	100	315.16		15.16
Amount carried forward				

	Pay recd.	What entitled to.	Amo due.	Amo overpaid.
Amount brought forward				
Chaplain John Hurt. 2 Mo pay in 1782 & 4 Mo 1783		450	300	
deduct: recd of John S. Dart		150		
Corn¹ Jasper Hughes. 3 Mo pay in 1782 & 4 Mo in 1783		186.60	160	
deduct: recd of John S. Dart	26.60	26.60		
Lt Peter Johnson. 3 Mo pay in 1782 & 4 Mo in 1783.		308.30		
Lees corps, deduct: recd of John Pierce	100			
" Col. Hen. Lee	18.30			
" John S. Dart	48.30			
Peter Johnson having already received more specie than he was entitled to is to be paid this bal. in certificates. " Gen. Greenes Bills	66.60	233.30	75	{To be paid in certificates.
Corn¹ John Jordan. 3 Mo pay in 1782 & 4 Mo in 1783		186.60		
Lees corps, deduct: recd of John Pierce	80			
" John S. Dart	26.60			
" Col. H. Lee	26.60			
" Gen. Greenes Bills	53.30			
" John Hamilton	56.53			
" Col. E. Carrington a horse	150	393.23		180.53
Surg. Mathew Irvine. 2 Mo pay in 1782 & 4 Mo 1783		366		
Lees corps, deduct: recd of John Pierce	120			
" Col. Hen. Lee	50			
" John S. Dart	60			
" Gen. Greenes Bills	130	366	6	
Cap. Churchill Jones. 2 Mo pay in 1782 & 4 Mo 1783		300	150	
deduct: recd of John S. Dart	50			
" Gen. Greenes Bills	100	150		

Cap. William Johnson. 2 Mo pay 1782 & 4 Mo 1783		240		
deduct: recd of John Pierce	40			
" Charles Stockley	200	240		
Cap. Abraham Kirkpatrick. 2 Mo 1782 & 4 Mo 1783		240		
deduct: recd of John Pierce	40			
" Chas Stockley	200	240		
Col. Henry Lee. *Lees corps,* 2 Mo pay 1782 & 4 Mo pay in 1783		702.45		102.45
deduct: recd of John Pierce	600			
Cornt James Lovell. *Lees corps,* 4 Mo in 1783		106.60		106.60
deduct: recd of John Pierce	213.30			
Lt Elias Langham. 3 Mo pay in 1782 & 4 Mo 1783		233.30		
deduct: recd of John Pierce	133.30			
" Charles Stockley	100	233.30		
Lt A. D. C. William Luderman. 3 Mo pay 1782 & 4 Mo 1783		252.60		
deduct: recd of John Pierce	26.60			
" Charles Stockley	24		72	
" Charles Stockley	230	280.60		
Lt John Linton. 3 Mo pay in 1782 & 4 Mo in 1783		233.30		
deduct: recd of John S. Dart	66.60			
" Gen. Greenes Bills	66.60	133.30	100	
Surg. George Munroe. 2 Mo pay in 1782 & 4 Mo in 1783		366		
deduct: recd of John S. Dart	60			
" Gen. Greene's Bills	130			
" Charles Stockley	130			
" Recd in certif. on settt but of his specie amo.	38			
" Samuel Hodgdon	8	366		
Amo carried forward				

	Pay recd.	What entitled to.	Amo due.	Amo overpaid.
Amount brought forward				
Lᵗ Thomas Martin. 3 Mᵒ pay in 1782 & 4 Mᵒ in 1783		186.60	5.9	
deduct: recᵈ of Chˢ Stockley	160			
" John Hamilton	21.51	181.51		
Lᵗ Javin Miller. 3 Mᵒ pay in 1782 & 4 Mᵒ in 1783		186.60		17.69
deduct: recᵈ of John S. Dart	53.30			
" Gen. Greenes Bills	53.30			
" Charles Stockley	97.69	204.39		
Lᵗ Thomas Miller. 3 Mᵒ pay in 1782 & 4 Mᵒ in 1783		186.60		
deduct: recᵈ of John Pierce	106.60			
" Charles Stockley	80	186.60		
Lᵗ James Merriweather. 3 Mᵒ pay in 1782 & 4 Mᵒ 1783		233.30	120.37	
deduct: recᵈ of John S. Dart	33.30			
" final settᵗ certifᵗ	12.83			
" Gen. Greenes Bills	66.60	112.83		
Lᵗ James Morton. 3 Mᵒ pay in 1782		80		
deduct: recᵈ of John Pierce		80		
B. Gen. Daniel Morgan. 2 Mᵒ pay in 1782 & 4 Mᵒ pay 1783		750		
deduct: recᵈ of John Pierce		750		
Lᵗ Lawrence Manning. 3 Mᵒ pay in 1782 & 4 Mᵒ 1783		233.30		
Lees corps. deduct: recᵈ of John Pierce	100			
" ditto	33.30			
" John S. Dart	33.30			
" Gen. Greenes Bills	66.60	233.30		

Cornt John Middleton. 3 Mo pay in 1782 & 4 Mo 1783.			186.60	100.85
Lees corps.				
deduct: recd of John Pierce	80			
" John S. Dart	26.60			
" Gen. Greenes Bills	53.30			
" do. Cash	46.60			
" Hamilton cloths	79.15		285.65	
B. Gen. Peter Muhlenburg. 2 Mo pay in 1782 and 4 1783			750	
deduct: recd of John Pierce	375			
" Charles Stockley	375		750	
Cornet John Masserg. 3 Mo pay in 1782 & 4 Mo 1783			228.60	107.13
deduct: recd of John S. Dart	115.30			
" Gen. Greenes Bills	113.30			
" Col. Carrington for horse.	107.13		335.33	
Ferdinand O'Neal, Cap. 2 Mo pay in 1782 & 4 Mo 1783.			300	
Lees corps.				
deduct: recd of John Pierce	150			
" John S. Dart	50			
" Gen. Greens Bills	100			
" Charles Stockley	150		450	150
Cap. William Parsons. 2 Mo pay 1782 & 4 Mo in 1783			300	
deduct: recd of John S. Dart	50			
" Gen. Greenes Bills	100	150	150	
Cornet Robert Power. 3 Mo pay in 1782 & 4 Mo in 1783			186.60	
Lees corps.				
deduct: recd of John Pierce	106.60			
" John S. Dart	26.60			
" Gen. Greens Bills	53.30		186.60	
Cap. Alexander Parker. 2 Mo pay 1782 & 4 Mo in 1783			240	171.28
deduct: recd of John S. Dart.	40			
" Gen. Greenes Bills	80			
" Charles Stockley	200			
" ditto.	42			
" John Hamilton	49.28		411.28	
Amo carried forward				

	Pay rec'd.	What entitled to.	Am'o due.	Am'o overpaid.
Amount brought forward				
Cap. William Pierce, A. D. C.　2 M° pay in 1782 & 4 M° 1783		328		
rec'd John Hamilton	83.77			
" John Pierce pay	187.45			
" Col Carrington, cash	69.82			
" Gen. Greene Priv. au°	560.77			
" d° Public service	214.30	1116.41		
Cornet John Perry.　pay in 1782 & 4 M° pay in 1783		240		
ded': rec'd of John S. Dart	53.30			
" " Gen. Greenes Bills...	53.30			
John Perry having been credited by Mr Dunscomb w'h too much specie—is entitled to only half this bal. in specie and the other half is to be paid in certificates.　" Charles Stockley......	26.60	133.30	106.60	{53° of this to be p'd in certif.
Maj' John Rudulph.　2 M° pay in 1782 & 4 M° in 1783		360		
Lees corps,　deduct: Sundry paym'ts in cash		360		
Cap. Michael Rudulph.　2 M° pay in 1782 & 4 M° 1783		300		
Lees corps,　deduct: Sundry payment cash		300		
L' Robert Quarles.　pay as Ens. 1782		106		
deduct: rec'd of John S. Dart	26.60			
" Gen. Greenes Bills	79.30			
" Charles Stockley	60			
" John Hamilton	49.34	215.34		109.34
Surg. Robert Rose.　2 M° pay in 1782 & 4 M° 1783		366		
ded': rec'd of John Hamilton cl'g......	44.26			
deduct: rec'd of Gen. Greenes Bills...	130	174.26	191.64	

Lt Alexander Skinner. *Lees corps,*			
3 M° pay 1782 & 4 M° 1783		366	
of Gen. Greene—cash..........	116	116	
deduct: rec^d of John Pierce	250	250	
S. Mate Nathan Smith.			
2 M° pay in 1782 & 4 M° 1783..........		258	
deduct: rec^d of John S. Dart	40		
" clothing of Hamilton	73.22		
" Gen. Greenes Bills	130	243.22	14.68
Cap. Clough Shelton.			
2 M° pay in 1782 & 4 M° in 1783		240	
deduct: rec^d of John S. Dart	40		
" Gen. Greenes Bills	80		
" clothing of Hamilton..........	40		
" Charles Stockley	80	240	
Lt Stephen Southall.			
3 M° pay in 1782 & 4 M° in 1783		303	
deduct: rec^d of John S. Dart	33.30		
" Gen. Greenes Bills	116.60		
" Charles Stockley	100	250	53
This off^r has been credited in M^r D^s settlement with too much specie therefore the bal. found due him must be paid in certificates — as he has already had his full comp° of specie.			
Cornet Charles Scott.			
3 M° pay 1782 & 4 M° 1783..........		186.60	
deduct: rec^d of John S. Dart	53.30		
" Gen. Greenes Bills..........	53.30	106.60	80
Lt Philip Stuart.			
3 M° pay in 1782 & 4 M° 1783		200	
ded^t: rec^d of John S. Dart	33.30		
" ditto.	33.30		
" Gen. Greenes Bills..........	66.60	133.30	66.60
Cap. John Stith.			
2 M° pay in 1782 & 4 M° pay in 1783		240	
deduct: rec^d of John Pierce..........	40		
" Charles Stockley..........	200	240	
Am° carried forward			

10

	Pay recᵈ.	What entitled to.	Amᵒ due.	Amᵒ overpaid.
Amount brought forward				
Lᵗ Jonathan Snowden. *Lees corps.* 3 Mᵒ pay in 1782 & 4 Mᵒ 1783 .... dedᵗ: recᵈ of John Pierce		233.30 233.30		
B. Gen. Charles Scott. 2 Mᵒ pay in 1782 & 4 Mᵒ 1783 .... deduct: Recᵈ of John Pierce.........		750 750		
Lᵗ Charles Stockley, P. M. 3 Mᵒ pay in 1782 & Mᵒ 1783 .... dedᵗ: Recᵈ of John Pierce		396 396		
S. Mate Claiboine Vaughn. 2 Mᵒ pay 1782 & 4 Mᵒ 1783 .... deduct: recᵈ of John Pierce .... " Gen. Greenes Bills	168 80	248 248		
Lᵗ A. D. C. George A. Washington. 3 Mᵒ pay in 1782 & 4 Mᵒ 1783 .... deduct: recᵈ of John Pierce		352 352		
Lᵗ William Winston, Adjᵗ. *Lees corps.* 3 Mᵒ in 1782 & 4 Mᵒ in 1783... deduct: recᵈ of John Pierce .... " John S. Dart .... " Gen. Greens Bills......... " Chaˢ Stockley	100 48.30 66.60 26.60	260 241.60	18.30	
Lᵗ William Whitaker. 3 Mᵒ pay 1782 & 4 Mᵒ 1783 .... deduct: recᵈ of John Pierce .... " John S. Dart.... " Charles Stockley	33.30 66.60 100	233.30 200	33.30	
B. Gen. George Weedon. 2 Mᵒ pay 1782 & 4 Mᵒ 1783 .... dedᵗ: recᵈ of John Pierce		750 750		

Lt David Walker. 3 M^o pay in 1782 & 4 M^o in 1783......		186.60	
ded^t rec^d of John Pierce......	26.60	106.60	80
" Charles Stockley......	80		
Lt Francis Whiting. 3 M^o pay in 1782 & 4 M^o in 1783......		233.30	
deduct rec^d of John S. Dart......	33.30	133.30	100
charged by Mr A. Dunscomb w^h......	100		
Lt Col. William Washington. 2 M^o pay in 1782 & 4 M^o 1783......		450	
deduct rec^d of John S. Dart......		75	375
Col. James Wood. 2 M^o pay in 1782 & 4 M^o in 1783......		450	
deduct Rec^d of John Pierce......	225		
" Charles Stockley......	225	450	
Cap. James Williams. 2 M^o pay in 1782 & 4 M^o in 1783		240	
ded^t rec^d of John Pierce......	40		
" Charles Stockley......	200	240	
Cap. John Watts. 2 M^o pay in 1782 & 4 M^o in 1783		300	
deduct Gen. Greenes Bills......		100	200
Lt Charles Yarbrough. 3 M^o pay in 1782 & 4 M^o 1783......		290	
deduct rec^d of John S. Dart......	96.60		
" Gen. Greenes Bills......	92.60	189.30	100.60
Lt Benjamin Ashby. 3 M^o Pay in 1782......			80
Lt David Allen. 3 M^o Pay in 1782......		80	
ded^t Rec^d of Ch^s Stockley		80	
Lt Peter F. Archer. 3 M^o Pay in 1782......		80	
deduct rec^d of Ch^s Stockley......		80	
Carried forward			

	Pay recd.	What entitled to.	Amo due.	Amo overpaid.
Amount brought forward				
Ens. Richard Archer. 3 Mo pay in 1782		60		
deduct recd of Chs Stockley.....		60		
Lt Daniel Bedinger. 3 Mo pay as Ensign in 1782	26.60	60		
deduct recd of John S. Dart......				
" Gen. Greens Bills......	60			
" Chs. Stockley......	58.34			
" John Hamilton		145.4		85.4
Cap. Nathaniel Burwell. 2 Mo pay in 1782		100		
deduct recd of John Pierce......		100		
Ens. Henry Bayless. 3 Mo pay in 1782......		60		
deduct recd of Chs Stockly		60		
Cap. Joseph Blackwell. 2 Mo pay in 1782		80		
recd of John Pierce		80		
Capt Thomas Barbee. 2 Mo pay in 1782		80		
deduct recd of John Pierce		80		
Maj. John Belfield. 2 Mo pay in 1782	24	120		
deduct recd of Gen. Greene.	96			
" in final sett. certificates		120		
Chaplain Alex. Balmain. 2 Mo pay in 1782......		150		
ded recd of John Pierce......		150		
Ens. Daniel Ball. 3 Mo pay in 1782		60		
deduct recd of Chs Stockley		60		
Lt Thomas Browne. 3 Mo pay in 1782		80		
deduct recd of Chs Stockley......		80		

Lt Henry Bell. 3 Mo pay in 1782		100	
deduct Gen. Greene cash	24		
final settt certificates recd	76	100	
Ens. John Beck. 3 Mo pay in 1782		60	
deduct recd of John Pierce		60	
Ens. Henry Bedinger. 3 Mo pay in 1782		60	
deduct recd of John Pierce		60	
Cap. Thomas Bowyer. 2 Mo pay in 1782		80	
deduct recd of Charles Stockley		80	
S. Mate John Brownley. 2 Mo pay in 1782		90	
deduct recd of John Pierce		90	
Lt Luke Cannon. 3 Mos pay in 1782		80	
deduct recd of Chs Stockley			
" John Hamilton		80	
Lt Robert Craddock. 3 Mo pay in 1782		80	
deduct recd of Gen. Greene			
" John Hamilton			
" Charles Stockley		80	
Cap. Whitehead Coleman. 2 Mo pay in 1782		100	
deduct recd of Chs Stockley		100	
Ens. & Adjt Jacob Coleman. 2 Mo pay in 1782 & 3 Mo 8 days '83		167.72	
deduct recd of John Pierce	99		
" clothing recd at Fort Pitt	33.42	132.42	35.30
Lt Mathew Clay. 3 Mo pay in 1782		80	
deduct recd of Chs Stockley		80	
Lt Philip Clayton. 3 Mo pay in 1782		80	
deduct recd of Charles Stockley		80	
Amount carried forward			

	Pay rec^d.	What entitled to.	Am° due.	Am° overpaid.
Amount brought forward				
Cap. Francis Cowherd. 2 m° pay in 1782		80		
deduct rec^d of Ch^s Stockley......		80		
Lt John Crawford. 3 m° pay in 1782......		80		
ded^t rec^d of John Pierce......		80		
Ens. William Connor. 3 m° pay in 1782		60		
deduct rec^d of John Pierce		60		
Surg. Mace Clements. 2 m° pay 1782		130		
deduct rec^d of Ch^s Stockley......		130		
Cap. John Dandridge. 2 m° pay in 1782		100		
deduct rec^d of Ch^s Stockley......		100		
Cap. Thomas Dix. 2 m° pay in 1782......		100		
deduct rec^d of Chas Stockley		100		
Surg. Joseph Davis. 2 m° pay in 1782 & 3 m° 20 days '83	216.30	346.30		
final settlement certificates......	130			
deduct rec^d of Ch^s Stockley......		346.30		
Ens. Q. Mr Henry Dawson. 3 m° pay 1782 & 3 m° 8 days 1783		167.72		
deduct rec^d of John Pierce......		99	68.72	
" clothing rec^d at Fort Pitt......				
Lt James Delaplaine. 3 m° pay in 1782......	80	80		
deduct rec^d of John Pierce......	26.60			
" ditto.	80			
" Charles Stockley......	21			
" Samuel Hodgdon......		207.60		127.60

Col. William Davis.	2 m⁰ pay in 1782 .... deduct recᵈ of Charles Stockley........	150 150
Lᵗ William Evans.	3 m⁰ pay in 1782................. deduct recᵈ of John Pierce.........	80 80
Cap. Samuel Eddings.	2 m⁰ pay in 1782 .... deduct received of Chˢ Stockly	100 100
Lᵗ Phillip Eastin.	3 m⁰ pay in 1782................. dedᵗ recᵈ of Chˢ Stockley..........	80 80
Lᵗ John H. Foster.	3 m⁰ pay 1782 as Ensign .... deduct recᵈ of Chˢ Stockley	60 60
Cap. Lᵗ Thomas Fenn.	3 m⁰ pay 1782 .... dedᵗ recᵈ of Chˢ Stockley	100 100
Cap. Reuben Field.	2 m⁰ pay in 1782 .... deduct recᵈ of Chˢ Stockley.......	80 80
Col. Christʳ Febiger.	2 m⁰ pay in 1782................. dedᵗ recᵈ of Chˢ Stockley	150 150
Cap. Thomas Fox.	2 m⁰ pay in 1782................. deduct recᵈ of Chˢ Stockley	80 80
Lᵗ William F. Gains.	3 m⁰ pay in 1782................. dedᵗ John Pierce	100 100
Cap. Robert Gamble.	2 m⁰ pay in 1782................. dedᵗ recᵈ of Charles Stockley	120 120
Cap. John Gilleson.	2 m⁰ pay in 1782 .... deduct recᵈ of John Pierce.........	80 80
	Amount carried forward.............	

	Pay recd.	What entitled to.	Amo due.	Amo overpaid.
Amount brought forward				
Lt Francis Gray. 3 Mo pay in 1782		80		
deduct recd of Chs Stockley		80		
Col. John Gibson. 2 Mo pay in 1782....	150	150		
deduct recd of John Pierce.....	8			41.42
" Saml Hodgdon	33.42	191.42		
" clothing at Fort Pitt.				
Ens. John Gibson. 3 Mo pay in 1782, 4 Mo 83	60	140		
deduct recd of John Pierce.....	7		73	
" Sam. Hodgdon		67		
Col. John Greene. 2 Mo pay in 1782		150		
deduct recd of John Pierce		150		
Lt Robert Green. 3 Mo pay in 1782		80		
deduct recd of John Pierce		80		
Lt Gabriel Green. 3 Mo pay in 1782		80		
deduct recd of Chs Stockley		80		
Lt Col. Thomas Gaskins. 2 Mo pay in 1782....		120		
deduct recd of Chs Stockley		120		
Lt William Gray. 3 Mo pay in 1782.....	100	100		
deduct recd of Charles Stockley....	13.83	113.83		13.83
" John Hamilton....				
Lt Benjamin Garnett. 2 Mo pay in 1782.....			66.60	
Ens. Henry Hughes. 3 Mo pay in 1782.....		60		
recd of Chas Stockley.....		60		

Lt Peter Higgins.	3 Mo pay in 1782	80	80	
	deduct recd of Charles Stockley......		80	
Surg. David Holmes.	2 Mo pay in 1782 & 3 Mo 8 days 1783		322.66	
	deduct recd of John Pierce	130	163.42	159.24
	" clothing at Fort Pitt	33.42		
Lt James Holt.	3 Mo pay in 1782		80	
	deduct recd of Chs Stockley......		80	
Cap. Samuel Hogg.	2 Mo pay in 1782		80	
	deduct recd of Chs Stockley......		80	
Lt Isaac Hite.	3 Mo pay in 1782......		80	
	deduct recd of Chs Stockley		80	
Lt Lawrence Harrison.	3 Mo pay in 1782......		80	
	deduct recd of John Pierce......		80	
Ens. Jordan Harris.	3 Mo pay in 1782......		60	
	deduct recd of Chs Stockley		60	
Surgeon Arthur Lind.	2 Mo pay in 1782......		130	
	deduct recd of Chs Stockley		130	
Cap. John Jordan.	2 Mo pay in 1782	80	80	27.42
	deduct recd of Chas Stockley	27.42	107.42	
	" John Hamilton			
Lt Albrighton Jones.	3 Mo pay in 1782		80	
	deduct recd of Chs Stockley		80	
Cap. John B. Johnson.	2 Mo pay in 1782		80	
	deduct recd of Chs Stockley		80	
Lt Robert Kayes.	3 Mo pay in 1782		80	
	Recd of Mr D. final settlt		80	
	Amount carried forward......			

	Pay rec⁴.	What entitled to.	Amᵒ due.	Amᵒ overpaid.
Amount brought forward				
L⁺ Elisha King. 3 Mᵒ pay in 1782.		100	76	
deduct cash rec⁴ of Gen. Greene	48	100		
" final sett certificates rec⁴	52			
L⁺ Robert Kirk. 3 Mᵒ pay in 1782		100		
deduct cash rec⁴ of Gen. Greene		24		
L⁺ John Kelty. [Left out.]				
Cap. William Lovely. 2 Mᵒ pay in 1782		80		
deduct rec⁴ of Chˢ Stockley		80		
L⁺ Benjamin Lawson. 3 Mᵒ pay in 1782 & 4 Mᵒ 1783		186.60	106.60	
deduct rec⁴ of Chˢ Stockley	80	80		
" Gen. Greene cash				
L⁺ Reuben Long. 3 Mᵒ pay in 1782		80		
deduct rec⁴ of Charles Stockley		80		
L⁺ James Maybon. 3 Mᵒ pay in 1782		80		21.80
deduct rec⁴ of Chas. Stockley	80	101.80		
" John Hamilton	21.80			
L⁺ William Miller. 3 Mᵒ pay in 1782		100	100	
L⁺ Benjamin Moseley. 3 Mᵒ pay in 1782		80		
deduct rec⁴ of Chˢ Stockley		80		
L⁺ David Merriweather. 3 Mᵒ pay in 1782.		80		
deduct rec⁴ of John Pierce		80		
Cap. Robert Morrow. 2 Mᵒ pay in 1782.		100		
ded⁺ Rec⁴ of John Pierce		100		

Description			To be paid in certificates.
Cap. Hezekiah Morton. 2 Mo pay in 1782		80	
deduct recd of Chs Stockley		80	
Surg. Bazil Middleton. 2 Mo pay in 1782		130	
deduct recd of John Pierce		130	
Cap. Simon Morgan. 4 Mo pay in 1782		160	
deduct recd of John Pierce			
" John Hamilton	160	160	
Lt Lipscomb Norwell. 3 Mo pay in 1782		80	
deduct recd of Chas Stockly		80	
Cap. Andrew Nixon. 2 Mo pay in 1782		150	
deduct: John Pierce	100		
" Sam. Hodgdon	11.60		11.60
" Chs Stockley	50	161.60	
Cap. John Nelson. 2 Mo pay in 1782		80	
deduct recd of Chs Stockley		80	
Lt Roger Nelson. 2 Mo pay in 1782		66.60	
deduct recd of Gen. Greenes Bills		66.60	
Cap. John Overton. 2 Mo pay in 1782		80	
deduct recd of Chs Stockley		80	
Lt Col. Thomas Posey. 2 Mo pay in 1782		120	
deduct recd of Charles Stockley		120	
Cap. Thomas Parker, 5th Regt. 2 Mo pay in 1782		80	
deduct recd of Charles Stockley		80	
Cap. Thomas Parker, 2d Regt. Pay in 1782		160	
deduct clothing of Hamilton	20.21		
deduct recd of Chs Stockley	80	100.21	59.69
Cap. Parker has recd too much specie, and the bal. made due to him must be paid in certificates.			
Amount carried forward			

	Pay rec⁴.	What entitled to.	Amᵒ due.	Amᵒ overpaid.
Amount brought forward				
Lᵗ John Prior. 3 Mᵒ pay in 1782		100		
deduct rec⁴ of John Pierce		100		
Ens. Josias Payne. 3 Mᵒ pay in 1782		60		
deduct rec⁴ of Chas. Stockley		60		
Cap. Thomas Pemberton. 2 Mᵒ pay in 1782		100		
deduct rec⁴ of John Pierce		100		
Lᵗ Peyton Powell. 3 Mᵒ pay in 1782		80		
deduct rec⁴ of Charles Stockley		80		
Cap. Archelaus Perkins. 2 Mᵒ pay in 1782		80		
deduct rec⁴ of Charles Stockley		80		
Maj. John Poulson. 2 Mᵒ pay in 1782		100		
deduct rec⁴ of Chˢ Stockley		100		
Lᵗ Thomas Payne. 3 Mᵒ pay in 1782		80		
deduct rec⁴ of Chˢ Stockley		80		
Ens. William P. Quarles. 3 Mᵒ pay in 1782				
deduct rec⁴ of Cha. Stockley	60	60		
" John Hamilton	12.85	72.85		12.85
Lᵗ Beverly Roy. 3 Mᵒ pay in 1782		80		
deduct rec⁴ of Cha. Stockley		80		
Cap. Drury Ragsdale. 2 Mᵒ pay in 1782		100		
dedᵗ rec⁴ of John Pierce		100		
Cap. Thomas Ransdale. 2 Mᵒ pay in 1782		80		
dedᵗ rec⁴ of John Pierce		80		

Lᵗ John Rooney. 3 Mᵒ pay in 1782......		80		
dedᵗ recᵈ Chˢ Stockley		80		
Lᵗ Albert Russell. 3 Mᵒ pay in 1782......		80		106.60
dedᵗ recᵈ of John Pierce.	26.60	186.60		
" Char. Stockley	160			
Lᵗ Mathew Rhea. 3 Mᵒ pay in 1782		80		
dedᵗ recᵈ Chaˢ Stockley .		80		
Lᵗ Robert Rankins. 3 Mᵒ pay in 1782		80		
dedᵗ recᵈ of Char. Stockley		80		
Lᵗ William Robinson. 3 Mᵒ pay in 1782......		80		
dedᵗ recᵈ of Chˢ Stockley.....		80		
Lᵗ John Robinson. 3 Mᵒ pay in 1782		80		
deduct recᵈ of Chˢ Stockley		80		
Cap. Joseph Scott. 2 Mᵒ pay in 1782		80		
deduct recᵈ of Chˢ Stockley		80		
Ens. John Scott. 3 Mᵒ pay in 1782		60		
deduct recᵈ of Chˢ Stockley		60		
Lᵗ Ballard Smith. 3 Mᵒ pay in 1782......		80		
deduct recᵈ of Chˢ Stockley		80		
Cap. Philip Sansum. 2 Mᵒ pay in 1782		80		
deduct recᵈ of Chˢ Stockley		80		
Lᵗ Richard Starke. 3 Mᵒ pay in 1782......		80		
deduct recᵈ of Charles Stockley		80		
Lᵗ John Scott. 3 Mᵒ pay in 1782		100	81.84	
deduct recᵈ of John Hamilton		18.6		
Amount carried forward......				

	Pay rec^d.	What entitled to.	Am^o due.	Am^o overpaid.
Amount brought forward				
Lt William S. Smith. 3 M^o pay in 1782		80		
ded^t rec^d of Ch^s Stockley		80		
Lt Francis Smith. 3 M^o pay in 1782		80		
ded^t rec^d of Ch^s Stockley		80		
Lt Strother Settle. 3 M^o pay in 1782		80		
deduct rec^d of John Pierce		80		
S. Mate Joseph Savage. 2 M^o pay in 1782	90	90		
deduct rec^d of Ch^s Stockley	4.60	94.60		4.60
" Col. Carrington..				
Lt Samuel Selden. 3 M^o pay in 1782.....		80		
deduct rec^d of Chas Stockley.....		80		
Maj. Smith Snead. 2 M^o pay in 1782		100		
ded^t Ch^s Stockley paid him		100		
Lt John Scarborough. 3 M^o pay in 1782	26.60	80		
deduct rec^d of John Pierce	80	106.60		26.60
" Chas. Stockley				
Cap. Segismund Stribling. 3 M^o pay in 1782.....		80		
deduct rec^d of John Pierce		80		
Lt John Steele. 3 M^o pay in 1782		80		
deduct rec^d of Ch^s Stockley.....		80		
Cap. Beverly Stubblefield. 3 M^o pay in 1782		80		
ded^t rec^d of Ch^s Stockley		80		
Maj. John Swan. 2 M^o pay in 1782		120		
ded^t Gen. Greenes Bills		120		

Entry				
Lᵗ Jonathan Smith. 3 Mᵒ pay in 1782		80		
dedᵗ recᵈ of Chˢ Stockley		80		
Ens. Thomas Sayers. 3 Mᵒ pay in 1782			60	
Ens. John Trabree. 3 Mᵒ pay in 1782		60		
dedᵗ recᵈ of Chˢ Stockley		60		
Cornᵗ Albion Throckmorton. 3 Mᵒ pay in 1782		80		
dedᵗ recᵈ of John S. Dart	26.60	80		
" Gen. Greenes Bills	53.30			
Ens. Zachariah Tatum. 3 Mᵒ pay in 1782		60		4
dedᵗ recᵈ of Charles Stockley	60	64		
" John Hamilton	4			
Lᵗ Nicholas Tailefaro. 3 Mᵒ pay in 1782		80		
deduct recᵈ of Chˢ Stockley		80		
Lᵗ Lewis Thomas. 3 Mᵒ pay in 1782		80		
deduct recᵈ of John Pierce		80		
Lᵗ Marks Vanderwall. 3 Mᵒ pay in 1782		80		
deduct recᵈ of Chˢ Stockley		80		
Maj. John Willis. 2 Mᵒ pay in 1782		100		
Charged by Mʳ Dunscomb wʰ		100		
Cap. Thomas Warman. 2 Mᵒ pay in 1782		80		
deduct recᵈ of Chˢ Stockley		80		
Lᵗ David Williams. 3 Mᵒ pay in 1782		80		
dedᵗ recᵈ of John Pierce		80		
Cap. Robert Woodson. 2 Mᵒ pay in 1782		80		
dedᵗ recᵈ of John Pierce	40			
" Charles Stockley	80			
Amᵗ carried forward		120		40

	Pay rec^d.	What entitled to.	Am^o due.	Am^o overpaid.
Amount brought forward				
Lt George Winchester. 3 M^o pay in 1782............		80		
ded^t rec^d of Th^o Bradford		80		
Lt John White. 3 M^o pay in 1782............		80		
deduct rec^d Ch^s Stockley		80		
Lt Col. Anth^y Walton White. 2 M^o pay in 1782............		187.45		
deduct rec^d of John Pierce		187.35		
Cap. Richard Worsham. 2 M^o pay in 1782.........	26.60	80		
ded^t rec^d of John Pierce	80			
" Ch^s Stockley.........		106.60		26.60
Surg. James Wallace. 2 M^o pay in 1782	24	130		
deduct rec^d of Gen. Greene.......	41.53			
" John Hamilton .	64.26			
" Col. Carrington a horse		129.79		
S. Mate George Yates. 2 M^o pay in 1782......		90		
deduct rec^d of Ch^s Stockley		90		
Lt Charles Erskine. 3 M^o pay in 1782.........	24	100		
deduct rec^d of Gen. Greene.........	28.54			
" John Hamilton		52.54	47.36	
Cap. James Gunn. 2 M^o pay in 1782.........		100		
ded^t rec^d of John Hamilton		73.10	26.80	
Maj. Richard Call. 2 M^o pay in 1782		120	120	
Cap. John Anderson. 2 M^o pay in 1782 & 4 M^o in 1783	40	240		
ded. rec^d of John Pierce	80			
" Charles Stockley		120	120	

Lt A. D. C. Samuel K. Bradford. 3 Mo pay in 1782 & 4 Mo 1783 .... ded't rec'd of John Pierce.....		300 300	
Lt Samuel Baskerville. 3 Mo pay in 1782 & 4 Mo 1783... ded't rec'd of John Pierce ..... " Charles Stockley	106.60 80	186.60 186.60	
Cap. John Blackwell. 2 Mo pay in 1782 & 4 Mo in 1783 deduct rec'd of John Pierce		240 80	160
Cap. Robert Beale. 2 Mo pay in 1782 & 4 Mo 1783 ded't rec'd of Thomas Bradford.....		240 80	160
Cap. Lawrence Butler. 2 Mo pay in 1782 & 4 Mo in 1783..... ded't rec'd of Ch' Stockley		240 80	160
Lt Col. Com. Burgos Ball. 2 Mo pay in 1782 & 4 Mo in 1783 ded't rec'd of John Pierce		450 450	
Cap. Benjamin Biggs. 2 Mo pay in 1782 & 4 M' in 1783 ded't rec'd of John Pierce		240 240	
Cap. William Bentley. 2 Mo pay in 1782 & 4 Mo in 1783..... ded't rec'd of John Pierce..... " Charles Stockley	160 80	240 240	
Cap. Thomas Buckner. 2 Mo pay in 1782 & 4 Mo 1783..... ded't rec'd of John Pierce ..... " Charles Stockley	40 80	240 120	120
Lt John Bowen. 3 Mo pay in 1782 & 4 Mo in 1783 ..... deduct rec'd of Cha' Stockley.....		186.60 80	106.60
Cap. Mayo Carrington. 2 Mo pay in 1782 & 4 Mo 1783..... ded't rec'd of John Pierce " Maj. Wm Lewis ..... " Charles Stockley	40 40 80	240 160	80
Amount carried forward.....			

11

	Pay rec^d.	What entitled to.	Am^o due.	Am^o overpaid.
Amount brought forward				
Cap. John C. Carter. 2 M° pay in 1782 & 4 M° 1783. ded^t rec^d of John Pierce	100	300 100	200	
Lt Samuel Coleman. 3 M° pay in 1782 & 4 M° 1783 ded^t Rec^d of John Pierce		233.30 100	133.30	
Lt John Crute. d° 3 M° pay in 1782 & 4 M° in 1783 ded^t rec^d of Ch^s Stockley		186.60 80	106.60	
Cap. James Curry. 2 M° pay in 1782 & 4 M° in 1783 deduct rec^d of Ch^s Stockley		240 80	160	
Lt Col. Samuel I. Cabell. 2 M° pay in 1782 & 4 M° 1783 ded^t rec^d of Ch^s Stockley		360 120	240	
Lt Col. Jonathan Clark. 2 M° pay in 1782 & 4 M° in 1783 ded^t rec^d of John Pierce .... " Ch^s Stockley	120 120	360 240	120	
Lt Col. Edward Carrington. 2 M° pay in 1782 & 4 M° in 1783. ded^t rec^d of John Pierce.......... " Gen. Greene ..... " Q^r M. Gen^{ls} department	150 30 270	450 450		
By his acknowledgment.				
Maj. William Croghan. 2 M° pay in 1782 & 4 M° 1783. ded^t Rec^d of Ch^s Stockley.......... " Thomas Bradford ..... " John Pierce	150 100 50	300 300		
Cap. Collin Cocke. 2 M° pay in 1782 & 4 M° 1783. deduct rec^d of Ch^s Stockley		240 80	160	
Cap. Leroy Edwards. 2 M° pay in 1782 & 4 M° 1783 deduct rec^d of Chs. Stockley		240 80	160	

Cap. John Fitzgerald.	2 Mᵒ pay in 1782 & 4 Mᵒ 1783.........		240	133.30
	dedᵗ recᵈ of John Pierce	26.60	106.60	133.30
	dedᵗ recᵈ of Chˢ Stockley.........	80		
Lᵗ Thomas Glasscock.	3 Mᵒ pay in 1782 & 4 mo. 1783.........		233.30	
	dedᵗ chᵈ by Mʳ Dunscomb.........		100	
Col. Charles Harrison.	2 Mᵒ pay in 1782.........	100	200	
	dedᵗ recᵈ of John Pierce.........	100	200	
	" John S. Dart.........			
Maj. Christian Holmer.	2 Mᵒ pay in 1782.........		125	
	deduct recᵈ of Chˢ Stockley.........		125	
Cap. Thomas Hord.	2 Mᵒ pay in 1782 & 4 Mᵒ 1783.........		240	160
	deduct recᵈ of Chˢ Stockley.........		80	
Cap. Abraham Hite.	2 Mᵒ pay 1782 & 4 Mᵒ 1783.........		240	120
	deduct recᵈ of John Pierce.........		120	
Lᵗ John Harrison.	3 Mᵒ pay in 1782 & 4 Mᵒ 83.........		186.60	80
	deduct recᵈ of John Pierce [erasure on original].	106.60	106.60	
	Charged by Mʳ Dunscomb [erasure on original].			
Col. William Heth.	2 Mᵒ pay in 1782 & 4 in 1783.........		450	
	dedᵗ Recᵈ of John Pierce.		450	
Lᵗ Col. Samuel Hawes.	2 Mᵒ pay in 1782 & 4 Mᵒ in 1783.........		360	
	deduct recᵈ of John Pierce.........	60	360	
	" Charles Stockley	300		
Cap. Thomas Holt.	2 Mᵒ pay in 1782 & 4 Mᵒ in 1783.........		360	240
Maj. David Hopkins.	2 Mᵒ pay in 1782 & 4 Mᵒ in 1783.........		360	
	dedᵗ Recᵈ on full a/c currᵈ.........	240	360	
Lᵗ Col. Samuel Hopkins.	2 Mᵒ pay in 1782 & 4 Mᵒ in 1783.........		360	
	dedᵗ recᵈ of John Pierce.........	120	360	
	" Charles Stockley.........			
	Amount carried forward.........			

	Pay rec	What entitled to.	Am due.	Am overpaid.
Amount brought forward				
L^t Pm. Charles Jones. 3 M^o pay in 1782 & 4 M^o in 1783....	143.30	416.60		
ded^t rec^d of John S. Dart....	113.30			
" Gen. Greenes Bills....				
" Chas Stockley....	160	416.60		
Cap. Custus Kendall. 2 M^o pay in 1782 & 4 M^o 1783	160	240		
ded^t rec^d of John Pierce......				
" Charles Stockley	80	240		
S. Mate John Knight. 2 M^o pay in 1782 & 4 M^o 1783		258		
deduct rec^d of John Pierce		132	126	
Maj. William Lewis. 2 M^o pay in 1782 & 4 M^o 1783....	200	300		
ded^t rec^d of John Pierce				
" Ch^s Stockley	100	300		
Col. George Mathews. 2 M^o pay in 1782	150	150		
ded^t Gen. Greenes Bills....				
" Gen. Greenes cash	40			
" Bal. due U. S. on sett^t of a/c of 1782	111.66	301.66		151.66
Cap. Henry Moss. 2 M^o pay in 1782 & 4 M^o in 1783....	80	240		
deduct rec^d of Charles Stockley....	56			
Bal. of specie rec^d of Duns. in certif	80			
deduct Gen. Greenes Bills....	24			
do. cash		240		
Cap. William Meredith. 2 M^o pay in 1782 & 4 M^o 83	200	300		
ded^t rec^d of John Pierce				
" Ch^s Stockley....	100	300		
Lt Artil. Benjamin Mosely. 3 M^o pay in 1782		100		
deduct rec^d of Ch^s Stockley		100		

Lt William McGuire. 3 M^o pay in 1782 & 4 in 1783	133.33	233.30	
deduct rec^d of John Pierce	100	233.30	
" Ch^s Stockley			26.60
Ens. John Mills. 3 M^o pay in 1782 & 4 M^o 1783		166.60	
deduct rec^d of John Pierce		140	160
Cap. Philip Mallery. 2 M^o pay in 1782 & 4 M^o 1783............		240	
deduct rec^d of Ch^s Stockley		80	
Cap. Isaiah Marks. 2 M^o pay in 1782 & 4 M^o in 1783		240	
deduct rec^d of John Pierce		240	
Cap. Holman Mennis. 2 M^o pay 1782 & 4 M^o 1783		240	
ded^t rec^d of John Pierce	40	120	120
" Ch^s Stockley	80		
Cap. Callowhille Mennis. 2 M^o pay in 1782 & 4 M^o 1783............		240	
ded^t rec^d of John Pierce	40	120	120
" Charles Stockley	80		
Col. John Nevil. 2 M^o pay in 1782 & 4 M^o in 1783		450	
ded^t rec^d of Th^o Bradford............	150	450	
" John Pierce	300		
Lt Col. Pressley Nevil. 2 M^o pay in 1782............		360	
ded^t rec^d of Th^o Bradford	120	360	
" John Pierce............	240		
Lt William Porter. 3 M^o pay in 1782 & 4 M^o 83		186.60	
ded^t rec^d of Ch^s Stockley		80	106.60
Cap. Tarleton Payne. 2 M^o pay in 82 & 4 M^o 83		240	
ded^t rec^d of John Pierce	40	120	120
" Ch^s Stockley	80		
Amount carried forward............			

		Pay recd.	What entitled to.	Amo due.	Amo overpaid.
	Amount brought forward				
Cap. Robert Porterfield.	2 Mo pay in 1782 & 4 Mo 1783		346.60		
[Illegible mem.]	ded: recd of John Pierce	186.60	186.60	160	
Maj. Charles Pelham.	2 Mo pay in 1782 & 4 Mo 1783		300		
	dedt recd of John Pierce	50			
	" Chs Stockley	100	150	150	
Lt Thomas Pearson.	3 Mo pay in 1782 & 4 in 83		186.60		
	dedt recd of Chs Stockley		80	106.60	
Col. William Russell.	2 Mo in 82 & 4 Mo 1783		450		
	dedt recd of John Pierce	300			
	" Charles Stockley	150	450		
Cap. Anthony Singleton.	2 Mo pay in 1782 & 4 Mo 1783		300		
	dedt recd of Gen. Greenes Bills	100			
	" Charles Stockley	100	200	100	
Cap. Uriah Springer.	2 Mo pay in 1782 & 4 Mo pay in 1783		240		
	dedt recd of John Pierce		240		
Lt Jacob Springer.	3 Mo pay in 1782 & 4 Mo 1783		186.60		
	dedt recd of John Pierce		186.60		
Lt William Stevens.	3 Mo pay in 1782 & 4 Mo in 1783		186.60		
	dedt recd of Charles Stockley		80	106.60	
Cap. Joseph Swearinger.	2 Mo pay in 1782 & 4 Mo 1783		240		
	dedt recd of John Pierce		120	120	
Cap. John Stokes.	2 Mo pay in 1782 & 4 Mo 1783		240		
	deduct recd of Ch. Stockley		80	160	

Description				54.30
Ens. P. M. Josiah Tannehill. 3 Mo pay in 82 & 3 Mo & 8 day: 83......	270		313.30	
deduct recd of John Pierce	80			
Charged by Mr Dunscomb	17.60			
" sundr of Sam: Hodgdon......				
Cap. Nathaniel Terry. 2 Mo pay in 1782 & 4 Mo 1783			367.60	160
dedt Recd of Chs Stockley......			240	
			80	
Cap. Benjamin Tailofar. 2 Mo pay in 1782 & 4 Mo 1783			240	160
dedt Recd of Chs Stockly......			80	
Cap. Richard C. Waters. 3 Mo pay in 1782 & 4 Mo 1783			233.30	
dedt Recd of John Pierce......			233.30	
Lt William B. Wallace. 3 Mo pay in 1782 & 4 Mo 1783			233.30	
deduct recd of John Pierce......			233.30	
Ens. Joseph Winlock. 3 Mo pay in 1782 & 4 Mo 1783			166.60	26.60
dedt recd of John Pierce......			140	
Lt Col. Gustavus B. Wallace. 2 Mo pay in 1782 & 4 Mo 83			360	
dedt recd of John Pierce......			360	
Lt Willis Willson. 3 Mo pay in 1782 & 4 Mo in 1783......			186.60	106.60
dedt recd of Charles Stockley......			80	
Cap. William White. 2 Mo pay in 1782 & 4 Mo in 1783	80		240	
Charged by mistake to Rob. White. recd of John Pierce by Col. Febiger	80			
deduct recd of Chs Stockley......			160	
Cap. James Wright. 2 Mo pay in 1782 & 4 Mo in 1783......			240	160
decuct recd of John Pierce......			80	
Maj. Andrew Waggoner. 2 Mo pay in 1782 & 4 Mo in 1783......			300	150
dedt recd of John Pierce......			150	
Amount carried forward......				

	Pay recᵈ.	What entitled to.	Amᵉ due.	Amᵉ overpaid.
Amount brought forward				
Cap. Robert Yancey. 2 M° pay in 1782 & 4 M° 1783		300		
dedᵗ recᵈ of John Pierce		100	200	
Lᵗ Layton Yancey. 2 M° pay in 1782 & 4 M° 1783		233.30		
deduct recᵈ of John Pierce		100	133.30	
Cap. James Pendleton. 2 M° pay in 1782 & 4 M° 1783		300		
deduct recᵈ of Chˢ Stockley		100	200	
Lᵗ Epaphroditus Rudder. 3 M° pay in 1782 & 4 M° 1783		233.30	233.30	
Lᵗ George Blackmore. 3 M° pay in 1782			80	
Lᵗ Col. Oliver Towles. 2 M° pay in 1782		120		
deduct recᵈ of Chˢ Stockley		120		
Lᵗ James Hamilton. 3 M° pay in 1782		80		
dedᵗ recᵈ of Charles Stockley		80		
Cap. Nathan Reed. 2 M° pay in 1782		80		
dedᵗ recᵈ of Chˢ Stockley		80		
Maj. David Stephenson. 2 M° pay in 1782		100		
dedᵗ recᵈ of Chˢ Stockley		100		
Cap. John Spotswood. 2 M° pay in 1782		80		
dedᵗ recᵈ of John Pierce		80		
Lᵗ John Towns. 3 M° pay in 1782		80		
deduct recᵈ of John Pierce		80		

Name / Description	Deductions	Amount	Balance	
Ens. Thomas Wallace. 3 Mo pay in 1782		60		
ded' rec'd of John Pierce		60		
Cor'nt John Waities. 3 Mo pay in 1782		80		
ded' rec'd of John Hamilton	11.83			
" Gen. Greenes Bills	53.30			
Charged w' cash rec'd of Gen. Greene for pub. Serv.	132	197.23		117.23
Cap. Henry Young. 2 Mo pay in 1782		80		
ded' rec'd of Ch' Stockley		80		
L' David Miller. 3 Mo pay in 1782		80		
ded' rec'd of Ch' Stockley		80		
L' John Hackley. 3 Mo pay in 1782 & 4 Mo 1783		186.60	41.49	
ded' rec'd of John Pierce	26.60			
" Goods of Col. Carrington	38.41			
Charles Stockley	80	145.11		
Cap. Peregrine Fitzhugh. 3 Mo pay in 1782		100		
deduct rec'd of John Pierce		100		
L' James Barbour. 3 Mo pay in 1782		80		
Rec'd certificates in full		80		
L' Col. Com't William Darke			150	
Of the foregoing sums there is to be paid in certificates			11,652.24	2388.5
			457.63	
Remains due in Specie			11,194.51	

NOTE.—Ensign Henry Bedinger in page 10 Should be called Captain and credited 80 dollars instead of 60—and also charged with 80 dollars instead of 60....his ano Ballances.

In many cases M[r] Dunscomb has credited in his settlements more specie than the officer was entitled to. Where I find an officer has actually drawn more specie than he was entitled to receive—I have admitted the credits which have been given them by Dunscomb—because they have been finally settled with and received their certificates—and there is no hold left upon them—this appears to have been wrong in M[r] Dunscomb, for, in Justice, an officer in this situation should return such [torn out] of specie—and receive certificates in   (?)   — Where he has credited too much to an officer—and the officer has not received the full am° of such credit—the supposed balance in specie should be paid in certificates—for instance:

		Doll[s].
He credits Col. Nat. Gist with 7 m[os] pay in 1782 & 3, which is..		525
Col. Gist has actually rec[d] 6 M° in specie, which is all he ought to have—and amounts to	450	
The remainder [torn out]		
Paid in certificates	75	
		525

The above example, and the following one of M[r] Breckenridge, which I believe elucidate the general principles on which I have proceeded in the business—without the trouble of going into particulars—

ROB. BRECKENRIDGE. See page 1.

Pay due him in 1782.	385	By Gen. Greens Bills	79.30
		Cha[s] Stockly, cash.......	80
		Certificates Rec[d]	225.60
	385		385

Pay due in 1783.	416.45	By Certificates Rec[d]	257.75
		clothing	50.84
		Gen. Greens Bills........	79.30
		Ch[s] Stockley...............	26.60
		Bal. due.....................	1.66
	416.45		416.45

M[r] Pierce.

C. S.

[Mem. on fold of back]   turn of specie pay   [torn]
Officers of the Virginia
for 1782 & 1783, for which drf[t]
on the Loan Officer of Virginia
have been given.

A PARTIAL LIST OF CAPT. DANIEL MORGAN'S RIFLE COMPANY OF WINCHESTER, FREDERICK CO., VA., JULY, 1775.

OFFICERS.

Capt., Daniel Morgan.
1st Lieutenant, John Humphreys.
2nd Lieutenant, William Heth (Heath).
1st Sergt., George Porterfield.

PRIVATES.

Anderson, Robert.	
Ball, William.	
Greenway, George.	
Greenway, William.	
Grim, Charles.	Buried at Winchester.
Heiskell, Adam.	Buried at Romney, Va.
Heiskell, George.	
Hayes, Mark.	
Kurtz, Frederick.	
Kurtz, Adam.	Buried at Winchester.
Lauck, Peter.	" " "
Lauck, Simon.	" " "
Schultz, John.	" " "
Sperry, Jacob.	" " "
Stratton, Seth.	

This company was organized in the Spring of 1775; consisted of 96 men from Winchester and vicinity; left Winchester July 14, 1775, arrived at Cambridge, Mass., Aug. 7, 1775, and joined the army under Gen. Wasnington.

PETITION FROM FAIRFAX COUNTY, VA., FOR IM PORTATION OF SALT.

VIRGINIA, FAIRFAX COUNTY, }
Nov. 23, 1775. }

Sir : The Committee of this county, informed of the present scarcity of salt in the colony in general, and in this part of it in particular, sensible of the Difficulty, perhaps impracticability, of procuring it if not done this winter, and apprehensive of the great distress and Discontent that the want of this necessary article may occasion among the people, as well as the impossibility of furnishing proper provisions for the Regiments of minute men and draughts from our militia which may be called into service next spring, have directed us to apply to the Honorable, the Continental Congress, praying them to encourage the Importation of salt, either by permitting the exportation of Country produce in return, in such manner as is allowed upon the importation of military stores, or in such other manner as that Honorable Board shall judge best. We beg leave, sir, thro' you, to lay this request, as a matter of the utmost importance to the good people of this colony and the public service, before the gentlemen of the Congress, and are,

With greatest respect, sir,

Your most obedient servants,

G. MASON, }
JOHN DALTON, } *Committee of*
WM. RAMSAY, } *Correspondence*
JOHN CARLYLE, } *of Fairfax*
JOHN MUIR, } *county.*
JAMES KIRK. }

To JOHN HANCOCK, ESQ.,
President of the Congress.

This petition at the opening of the Revolutionery struggle incidentally presents several matters of importance : 1. It shows the value of salt as a household commodity, and the difficulty of procuring it at a time when means of rapid and easy communication were wanting.   2. It also shows that at this early period the military strength was supplied by "minute-men" and by drafts from the "militia."

In the list of signers will be found the names of persons in whom posterity will doubtless be interested.

CORRESPONDENCE OF WASHINGTON AND GATES WITH COLONEL BEDEL.

CAMBRIDGE, *1st February, 1776.*

Sir : The Continental Congress, haveing calld upon the Government of New Hampshire to raise a Regiment for the Service of the United Colonies, which they have accordingly complied with, and appoint you to the command, I have to desire, that you will use all the deligence & dispatch possible, to raise the said Regiment & march it into Canada takeing your Rout by Number four and Onion River, where a Suply of provisions will be laid up, by order of Major General Schuyler.

This Regiment is to be raised upon the Continental establishment, agreeable to the terms & requisitions of the Congress as transmitted to the Honble Convention of New Hampshire, the necessity of reinforceing our troops, posted before & forming the Blockade of Quebec, is too apparent to need being dwelt on, I would therefore have you order each Company to March, as fast as they are raised, and on their arrival put themselves under the Command of the General or Commanding officer in Canada.

Your Colony will provide you with such necessarys, as are indespensably wanting for the use of your Regiment, in the takeing up of which, and your expences on the March I recommend the utmost Oeconomy, that can be used consistant with dispatch—

You will take under your care the Coghnawaga Indians, who are now here and conduct them in the safest and most agreeable manner to themselves, into Canada. You are to bear their expenses, for which purpose I now give you a warrant on the paymaster General for the sum of £100.—D. M.³

You must keep a just account of its expenditure, & render the same to the Commissary of the Northern department when you get there he will be advertized of this matter and directed to settle with you,—

these sir, are your Instructions, to which I doubt not you will pay a proper attention that you may have a share in the Gory of expelling the instruments of Ministerial Tyranny from that fair province, is the Sincere wish of

Sir, Your most H. Sᵗ.,

(Signed) Gᵒ. Washington.

COLONEL BEDEL,

  on the service of the United Colonies.

CAMP, 4th October, 1777.

Dear Bedel: I sent your faithful friend Louis to assist you in immediately bringing forward to my assistance all The St. Francis Indians who have lately come to Co'hos, with all those who, from Friendship to you and affection to Our Noble Cause, are ready to step forth at this important Crisis to put a finishing Stroke to this Campaign. The Enemy are at their last Gasp in every Question ; A Bold Stroke in Each Gives peace & Freedom to America. that you & I may live to see & Enjoy that Blessing is the anxious Wish of your affectionate Friend

and Humble Servant,

[Signed]   HORATIO GATES.

COL. BEDEL, Co'hos.

WAR OFFICE, *March 4, 1778.*

Sir: As the irruption intended to be made into Canada is suspended by a resolve of Congress, on account of the insuperable difficulties in getting the necessaries in so short a period as the advanced season would admit, the raising your regiment is needless and improper. You will, therefore, cease your proceedings on this account and dismiss any men you may have inlisted, that the continent may be put to no unnecessary expence.

Such charges as you have incurred in preparing for the expedition you will exhibit a State of to the Dep. Pay Master General at Albany, who will settle with you for the same.

I am, Sir, your most h'ble servt.,

[Signed]   HORATIO GATES,
President of the War Office.

P. S.   It will be proper that Major Whitcomb rejoin his Companies, with his present rank.

To COL. TIM° BEDEL, at Coos.

WAR OFFICE.

Col. Timothy Bedel was a prominent Revolutionary officer from New Hampshire. He served as lieutenant in Goffe's regiment in 1760, in Canada. July 6, 1775, he was appointed captain of rangers, and on the 20th of January, 1776, was made Colonel of the 1st N. H. regiment, joining the Northern army under General Schuyler.

For neglect of duty he was tried by Court martial in August, 1776, and cashiered. Despite this action, however, he was shown great consideration by Generals Washington and Gates, as will appear from the foregoing letters, and from the additional fact that he was subsequently made a Major General of his state militia. He died in Haverhill, N. H., in February, 1787.

A PAY ROLL FOR THE TRAVELING EXPENCES FOR A DETACHMENT OF THE 3ᵈ VIRGᵃ REGᵗ THAT WERE DISCHARG'D FROM THE CAMP AT THE VALLEY FORGE TO THEIR DIFFERENT COUNTIES.   FEBʸ 16ᵗʰ, 1776.

No.	Names.	Rank.	County's.	Distance.	£	s.	D.
1	Jaˢ Hansborough	Q. M.	Stafford.	220	2	19	8
2	Lewis Young	Sergᵗ.	Louisa.	267	1	18	
3	Armstid White	Do.	Culpeper.	230	0	18	
4	Paul Leatherer		Ditto.	Ditto.	0	15	
5	Nathaˡ Tylor		Prince Wilm.	190	0	15	
1	Samuel Love	Privᵉ.	Do.	Do.	0	14	8
2	Jaˢ Primm	Do.	Stafford.	220	0	14	8
3	John King		Do.	Do.	0	14	8
4	Volentine King			Do.	0	14	8
5	Moses Baker			Do.	0	14	8
6	Peter Byram			Do.	0	14	8
7	John Nicholson			Do.	0	14	8
8	Richᵈ Simms			Do.	0	14	8
	Wᵐ Culley			Do.	0	16	
1	Geo. Jones		King George.	240	0	16	
2	Geo. Patton			Ditto.	0	16	
3	Weedon Wilkerson			Do.	0	16	
4	Wᵐ Oliver			Do.	0	16	
5	John Rogers	Privᵉ.		240	0	16	
6	Samˡ Wharton			Do.	0	16	
7	Jonathon Jackson			Do.	0	16	
1	John Cullins		Prince Wilm.	120	0	12	8
2	Wᵐ Mathews			Do.	0	12	8
3	Wᵐ Conner			Do.	0	12	8
4	Ezekiel Cowert			Do.	0	12	8
5	Jonathon Williams			Do.	0	12	8
6	Henry Garvey			Do.	0	12	8
7	John Mathews			Do.	0	12	8
					£23	3	8

A PAY ROLL FOR THE TRAVELING EXPENCES FOR A DETACHMENT OF THE 3ᵈ VIRGᵃ REGᵗ, ETC.

No.	Names.	Rank.	County's.	Distance.	£	s.	D.
	Brought over...............				23	3	8
8	Lewis Murphey............	Private.	Prince Wᵐ.	120		12	8
9	Wᵐ Baily..................			Ditto.		12	8
10	Wᵐ Lent..................			Ditto.		12	8
11	John Aithey			Ditto.		12	8
1	Chaˢ Lander		Loudoun.	160		10	8
2	Geo. May			Ditto.		10	8
3	Jamˢ Murrey			Ditto.		10	8
4	Seboston Lush.............			Ditto.		10	8
5	Jnᵒ Sidebothom............		Loudoun.	160		10	8
6	Jos. Sidebothom...........			Ditto.		10	8
7	Jnᵒ Bruton................			Ditto.		10	8
8	Evan Thomas..............			Ditto.		10	8
9	John Moreland			Ditto.		10	8
1	Clough Overton............		Louisa.	267		17	6
2	Nichoˢ Johnston...........			Ditto.		17	6
3	Geo. Thomason............			Ditto.		17	6
4	John Durvin			Ditto.		17	6
1	Edmond Bowling		Stafford.	220		17	6
1	Robᵗ Moderwill............		Fairfax.	182		12	6
2	Wᵐ Berrey.................			Ditto.		12	8
					£35	19	0

E. P. J. P.

THOMAS HUNGERFORD, *Lᵗ 3ᵈ Virgᵃ Regᵗ.*

YORKTOWN, *February 18, 1778.*

Received of Mʳ Joseph Nourse Paymaster to the Board of War & Ordnance, One hundred and nineteen dollars and two-thirds of a dollar being in full for the within warrant, and which I promise to divide among the men with my Detachment agreable to the pay roll annexᵈ.   [Copy]

THOMAS HUNGERFORD, *Lᵗ 3ᵈ Virginia Regᵗ.*

[On outside] { No 141. / Enterᵈ in the Audʳˢ Books. / No. 141.

12

Valley Forge is a village in Chester County, Pa., twenty-four miles west of Philadelphia.

It was the location of Washington's army from the middle of December, 1777, to June 18, 1778. It was selected to protect Congress at York, Pa., whither that body had adjourned from Philadelphia in consequence of the occupation of the latter place by the British.

At this place Baron Steuben assumed the duties of Inspector-General of the American army. Here, also, Washington announced, on the 6th of May, 1778, the treaty of our alliance with France.

The American forces numbered about 11,000, only about one-half of whom, however, were in condition for service. Their sufferings were intense—a fact known to every tyro in history.

ROSTER OF CAPTAIN THOMAS BUCK'S COMPANY IN REVOLUTION.

ENLISTED FROM DUNMORE (NOW SHENANDOAH) COUNTY, VA.

Copied from the original roll filed by said Buck, with his application for pension, in the U. S. Pension Office, with date of enlistment of each officer and soldier.

First lieutenant, John Crookshank, Sept. 6, 1777.
Second   "   Jacob Yost, Sept. 6, 1777.
Lionel Branson, Ensign, Aug. 29, 1777.
William Reed, Sergent,   "   "
Jacob Lambert, 2nd Sergent, Aug. 29, 1777.
Christian Tush, 2nd sergent,   "   "
John Steel, 3rd sergent, Sept. 9, 1777.
Jermiah Philips, 4th sergent, Sept. 28, 1777.
Henry Pangle, Drummer, Sept. 10, 1777.

Frederick Honaker, Private,	Aug. 29.	
William Hoover,	" 30.	
John Bently,	" 29.	
William Slack,	" 29.	
Valentine Lockmiller,	" 29.	
Philip Smith,	" 29.	
Martin Say,	" 29.	
Gasper Lutz,	" 29.	
David Piper,	" 30.	
Christian Sapington,	" 22.	
Martin Miller,	" 29.	Appointed Corporal.
Abraham Grable,	" 30.	
William Moredock,	" 29.	
John Middleton,	" 22.	
George Lockmiller,	" 29.	
William Bagnall,	" 29.	
George Miller,	" 30.	
Henry Shumaker,	" 29.	
Harbert Stockbridge,	" 29.	Appointed Corporal.
William Copeman,	Sept. 8.	
Christian Bowerman,	" 29.	
Andrew Copeman,	" 29.	
Michael Setser,	" 10.	
Randolp Bizant,	Aug. 22.	
John Snider,	Sept. 10.	
John Sonner,	" 10.	
Samuel Dust,	" 12.	
John Hoover,	" 12.	Appointed Corporal
Elijah Aadell,	" 6.	
Conard Hansbager,	Aug. 28.	
William Harris,	" 28	
Thomas Price,	" 28.	
Zachriah Price,	" 28.	
John Marshall Taylor,	" 22.	

DUNMORE SET, *Sept. 5, 1777.*

At a meeting of the volunteers of the Town of Woodstock, Thomas Buck, Gentleman, was unanimously chosen Captain, Given under my hand,   JOSEPH PUGH, C. L.

DUNMORE SET.

I do hereby enlist the above Men under the command of Capt. Thomas Buck, Given under my hand this 16th of Sept., 1777.   JOSEPH PUGH, C. L.

Capt. Thomàs Buck was born in Frederick Co., Virginia, Jan. 9, 1756, son of Charles and Letitia Wilcocks, nee Sorrell, widow. At age of 18 was one of the surveyors for Frederick Co., Va.; magistrate at 21, and on Jan. 11, 1776, commissioned Lieutenant of Militia for Dunmore county, now Shenandoah, Va., Sept. 5, 1777—commissioned Capt. of a company which he himself enlisted from the vicinity of Woodstock, now in Shenandoah Co. He married Ann, daughter of Marquis Calmes, Jr., and Winnifred (Waller) Calmes, of Frederick county, Va. He died in Shenandoah county, Va., June 4, 1842, in the 86th year of his age. Had issue 13 children. For his complete military record and the history of the descendants of his children, see Richardson and their kin, by the author hereof.

LIST OF BALANCES DUE THE DEAD AND DESERTED OF THE 1st
VIRGINIA STATE REGT., COMMANDED BY COL. GEORGE
GIBSON, FROM 16TH SEPT., 1777, TO 1st JAN., 1778.

NAMES.	RANK.	DEAD.	DESERTED.	
Captain John Lees.				
John Bury.....................	Sergt.	Dead.	....	$8.00
Joseph Brim...............	Corpl.	"	....	7.30
Robert Wilkins..............	Private.	"	....	13.30
Anthony Salmitro...........	"	"	....	18.00
Joseph Little.............	"	"	....	22.50
Nathan Cannady	"	"	....	23.50
Thomas Barham.........	"	"	....	6.60
Daniel McCarta.......................	"	"	....	6.60
William Hicks.........	"	"	....	6.60
Richard Taylor............	"	"	....	13.30
John McFarley............	"	"	....	6.60
William Thacker............	"	....	Deserted.	4.15
Arch Cash, paid	"	....	"	6.60
Thomas Gardner	"	....	{ Put on board a galley. }	4.00
Capt. T. Misonthe.				
John Carnall	Corpl.	"	....	22.00
Henry Small................	Privt.	"	....	6.60
John Sammond............	"	"	....	20.00
John Steel.................	"	....	"	3.30
Capt. Wᵐ Hofflers.				
James Forrister.................	"	"	....	6.60
Samson Randolph	"	"	....	6.60
Henry Trent............	"	"	....	6.60
Charles Carter...........	"	"	....	13.30
John Randolph	"	"	....	13.30
Capt. T. Evertts.				
Pervis Griffin	Corpl.	"	....	7.30
Edward Whittield............	Private.	"	....	13.30
Thomas Moor	"	"	....	13.30
Burnitt Jiffriss............	"	"	"	6.60
James Banks............	"	"	....	6.60
John Moor.............	"	"	....	13.30
Capt. T. Nicholson.				
Soloman Jinnings............	Sergt.	"	....	8.00
Almond Addleton............	Corpl.	"	....	10.20
Peter Richeson............	Private.	"	....	13.50
George Judd............	"	"	....	11.30
James Orzlin............	"	"	....	13.30

LIST OF BALANCES DUE DEAD AND DESERTED.—*Continued.*

NAMES.	RANK.	DEAD.	DESERTED.	
Cap. William Cayors.				
James Beach	Private.	Dead.		$6.60
Searlett Church	"	"		6.60
William Taylor	"	"		6.60
John Scott	"	"		13.30
John Dunn	"	"		6.60
James Little	"	"		6.60
Samuel Monathaw	"	"		6.60
Henry Bronaugh	"	"	Deserted.	6.60
Capt. Windsor Browne.				
Thomas Cooper	"	"		13.50
James Gary	"	"		6.60
James Nemo	"	"		15.60
Christopher Critindon	"	"		13.30
James Duford	"	"		6.60
Edward Dearing	"	"		13.30
John Grushaun	"	"		13.30
John Wager	"	"		6.60
John Burk	"	"		13.30
Joseph Rankins	"	"		20.00
John Harris	"	"	"	20.00
John Waldin	"	"	"	20.00
Capt. John Camps.				
John Morgan	Sergt.	"		14.30
George Corneleous	Corpl.	"		3.50
Nathaniel Parish	Private.	"		6.60
William Lamkin	"	"		6.60
Lewis Powers	"	"		6.60
Henry Majors	"	"		6.60
Nicholas Balf	"	"		13.30
Humphrey Wayne	"	"		13.30
Henry M. Lood	"	"		13.30
William Taylor	"	"		26.60
William Merryman	"	"		15.45
George Whale	"	"		26.60
James Jones	"	"		26.60
John Oneal	"	"		26.60
John Garvill	"	"		13.30
Capt. Thomas Hamilton.				
Timothy Sulavin	Sergt.	"		2.41
Abraham Davis	Corpl.	"		7.30
John Aetkinson	Private.	"		6.60
Isaac Higden	"	"		6.60
Thomas Allexon	"	"		6.60
Thomas Boswell	"	"		6.60
James Williamson	"	"		13.30

LIST OF BALANCES DUE DEAD AND DESERTED.—*Concluded.*

NAMES.	RANK.	DEAD.	DESERTED.	
Capt. Thomas Hamilton, *continued.*				
Thomas Wakdin	Private.	Dead.	....	$13.30
Morning Hay	"	"	....	6.60
Joseph Chamberlin	"	"	....	16.80
Spencer Waldin...........................	"	"	....	6.60
William Allexon	"	"	....	13.30
Capt. Abner Crumps.				
James Martin	"	"	....	13.30
John Roundton............................	"	"	....	6.60
Joseph Sherman	"	"	....	6.60
Thomas Pinn..............................	"	"	....	6.60
Richard Brim	"	"	....	6.60
Jesse Goldin	"	"	....	13.30
Zachariah Harris	"	"	....	2.60
John Bullington	"	"	....	6.60
Zedekiah Saxton	"	"	....	6.60
Thomas Brim	"	"	....	6.60
John Thurston	"	"	....	6.60
Ansalm Baley	"	"	....	6.60
Robert Holdings	"	"	....	1 60
James Ladd	"	"	....	22.60
				1045\frac{10}{94}$

[Signed] JOHN LEE.

Received, 20th May, 1778, of Captain John Lee, Acting Pay Master of the Virginia State Regiment, Commanded by Col. George Gibson, the sum of one thousand and forty-five dollars and $\frac{86}{90}$ parts of a dollar—being money in his hand belonging to Dead men, prisoners, and deserters.

[Signed] THOS. REED,
Asst. PayM. Gen'l.

1778
Entered & Ex^d
by J. O.

Col. George Gibson was born in Lancaster, Pa., in October, 1747, and died at Fort Jefferson, Dec. 14, 1791.

His scholastic education was secured at an Academy, but it was subsequently made practical by business training in a mercantile house in Philadelphia.

At the opening of the Revolution he formed a company of a hundred men at Fort Pitt, and marching to Williamsburg, Va., was commissioned a captain in the Virginia line. Owing to the scarcity of powder and lead, he was selected by the governor to negotiate secretly with Spain, for a supply of these materials. He was successful in procuring supplies not only for Virginia, but for the other Colonies. For his services in this matter he was subsequently appointed colonel of the first Virginia regiment.

His men, known as "Gibson's lambs," were skilled sharpshooters; and being distinguished for independence and personal bravery, assisted in repelling Lord Dunmore's attack on Hampton, October 25, 1775.

He served with Washington through much of the Revolution, his command of the first regiment extending from June 5, 1777, to January, 1782. As a supernumerary officer he conducted the march of the British captured at Yorktown to the town of York, Pa., where they remained under his command until they were sent to England.

The war being over, Gibson retired to his farm in Cumberland county, Penn., where, for a time, he held the position of county lieutenant. He was not permitted, however, to remain in retirement. In 1791 he was made Colonel of Penn. and New Jersey troops, and participated in St. Clair's Defeat near Fort Recovery, Ohio, on the 4th of November of that year. In this battle he was mortally wounded, and his death occurred on the 14th of the following December.

Col. Gibson was a brave and meritorious officer.

PAY ROLL BOOK, No. 1. 1ST REG. L. DRAGOONS, NOVEMBER & DECEMBER, 1777, & EXTRA MONTH.

PAY ROLL FOR THE FIELD & STAFF OFFICERS OF THE FIRST REGIMENT LIGHT DRAGOONS. COMMANDED BY COL° THEODORICK BLAND FOR THE MONTH OF NOVEMBER, ONE THOUSAND SEVEN HUNDRED & SEVENTY-SEVEN.

Names, Rank, &c.	N° Days.	N° Doll^s.	£	S.	D.	Virginia Currency.	
Theodorick Bland, Col°	30	93¾	28	0	0	Rec^d in full.	[Signature.]
Benjamin Temple, Lt. Col°	30	75	22	10	0	Do.	"
John Jameson, Maj^r	30	60	18	0	0	Do.	"
*Robert Rose, Surgeon	30	60	18	0	0	Do.	[Signature of Berryman Green.]
Andrew Nixon, Adj^t	30	50	15	0	0	Do.	"
Berryman Green, Q^r M^r	30	50	15	0	0	Do.	"
John Gordon, R^s Master	30	33¾	10	0	0	Do.	"
*Pat^k Carnes, Surg. Mate	30	40	12	0	0	Do.	By order [signature of John Jameson].
John McLean, T^r Major	30	11⅔	3	10	0	Do.	"
Joseph Eggleston, P. Master	30	50	15	0	0	Do.	{Being for so much Advanced Joseph Eggleston previous to his resignation, & which was in full due him at the time of his resignation. Pr Wm Palfry, P. M. G.
Berryman Green, Q^r Master	a						
Deficiency of 16⅔ Dollars not drawn in April last		16⅔	5	0	0	V. C.	[Signature of Berryman Green.]
Dollars		510	162	20	0		

Doll^s.
Amount of Payment to Field & Staff ... 540.
ditto. first Troop ... 332.30
d° second d° ... 376.60
d° third ditto. ... 301.60
d° fourth d° ... 381.60
d° fifth d° ... 480.35
d° sixth d° ... 326.80
2739.55
Amount of absentees ... 25.
2764.25

*Exam^d.

PAY ROLL OF FIRST TROOP OF VIRGINIA LIGHT DRAGOONS, IN THE FIRST REGIMENT COMMANDED BY COL° THEODORICK BLAND, FOR THE MONTH OF NOVEMBER, ONE THOUSAND SEVEN HUNDRED & SEVENTY-SEVEN.

Names, Rank, &c.	No. of Days.	No. of Dollars.	£.	s.	D.	Virginia Currency.	
Richd Call, Capt	30	50	15	0	0	Rec^d in full.	[Signature.]
Thomas Pemberton, Lieut	20	22	6	12	0	do.	"
Ditto, Cornet	10	8⅔	2	12	0	do.	"
William Morsham, D. M. S	30	15	4	10	0	do.	"
Henry Heath. Serg^t	30	11⅓	3	10	0	do.	"
Minson Proby, Corp^l	30	10	3	0	0	do.	"
Robert Oliver, ditto	30	10	3	0	0	do.	"
William Jordan, ditto	30	10	3	0	0	do.	"
Phillip Webber, ditto	30	10	3	0	0	do.	pr. order [Signature of Wm Morsham].
*Drury Hobbs, Trump^t	30	10	3	0	0	do.	[Signature.]
*Keal McCaffry, Farrier	30	8⅓	2	10	0	do.	[Mark of Daniel Benn.]
Daniel Benn. private	30	8⅓	2	10	0	do.	[Signature.]
William Epps	30	8⅓	2	10	0	do.	"
James Gunn	30	8⅓	2	10	0	do.	pr. order [Signature of Thomas Pemberton].
*James Cureton	30	8⅓	2	10	0	do.	[Signature.]
John Craigg	30	8⅓	2	10	0	do.	pr. order [Signature of Richd Call].
*Edward Bertchet	30	8⅓	2	10	0	do.	[Signature.]
John Lang	30	8⅓	2	10	0	do.	"
Richard Poindexter	30	8⅓	2	10	0	do.	[Mark of Anthony Sonn.]
Anthony Sonn	30	8⅓	2	10	0	do.	" " John Kirkland.]
John Kirkland	30	8⅓	2	10	0	do.	[Signature.]
David Organ	30	8⅓	2	10	0	do.	"
Bolling Bolton	30	8⅓	2	10	0	do.	"
David Bradley	30	8⅓	2	10	0	do.	"
Enoch Vaughn	30	8⅓	2	10	0	do.	[Mark of David Lee.]
David Lee	30	8⅓	2	10	0	do.	[Signature.]
John White	30	8⅓	2	10	0	do.	

	Dollars					V. C.	
Benjamin Hobbs	30	8	2	10	0	do.	[Mark of Benjamin Hobbs.]
*John Tinney	30	8	2	10	0	do.	pr. order [Signature of And^w Nixon, Adj^t].
Peter Leath	30	8	2	10	0	do.	[Signature.]
George Vest	30	8	2	10	0	do.	[" George vst.]
Dollars	332		99	14	0		

PAY ROLL OF THE SECOND TROOP, VIRGINIA LIGHT DRAGOONS, IN THE FIRST REGIMENT, COMMANDED BY COL° THEODORICK BLAND, FOR THE MONTH OF NOVEMBER, ONE THOUSAND SEVEN HUNDRED & SEVENTY-SEVEN.

Cuthbert Harrison, Capt.	30	50	15	0	0	Rec'd in full.	[Signature.]
Bailor Hill, Lieut.	30	33¾	10	0	0	do.	"
Alex^r Gordon, Q. M. S.	30	15	4	10	0	do.	"
John Waite, Serjt	30	11⅞	3	0	0	do.	"
George Nowell, Corpl.	30	10	3	0	0	do.	"
Sandford Edwards, ditto	30	10	3	0	0	do.	"
Thomas New, ditto	30	10	3	0	0	do.	"
Thomas Sanders, ditto	30	10	3	0	0	do.	Pr. order [Mark of George Abrams].
*John Powers, Trumpt^r	30	8	3	0	0	do.	[Signature.]
Major Winfry, Farrier	30	8	2	10	0	do.	"
Robert Smith, private	30	8	2	10	0	do.	"
*William Edmundson	30	8	2	10	0	do.	[Signature of Thomas Madison.]
Richard Bowcock	30	8	2	10	0	do.	[Signature.]
Thomas Bagley	30	8	2	10	0	do.	"
Ambrose Maddison	30	8	2	10	0	do.	"
William Johnston	30	8	2	10	0	do.	"
*Edward Fleet	30	8	2	10	0	do.	Pr. Edwin Fleets order. John Turner.
William Bowler	30	8	2	10	0	do.	[Signature.]
Benjamin Timberlake	30	8	2	10	0	do.	"
*Thomas Maddison	30	8	2	10	0	do.	Pr. order [Signature of Sanford Edwards].
George Abrams	30	8	2	10	0	do.	[Mark of George Abrams.]
John Houchings	30	8	2	10	0	do.	[Signature.]
Archer Henley	30	8	2	10	0	do.	"

* Exam^d.

Names, Rank, &c.	N° Days.	N° Dollars.	£	S.	D.	Virginia Currency.	
John Lipscomb	30	8⅓	2	10	0	Rec'd in full.	[Signature.]
Richard Johnson	30	8⅓	2	10	0	do.	"
John Turner	30	8⅓	2	10	0	do.	"
Thomas Williams	30	8⅓	2	10	0	do.	[No signature.]
William Layton	30	8⅓	2	10	0	do.	[Signature.]
John Boltenhouse	30	8⅓	2	10	0	do.	"
William McCombs	30	8⅓	2	10	0	do.	"
Samuel French	30	8⅓	2	10	0	do.	"
David Lewis	30	8⅓	2	10	0	do.	P^r order [signature of John Waide].
*John Freeman	30	8⅓	2	10	0	do.	[Signature.]
Edward Luzader	30	8⅓	2	10	0	do.	"
John Sellers	30	8⅓	2	10	0	do.	"
John Sellers (omitted in pay Roll for October).	31	8⅔	2	10	0	do.	
Dollars		385	115	10	0	V. C.	

PAY ROLL OF THE THIRD TROOP OF VIRGINIA LIGHT DRAGOONS IN THE FIRST REGIMENT, COMMANDED BY COL° THEODORICK BLAND, FOR THE MONTH OF NOVEMBER, ONE THOUSAND SEVEN HUNDRED & SEVENTY-SEVEN.

Names, Rank, &c.	N° Days.	N° Dollars.	£	S.	D.	Virginia Currency.	
Alex. S. Dandridge, Capt.	30	50	15	0	0	Rec'd in full.	[Signature.]
William Lindsay, Lieut.	30	33⅓	10	0	0	do.	"
Cole Diggs, Cornet.	30	26⅔	8	0	0	do.	P^r order [signature of John Jameson].
*John Robertson, Q. M. S.	30	15	4	10	0	do.	P^r order [signature of Tho' Andrews].
*Francis Slaughter, Serjt.	30	11⅓	3	10	0	do.	[Signature.]
John Zackary, Corp^1	30	10	3	0	0	do.	"
James Finnell, ditto.	30	10	3	0	0	do.	"
John Long	30	10	3	0	0	do.	"
John Black, Trumpt^r	30	10	3	0	0	do.	"
Charles Slaughter, Private	30	8⅓	2	10	0	do.	"

Phillip Clayton	30	8⅓	2 10 0	Recᵈ in full	[Signature.]
Samuel Yager	30	8⅓	2 10 0	do.	[Mark of Samuel Yager.]
John Long, Junʳ	30	8⅓	2 10 0	do.	[Signature.]
William Benson	30	8⅓	2 10 0	do.	"
Samuel Tankersley	30	8⅓	2 10 0	do.	"
Thomas Andrews	30	8⅓	2 10 0	do.	"
David London	30	8⅓	2 10 0	do.	"
John Webster	30	8⅓	2 10 0	do.	"
Richard Pendleton	30	8⅓	2 10 0	do.	"
James Clements	30	8⅓	2 10 0	do.	"
William Cook	30	8⅓	2 10 0	do.	[Mark of Willᵐ Cook.]
William Lawrance	30	8⅓	2 10 0	do.	[Signature.]
*Samuel Knap	30	8⅓	2 10 0	do.	Pr. order [signature of Wᵐ Lawrence].
Jonathan Prowty	30	8⅓	2 10 0	do.	[Signature.]
Dollars		301⅔	90 10 0		

PAY ROLL OF THE FOURTH TROOP, VIRGINIA LIGHT DRAGOONS, IN THE FIRST REGIMENT, COMMANDED BY COLᵒ THEODORICK BLAND, FOR THE MONTH OF NOVEMBER, ONE THOUSAND SEVEN HUNDRED & SEVENTY-SEVEN.

*Lewellen Jones, Capt.	30	50	15 0 0	Recᵈ in full	[Signed: Pʳ order John Watts.]
John Watts, Lieut.	30	33⅓	10 0 0	Recᵈ in full	" John Watts.]
*Robert Yancy, Cornet.	30	26⅔	8 0 0	Recᵈ in full	" Pʳ order John Watts.]
*John Hamlin, Q. M. S.	30	15	4 10 0	Recᵈ in full	" Pʳ order Billington Dun.]
John Timberlake, Serjt.	30	11⅔	3 10 0	Recᵈ in full	" John Timberlake.]
James Crosby, Corpˡ	30	10	3 0 0	Recᵈ in full	" James Crosby.]
John Evans, ditto.	30	10	3 0 0	Recᵈ in full	" John Evans.]
Thomas Hewlet, ditto.	30	10	3 0 0	Recᵈ in full	" Thomas Hewlet.]
Jeremiah Bradshaw, ditto.	30	10	3 0 0	Recᵈ in full	" Jeremiah Bradshaw.]
John McClain, Ta. Major	30	11⅔	3 10 0	Recᵈ in full	" John McLean.]
Thomas Green, Trumpʳ	30	10	3 0 0	Recᵈ in full	" Thomas Green.]
Julius Powers, Private	30	8⅓	2 10 0	Recᵈ in full	" Julius Powers.]
Lewis Powers	30	8⅓	2 10 0	Recᵈ in full	" Lewis Powers.]

*Exam'd.

Names, Rank, &c.	N^{o} Days.	N^{o} Dollars.	£.	S.	D.	Virginia Currentcy.	
Peter Grigg	30	$8\frac{1}{3}$	2	10	0	Rec^{d} in full.	[Mark of Peter Grigg.]
Charles Stainback	30	$8\frac{1}{3}$	2	10	0	Rec^{d} in full.	[Signed: P^{r} order Ranson Colquit.]
John Morris	30	$8\frac{1}{3}$	2	10	0	Rec^{d} in full.	[" John Morris.]
Austin Hewlet	30	$8\frac{1}{3}$	2	10	0	Rec^{d} in full.	[" Austin Hewlitt.]
*John Cann	30	$8\frac{5}{8}$	2	10	0	Rec^{d} in full.	[" P^{r} order Thomas Green.]
Holman Rice	30	$8\frac{1}{3}$	2	10	0	Rec^{d} in full.	[" Holman Rice.]
Edmund Singleton	30	$8\frac{1}{3}$	2	10	0	Rec^{d} in full.	[Mark of Edmund Singleton.]
Thomas Gibson	30	$8\frac{1}{3}$	2	10	0	Rec^{d} in full.	[Mark of Thomas Gibson.]
John George	30	$8\frac{1}{3}$	2	10	0	Rec^{d} in full.	[Signed: John George.]
Jessee Harper	30	$8\frac{1}{3}$	2	10	0	Rec^{d} in full.	[" Jessee Harper.]
John Carter	30	$8\frac{1}{3}$	2	10	0	Rec^{d} in full.	[" John Carter.]
Josiah Foster	30	$8\frac{1}{3}$	2	10	0	Rec^{d} in full.	[" Josiah Foster.]
James Collier	30	$8\frac{1}{3}$	2	10	0	Rec^{d} in full.	[" James Collier.]
Ransom Colquitt	30	$8\frac{1}{3}$	2	10	0	Rec^{d} in full.	[" Ransom Colquit.]
John Wallis	30	$8\frac{1}{3}$	2	10	0	Rec^{d} in full.	[" John Wallis.]
Billington Dunn	30	$8\frac{1}{3}$	2	10	0	Rec^{d} in full.	[" Billington Dun.]
John Harrison	30	$8\frac{1}{3}$	2	10	0	Rec^{d} in full.	[Mark of John Harrison.]
William Payne	30	$8\frac{1}{3}$	2	10	0	Rec^{d} in full.	[Mark of William Payne.]
Isaac Chapman	30	$8\frac{1}{3}$	2	10	0	Rec^{d} in full.	[Mark of Isaac Chapman.]
*Charles Lovey	30	$8\frac{1}{3}$	2	10	0	Rec^{d} in full.	[Pr. order. Mark of Shadrach Lovey.]
Dollars		$381\frac{2}{3}$	114	10	0		

PAY ROLL OF THE FIFTH TROOP, VIRGINIA LIGHT DRAGOONS, IN THE FIRST REGIMENT, COMMANDED BY COL^{o} THEODORICK BLAND, FOR THE MONTH OF NOVEMBER, ONE THOUSAND SEVEN HUNDRED & SEVENTY-SEVEN.

Henry Lee, Capt	30	50	15	0	0	Rec^{d} in full.	[Signed Hen^{y} Lee.]
Henry Peyton, Lieut	30	$33\frac{1}{3}$	10	0	0	Rec^{d} in full.	[" Henry Peyton.]

John White, Cornet	30	26$\frac{2}{3}$	8	0	0	Rec^d in full.	[Signed: John White.]
William Peake, Q. M. S	30	15	4	10	0	Rec^d in full.	[" Wm Peake.]
William Brooks, Serjt	30	11$\frac{2}{3}$	3	10	0	Rec^d in full.	[" Wm Brooke.]
John Longdon, Corp^l	30	10	3	0	0	Rec^d in full.	[" John Longden.]
*John Watters, ditto	30	10	3	0	0	Rec^d in full.	[" p. ord^r Hen^y Lee.]
Fardiendo Neal, ditto	30	10	3	0	0	Rec^d in full.	[" Fardino Neal]
Robert Powers, ditto	30	10	3	0	0	Rec^d in full.	[" Robert Power.]
Joseph Benjamin, Trump^r	30	10	3	0	0	Rec^d in full.	[" Joseph Benjamin.]
*Zachariah Wells, Farrier	30	8$\frac{1}{3}$	2	10	0	Rec^d in full.	p^r order [Mark of Coleman Leonard].
Robert Rosamond, private	30	8$\frac{1}{3}$	2	10	0	Rec^d in full.	[Mark of Robert Rosamond.]
Ditto, omitted in October	30	8$\frac{1}{3}$	2	10	0	Rec^d in full.	[" " " "]
Coleman Ausberry	30	8$\frac{1}{3}$	2	10	0	Rec^d in full.	[Signed: Coalmon Asbury.]
John Allia	30	8$\frac{1}{3}$	2	10	0	Rec^d in full.	[" J. Allier.]
Joseph Bond	30	8$\frac{1}{3}$	2	10	0	Rec^d in full.	[" Joseph Bond.]
William Bilson	30	8$\frac{1}{3}$	2	10	0	Rec^d in full.	[Mark of William Bilson.]
Israel Coon	30	8$\frac{1}{3}$	2	10	0	Rec^d in full.	[Signed: Israel Coon.]
John Brewer	30	8$\frac{1}{3}$	2	10	o	Rec^d in full.	[" John Brewer.]
John Champ	30	8$\frac{1}{3}$	2	10	0	Bec^d in full.	[" John Champ.]
Isaac Dehavin	30	8$\frac{1}{3}$	2	10	0	Rec^d in full.	[" Isaac Dehaven.]
Annanias Freeman	30	8$\frac{1}{3}$	2	10	0	Rec^d in full.	[" Annes Freman.]
Robert Ferguson	30	8$\frac{1}{3}$	2	10	0	Rec^d in full.	[" Robt Fergusson.]
Peter Faulkner	30	8$\frac{1}{3}$	2	10	0	Rec^d in full.	[" Peter Faulkner.]
George Guthery	30	8$\frac{1}{3}$	2	10	0	Rec^d in full.	[" George Guthery.]
John Humphrys	30	8$\frac{1}{3}$	2	10	0	Rec^d in full.	[" John Humphrey.]
Downing Herndon	30	8$\frac{1}{3}$	2	10	0	Rec^d in full.	[" Downin Hendun.]
William Halbert	30	8$\frac{1}{3}$	2	10	0	Rec^d in full.	[" William Halbert.]
John Harrison	30	8$\frac{1}{3}$	2	10	0	Rec^d in full.	[" John Harrisson.]
Thomas Hogan	30	8$\frac{1}{3}$	2	10	0	Rec^d in full.	[Mark of Thomas Hogan.]
William Kichson	30	8$\frac{1}{3}$	2	10	0	Rec^d in full.	[" " William Kichson.]
Stephen Lewis	30	8$\frac{1}{3}$	2	10	0	Rec^d in full.	[Signed: Stephen Lewis.]
Coleman Leonard	30	8$\frac{1}{3}$	2	10	0	Rec^d in full.	[Mark of Coleman Leonard.]
*Michael McKrum	30	8$\frac{1}{3}$	2	10	0	Rec^d in full.	[Signed: p^r order Wm Peake.]
Carried over							

* Exam^d.

Names, Rank, &c.	N° Days.	N° Doll^s.	£	S.	D.	Virginia Currentcy.	
Brought over							
William McDonald	30	$8\frac{1}{3}$	2	10	0	Rec^d in full.	[Signed: William Mackdanileel.]
William Newman	30	$8\frac{1}{3}$	2	10	0	Rec^d in full.	[" William Newman.]
Mark Kenton	30	$8\frac{1}{3}$	2	10	0	Rec^d in full.	[Mark of Mark Kenton.]
George Painter	30	$8\frac{1}{3}$	2	10	0	Rec^d in full.	[Signed: George Painter.]
George Rush	30	$8\frac{1}{3}$	2	10	0	Rec^d in full.	[" George Reush.]
John Wright	30	$8\frac{1}{3}$	2	10	0	Rec^d in full.	[" John Wright.]
William Stillwell	30	$8\frac{1}{3}$	2	10	0	Rec^d in full.	[" William Stillwell.]
William Crookshanks	30	$8\frac{1}{3}$	2	10	0	Rec^d in full.	[Mark of William Crookshanks.]
John Ben Ward	30	$8\frac{1}{3}$	2	10	0	Rec^d in full.	[Signed: John Ben Ward.]
William Bigbie	25	$6\frac{58}{72}$	2	0	10	Rec^d in full.	[" William Bigby.]
James White	29	$8\frac{9}{72}$	2	8	2	Rec^d in full.	[Mark of James White.]
David Stewart	3	$\frac{5}{6}$	"	5	0	Rec^d in full.	[" David Stewart.]
Joseph Chapman	2	$\frac{40}{72}$	"	3	4	Rec^d in full.	[Signed: Joseph Chapman.]
*Levi Sharp	3	$\frac{5}{6}$	"	5	0	Rec^d in full.	[" p^r ord^r Hen^y Lee.]
*James Casey	2	$\frac{40}{72}$	"	3	4	Rec^d in full.	[" " "]
Isaac Conroe	2	$\frac{40}{72}$	"	3	4	Rec^d in full.	[" Isaac Consoe.]
*John Robinson	2	$\frac{40}{72}$	"	3	4	Rec^d in full.	[" p^r ord^r Hen^y Lee.]
Jacob Collater	7	$1\frac{68}{72}$	"	11	8	Rec^d in full.	[" Jacob Callatter.]
		$482\frac{1}{3}$	144	14	0	V. C.	
Deduct: Robt Rosamond 1 month & Jacob Collatter 11/8^d, not added in the pay roll, of which this is a copy	....	$10\frac{20}{72}$	3	1	8		
Dollars	....	$472\frac{4}{72}$	141	12	4		

* Exam^d.

PAY ROLL OF THE SIXTH TROOP, VIRGINIA LIGHT DRAGOONS, IN THE FIRST REGIMENT, COMMANDED BY COL° THEODORICK BLAND, FOR THE MONTH OF NOVEMBER, ONE THOUSAND SEVEN HUMDRED & SEVEN-SEVEN.

*John Belfield, Capt.	30	50	15	0	0	Rec[d] in full.	[Signed: p[r] order Berryman Green.]
Addison Lewis, Lieu[t]	30	$33\frac{1}{3}$	10	0	0	" "	[" Addison Lewis.]
*Griffen Fauntleroy, Corn[t]	19	$16\frac{2}{3}$	5	1	4	" "	[" p[r] order Alex[r] S. Dandridge.]
John Hughes, Q. M. S.	30	15	4	10	0	" "	[" Jn[o] Hughes.]
Leonard Henley, Serj[t]	30	$11\frac{2}{3}$	3	10	0	" "	[" Leonard Henley.]
Christopher Garland, Corp[l]	30	10	3	0	0	" "	[" Christopher Garland.]
John Plumer, ditto.	30	10	3	0	0	" "	[" John Plummer.]
Isaac Howlet, ditto.	30	10	3	0	0	" "	[" Isaac Howlitt.]
William Plumer, ditto.	30	10	3	0	0	" "	[" W[m] Plummer.]
William Read, Trump[tr]	30	10	3	0	0	" "	[" William Reade.]
*John Jones, private	30	$8\frac{1}{3}$	2	10	0	" "	[" p[r] order John Watts.]
Henry Allen	30	$8\frac{1}{3}$	2	10	0	" "	[" Henry Allen.]
Robert Ransone	30	$8\frac{1}{3}$	2	10	0	" "	[" Rob[t] Ransone.]
Armistead Plumer	30	$8\frac{1}{3}$	2	10	0	" "	[" Armistead Plummer.]
Jacob Rhoades	30	$8\frac{1}{3}$	2	10	0	" "	[Mark of Jacob Rhoades.]
*James Tyree	30	$8\frac{1}{3}$	2	10	0	" "	[Signed: p[r] order Leonard Henley.]
*William Throckmorton	30	$8\frac{1}{3}$	2	10	0	" "	[" " Armistead Plummer.]
*Johnston Allen	30	$8\frac{1}{3}$	2	10	0	" "	[" " Leonard Henley.]
Jasper Hughes	30	$8\frac{1}{3}$	2	10	0	" "	[" Jasper Hughes.]
Edmund Hobday	30	$8\frac{1}{3}$	2	10	0	" "	[" Edmund Hobday.]
*William Callis	30	$8\frac{1}{3}$	2	10	0	" "	[" p[r] order Alex[r] Gordon.]
*Edward Wilson	30	$8\frac{1}{3}$	2	10	0	" "	[" " Leonard Henley.]
*Humphrey Givin	30	$8\frac{1}{3}$	2	10	0	" "	[" " Addison Lewis.]
*John Stubbs	30	$8\frac{1}{3}$	2	10	0	" "	[" " John Jameson.]
John Wright	30	$8\frac{1}{3}$	2	10	0	" "	[" John Wright.]
William Davis	30	$8\frac{1}{3}$	2	10	0	" "	[" William Davis.]
*Thomas Braden	30	$8\frac{1}{3}$	2	10	0	" "	[" p[r] order Rob[t] Ransone.]
Joseph Smelt	30	$8\frac{1}{3}$	2	10	0	" "	[" Joseph Smelt.]
Major Waller	30	$8\frac{1}{3}$	2	10	0	" "	[No signature.]
Francis Scott	30	$8\frac{1}{3}$	2	10	0	" "	[No signature.]
Dollars		$343\frac{20}{72}$	103	1	1	V. C.	

* Exam[d].

PAY ROLL OF FIELD & STAFF OFFICERS IN THE FIRST REGIMENT OF LIGHT DRAGOONS, COMMANDED BY COLº THEODORICK BLAND, FOR THE MONTH OF DECEMBER, 1777.

	Days.	Dollˢ.	£	S.	D.		
Theodorick Bland, Colº	31	93¾	28	0	0	Recᵈ in full.	[Signed: Theoᵏ Bland.]
Benjamin Temple, Lt. Colº	31	75	22	10	0	Recᵈ in full.	" Benj. Temple.]
*John Jameson, Major	31	60	18	0	0	Recᵈ in full.	p. order [signed: Berryman Green].
*Robert Rose, Surgeon	31	62	18	12	0	Recᵈ in full.	p. order " Berryman Green].
Berryman Green, Qr Master	31	50	15	0	0	Recᵈ in full.	[Signed: Berryman Green.
Andrew Nixon, Adjt	31	50	15	0	0	Recᵈ in full.	" Andʷ Nixon, Adjt.]
*Patrick Carnes, S. Mate	31	41⅓	12	8	0	Recᵈ in full.	{ p. order of Majr Jameson. [Signed: Berryman Green.]
*John Gordon, R. Q. Master	31	33⅓	10	0	0	Recᵈ in full.	p. order [signed: Berryman Green].
John McLean, Trump. Majr	31	11⅓	3	10	0	Recᵈ in full.	[Signed: John McLean.]
Berryman Green, Qr. Mr., for Deficiency of 16⅔ Dollars not drawn in May last.		16⅔	5	0	0	Recᵈ in full.	[Signed: Berryman Green.]
Dollars		493	148	0	0		

Paid The field & Staff 493.30
1ˢᵗ Troop 320.50
2ⁿᵈ do. 368.30
3ʳᵈ do. 291.60
4ᵗʰ do. 381.60
5ᵗʰ do. 559.72
6ᵗʰ do. 336.60
　　　　　　　　　　　2752. 2
Absentees 25
　　　　　　　　　　　2777. 2
Wanting to balance...... 3.33
　　　　　　　　　　　2780.35

*Examᵈ.

PAY ROLL of 1st TROOP in the FIRST REGIMENT LIGHT DRAGOONS, COMMANDED BY COL° THEODORICK BLAND, FOR THE MONTH OF DECEMBER, ONE THOUSAND SEVEN HUNDRED & SEVENTY-SEVEN.

Name		Dollars					Signed
Richard Call, Capt	31	50	15	0	0	Rec^d in full.	[Signed: Richd Call.]
Thomas Pemberton, Lieut.	31	33⅓	10	0	0	Rec^d in full.	" Thomas Pemberton.
*William Worsham, Q. M. S.	31	15¾	4	10	0	Rec^d in full.	" P^r order Berryman Green.
Henry Heath, Serj^t	31	11⅔	3	10	0	Rec^d in full.	" Henry Heeth.
Minson Proby, Corp^l	31	10	3	0	0	Rec^d in full.	" Minson Proby.
Robert Oliver, Corp^l	31	10	3	0	0	Rec^d in full.	" Robert Oliver.
William Jordan, Corp^l	31	10	3	0	0	Rec^d in full.	" Wm Jordan.
Phillip Webber, Corp^l	31	10	3	0	0	Rec^d in full.	" Phillip Webber.
*Drury Hobbs, Trump^tr	31	10	3	0	0	Rec^d in full.	P^r order Thos Pemberton.
Niel McCaffry, farrier	31	8 8/30	2	10	0	Rec^d in full.	Signed: Neal McCaffry.
Daniel Bem, private	31	8 8/30	2	10	0	Rec^d in full.	Mark of Daniel Benn.
Benjamin Hobbs	31	8 8/30	2	10	0	Rec^d in full.	Signed: Bengamine Hobbs.
Boling Bolton	31	8 8/30	2	10	0	Rec^d in full.	" Boling Bolton.
Peter Leath	31	8 8/30	2	10	0	Rec^d in full.	" Peter Leath.
Anthony Sonn	31	8 8/30	2	10	0	Rec^d in full.	Mark of Anthony Sonn.
James Gunn	31	8 8/30	2	10	0	Rec^d in full.	Signed: James Gunn.
*James Cureton	31	8 8/30	2	10	0	Rec^d in full.	" Pr Order Thomas Pemberton.
William Epps	31	8 8/30	2	10	0	Rec^d in full.	" William Epps.
John Lang	8	2 6 2/30	2	13	4	Rec^d in full.	" John Lang.
David Lee	31	8 8/30	2	10	0	Rec^d in full.	" David Lee.
Enoch Vaughn	31	8 8/30	2	10	0	Rec^d in full.	" Enouck Vaughn.
Richard Poindexter	31	8 8/30	2	10	0	Rec^d in full.	" Richard Poindexter.
*John Tinney	31	8 8/30	2	10	0	Rec^d in full.	" P^r order Henry Heeth.
*David Bradley	31	8 8/30	2	10	0	Rec^d in full.	" P^r order Henry Heeth.
David Organ	31	8 8/30	2	10	0	Rec^d in full.	" David Organ.
John Craigg	31	8 8/30	2	10	0	Rec^d in full.	" John Craig.
George Vest	31	8 8/30	2	10	0	Rec^d in full.	" George Vest.
John White	31	8 8/30	2	10	0	Rec^d in full.	" John White.
*Edward Birtchet	31	8 8/30	2	10	0	Rec^d in full.	" P^r order Richd Call.
Dollars		320 9/12	96	3	4	V. C.	

*Exam^d.

Pay Roll of the Second Troop in the First Regiment Light Dragoons, Commanded by Colonel Theodorick Bland, for the Month of December, One Thousand Seven Hundred & Seventy-seven.

	Days.	Dolls.	£.	S.	D.		
Cuthbert Harrison, Capt	31	50	15	0	0	Rec^d in full.	[Signed: Cuth^bt Harrison.]
Bailor Hill, Lieut	31	33⅓	10	0	0	Rec^d in full.	[" Baylor Hill.]
Alexander Gordon, Q. M. S	31	15	4	10	0	Rec^d in full.	[" Alex^r Gordon.]
John Waide, Serjt	31	11⅔	3	10	0	Rec^d in full.	[" John Waide.]
*George Norvell, Corp^l	31	10	3	0	0	Rec^d in full.	[" P^r order Sanford Edwards.]
Sandford Edwards, d^o	31	10	3	0	0	Rec^d in full.	[" Sanford Edwards.]
Thomas New, ditto	31	10	3	0	0	Rec^d in full.	[" Thos New.]
Thomas Sanders, ditto	31	10	3	0	0	Rec^d in full.	[" Tho. Sanders.]
Robert Smith, private	31	8⅓	2	10	0	Rec^d in full.	[" Robert Smith.]
William Edmundson	31	8⅓	2	10	0	Rec^d in full.	[" William Edmondson.]
Samuel French, Trumpt^r	31	10	3	0	0	Rec^d in full.	[" Samuel French.]
Major Winfree, Farrier	31	8⅓	2	10	0	Rec^d in full.	[" Major Winfree.]
Richard Bowcock, private	31	8⅓	2	10	0	Rec^d in full.	[" Richard Bowcock.]
Thomas Bagby	31	8⅓	2	10	0	Rec^d in full.	[" Thomas Bagby.]
Ambrose Maddison	31	8⅓	2	10	0	Rec^d in full.	[" Ambrose Madison.]
William Johnston	31	8⅓	2	10	0	Rec^d in full.	[" William Johnson.]
Edwin Fleet	31	8⅓	2	10	0	Rec^d in full.	[" Edwin Fleet.]
William Bowler	31	8⅓	2	10	0	Rec^d in full.	[" Wm Bowler.]
*Benjamin Timberlake	31	8⅓	2	10	0	Rec^d in full.	[" p^r order Thomes Wilmes.]
Thomas Maddison	31	8⅓	2	10	0	Rec^d in full.	[" Thomas Madison.]
George Abrams	31	8⅓	2	10	0	Rec^d in full.	[Mark of George Abrams.]
John Houchings	31	8⅓	2	10	0	Rec^d in full.	[Mark of John Houching.]
Archer Henley	31	8⅓	2	10	0	Rec^d in full.	[Signed: Archer Henley.]
*John Lipscomb	31	8⅓	2	10	0	Rec^d in full.	Rec^d 3⅔ Dollars p^r order Thos Sanders; also Rec^d 4⅔ @ Dollars. [Signed] John Lipscomb.
Richard Johnston	31	8⅓	2	10	0	Rec^d in full.	[Signed: Richd Johnston.]
John Turner	31	8⅓	2	10	0	Rec^d in full.	[" John Turner.]

Thomas Williams	31	$8\frac{1}{3}$	2	10	0	Rec^{d} in full.	[Signed: Thomes Wilmes.]
William Layton	31	$8\frac{1}{3}$	2	10	0	Rec^{d} in full.	[No signature.]
*John Powers	31	$8\frac{1}{3}$	2	10	0	Rec^{d} in full.	[Signed: p^{r} order [Mark of] George Abrams].
*John Boltenhouse	31	$8\frac{1}{3}$	2	10	0	Rec^{d} in full.	[" p^{r} order Alex. Gordon.]
William McCombs	31	$8\frac{1}{3}$	2	10	0	Rec^{d} in full.	[" William McCombs.]
David Lewis	31	$8\frac{1}{3}$	2	10	0	Rec^{d} in full.	[" David Lewis.]
John Freeman	31	$8\frac{1}{3}$	2	10	0	Rec^{d} in full.	[" John Freman.]
Edward Luzader	31	$8\frac{1}{3}$	2	10	0	Rec^{d} in full.	[Mark of Edward Luzader.]
John Sellers	31	$8\frac{1}{3}$	2	10	0	Rec^{d} in full.	[Signed: John Sellers.]
Dollars		$376\frac{2}{3}$	113	0	0		

PAY ROLL OF THE THIRD TROOP IN THE FIRST REGIMENT LIGHT DRAGOONS, COMMANDED BY COL^{o} THEODORICK BLAND, FOR THE MONTH OF DECEMBER, ONE THOUSAND SEVEN HUNDRED & SEVENTY-SEVEN.

Alexander Spots^{o} Dandridge	31	50	15	0	0	Rec^{d} in full.	[Signed: Alex^{r} S. Dandridge.]
William Lindsay, Lieut	31	$33\frac{1}{3}$	10	0	0	Rec^{d} in full.	[" Wm Lindsay.]
Cole Diggs, Cornet	31	$26\frac{2}{3}$	8	0	0	Rec^{d} in full.	[" Cole Diggs.]
*Francis Slaughter, Q. M. S	31	15	4	10	0	Rec^{d} in full.	[" Alex^{r} S. Dandridge p^{r} order.]
John Zackary, Serjt	31	$11\frac{2}{3}$	3	10	0	Rec^{d} in full.	[" John Zachary.]
James Finnel, Corp^{l}	31	10	3	0	0	Rec^{d} in full.	[" James Finnell.]
John Long, ditto	31	10	3	0	0	Rec^{d} in full.	[" John Long.]
John Black, Trump^{r}	31	10	3	0	0	Rec^{d} in full.	[" John Black.]
William Benson, private	31	$8\frac{1}{3}$	2	10	0	Rec^{d} in full.	[" William Benson.]
Samuel Yager	31	$8\frac{1}{3}$	2	10	0	Rec^{d} in full.	[" Samuel Yager.]
Charles Slaughter	31	$8\frac{1}{3}$	2	10	0	Rec^{d} in full.	[" Charles Slaughter.]
Phillip Clayton	31	$8\frac{1}{3}$	2	10	0	Rec^{d} in full.	[" Phil Clayton.]
John Long, Jr	31	$8\frac{1}{3}$	2	10	0	Rec^{d} in full.	[" John Long.]
Samuel Tankersley	31	$8\frac{1}{3}$	2	10	0	Rec^{d} in full.	[" Samuel Tankersley.]
Thomas Andrews	31	$8\frac{1}{3}$	2	10	0	Rec^{d} in full.	[" Thos Andrews.]
David London	31	$8\frac{1}{3}$	2	10	0	Rec^{d} in full.	[" David London.]
John Webster	31	$8\frac{1}{3}$	2	10	0	Rec^{d} in full.	[" John Webster.]
Richard Pendleton	31	$8\frac{1}{3}$	2	10	0	Rec^{d} in full.	[" Richard Pendleton.]

* Exam^{d}.

	Days.	Doll^s.	£.	S.	D.		
James Clements	31	$8\frac{1}{3}$	2	10	0	Rec^d in full.	[Signed: James Clements.]
William Cook	31	$8\frac{1}{3}$	2	10	0	Rec^d in full.	[Mark of William Cook.]
*William Lawrance	31	$8\frac{1}{3}$	2	10	0	Rec^d in full.	[Signed: p^r order Thomas Bagby.]
Samuel Knapp	31	$8\frac{1}{3}$	2	10	0	Rec^d in full.	[" Samuel Knapp.]
Jonathan Prouty	31	$8\frac{1}{3}$	2	10	0	Rec^d in full.	[" Jonathan Prouty.]
Dollars		$291\frac{2}{3}$	87	10	0	V. C.	

Pay Roll of the 4th Troop in the First Regiment, Light Dragoons, Commanded by Col^o Theodorick Bland, for the Month of December, One Thousand Seven Hundred & Seventy-seven.

*Lewellen Jones, Capt^t	31	50	15	0	0	Rec^d in full.	[Signed: p. John Watts.]
John Walls, Lieut	31	$33\frac{1}{3}$	10	0	0	" "	[" John Watts.]
*Robert Yancey, Cornet	31	$26\frac{2}{3}$	8	0	0	" "	[" p. John Watts.]
*John Hamlin, Q. M. S	31	15	4	10	0	" "	[" p. order Billington Dun.]
John Timberlake, Serj^t	31	$11\frac{2}{3}$	3	10	0	" "	[" John Timberlake.]
John McLean, Tr. Major	31	$11\frac{2}{3}$	3	10	0	" "	[" Jno McLean.]
James Cosby, Corp	31	10	3	0	0	" "	[" James Cosby.]
John Evans, ditto	31	10	3	0	0	" "	[" John Evans.]
Thomas Hewlet, ditto	31	10	3	0	0	" "	[" Thomas Hewlet.]
Jeremiah Bradshaw	31	10	3	0	0	" "	[" Jeremiah Bradshaw.]
John Wallis, Private	31	$8\frac{1}{3}$	2	10	0	" "	[" John Wallis.]
Austin Hewlet	31	$8\frac{1}{3}$	2	10	0	" "	[" Austin Hewlet.]
William Payne	31	$8\frac{1}{3}$	2	10	0	" "	[Mark of Wm Payne.]
John Harrison	31	$8\frac{1}{3}$	2	10	0	" "	" " John Harrison.]
John George	31	$8\frac{1}{3}$	2	10	0	" "	[Signed: John George.]
Julius Powers	31	$8\frac{1}{3}$	2	10	0	" "	[" Julius Powers.]
Lewis Powers	31	$8\frac{1}{3}$	2	10	0	" "	[" Lewis Powers.]
Peter Grigg	31	$8\frac{1}{3}$	2	10	0	" "	[Mark of Peter Grigg.]
Charles Stainback	30	$8\frac{1}{3}$	2	10	0	" "	[Signed: Charles Stainback.]

John Morris	30	$8\frac{1}{3}$	2	10	0	Rec[d] in full.	[Signed: John Morris.]
*John Cann	30	$8\frac{1}{3}$	2	10	0	" "	rec[d] $2\frac{2}{3}$[d] Dollars. Thomas Green. also rec[d] $5\frac{2}{3}$[d] Dollars, p. acc[t]. John Watts.
Holman Rice	30	$8\frac{1}{3}$	2	10	0	" "	[Signed: Holeman Rice.]
Edmund Singleton	30	$8\frac{1}{5}$	2	10	0	" "	[" Edmund Singleton.]
Thomas Gibson	30	$8\frac{1}{3}$	2	10	0	" "	[" Thomas Sig[l] P. Gibson.]
Josiah Foster	31	$8\frac{1}{3}$	2	10	0	" "	[" Josiah Foster.]
James Collier	31	$8\frac{1}{3}$	2	10	0	" "	[" James Collier.]
Ransom Colquitt	31	$8\frac{1}{3}$	2	10	0	" "	[" Ranson Colquit.]
Billington Dunn	31	$8\frac{1}{3}$	2	10	0	" "	[" Billington Dun.]
Isaac Chapman	31	$8\frac{1}{3}$	2	10	0	" "	[Mark of Isaac Chapman.]
*Charles Lovey	31	$8\frac{1}{3}$	2	10	0	" "	[p[r] order Shadrack Lovey.]
John Carter	31	$8\frac{1}{3}$	2	10	0	" "	[Signed: John Carter.]
Jessee Harper	31	$8\frac{1}{3}$	2	10	0	" "	[" Jesse Harper.]
Thomas Green, Trump[tr]	31	10	3	0	0	" "	[" Thomas Green.]
Dollars		$381\frac{2}{3}$	114	10	0		

PAY ROLL OF THE FIFTH TROOP IN THE FIRST REGIMENT, LIGHT DRAGOONS, COMMANDED BY COL[o] THEODORICK BLAND, FOR THE MONTH OF DECEMBER, ONE THOUSAND SEVEN HUNDRED & SEVENTY-SEVEN.

*Henry Lee, Capt	31	50	15	0	0	Rec[d] in full.	[Signed: P. order John Jameson.]
*Henry Peyton, Lieut	31	$33\frac{1}{3}$	10	0	0	" "	[" p[r] ord[r] Hen[y] Lee.]
John White. Cornet	31	$26\frac{2}{3}$	8	0	0	" "	[" John White.]
William Peake, Q. M. S.	31	15	4	10	0	" "	[" Wm. Peake.]
William Brooks, Serjt	31	$11\frac{2}{3}$	3	10	0	" "	[" W[m] Brooks.]
John Longdon, Corpl	31	10	3	0	0	" "	[" John Longden.]
*John Waters, ditto	31	10	3	0	0	" "	[" p. ord[r] Hen[y] Lee.]
Fardiendo Neal, ditto	31	10	3	0	0	" "	[" Fardiendo Neal.]
Mark Kenton, ditto	31	10	3	0	0	" "	[Mark of Mark Kenton.]
Joseph Benjamin, Trumpt[r]	31	10	3	0	0	" "	[Signed: Joseph Benjamin.]
Continued on other side							

* Exam[d].

Name	Days	Dollars	£	S.	D.		Signed
Broᵗ over....		10	3	0	0	Recᵈ in full	[Signed: Zachariah Wells.
Zachariah Wells, farrier	31	8	2	10	0	"	" Jo. Allier.]
John Allia, private	31	8	2	10	0	"	[Mark of Thomas Hogan.]
Thomas Hogan	31	8	2	10	0	"	[Signed: Coalmon Asbury.
Coleman R. Ausberry	31	8	2	10	0	"	" Downin Hendren.
Downing Hendron	31	8	2	10	0	"	" George Guthery.
George Guthery	31	8	2	10	0	"	[Mark of Coleman Leonard.
Coleman Leonard	31	8	2	10	0	"	" Robert Rosamond
Robert Rosamond	31	8	2	10	0	"	[Signed: William Newman.
William Newman	31	8	2	10	0	"	" John Brewer.]
John Brewer	31	8	2	10	0	"	[Mark of William Kichson.]
William Kichson	31	8	2	10	0	"	[Signed: pʳ order Wᵐ Peake.
*Robert Power	31	8	2	10	0	"	" Isaac Dehaven.]
Isaac Dehaven	31	8	2	10	0	"	" John Champ.]
John Champe	31	8	2	10	0	"	" John Humphrey.]
John Humphry	31	8	2	10	0	"	" Stephen Lewis.]
Stephen Lewis	31	8	2	10	0	"	" pʳ order Wᵐ Peake.
*Michael McKrum	31	8	2	10	0	"	" John Wright.]
John Write	31	8	2	10	0	"	" George Painter.]
George Painter	31	8	2	10	0	"	" George Rush.]
George Rush	31	8	2	10	0	"	" Anaes freeman.]
Annanias Freeman	31	8	2	10	0	"	" William Mackdanial.]
William McDonald	31	8	2	10	0	"	[Mark of William Bilson.]
William Bilson	31	8	2	10	0	"	[Signed: pʳ order Henʸ Lee.
*William Stilwell	31	8	2	10	0	"	" John Harrison.] } Names so transposed on original.
Joseph Bond	31	8	2	10	0	"	" Joseph Bond.]
John Harrison	31	8	2	10	0	"	" Israel Coon.]
Israel Coon	31	8	2	10	0	"	" John Benward.]
John Ben Ward	31	8	2	10	0	"	[Mark of James White.]
James White	31	8	2	10	0	"	[Signed: William Bigby.]
William Bigbie	31	8	2	10	0	"	

Peter Faulkner	31	$8\frac{1}{3}$	2	10	0	Rec[d] in full.	[Signed: Peter Faulkner.]
William Halbert, Private	31	$8\frac{1}{3}$	2	10	0	" "	[" William Halbert.]
Robert Ferguson	31	$8\frac{1}{3}$	2	10	0	" "	[" Rob[t] Fergusson.]
William Crookshanks	31	$8\frac{1}{3}$	2	10	0	" "	[Mark of William Crookshanks.]
Joseph Chapman	31	$8\frac{1}{3}$	2	10	0	" "	[Signed: Joseph Chapman.]
*James Casey	31	$8\frac{1}{3}$	2	10	0	" "	[" p[r] ord[r] Hen[y] Lee.]
Isaac Conroe	31	$8\frac{1}{3}$	2	10	0	" "	[" Isaac Conroe.]
Jacob Colater	31	$8\frac{1}{3}$	2	10	0	" "	[" Jacob Collatter.]
John Kendall	31	$8\frac{1}{3}$	2	10	0	" "	[Mark of John Kendall.]
*John Robinson	31	$8\frac{1}{3}$	2	10	0	" "	[Signed: p[r] ord[r] Hen[y] Lee.]
*Levi Sharp	31	$8\frac{1}{3}$	2	10	0	" "	[" " Hen[y] Lee.]
David Stewart	31	$8\frac{1}{3}$	2	10	0	" "	[Mark of David Stewart.]
James Wheeler	5	$1\frac{1}{4}$	"	7	6	" "	[Signed: James Wheler.]
John Wheeler	5	$1\frac{1}{4}$	"	7	6	" "	[" John Wheler.]
Thomas Davis	28	$7\frac{5}{6}$	2	7	0	" "	[" Tho[s] Davis.]
John Hopper	25	$7\frac{1}{6}$	2	3	0	" "	[Mark of John Hopper.]
Richard Johnston	5	$1\frac{1}{4}$	"	7	6	" "	[Signed: Richard Johnson.]
*William Ansley	5	$1\frac{1}{4}$	"	7	6	" "	[" p[r] ord[r] Hen[y] Lee.]
*John Briggs	3	$\frac{3}{4}$	"	4	6	" "	[" " Julius Hite.]
Julius Hite	3	$\frac{3}{4}$	"	4	6	" "	[" Julius Hite.]
Dollars		$559\frac{5}{6}$	167	19	0	V. C.	

PAY ROLL OF THE SIXTH TROOP IN THE FIRST REGIMENT LIGHT DRAGOONS, COMMANDED BY COLO. THEODORICK BLAND, FOR THE MONTH OF DECEMBER, ONE THOUSAND SEVEN HUNDRED & SEVENTY-SEVEN.

*John Belfield, Cap[t]	31	50	15	0	0	Rec[d] in full.	[Signed: p[r] order Berryman Green.]
Addison Lewis, Lieut.	31	$33\frac{1}{3}$	10	0	0	" "	[" Addison Lewis.]
*Griffen Fauntleroy, Cornet	31	$26\frac{2}{3}$	8	0	0	" "	[" { Rec[d] p[r] order $3\frac{1}{3}$ dollars. Alex[r] S. Dandridge. also Rec[d] $23\frac{1}{3}$ Dollars. Griffin Fauntleroy].
John Hughes, Q. M. S.	31	15	4	10	0	" "	[" John Hughes.

* Exam[d].

	Days.	Dollars.	£	S.	D.		
Leonard Henley, Serjt.	31	11⅔	3	10	0	Rec[d] in full.	[Signed: Leonard Henley.]
Christopher Garland, Corp[l]	31	10	3	0	0	" "	[" Christopher Garland.]
John Plummer, ditto.	31	10	3	0	0	" "	[" John Plummer.]
Isaac Howlet, ditto.	31	10	3	0	0	" "	[" Isaac Howlet.]
William Plummer, ditto.	31	10	3	0	0	" "	[" W[m] Plummer.]
William Read, Trump[tr]	31	10	3	0	0	" "	[" William Reade.]
Henry Allen, private	31	8⅓	2	10	0	" "	[" Henry Allen.]
John Jones	31	8⅓	2	10	0	" "	[" John Jones.]
Robert Ransone	31	8⅓	2	10	0	" "	[" Rob[t] Ransone.]
Armstead Plummer	31	8⅓	2	10	0	" "	[" Annistead Plummer.]
*Jacob Rhoades	31	8⅓	2	10	0	" "	[" { rec[d] six Dollars.† John Plummer. also rec[d] 2⅓[d] Dollars. (Mark of) Jacob Rhoades.
*James Tyree	31	8⅓	2	10	0	" "	[" ¢ James Tyree p[r] order John Jones.]
*William Throckmorton	31	8⅓	2	10	0	" "	[" p[r] order Johnson Allen.]
Johnston Allen	31	8⅓	2	10	0	" "	[" Johnson Allen.]
Jasper Hughes	31	8⅓	2	10	0	" "	[" Jasper Hughes.]
*Edmund Hobday	31	8⅓	2	10	0	" "	[" p. order Leonard Henley.]
William Callis	31	8⅓	2	10	0	" "	[" W[m] Callis.]
*Edward Wilson	31	8⅓	2	10	0	" "	[" p. order Leonard Henley.]
Humphry Gwin	31	8⅓	2	10	0	" "	[" Humphrey Gwyn.]
John Stubbs	31	8⅓	2	10	0	" "	[Mark of John Stubbs.]
*John Wright	31	8⅓	2	10	0	" "	[Signed: p. order Leonard Henley.]
William Davis	31	8⅓	2	10	0	" "	[" William Davis.]
Thomas Braden	31	8⅓	2	10	0	" "	[" Thomas Bradin.]
Joseph Smelt	31	8⅓	2	10	0	" "	[" Joseph Smelt.]
Major Waller	31	8⅓	2	10	0	" "	[No signature.]
Francis Scott	31	8⅓	2	10	0	" "	["]
Dollars.		353⅓	106	0	0	V. C.	

* Exam[d].

† See Capt. Harrison's order for this as Com[d] the Regim[t].

PAY ROLL of FIELD & STAFF OFFICERS in the FIRST REGIMENT LIGHT DRAGOONS, COMMANDED BY Col° THEODORICK BLAND, FOR 1 MONTH'S EXTRAORDINARY PAY BESTOWED BY CONGRESS, DECEMBER, 1777.

Theodorick Bland, Col°	30	93⅜	28	0	Rec'd in full.	[Signed: Theo⁴ Bland.]
Benjamin Temple, L' Col°	30	75	22	10	"	Benj. Temple.]
*John Jameson, Major	30	60	18	0	"	p. order Berryman Green.]
*Robert Rose, Surgeon	30	60	18	0	"	p. order Berryman Green.]
Berryman Green, P. Master	30	50	15	0	"	Berryman Green.]
Andrew Nixon, Adjutant	30	50	15	0	"	And'w Nixon, Adj't.]
John Hughes, Q. Master	30	50	15	0	"	John Hughes.]
*John Gordon, R. J. Master	30	33⅜	10	0	"	pr. order Berryman Green.]
*Patrick Carnes, S. Mate	30	40	12	0	"	{ pr. order Capt. Harrison, Moses Van Court.
John McLean, Trump. Maj'	30	11⅞	3	10	"	John McLean.]
Berryman Green, Q' M', a Deficiency of 16⅞ Dollars not drawn in June last		16⅞	5	0	"	Berryman Green.]
Dollars		540	102	0	V. C.	

N. B. this ought to have been enter'd under December: with Deficiency in May. See, Berry: Green.

Paid the field & staff .... 540:—
do 1st Troop 326:60
2nd ditto. 368:30
3rd ditto. 393:30
4th ditto. .... 370:—
5th ditto. .... 603:—
6th ditto. 528:30
                              3129:60
absentees 25:
                              3154:60
                              3008:30
Rec'd from the P. M. Gen' 146:30

* Exam'd.

Pay Roll of 1st Troop in the First Regiment Light Dragoons, Commanded by Col° Theodorick Bland, for 1 Month's Extraordinary Pay Bestowed by Congress, December, 1777.

	Days.	Dolls.	£.	S.	D.		
Richard Call, Captain	30	50	15	0	0	Recd in full.	[Signed: Richd Call.]
Thomas Pemberton, Lieut	30	33⅓	10	0	0	" "	[" Thomas Pemberton.]
*William Worsham, Q. M. S	30	15	4	10	0	" "	[" pr order Berryman Green.]
Henry Heath, Sergt	30	11⅔	3	10	0	" "	[" Henry Heeth.]
Minson Proby, Corpl	30	10	3	0	0	" "	[" Minson Proby.]
Robert Olliver, ditto	30	10	3	0	0	" "	[" Robert Oliver.]
William Jordan, ditto	30	10	3	0	0	" "	[" Wm Jordan.]
Phillip Webber, ditto	30	10	3	0	0	" "	[" Philip Webber.]
*Drury Hobbs, Trumptr	30	10	3	0	0	" "	[" pr order Thomas Pemberton.]
Niel McCaffry, farrier	30	8⅓	2	10	0	" "	[" Neale Mcaffry.]
Daniel Benn, private	30	8⅓	2	10	0	" "	[Mark of Daniel Benn.]
William Epps	30	8⅓	2	10	0	" "	[Signed: Wm Eppes.]
James Gunn	30	8⅓	2	10	0	" "	[" James Gunn.]
John Craigg	30	8⅓	2	10	0	" "	[" John Craig.]
James Cureton	30	8⅓	2	10	0	" "	[" James Cureton.]
*Edward Birchet	30	8⅓	2	10	0	" "	[" p. order Richd Call.]
Richard Poindexter	30	8⅓	2	10	0	" "	[" Richard Poindexter.]
Anthony Sonn	30	8⅓	2	10	0	" "	[Mark of Anthony Sonn.]
John Kirkland	30	8⅓	2	10	0	" "	[" " John Kirkland.]
David Organ	30	8⅓	2	10	0	" "	[Signed: David Organ.]
*David Bradley	30	8⅓	2	10	0	" "	[" pr order Henry Heeth.]
Bolling Bolton	30	8⅓	2	10	0	" "	[" Boling Bolton.]
Enoch Vaughn	30	8⅓	2	10	0	" "	[" Enouck Vaughn.]
David Lee	30	8⅓	2	10	0	" "	[" David Lee.]
John White	30	8⅓	2	10	0	" "	[" John White.]
Benjamin Hobbs	30	8⅓	2	10	0	" "	[" Bengamine Hobbs.]
*John Tinney	30	8⅓	2	10	0	" "	[" pr order Henry Heeth.]

Peter Leath	30	$8\frac{1}{3}$	2	10	0	"	"	[Signed: Peter Leath.]
George Vest	30	$8\frac{1}{3}$	2	10	0	"	"	[" Goege Vest.]
Dollars		$326\frac{2}{3}$	98	0	0			

Pay Roll of Second Troop in the First Regiment, Light Dragoons, Commanded by Colonel Theodorick Bland, for One Month's Extraordinary Pay Bestowed by Congress, December, 1777.

Cuthbert Harrison, Capt	30	50	15	0	0	Rec^{d}	in full.	[Signed: Cuth^{t} Harrison.]
Bailor Hill, Lieut	30	$33\frac{1}{3}$	10	0	0	"	"	[" Baylor Hill.]
Alexander Gordon, Q. M. S	30	15	4	10	0	"	"	[" Alex^{r} Gordon.]
John Waide, Serjt	30	$11\frac{2}{3}$	3	10	0	"	"	[" John Waide.]
*George Nowell, Corpl	30	10	3	0	0	"	"	[" { rec^{d} 4 Dollars Sanford Edwards.] { rec^{d} 6 Dollars Geo. Norvell.]
Sandford Edwards, ditto	30	10	3	0	0	"	"	[" Sanford Edwards.]
Thomas New, ditto	30	10	3	0	0	"	"	[" Thos New.]
Thomas Saunders, ditto	30	10	3	0	0	"	"	[" Tho. Sanders.]
Robert Smith, Private	30	$8\frac{1}{3}$	2	10	0	"	"	[" Robert Smith.]
William Edmundson	30	$8\frac{1}{3}$	2	10	0	"	"	[" William Edmondson.]
Richard Bowcock	30	$8\frac{1}{3}$	2	10	0	"	"	[" Richard Bowcock.]
Thomas Bagby	30	$8\frac{1}{3}$	2	10	0	"	"	[" Thomas Bagby.]
Ambrose Maddison	30	$8\frac{1}{3}$	2	10	0	"	"	[" Ambrose Madison.]
William Johnson	30	$8\frac{1}{3}$	2	10	0	"	"	[" William Johnson.]
*Edwin Fleet	30	$8\frac{1}{3}$	2	10	0	"	"	[" p^{r} order John Turner.]
William Bowler	30	$8\frac{1}{3}$	2	10	0	"	"	[" Wm Bowler.]
*Benjamin Timberlake	30	$8\frac{1}{3}$	2	10	0	"	"	[" p^{r} order Thomes Wilmes.]
Thomas Maddison	30	$8\frac{1}{3}$	2	10	0	"	"	[" Thomas Madison.]
George Abrams	30	$8\frac{1}{3}$	2	10	0	"	"	[Mark of George Abrams.]
John Houchings	30	$8\frac{1}{3}$	2	10	0	"	"	[Signed: John Houching.]
Archer Henley	30	$8\frac{1}{3}$	2	10	0	"	"	[" Archer Henley.]
*John Lipscomb	30	$8\frac{1}{3}$	2	10	0	"	"	[" per order Tho. Sanders.]
Richard Johnston	30	$8\frac{1}{3}$	2	10	0	"	"	[" Richd Johnston.]
William Layton	30	$8\frac{1}{3}$	2	10	0	"	"	[No signature.]

* Exam^{d}.

	Days.	Dollars.	£	S.	D.		
Thomas Williams	30	$8\frac{1}{3}$	2	10	0	Rec^{d} in full.	[Signed: Thomas Wilmes.]
John Turner	30	$8\frac{1}{3}$	2	10	0	" "	[" John Turner.]
William McComb	30	$8\frac{1}{3}$	2	10	0	" "	[" William McCombs.]
*John Boltenhouse	30	$8\frac{1}{3}$	2	10	0	" "	[" p^{r} order David Lewis.]
David Lewis	30	$8\frac{1}{3}$	2	10	0	" "	[" David Lewis.]
*John Freeman	30	$8\frac{1}{3}$	2	10	0	" "	[" p^{r} order Thomas Madison.]
Edward Luzader	30	$8\frac{1}{3}$	2	10	0	" "	[Mark of Edward Luzader.]
John Sellers	30	$8\frac{1}{3}$	2	10	0	" "	[" John Sellers.]
*John Powers	30	$8\frac{1}{3}$	2	10	0	" "	[" { rec^{d} $1\frac{2}{3}$^{ds} Dollars. p^{r} order (Mark of George Abrams.) also $6\frac{2}{3}$ Dollars. p^{r} order (Signature) David Organ.]
Samuel French, Trump^{tr}	30	10	3	0	0	" "	[" Samuel French.]
Major Winfree	30	$8\frac{1}{3}$	2	10	0	" "	[" Major Winfree.]
Dollars	....	$376\frac{2}{3}$	113	0	0		

PAY ROLL OF THE THIRD TROOP, IN THE FIRST REGIMENT LIGHT DRAGOONS, COMMANDED BY COL^{o} THEODORICK BLAND, FOR ONE MONTH'S EXTRAORDINARY PAY BESTOWED BY CONGRESS, DECEMBER, 1777.

	Days.	Dollars.	£	S.	D.		
Alex^{r} Spots^{d} Dandridge, Capt	30	50	15	0	0	Rec^{d} in full.	[Signed: Alex^{r} S. Dandridge.]
William Lindsay, Lieut.	30	$33\frac{1}{3}$	10	0	0	" "	[" Wm Lindsay.]
Cole Diggs, Cornet	30	$26\frac{2}{3}$	8	0	0	" "	[" Cole Diggs.]
*Francis Slaughter, Q. M. S.	30	15	4	10	0	" "	[" p^{r} order Alex^{r} S. Dandridge.]
John Zackary, Serjt.	30	$11\frac{2}{3}$	3	10	0	" "	[" John Zachary.]
James Finnel, Corp^{l}	30	10	3	0	0	" "	[" James Finnell.]
John Long, ditto	30	10	3	0	0	" "	[" John Long]
Thomas Andrews, ditto.	30	10	3	0	0	" "	[" Thos Andrews.]
John Black, Trumpt^{r}	30	10	3	0	0	" "	[" John Black.]
William Benson, Private	30	$8\frac{1}{3}$	2	10	0	" "	[" William Benson.]

Name						Rec'd in full	Signed
Samuel Yager	30	8⅓	2	10	0	Rec'd in full	[Signed: Samuel Yager.]
Phillip Clayton	30	8⅓	2	10	0	"	" Phil Clayton.]
John Long	30	8⅓	2	10	0	"	" John Long.]
Samuel Tankersley	30	8⅓	2	10	0	"	" Samuel Tankersley.]
David London	30	8⅓	2	10	0	"	" David London.]
John Webster	30	8⅓	2	10	0	"	" John Webster.]
Richard Pendleton	30	8⅓	2	10	0	"	" Richard pendleton.]
James Clements	30	8⅓	2	10	0	"	" James Clements.]
William Cook	30	8⅓	2	10	0	"	Mark of William Cook.]
*William Lawrance	30	8⅓	2	10	0	"	[Signed: pr. order Thomas Bagby.]
Samuel Knapp	30	8⅓	2	10	0	"	" Samuel Knapp.]
Jonathan Prouty	30	8⅓	2	10	0	"	" Jonathan Prouty.]
William Furbush	30	8⅓	2	10	0	"	" William furbush.]
Robert Deadman	30	8⅓	2	10	0	"	" Robt Dedman.]
William Arnold	30	8⅓	2	10	0	"	" William Arnold.]
Benjamin Head	30	8⅓	2	10	0	"	" Benjamin Head.]
William Listen	30	8⅓	2	10	0	"	Mark of William Lister.]
Ellis Sherfield	30	8⅓	2	10	0	"	[Signed: Ellis Sherfield.]
William Hicks	30	8⅓	2	10	0	"	" William Hicks.]
Rail Thompson	30	8⅓	2	10	0	"	Mark of Rial Thompson.]
Christopher Horn	30	8⅓	2	10	0	"	" Christopher Horn.]
John Hill	30	8⅓	2	10	0	"	[Signed: John Hill.]
James Harcum	30	8⅓	2	10	0	"	" James Harcum.]
Thomas Marsh	30	8⅓	2	10	0	"	Mark of Thomas Marsh.]
Charles Slaughter	30	8⅓	2	10	0	"	[Signed: Charles Slaughter.]
Dollars		393⅓	118	0	0		

PAY ROLL OF THE FOURTH TROOP, IN THE FIRST REGIMENT LIGHT DRAGOONS, COMMANDED BY COLº THEODORICK BLAND, FOR THE MONTHS EXTRAORDINARY PAY BESTOWED BY CONGRESS IN DECEMBER, ONE THOUSAND SEVEN HUNDRED & SEVENTY-SEVEN.

Name						Rec'd in full	Signed
*Lewellen Jones, Captain	30	50	15	0	0	Rec'd in full	[Signed: p. John Watts.]
John Walls, Lieutenant	30	33⅓	10	0	0	" "	" John Walls.]

*Exam.d

	Days.	Doll^{s}.	£.	S.	D.		
*Robert Yancey, Cornet	30	$26\frac{2}{3}$	8	0	0	Rec^{d} in full.	[Signed : p. John Watts.]
*John Hamlin, Q. M. S.	30	15	4	10	0	" "	[" rec^{d} $3\frac{1}{3}$ Dollars p. order Billington Dun.] also Rec^{d} $11\frac{2}{3}$ Dol^{s} John Hamlin.]
John Timberlake, Serjt	30	$11\frac{2}{3}$	3	10	0	" "	[" John Timberlake.]
James Cosby, Corp^{l}	30	10	3	0	0	" "	[" James Crosby.]
John Evans, ditto	30	10	3	0	0	" "	[" John Evans.]
Thomas Hewlet, ditto	30	10	3	0	0	" "	[" Thoms Hewlet.]
Jeremiah Bradshaw, ditto	30	10	3	0	0	" "	[" Jeremiah Bradshaw.]
Thomas Green, Trump^{r}	30	10	3	0	0	" "	[" Thomas Green.]
John Wallis, private	30	$8\frac{1}{3}$	2	10	0	" "	[" John Wallis.]
Austin Hewlet.	30	$8\frac{1}{3}$	2	10	0	" "	[" Austin Hewlett.]
William Payne	30	$8\frac{1}{3}$	2	10	0	" "	[Mark of William Payne.]
John Harrison	30	$8\frac{1}{3}$	2	10	0	" "	[" " John Harrison.]
John George	30	$8\frac{1}{3}$	2	10	0	" "	[Signed : John George.]
Julius Powers	30	$8\frac{1}{3}$	2	10	0	" "	[" Julius Powers.]
Lewis Powers	30	$8\frac{5}{8}$	2	10	0	" "	[" Lewis powers.]
Josiah Foster	30	$8\frac{1}{3}$	2	10	0	" "	[" Josiah Foster.]
Ransom Colquitt	30	$8\frac{1}{3}$	2	10	0	" "	[" Ransom Colquit.]
Peter Grigg	30	$8\frac{1}{3}$	2	10	0	" "	[Mark of Peter Grigg.]
Billington Dunn	30	$8\frac{1}{3}$	2	10	0	" "	[Signed : Billington Dun.]
James Collier	30	$8\frac{1}{3}$	2	10	0	" "	[" James Collier.]
Thomas Gibson	30	$8\frac{1}{3}$	2	10	0	" "	[Mark of Thomas Gibson.]
Isaac Chapman	30	$8\frac{1}{3}$	2	10	0	" "	[" " Isaac Chapman.]
Edmund Singleton	30	$8\frac{1}{3}$	2	10	0	" "	[Signed : Edmund Singleton.]
John Carter	30	$8\frac{1}{3}$	2	10	0	" "	[" John Carter.]
*John Cann	30	$8\frac{1}{3}$	2	10	0	" "	[" p^{r} order Ransom Colquit.]
Jessee Harper	30	$8\frac{1}{3}$	2	10	0	" "	[" Jesse Harper.]
Holman Rice	30	$8\frac{1}{3}$	2	10	0	" "	[" Holeman Rice.]
Charles Stainback	30	$8\frac{1}{3}$	2	10	0	" "	[" Charles Stainback.]

	30	8⅛	2 10 0		[Signed : { " " p. order (Mark of) Shadrack Lovey.]
*Charles Lovey.........	30	8⅛	2 10 0		[" John Morris.]
John Morris	30	8⅛	2 10 0		
Dollars	370		111 0 0		

14

PAY ROLL OF THE FIFTH TROOP IN THE FIRST REGIMENT, LIGHT DRAGOONS, COMMANDED BY COLº THEODORICK BLAND, FOR ONE MONTH'S EXTRA PAY BESTOWED BY CONGRESS, DECEMBER, 1777.

	30				
*Henry Lee, Capt.	30	50	15 0 0	Rec'd in full.	[Signed : p. order John Jameson.]
*Henry Peyton, Lieut.	30	33⅓	10 0 0	"	" pʳ ordʳ Henʸ Lee.]
John White, Cornet.	30	26³⁄₁₀	8 0 0	"	" John White.]
William Peake, Q. M. S.	30	15	4 10 0	"	" Wᵐ Peake.]
William Brookes, Serjt	30	11⅜	3 10 0	"	" Wᵐ Brooks.]
John Longdon, Corpl	30	10	3 0 0	"	" John Longden.]
Ferdiendo Neal, ditto	30	10	3 0 0	"	{ " [p. ordʳ Henʸ Lee.] This should have been Waters.
*John Waters, ditto......	30	10	3 0 0	"	" Fardiendo Neal]
Mark Kenton, ditto......	30	10	3 0 0	"	[Mark of Mark Kenton.]
Joseph Benjamin, Trumpʳ	30	10	3 0 0	"	[Signed : Joseph Benjamin.]
Zachariah Wells, farrier	30	8⁴⁄₆₉	2 10 0	"	" Zachariah Wells.]
John Allia, Private	30	8⁴⁄₆₉	2 10 0	"	" J. Allier.]
William Bilson	30	8⁴⁄₆₉	2 10 0	"	[Mark of William Bilson.]
John Champe	30	8⁴⁄₆₉	2 10 0	"	[Signed : John Champ.]
Joseph Chapman	30	8⁴⁄₆₉	2 10 0	"	" Joseph Chapman.]
William Newman......	30	8⁴⁄₆₉	2 10 0	"	" William Newman.]
John Brewer	30	8⁴⁄₆₉	2 10 0	"	" John Brewer.]
Robert Rosamond......	30	8⁴⁄₆₉	2 10 0	"	[Mark of Robert Rosamond.]
Coleman Leonard	30	8⁴⁄₆₉	2 10 0	"	" Coleman Leonard].
Thomas Hogan	30	8⁴⁄₆₉	2 10 0	"	" Thomas Hogan.]
George Guthery	30	8⁴⁄₆₉	2 10 0	"	[Signed : Georg Guthery.]
Downing Herndon	30	8⁴⁄₆₉	2 10 0	"	" Downin Hendren.]
John Humphry......	30	8⁴⁄₆₉	2 10 0	"	" John Humphrey.]

* Examᵈ.

	Days.	Doll.	£	S.	D.	Rec'd in full.	Signed.
*Robert Power	30	8⅓	2	10	0	Rec'd in full.	[Signed: p'r order W'm Peake.]
Stephen Lewis	30	8⅓	2	10	0	"	" Stephen Lewis.
George Painter	30	8⅓	2	10	0	"	" George Painter.
John Wright	30	8⅓	2	10	0	"	" John Wright.
*Michael M'cKum	30	8⅓	2	10	0	"	" p. order W'm Peake.
Annanias Freeman	30	8⅓	2	10	0	"	" Anenas feman.
*William Stilwell	30	8⅓	2	10	0	"	" p. ord'r Hen'y Lee.
Joseph Bond	30	8⅓	2	10	0	"	" Joseph Bond.
John Harrison	30	8⅓	2	10	0	"	" John Harrison.
Robert Fergusson	30	8⅓	2	10	0	"	" Rob't Fergusson.
William Halbert	30	8⅓	2	10	0	"	" William Halbert.
Israel Coon	30	8⅓	2	10	0	"	" Israel Coon.
John Ben Ward	30	8⅓	2	10	0	"	" John Benward.
Peter Faulkner	30	8⅓	2	10	0	"	" Peter Faulkner.
George Rush	30	8⅓	2	10	0	"	" George Rush.
Jacob Colater	30	8⅓	2	10	0	"	" Jacob Collatter.
James White	30	8⅓	2	10	0	"	Mark of James White.
William Crookshanks	30	8⅓	2	10	0	"	" William Crookshanks.
William M'cDonald	30	8⅓	2	10	0	"	Signed: William Mackdanieal.
David Stewart	30	8⅓	2	10	0	"	Mark of David Stewart.
*Levi Sharpe	30	8⅓	2	10	0	"	Signed: p'r ord'r Hen'y Lee.
John Kendal	30	8⅓	2	10	0	"	Mark of John Kendall.
Isaac Coonroe	30	8⅓	2	10	0	"	Signed: Isaac Conroe.
*John Robertson	30	8⅓	2	10	0	"	" "
*James Casey	30	8⅓	2	10	0	"	" "
*William Ansley	30	8⅓	2	10	0	"	" "
Bichard Johnson	30	8⅓	2	10	0	"	" Rich'd Johnson.
James Wheeler	30	8⅓	2	10	0	"	" James Wheler.
John Wheeler	30	8⅓	2	10	0	"	" John Wheler.
Julius Hite	30	8⅓	2	10	0	"	" Julius Hite.
John Hopper	30	8⅓	2	10	0	"	[Mark of John Hopper.]

Name		Days	£	s	d	Recᵈ	Signed
Thomas Davis	30	8¹⁰⁄₈	2	10	0	Recᵈ in full.	[Signed: Thoˢ Davis.]
Isaac Dehaven	30	8	2	10	0	" "	" Isaac Dehaven.]
Coleman R. Ausbery	30	8	2	10	0	" "	" Coalmon Asbury.]
William Kichson	30	8	2	10	0	" "	Mark of William Kichson.]
*John Briggs	30	8	2	10	0	" "	[Signed: pʳ order Julius Hite.]
William Bigbie	30	8⁵⁄	2	10	0	" "	" William Bigby.]
Dollars		603⅔	181	0	0		

PAY ROLL OF THE SIXTH TROOP, IN THE FIRST REGIMENT LIGHT DRAGOONS, COMMANDED BY COLᵒ THEODORICK BLAND, FOR ONE MONTH EXTRAORDINARY BESTOWED BY CONGRESS, DECEMBER, 1777.

Name		Days	£	s	d	Recᵈ	Signed
*John Belfield, Capᵗ	30	50	15	0	0	Recᵈ in full.	[Signed: pʳ order Berry. Green.]
Addison Lewis, Lieut.	30	33⅓	10	0	0	" "	" Addison Lewis.]
Griffin Fauntleroy, Cornet	30	26⅔	8	0	0	" "	" Griffin Fauntleroy.]
Leonard Henley, Q. M. S.	30	15	4	10	0	" "	" Leonard Henley.]
Christopher Garland, Serjᵗ	30	11⅔	3	10	0	" "	" Christopher Garland.]
John Plummer, Corpˡ	30	10	3	0	0	" "	" John Plummer.]
Isaac Howlet, ditto	30	10	3	0	0	" "	" Isaac Howlett.]
William Plummer, ditto	30	10	3	0	0	" "	" Wᵐ Plummer.]
John Jones, ditto	30	10	3	0	0	" "	" John Jones.]
William Read, Trump	30	10	3	0	0	" "	" William Reade.]
Henry Allen, Private	30	8⅓	2	10	0	" "	" Henry Allen.]
Robert Ransone	30	8⅓	2	10	0	" "	" Robt. Ransone.]
Armstead Plummer	30	8⅓	2	10	0	" "	" Armistead Plummer.]
*James Tyree	30	8⅓	2	10	0	" "	∮ James Tyree, p. order John Jones.]
*William Throckmorton	30	8⅓	2	10	0	" "	pʳ order Johnson Allen.]
Johnson Allen	30	8⅓	2	10	0	" "	" Johnson Allen.]
Jasper Hughes	30	8⅓	2	10	0	" "	" Jasper Hughes.]
*Edmund Hobday	30	8⅓	2	10	0	" "	p. order Leonard Henley.]
*Edward Wilson	30	8⅓	2	10	0	" "	" "]
Humphry Gwin	30	8³⁄	2	10	0	" "	" Humphry Gwin.]
*John Wright	30	8⁸⁄	2	10	0	" "	pʳ order Armistead Plummer.]

*Examᵈ.

	Days.	Doll^{s}.	£.	S.	D.		
William Davis	30	$8\frac{1}{3}$	2	10	0	Rec^{d} in full.	[Signed: William Davis.]
*Thomas Braden	30	$8\frac{1}{3}$	2	10	0	" "	[" { also 7/. over p^{r} order Samuel Knapp.]
Joseph Smelt	30	$8\frac{1}{3}$	2	10	0	" "	[" Joseph Smelt.]
Francis Scott	30	$8\frac{1}{3}$	2	10	0	" "	[No signature.]
Major Waller	30	$8\frac{1}{3}$	2	10	0	" "	[" " .]
Jessee Crump	30	$8\frac{1}{3}$	2	10	0	" "	[Signed: Jesse Crump.]
*Samuel Ware	30	$8\frac{1}{3}$	2	10	0	" "	[" p. order Richd Davis.]
John Johnson	30	$8\frac{1}{3}$	2	10	0	" "	[Mark of John Johnson.]
William Hollaby	30	$8\frac{1}{3}$	2	10	0	" "	[Signed: Wm Holderby.]
Richard Hobday	30	$8\frac{1}{3}$	2	10	0	" "	[" Richd Hobday.]
George Billops	30	$8\frac{1}{3}$	2	10	0	" "	[Signed: George Billups.]
John Rowe	30	$8\frac{1}{3}$	2	10	0	" "	[Mark of John Rowe.
Richard Davis	30	$8\frac{1}{3}$	2	10	0	" "	[Signed: Richard Davis.]
Lewis Belvin	30	$8\frac{1}{3}$	2	10	0	" "	[Mark of Lewis Belvin.]
John Eubank	30	$8\frac{1}{3}$	2	10	0	" "	[Signed: John Eubank.]
John Maddison	30	$8\frac{1}{3}$	2	10	0	" "	[Mark of John Maddison.]
William Hall	30	$8\frac{1}{3}$	2	10	0	" "	[Signed: Wm Hall.]
Reuben Layton	30	$8\frac{1}{3}$	2	10	0	" "	[Mark of Reuben Layton.]
Edmund Edmundson	30	$8\frac{1}{3}$	2	10	0	" "	[Signed: Edmund Edmondson.]
Larkin Lane	30	$8\frac{1}{3}$	2	10	0	" "	[" Larken Lane.]
Robert Pool	30	$8\frac{1}{3}$	2	10	0	" "	[Mark of Robert Pool.]
West Hert	30	$8\frac{1}{3}$	2	10	0	" "	[Signed: West Hurt.]
*John Carroll	30	$8\frac{1}{3}$	2	10	0	" "	[" { p. order (Mark of) William Alexander.]
Lewis Cook	30	$8\frac{1}{3}$	2	10	0	" "	[" Lewis Cook.]
John Brown	30	$8\frac{1}{3}$	2	10	0	" "	[Mark of John Brown.]
Richard Walker	30	$8\frac{1}{3}$	2	10	0	" "	[" " Richard Walker.]
Robert Angel	30	$8\frac{1}{3}$	2	10	0	" "	[" " Robert Angel.]
William Butlar	30	$8\frac{1}{3}$	2	10	0	" "	[Signed: William Buttler.]
George Forrest	30	$8\frac{1}{3}$	2	10	0	" "	[" George Forest.]
John Treakle	30	$8\frac{1}{3}$	2	10	0	" "	[" John Trekel.]

*Moses Hudgen	30	$8\frac{1}{3}$	2	10	0	" "	[Signed: pr order Christor Garland.]
Digges Weston	30	$8\frac{1}{3}$	2	10	0	" "	[Mark of Digges Western.]
Dollars		545	163	10	0		

Pay Roll of 5th Troop in the First Regiment, Light Dragoons, Commanded by Col° Theodorick Bland, for the Month of January, One Thousand Seven Hundred & Seventy-eight.

*Henry Lee, Captain	31	50	15	0	0	Recd in full.	[Signed: p. order John Jameson.]
*Henry Peyton, Lieut	31	$33\frac{1}{3}$	10	0	0	" "	[" p. order Heny Lee.]
John White, Cornet	31	$26\frac{2}{3}$	8	0	0	" "	[" John White.]
William Peake, Q. M. S.	31	15	4	10	0	" "	[" Wm Peake.]
William Brooks, Serjt	31	$11\frac{2}{3}$	3	10	0	" "	[" Wm Brooks.]
John Longdon, Corpl	31	10	3	0	0	" "	[" John Longden.]
*John Waters, ditto	31	10	3	0	0	" "	[" p. ordr Heny Lee.]
Ferdiendo Neal, ditto	31	10	3	0	0	" "	[" Fardiendo Neal.]
Mark Kenton, ditto	31	10	3	0	0	" "	[Mark of Mark Kenton.]
Joseph Benjamin, Trumptr	31	10	3	0	0	" "	[Signed: Joseph Benjamin.]
Coleman Ausberry, Private	31	$8\frac{1}{3}$	2	10	0	" "	[" Coalmon Asbury.]
William Newman, d°	31	$8\frac{1}{3}$	2	10	0	" "	[" William Newman.]
Zachariah Wells, Farrier	31	$8\frac{1}{3}$	2	10	0	" "	[" Zachariah Wells.]
*Robert Power, Private	31	$8\frac{1}{3}$	2	10	0	" "	[" pr order Wm Peake.]
John Champ	31	$8\frac{1}{3}$	2	10	0	" "	[" John Champ.]
Isaac Dehaven	31	$8\frac{1}{3}$	2	10	0	" "	[" Isaac Dehaven.]
Stephen Lewis	31	$8\frac{1}{3}$	2	10	0	" "	[" Stephen Lewis.]
John Humphry	31	$8\frac{1}{3}$	2	10	0	" "	[" John Humphry.]
Downing Herndon	31	$8\frac{1}{3}$	2	10	0	" "	[" Downin Hendren.]
Thomas Hogan	31	$8\frac{1}{3}$	2	10	0	" "	[Mark of Thomas Hogan.]
George Guthery	31	$8\frac{1}{3}$	2	10	0	" "	[Signed: George Guthery.]
Robert Ferguson	31	$8\frac{1}{3}$	2	10	0	" "	[" Robt. Fergusson.]
Coleman Leonard	31	$8\frac{1}{3}$	2	10	0	" "	[Mark of Coleman Leonard.]
William Halbert	31	$8\frac{1}{3}$	2	10	0	" "	[Signed: William Halbert.]
William Kichson	31	$8\frac{1}{3}$	2	10	0	" "	[" pr Mark of William Kichson.]
William Bigbie	31	$8\frac{1}{3}$	2	10	0	" "	[" William Bigby.]

* Examd.

	Days.	Dolls.	£	S.	D.	Rec'd in full.	
John Wright	31	8 5/6	2	10	0	Rec'd in full.	[Signed: John Wright.
*Michael McCrum	31	8 5/6	2	10	0	"	" p'r order Wm Peake.]
Annanias Freeman	31	8 5/6	2	10	0	"	" Annaes freeman.]
John Ben Ward	31	8 5/6	2	10	0	"	" John Benward.]
*William Stillwell	31	8 5/6	2	10	0	"	" p. order Hen^y Lee.]
George Rush	31	8 5/6	2	10	0	"	" George Rush.]
George Painter	31	8 5/6	2	10	0	"	" George Painter.]
John Harrison	31	8 5/6	2	10	0	"	" John harrisson.]
Israel Coon	31	8 5/6	2	10	0	"	" Israel Coon.]
Joseph Bond	31	8 5/6	2	10	0	"	" Joseph Bond.]
Peter Faulkner	31	8 5/6	2	10	0	"	" Peter Faulkner.]
William Bilson	31	8 5/6	2	10	0	"	Mark of William Bilson.]
William McDonald	31	8 5/6	2	10	0	"	Signed: William Mackdanieal.]
Robert Rosamond	31	8 5/6	2	10	0	"	Mark of Robert Rosamond.]
William Crookshank	31	8 5/6	2	10	0	"	" William Crookshanks.]
James White	31	8 5/6	2	10	0	"	" James White.]
Joseph Chapman	31	8 5/6	2	10	0	"	" Joseph Chapman.]
*William Ansley	31	8 5/6	2	10	0	"	" p. ord^r Hen^y Lee.]
John Wheeler	31	8 5/6	2	10	0	"	" John Wheler.]
James Wheeler	31	8 5/6	2	10	0	"	" James Wheler.]
Richard Johnson	31	8 5/6	2	10	0	"	" Richard Johnson.]
John Allia	31	8 5/6	2	10	0	"	[Signed: J. Allier.]
John Hopper	31	8 5/6	2	10	0	"	Mark of John Hopper.]
David Stewart	31	8 5/6	2	10	0	"	" David Stewart.]
*Levi Sharpe	31	8 5/6	2	10	0	"	" p. ord^r Hen^y Lee.]
*James Casey	31	8 5/6	2	10	0	"	" p. ord^r Hen^y Lee.]
Isaac Conroe	31	8 5/6	2	10	0	"	" Isaac Conroe.]
*John Robinson	31	8 5/6	2	10	0	"	" p. ord^r Hen^y Lee.]
Jacob Collatter	31	8 5/6	2	10	0	"	" Jacob Callatter.]
James Kendal	31	8 5/6	2	10	0	"	Mark of James Kendall.]
Dollars		570	171	0	0		

*Exam^d,

Memorandum of money rec^d p^r sundry officer's Acc^t, 1st Nov^r, 1778:

Doll^s.

Bland	101$\frac{74}{90}$
Temple	117$\frac{74}{90}$
Rose	92$\frac{58}{90}$
Nixon	51$\frac{46}{90}$
Watts	18$\frac{88}{90}$
Pemberton	34$\frac{18}{90}$
Yancey	22$\frac{40}{90}$
Hill	24$\frac{58}{90}$
Belfield	65$\frac{88}{90}$
Green	53$\frac{54}{90}$

583$\frac{10}{90}$

Mem^o of Moneys Drawn from The Paymaster-General:

For November, 1777...	2764$\frac{64}{90}$d Dollars.	Abstract for July after sundry Deductions............	2902$\frac{7}{8}$
For December	2780$\frac{28}{90}$ Ditto.		
For Extra Month	3008$\frac{1}{3}$d Ditto.	Deductions, viz:	
For Recruiting money, Jan., 78	800 Ditto.	*1st Troop, Edwd Birchet, sick in Virg^a...............	8$\frac{1}{3}$
For January's Pay, '78.	3218$\frac{74}{90}$ Ditto.	*1 Waggoner	7$\frac{2}{3}$
For February............	3109$\frac{10}{90}$ Ditto.	*Antone son overch^d	8$\frac{1}{3}$
For March	2543$\frac{64}{90}$ Ditto.	*2^d Troop, Saml French, Wagg^r	7$\frac{2}{3}$
For April	2888$\frac{1}{2}$ Ditto.	*W^m McCombs, d^o.	7$\frac{2}{3}$
For May.................	6487$\frac{37}{72}$ Ditto.	*3^d d^o, James Clements, d^o.	7$\frac{2}{3}$
Commissary's Certificate (part of the 6487$\frac{37}{72}$ mentioned to be drawn for May).	3916$\frac{46}{90}$ Ditto.	*4th d^o, John Wallis, sick in Hospital	8$\frac{1}{3}$
For June, after sundry deductions	840 Dollars.	*6th d^o, Wm Davis, Wagg^r.	7$\frac{2}{3}$
		*Surgeon & Mate ..	3$\frac{1}{3}$
			66$\frac{2}{3}$

*Deductions in June, viz:		*Abstract for August	3230$\frac{1}{3}$
		*Add for Diggs Western, omitted	8$\frac{1}{3}$
*John Craigg returnd, Sick, Absent, *46/. of which was for acting as Waggoner.....	£4 16		3238$\frac{1}{3}$
*Waggoner of 2^d Troop	2 6 0	*Deductions	
*D^o, 3^d Troop	2 6 0	*John Sellers, sick in hospital..................	8$\frac{1}{3}$
*D^o, 4th Troop, Charles Lovey.		*Ch^s Grigg, not mustered	8$\frac{1}{3}$ } 25
*D^o, Waggoner of 6th Troop.	[torn]	*John Wallis, sick in hospital..................	8$\frac{1}{3}$
*Am^t of Sunday due bills deducted..............................			
Total deducted £123		Ball^{es}............	3213$\frac{1}{3}$
		*Abstract for September...	2906
		*Add for Diggs Western, omitted	8$\frac{1}{3}$
			2914$\frac{1}{3}$
		*Deduct for John Wallis, sick in hospital ...	8$\frac{1}{3}$
			2906

Colonel Theodoric Bland, a revolutionary hero, was born in Prince George county, Va., January 28, 1742, and died in New York City, June 1, 1790.

His preparatory training was received in England, but his medical preparation was secured in the University of Edinburg. He began his practice of medicine in 1774. He was one of the number who petitioned the house of burgesses to enact a law forbidding any one not properly licensed to practice medicine within the province.

He continued to practice his profession until the breaking out of the Revolution. Joining the colonists he became captain of the first troop of Virginia cavalry. After the enrollment of six companies he entered the service regularly in 1777 with the rank of lieutenant-colonel. Subsequently he attained the rank of colonel, and rendered efficient service throughout the remainder of the war, enjoying the personal confidence and friendship of Washington.

He participated in the battle of Brandywine; and conducted to Charlottesville, Va., the prisoners captured at Saratoga, October 17, 1777.

In civil life he was active. He served one term in the Virginia Senate, and from 1780 to 1783 was a member of the Continental Congress. He opposed the adoption of the present Federal Constitution, but was a member of the first Congress convened under its provisions, his term beginning March 30, 1789. See "The Bland Papers," published 1840–3.

LOUDOUN COUNTY, VA., IN THE REVOLUTION.

The following list of Gentlemen Justices who composed the county Court of Loudoun county, Va., from 1778, to Jan., 1783, served in the following order: 1778, March Term, Thomas Lewis, James Kirk, John Lewis, Farling Ball, George West, and Joshua Daniel. 1778, May Term, Josias Clapham,

Samuel Love, John Orr, Chas. Eskridge, and Farling Ball. 1778, August Term, Josias Clapham, William Douglass, George Summers, John Orr, and John Alexander. 1778, September Term, Josias Clapham, John Orr, Earling Ball, John Lewis, and John Alexander. 1779, May Term, Josias Clapham, Francis Peyton, John Lewis, and Jonathan Davis. 1779, June Term, George West, Pierce Bayly, Farling Ball, Amos Hough, and John Alexander. 1779, July Term, Josias Clapham, Francis Peyton, William Douglass, Samuel Love, John Orr, Hardage Lane, Thomas Respass, Jonathan Davis, Amos Hough, and James Jennings. 1779, October Term, Jonathan Davis, James Jennings, and John Alexander. 1779, November Term, James Coleman, John Orr, John Alexander, and James Jennings. 1780, February Term, Josias Clapham, Samuel Love, John Orr, William Stanhope, and James McIlhaney. 1780, June Term, George Summers, Samuel Love, John Orr, Hardage Lane, Farling Ball, and Jonathan Davis. 1780, October Term, Josias Clapham, Samuel Love, John Orr, Jonathan Davis, and John Alexander. 1780, November Term, Josias Clapham, Samuel Love, John Orr, William Stanhope, Jonathan Davis, and John Tyler. 1781, February Term, John Tyler, John Alexander, Jonathan Davis, William Stanhope, and Thomas Respass. 1781, March Term, Samuel Love, Pierce Bayly, Robert Frier, and James McIlhaney. 1781, April Term, Josias Clapham, John Orr, Hardage Lane, William Stanhope, Francis Peyton, and Robert Frier. 1781, May Term, John Orr, John Tyler, William Stanhope, Cuthbert Harrison, and William Bronough. 1781, June Term, John Orr, Pierce Bayly, William Bronough, James McIlhaney, and Thomas Respass. 1781, September Term, Josias Clapham, John Orr, Jonathan Davis, John Tyler, and Robert Frier. 1782, January Term, Samuel Love, John Tyler, Pierce Bayly, John Lewis, and Farling Ball. 1782, March Term, Samuel Love, Hardage Lane, James Coleman, Thomas Respass, William Stanhope, and William Douglass. 1782, August Term, Francis Peyton, John Tyler, John Orr, James

James McIlhaney, and Robert Frier. 1782, December Term, Leven Powell, James Coleman, Thomas Respass, William Stanhope, and James McIlhaney.

The following list of militia officers were recommended by the Gentlemen Justices of the county Court for Loudoun county, Virginia, to the Governor for appointment from March, 1778, to December, 1782:

Abstract from Court Order Book G., pages 517–522. Persons recommended, with rank: March, 1778: James Whaley, Jr., 2d Lieutenant; William Carnan, Ensign; Daniel Lewis, 2d Lieut.; Josias Miles & Thos. King, Lieutenants; Hugh Douglass, Ensign; Isaac Vandeventer, Lieut.; John Dodd, Ensign. May, 1778: George Summers & Chas. G. Eskridge, Colonels; Wm. McClellan, Robert McClain & John Henry, Captains; Samuel Cox, Major; Frans Russell, Jas. Beavers, Scarlet Burkley, Moses Thomas, Henry Farnsworth, John Russell, Gustavus Elgin, John Miller, Samuel Butcher, Joshua Botts, John Williams, George Tyler, Nathaniel Adams, & Geo. Mason, Lieutenants; Isaac Grant, John Thatcher, William Elliott, Richard Shore, and Peter Benham, Ensigns. 1778, August: Thos. Marks, Wm. Robison, Joseph Butler, and John Linton, Lieutenants; Joseph Wildman and George Asbury, Ensigns. 1778, September: Francis Russeell, Lieut., and George Shrieve, Ensign. 1779, May: Joseph Wildman, Lieut., and Francis Elgin, Jr., Ensign. 1779, June 14: George Kilgour, Lieut., and Jacob Caton, Ensign. 1779, July 12: John Debell, Lieut., and William Hutchison, Ensign. 1779, Oct. 11: Francis Russell, Captain. 1779, Nov. 8th: James Cleveland, Capt.; Thomas Millan, Ensign. 1780, Feb. 14: Thos. Williams, Ensign. 1780, March: John Benham, Ensign. 1780, June: Wethers Smith and William Debell, 2d Lieuts; Francis Adams and Joel White, Ensigns. 1780, August: Robert Russell, Ensign. 1780, October: John Spitzfathem, 1st Lieut.; Thomas Thomas and Matthew Rust, 2d Lieuts.; Nicholas Minor, Jr., David Hopkins, Wm. McGeath and Samuel Oliphant, Ensigns; Charles Bennett, Captain. 1780, Nov.: James Coleman, Esq., Colo.; George West, Lt.-Colo.; James McIlhaney, Major. 1781, February : Simon Triplett, Colo.; John Alexander, Lt.-Colo.; Jacob Reed, Major ; John Linton, Capt.; Wm. Debell and Joel White, Lieuts.; Thomas Minor, Ensign ; Thomas Shores, Capt.; John Taylor and Thomas Beaty, Lieuts.; John McClain, Ensign. 1781, March : John McGeath, Capt.; Ignatius Burnes, Capt.; Hugh Douglass, 1st Lieut.; John Corneliscn, 2d Lieut.; Joseph Butler & Conn Oneale, Lieuts.; John Jones, Jr., Ensign ; William Taylor, Major 1st Battalion ; James Coleman, Colo.; George West, Lt.-Colo.; Josiah Maffett, Capt.; John Binns, 1st Lieut.; Charles Binns, Jr., 2d Lieut., and Joseph Hough, Ensign ; 1781, April : Samson Trammell, Capt.; Spence Wiggington & Smith King, Lieuts. 1781, May : Thomas Respess, Esq., Major ; Hugh Douglass, Gent, Capt.; Thos. King, Lieut.; Wm. T. Mason, Ensign ; Samuel Noland, Capt.; Abraham Dehaven & Enoch Thomas, Lieuts.; Isaac Dehaven and Thomas Vince, Ensigns ; James McIlhaney, Capt.; Thomas Kennan, Capt.; John Bagley, 1st Lieut. 1781, June : Enoch Furr & George Rust, Lieuts.; Withers Berry and William Hutchison (son of Benjamin), Ensigns. 1781, Sept.: Gustavus Elgin, Capt.; John Littleton, Ensign. 1782, Jan.: Wm. Mc-Clellan, Capt.; (Feb., 1782) Wm. George, Timothy Hixon and Joseph Butler, Capts. 1782, March : James McIlhaney, Capt.; George West, Colo.; Thos. Respess, Lt.-Colo. 1782, July : Samuel Noland, Major ; Jas. Lewin Gibbs, 2d Lieut., and Giles Turley, Ensign. 1782, August : Enoch Thomas, Capt.; Samuel Smith, Lieut.; Matthias Smitley, 1st Lieut.; Charles Tyler and David Beaty, Ensigns. 1782, Dec.: Thos. King, Capt.; Wm. Mason, 1st Lieut., and Silas Gilbert, Ensign.

Soldiers' wives and children, how supplied with the necessaries of life :

1778, November 9th. John Alexander to furnish Elizabeth Welch, her husband being in the army.

1778, Nov. 15. George Emrey to furnish the child of Jacob

Rhodes, said Jacob being in the Continental army.   William Douglass to furnish Mary Rhodes, her husband being in the army.   George Summers to furnish William Gilmore, his son being in the army.

1778, Dec. 14.   Leven Powell to furnish Andrew Laswell.

1779, Feb. 8th.   Samuel Triplett to furnish the wife of Hugh Henderson.   Josias Clapham to furnish Ann Philips.

1779, March 8th.   Farling Ball to furnish the widow of Joseph Collens and the wife of William Eaton.   William Stanhope to furnish Ann Barton.

1779, April.   John Lewis, Gent, to furnish the wife of Shadrack Reeder.   Hardage Lane to furnish Sarah Gilmore, wife of William, whose son is in the army.   William Ellzey to furnish wife of Shadrack Reeder.   Josiah Clapham appointed to apply to the Treasurer for 500 pounds to be placed in the hands of John Lewis, Gent, to supply the necessaries of life for those who have husbands or children in the Continental army.

1779, May.   Farling Ball to furnish Edward McGinnis and William Means.   John Alexander to furnish Ann Barton. (William Stanhope to furnish Ann Barton, July, 1779.)

August, 1779.   Robert Jamison to furnish Conard Shanks, whose son is in the army.   Jonathan Davis to furnish Mary Stoker.   Pierce Bayly do. wife of Joel Coleman.

1780, March.   John Tyler do. Jemima Coleman.

1780, July.   Simon Triplett to furnish Jemima Coleman, wife of Joel, not exceeding two barrels of flour and 200 pounds of Pork.

1780, September.   John Alexander to furnish Ann Barton one barrel of corn and fifty pounds of Pork.   Josias Clapham do. Catherine Henderson, widow of Adam Henderson.   William Cavans to furnish Ann Richards, her husband being in the army, and Isabella Collens, widow of Joseph.

1780, November.   Wm. Bronough do. Sarah Russell, wife of Samuel.

1781, April.   William Owsley to supply Hannah Rice &

two children, the family of James Rice, who died in the Continental Army.

1781, May. Adam Vincel to supply Mary Tritipoe, wife of Conrad, her husband being in the army.

1781, Sept. Joseph Thomas to supply the widow of David Hamilton (a soldier who was killed in the Continental army).

1782, Jan. John Tyler, Gent, to furnish the family of Cornelius Slacht, he being an 18 months' draft).

1782, Feb. John Lewis, Gent, to furnish Eleanor Wilcox (a soldier's wife).

1782, March. William Douglass to furnish Eleanor Wilcox, agreeable to an order of the last Court directed to John Lewis, Gent, the said Lewis declining.

Treasurer to pay sundry persons for furnishing supplies as per their several accounts:

1778, May 12. William Ellzey, Esq., £3–8–9 on account of wife of John Stoker and £2–10 ditto. for wife of Shadrack Reeder. Wm. Douglass, £50–14–6 as per acct.

1778, June 9. Andrew Adam, £13–5 for Margaret Hill (service).

1778, Aug. 10. Farling Ball, £4 16–9. John Alexander, £5.

1778, Sept. 14. Leven Powell, Gent, £6–1. William Douglass, Gent, £47–7. John Tyler, £3–19–6.

1778, Sept. 15. Farling Ball, Gent, £1–17–6.

1778, Nov. 9. Andrew Adam, £16–15.

1778, Nov. 15. Daniel Losh, £24–6–9. Geo. West, Gent, £3–10. Farling Ball, ditto., £2.

1778, Dec. 14. Joshua Daniel, Gent, £9–15. John Orr, £7–16.

1779, Feb. 9. Farling Ball, £18–13–9. Wm. Douglass, £53–9–1. Chas. Binns, £3 on acct. of widow of Hamilton.

1779, April. John Alexander, £68–15. Daniel Losh, £10–3 7. William Douglass, Gent, £28–16. Andrew Adam, £17–13. Wm. Ellzey, £24–2.

1779, May. Geo. West, Gent, £42–14.

1779, June. Andrew Adam, £12–3–6. John Orr, £43–16. Wm. Douglass, £18 16. Farling Ball, Gent, £175–5.

1779, July. John Alexander, £18.

1779, August. Jacob Tracey, £20 for nursing & Burying Sophia Harris, the wife of a continental soldier.

1779, Oct. Pierce Bayly, Gent, £10. Simon Triplett, £43–9–10. Robert Jamison, £30. Jonathan Davis, £32–10. Farling Ball, £61–10–6. Wm. Douglass, Gent, £51–15.

1779. John Orr, Gent, £93–8–3. Leven Powell, Gent, £69–10. Wm. Stanhope, Gent, £4–4.

1780, Jan. Jonathan Davis, Gent, £50. Wm. Stanhope, Gent, £4–4.

1780, February. Thomas George, £206. Israel Thompson, £119–2. George Emrey, £46–19.

1780, March. Hardage Lane, Gent, £83–8.

1780, April. Thomas George, £15. Farling Ball, Gent, £99–6. Wm. Douglass, Gent, £69–10.

1780, June. John Tyler, Gent, £40. Pierce Bayly, Gent, £20.

1780, August. John Orr, Gent, £500. Wm. Douglass, Gent, £44.

1780, November. Thomas George, £221. Farling Ball, £50. George Tyler, Gent, £8. George Emrey, Gent, £163–12.

1781, March. John Orr, Gent, £431–16· Wm. Cavans, £120.

1782, Feb. John Orr, as per acct. for furnishing Mary Butler, a soldier's wife, with necessaries.

VIRGINIA.

Clerk's Office of the County Court of Loudoun County, to wit: November 12th, 1902.

I, W. Dade Hempstone, Clerk of the County Court of the County aforesaid, certify that the foregoing is a true copy from the records of said County.

Given under my hand this 12th day of November, 1902.

W. D. HEMPSTONE, C. C.

LIST OF MILITIAMEN IN CAPTAIN JOHN GIVENS' COMPANY, AUGUSTA COUNTY, VIRGINIA, FROM OCTOBER 16, 1777, TO MARCH 15, 1782, INCLUSIVE.

Jacob Barrior,
Andrew Erwin,
Wm. Dickson,
Leonard Williams,
James Donohoe,
Samuel Givens, Sr.,
James Craig, Sr.,
Peter Bleake,
Lieutenant Robert Campbell,
James Lamb,
David Baird,
John Lockry,
John Lemmon,
John Givens,
Wm. Baird,
Robert Givens,
John Castle,
Robert Baird,
Thomas Baird,
Peter Carrol,
William Bell,
Wm. Patterson,
Christopher Liner,
Jacob Stull,
Zachariah Stull,
Robert Rankin,
James Henderson,
William Henderson,
John Morrison,
William Rankin,

James Rankin,
Joseph Hannah,
Neil Hughes,
Andrew Mitchell,
Moses Trapp,
David Hannah,
Samuel Bell,
George Hooke,
Robert Crawford,
John Harper,
William Craig,
Robert Reaburn,
James Craig, Jr.,
John Craig,
James Crawford,
James Patterson,
Boswell Halkett,
John Craig, 2nd,
George Crawford,
Robert Craig,
Joseph Henderson,
George Craig,
John Lilley,
Jacob Snowdon,
Thomas Price,
John Crawford
John Campbell,
William Crawford,
James Givens,
William Givens,

Joseph Gasper,	Samuel Carrol,
Richard Rankin,	David Laird,
Wm. Thompson,	John Hook,
Joseph Thompson,	Thomas Rhodes.
Isaac Rankin,	

PENSION DECLARATION OF ROBERT GIVENS, LINCOLN COUNTY, KY., SEPT. 24, 1824, AGED 75 YEARS.

I was drafted for 3 months' service as a militia Man in 1776 or 1777; was a private in Capt. John Lewis's company which I joined at Staunton, Va. From there we marched to Warm Springs; then to Back Creek; then we crossed the mountain to Levi Moor's; then to Warnk's Fort, and at the end of my time of services was discharged by my Captain.

In 1778 I entered the services as a volunteer in Capt. John Given's company, Augusta County militia, which I joined at Mr. McKetrick's at the foot of the mountain; from there we moved to Warm Springs, then to Col. Anderson's, then to the Big Level, then to the Big Savannah, then to Col. Donnely's Fort, where we joined the force of Col. Lewis and I was discharged.

Again in 1778 I volunteered in Capt. Richard May's company, which company I joined at Abbington, Washington county, Va., then marched to Logan's Fort, and continued in the service for eleven months, I was discharged by Lieutenant Samuel Crand of Capt. Richard May's company.

In 1781 I was called out to guard the prisoners taken at the battle of Cowpens, where I served for 15 days & discharged.

In 1781 I was ordered out as a militiaman; was at Charlotteville under Capt. John Givens, Col. Huggard commander; marched to Richmond in the presence of Cornwallis; had an engagement with the British. We then marched to old Jamestown where we had a second engagement with the British; we then marched to a point ten miles below Richmond, where I was discharged, July, 1781.

1782. Served as a sub-officer in the place of George Givens in Capt. John Daugherty's company; later under Capt. John Martin, in the command of Col. Logan, whose company I joined at Scotch's Station; went to Lexington, then to Brant Station, then to Blue Creek, where Col. Todd was defeated under Gen. Clarke.

Bible record of the family of Robert Givens, of Lincoln county, Kentucky, and Martha his wife, copied from a leaf out of their Bible, filed by his widow in the U. S. Pension Office, Sept. 24, 1824, with her application for a Pension :

1. Robert Givens,   b. May 22, 1759; d. Oct. 26, 1833.
                    m. Martha ——, July 4, 1782; b. July
                    31, 1761.

Their children :

1. John Allen,	b. Aug. 31, 1784.
2. James,	b. Jan. 22, 1786.
3. Rebecca Brown,	b. Apr. 19, 1788.
4. Martha,	b. Dec. 24, 1790.
5. Sarah Mitchell,	b. June 14, 1793.
6. Benjiman,	b. Apr. 14, 1796.
7. Robert,	b. Sept. 6, 1799.
8. Molly,	b. Feb. 27, 1802.

John Allen Givens settled in Monroe County, Ind.

The Courts Martial Record of Augusta county, Va., filed in the office of the clerk of The Corporation Court for the city of Staunton, shows that in the latter part of Sept., 1781, Capt. Givens' company was ordered to rendezvous under the command of Lieutenant-Col. Samuel Vance.

Palmer's *Calendar of Va. State Papers*, Vol. 2, page 514, shows that Col. Vance was, on Oct. 1, 1781, in camp four miles below Williamsburg with a reinforcement of militia

15

from Augusta, Co. In the Calendar Col. Vance's name is spelled Varne, which is clearly an error.

His command, including Capt. Givens' company, was then only a few miles distant from Yorktown, in the siege, of which they participated.

REVOLUTIONARY ARMY PRISONERS.

List of American prisoners confined on board the British ship "Torbay" in the harbor of Charleston, South Carolina, during the war of the Revolution, 1780–1, many of whom were from the State of Virginia, filed by the heirs of Capt. Jacob Cohen (Cowen), of Cumberland county, Virginia, with their Memorial to the 26th Congress for compensation for the service of their father as captain of a company of troopers of the Virginia Continental Line, of which the following is a copy, spelling included (Pub.):

TORBAY PRISON SHIP, CHARLES TOWN HARBOUR, }
                                    18th May, 1781. }

Roll of the militia Prisoners on board said ship:

William Axon, Jr., Samuel Ash, George Authur, John Anthony, Ralph Atmore, Major John Barnwell, Major John Baddely, Capt. Edward Barnwell, Capt. Peter Bounethean, Henry Bembridge, Lieut. John Black, William Branford, Joseph Ball, Robert Branwell, Joseph Bee, Nath. Blindell, James Bricker, Francis Bailey, William Basquin, Johnathan Clarke, Thos. Cockeran, Thos. Cooke, John Calhoone (protection), Capt. Jos. Cray Aug. 16, '80, Norwood Conyers, James Cox, Richard Cummings, Jacob Cohen, Robert Dewar, Wm. Depanseure, Joseph Dunlap, Richard Edmonds, Thomas Eueleigh, John Edwards, Jr., John Warren Edwards, Thomas Elliott, Sr., Joseph Elliott, Jr., John Evans, John Eberly, John Egan (protection), Wm. Elliott, Benjamin Guerard,

John Gibbons, Thos. Grayson, Peter Guerard, William Graves, Christian Geir, Philip Gadsden, John Graves, Joseph Glover, Francis Geott, Mitchell George, Lieut. Wm. Harvey, Jacob Henry, David Hamilton, John B. Holmes, Wm. Holmes, Thos. Hughes, James Heward, Thos. Harris, Wm. Hornby, George Jones, Daniel Jacobs, Charles Kent, Henry Keunon, John Kain, Capt. Sam. Lockhart (Aug. 16, '80), Nathaniel Libby, Thos. Listen, Lieut. Stephens Lee, Thos. Legare, John Leperne, Henry Leybert, Philip Meyers, John Michael, John Minott, Sr., John Moncrief, Chas. Magdalen, John Minott, Jr., Samuel Miller, Col. Stephen Moore (Aug. 16, '80), William Murphy, George Monks, John Morgan, Dr. George Moss, Alfred Merriett, Lieut. Samuel Miller, John Neville, Jr., Wm. Neville, John Owen, Samuel Priolean, Sr., Philip Priolean, Chas. Pickney, Jr., James Poyas, Job Palmer, Jos. Robinson, Thos. Revin, Daniel Rhodes, Joseph Righton, Jon. Scott, Sr., Wm. Snelling, John Stephenson, Jr., Daniel Stephenson, Paul Snyder, Samuel Smith, Abraham Seavers, Rippely Singleton, Samuel Scotton, William Sayle (protection, 61 yrs. of age, does not want to be exchanged), Stephen Shrewsbury, James Sonsiger, John Tandus, Paul Tayloe, Lieut. Sim. White, William Wigg, Jas. Williams, Chas. Warham (ct. dst.), Thos. Waring, Sr., Richard Waring, Isaac White, Geo. Welch, Benj. Wheeler, John Waters, Jr., Wm. Wilcocks, David Warham, Wm. Wilkie, Thos. You, Richard Yeadon.

A LIST OF THE OFFICERS OF THE VIRGINIA LINE WHO SERVED AT THE SIEGE OF YORK, OCTOBER 30TH, 1781.

Lt.-Colonel Gaskens.   Cr. as received by Cap. Parker.
Major Willes.*

* Not credited.

Major Paulson. { Credited on settlement with Audrs. Va.
Not mentioned of whom received.

Capts. Overton,   ditto.   ditto.

Cap. Thos. Parker,   ditto.   ditto.
  of 2d V. Regt.

  Woodson,   ditto.   ditto. } each $66\frac{60}{90}$
  Lamme,   ditto.   ditto. } dollars.
  Fields,   ditto.   ditto.
  Williams,   ditto.   ditto.
  Lovely,   ditto.   ditto.
  Warman,*   ditto.   ditto.
  Crane,*
  Russell,†   Credited with the Audrs. Virg., $66\frac{60}{90}$.
  Alex. Parker,   ditto.
  Delplane,   ditto.
  Mayborn,   ditto. } each $66\frac{60}{90}$ Dollars.
  Coverly,   ditto.
  Andw. Lewis,   ditto.

LIST OF OFFICERS.

Lieuts.   Askredge,   Audrs. Va.
          Stokely,‡
          Scarborough, $66\frac{60}{90}$.
          Miller,§
          Hays,‡
          Clayton,*
          Darby.* ‡
Ensigns   Barbour,*
          Eustace.*
Cap.   Thos. Payne. $66\frac{60}{90}$.

* Not credited.

† Do. settled with me nor Cr. with Auditors.

‡ Not settled with me.

§ Lieutenant William Miller, of Artillery, has credited on settlement with
Audrs. Virg. sundries received at York Town to the amount of £22 7s. 10d., Va.
Currency, equal to $47\frac{57\frac{1}{2}}{90}$ dollars.

Lieut.   Jno. Harris, dragoons, cred. with A. Dunscomb.
              Trabue,   ditto.   ditto.
              Bailis.*
Chaplains   Alexander Balmain,*
              John Hart.*
Surgeon   George Monro, Audrs. Va.
Do. mate   George Yates.*
                   Total, 35.

The above is a Copy of a list of officers Contained among the papers of Capt. Williams, of the Maryland line, and who received goods of him at Yorktown, in Virginia, the Vouchers for which he says he delivered to Col. Carrington, Agreeably to a General order.

                                   JOHN WHITE, *Ast. Comiss.*

June 28th, 1785.

GARRISON AT WEST POINT, JUNE 21, 1784.

GARRISON OF WEST POINT, }
June 21st, 1784. }

Sir : We the late officers of the American Army, deranged by the Resolution of Congress of the 2nd instant having been reduced to the necessity of adopting a measure, which may possibly by some be thought unjustifiable without the motives and reasons of our conduct being fully explained have thought proper in this collective manner to communicate the transaction and the reasons on which it is grounded.

From the assurances of the Commander-in-Chief, and the other characters who were intrusted by Congress to arrange the troops who were to remain in service after the 1st of January, 1784, and in whom we placed the fullest confidence, we

* Not credited.

had every prospect of Punctual Payment for our Services.
With this view we gave up every idea of business and were at
very great Expense in making our arrangements as military
Characters. Having made every Preparation for the year
The Resolution of Congress which dismissed us, arrived at a
very unexpected period. Being made however by the Sov-
ereign power of the Country we acquiessed with that cheerfull-
ness and obedience which becomes Servants of the public.
The same Resolution of Congress by which we obtained our
dismission granted us only two months pay in notes of the
Financier, and directed final settlement Certificates for the
discharge of the other four—upon an adjustment of our
accounts we found this sum by no means sufficient to satisfy
those demands which had necessarily incurred during a service of six months. In a situation so distressing we looked
around for a possibility of Relief—Nothing presented itself
but an order on Mr. Lovell, which you had placed in the
hands of the Pay master for the officers subsistence, after de-
ducting three months subsistence for those who were to remain
in service, including the Invalids we found there was a
sufficient sum to furnish us with six weeks pay, and on an
application to the person with whom it was intrusted for the
purpose of exchange, he delivered the money, taking our receipts to that amount received of the Regimentel Pay Master
on account of our four months pay for the year 1784.

Thus Sir have we stated to you in the clearest manner the
measures we have taken and the necessity which induced
them. We fully persuaded ourselves they will be considered
as perfectly just on our part and meet the approbation of all
Concerned.

            We are, Sir, with great regard and Esteem,
                Your most obedient humble Servants,
                NAT. STONE,   HENRY JACKSON,
                JOB. SUMMER,   C. GIBBS,
                ISAAC FORYE,   WM. HUTT,
                NATHAN LEAVENWORTH, G. BAUMAN,

JOHN MILLS,	J. WOFFY,
JONATHAN HASKELL,	S. HUKSON,
GAM. BRADFORD,	E. FENNO,
JAMES SAWYER,	WM. RICHARD,
C. SELDEN,	JOSEPH BLISS,
JOSEPH POTTER,	CALEB SWAN,
I. MORROW,	JOHN ADAMS,
HENRY NELSON,	JAMES SEVER,
H. CUNNINGHAM,	E. HASKELL,
THOMAS SMITH,	J. LARD,
JOHN REED,	ROBT. H. W. BOWLES,
P. PHELON,	JAMES BRADFORD.

On the back of the above letter the following is written:

From the late officers of the Garrison at West Point, July 11, 1784.

WEST POINT.

West Point, the seat of the United States Military Academy, is situated on the Hudson River, 52 miles north of New York City.

Its importance as a strategic point for the defense of the Hudson river and the circumjacent country was early appreciated. Accordingly it was carefully fortified at the opening of the Revolution.

The establishment of a military training school dates back to 1776, when a committee of the Continental Congress was appointed "to prepare and bring in a plan of a military Academy at the Army."

Washington called attention to the subject in 1793 and again in 1796. The final act establishing such a school is dated March 16, 1802.

The accompanying letter, written after the close of the war and addressed presumably to the War office of the government, plainly indicates that official promises were not scrupulously observed, even by the fathers of the Republic.

LETTER OF LIEUT.-COL. EDW. ANTILL TO PAYMASTER-GENERAL OF THE ARMY.

NEW YORK, *July 17th, 1784.*

Sir : Major Lloyd informs me you wished for an explanation relative to some charges in my public account against certain officers then belonging to the Regiment. I will take up that of Captain McConnel for instance (the others are in the same predicament). I advanced Captain McConnel for the recruiting service at different times as per receipts 1104 dollars, together with twenty dollars as per memorandum Book dated in Feb., 1777. The whole of these 1124 dollars were given him from the time he received his recruiting instructions in 76 to March, 77—In the beginning of March, 1777. I received a letter from Mr. R. Peters,* Secretary of war, dated Baltimore, Feb. 24, 1777, in the following words : "Sir, congress having received intelligence of the enemy's being reinforced in New Jersey Very considerably it becomes absolutely necessary both for the preservation of the army under General Washington and to check the progress of a cruel and remorseless enemy that he be joined immediately by all the forces that can possibly be procured. You have the resolve of Congress on that head inclosed by Direction of the Board of War with which they request you will instantly comply by sending all the men raised in your Regiment. Let them bring what Arms Blankets and clothes they have or *can by any means obtain* and the deficiency will be supplied at

---

* Richard Peters, a prominent jurist and agriculturist, was born at Blockley, near Philadelphia, August 22, 1744, and died there August 21, 1828. Lanman says 1824.

He spoke German fluently and was noted for his wit and humor. He achieved some success in the legal profession. At the opening of the Revolution he became a captain of a company of volunteers. This position, however he held but a short time, when he was assigned by Congress to the Board of War, of which he was made Secretary, from June 13, 1776, to Dec., 1781. He was a member of Congress in 1782–3. From 1789 to the time of his death he was a Federal Judge in Pennsylvania.

Philadelphia or Head Quarters. *Let nothing delay your* immediate march either by companies or parts of companies as you can get them together as the safety of our country much depends on the exertions of its army at this trying period and it is hoped no care or pains of yours will be wanting when all we hold dear and valuable demands them. Signed Richard Peters Secry." Upon receipt of this letter anxious to comply with its contents, and unable to remove the troops without a considerable sum of money, they having received neither pay or subsistence since engaged, many of them in Nov. and Dec., 1776, I procured a loan from Lowman and Hubley of 6,000 Dollars, and from Mr. Atlee of 4,000 Dollars, 14th of March or thereabout, for which I gave them my Draughts on Congress, which were accepted, and for which sum I stand charged on the same day being hurried thro' my wish to meet the requests of Congress and not having time to take Receipts I began to pay out this money, and as I paid it Entered it in my book, I was obliged to received the money from those Gentlemen in such as they had, and I paid to Capt. McConnel that Day.

801	Continental	Dollars.
49	Maryland	Do.
58	Do.	Do.
37	Continental	Do.
55	Continental	Do.

1,000 making in the whole.

Thus stands the matter as to this charge, and I am ready and willing to give you or Capt. McConnel any further light in the business in my power. The entry in my book is fair and clear, and I am willing to sware to the best of my knowledge and belief to its Justice.

I am with regard,

Your Very Humble Servant,

EDW. ANTILL.

The foregoing letter was addressed to John Pierce,* Pay-Master-General, Philadelphia, and seems to be post-marked New York, August 1st.

Lieutenant-Colonel Edward Antill was an officer in the 2d Canadian (known also as "Congress Own") regiment, from the 22d of January, 1776, to the first of January, 1783. He was captured during his time of service, but was exchanged November 2, 1780. His retirement from the army occurred January 1, 1783.

The other field officers of his regiment in the order of service were:

Colonel Moses Hazen, January 22, 1776, to January 1, 1783.
Major John Taylor, Nov. 13, 1776, to ———.
Major Joseph Torrey, Jan. 9, 1777, to ———.
Major Tarlton Woodson, May 1, 1777, to March 1, 1782.
Major James R. Reid, Sept. 1, 1777, to ———.
Major Anthony Slin, ——— to Jan. 1, 1783.

A. DUNCOMB TO JOS. HOWELL, ESQ.

RICHMOND, *March 27, 1791.*

Dear Sir : I suppose if I were to write you a letter in which you would be told that fate, fortune, or something, or somebody else has left, or given, or put in the power of you to command a good chew of Tobacco, that you would be attentive to give me thanks for the information. Why I thus write and why the real cause judge you? upon looking over my files I can boast of receiving one letter from you since my arrival at this place, but it is equal with other great men who

---

* John Pierce, from Connecticut, was an Assistant Paymaster-General in the Continental army during the early part of the Revolution. He is reported, June 1, 1779, Deputy Paymaster-General; and on January 17, 1781, Paymaster-General. He died in New York about August, 1788.

have not given me more—enough. Will you look into the return of Posey's Detachment? and there you will find that Capt. Scott was only settled for up to the rank of the commencement of his account—this happened in consequence of his having been Mustered on Command, which not being fully explained to me at the time the agent *made the claim for all pay due the Detachment*, remained to be settled thereafter, and various are the instances of after-settlements. to this and other matters let me call your *serious attention.* if you will examine thoroughly, you will find that I have lodged many accounts with you that remain as yet unsettled and which are the sources of disagreeable and fruitless applications. pray have all closed that can be and inform those that cannot, and give me a power of satisfying the minds and wishes of the needy and the concerned, for I am almost daily applyed to on one score or the other. Subsistence, Pay, &c., are the themes.

In haste yours,

[Signed]   A. Duncomb.

Jos. Howell, Esqr.,
  Acting Pay Master General,
    Philadelphia, Pa.

[copy.]

Thomas Posey was born on the Potomac river, in Fairfax Co., Va., July 9, 1750, and died in Shawneetow, Ill., March 19, 1818. His education was acquired in the common schools. At the age of nineteen he removed to what is now West Virginia.

As quarter-master in Colonel Andrew Lewis's command, he participated in the defeat of the Indians at Point Pleasant, October 10, 1774, during Dunmore's War. The following year he was commissioned captain in the 7th Virginia Continental regiment, and was present at the defeat of Lord Dunmore, July 8, 1776.

During the remainder of the war he served in New Jersey with Daniel Morgan and Horatio Gates.

The war having closed, he settled in Spottsylvania county, Va., and was made colonel of the county militia. In 1793 he was commissioned a brigadier-general and assigned to duty under Wayne in the Northwest. He resigned Feb. 28, 1794, and located in Kentucky, where he served a term in the State Senate. He was finally made major-general and assigned to the organization of state troops. Having removed to Louisiana, he served, by appointment, as U. S. Senator in 1812–13. Subsequently, he acted as governor of Indiana Territory to the date of its admission as a state.

His life was active and productive, the legitimate results of innate ability. In his sphere he was the equal of any of his contemporaries.

NEWMAN FAMILY OF VIRGINIA.

THE family name Newman is of the same origin as that of Newcome—"stranger newly arrived." It was originally spelled Nieuweman ; Latinized, Novus Homo. (See Patronymica Britannica, by Mark Antony Lower, page 237.) The original spelling would seem to indicate an Anglo-Saxon origin.

Among the members of the family who came to Virginia and left their impress upon the early history of the colony were Robert, William, John, and Thomas Newman. They were, doubtless, relatives of John Newman, grocer, a member of the London Virginia Company in 1609, and in all probability came to Virginia at his suggestion in order to better their fortunes. Their descendants are now scattered throughout the South and West; many of them are prominent in the walks of social and business life.

First. Robert Newman arrived in Virginia in the ship "Furtherance," in 1618, aged 19 years. He was living in Elizabeth City county in 1624. On May 11, 1635, he obtained a patent for 450 acres of land, which he afterwards assigned to Richard Bennett. (See William and Mary College Quarterly, Vol. 9, page 139.) This is the earliest patent granted to any one of the name of which the compiler has record.

Robert Newman undoubtedly married and left, with other children, two sons, William and John. William was living in York county in 1698. (See William and Mary Quarterly, Vol. 4, page 250.) It is believed that he married and was the father of John, who in 1709 was "summoned to answer a

238

presentment of the grand jury against him for absenting himself from Divine Service." (York county records.)

Second. John Newman, second son of Robert, married Ruth Taberer, daughter of Thomas, of Isle of Wight county. The will of Thomas Taberer, dated Jan. 14, 1692, and proven in 1699, refers to his "son" John Newman, and his grandchildren, Thomas and Isabella Newman, to whom he leaves Basses' Choice. John Newman died about 1700; his will, bearing date Dec. 11, 1695, was proven in Isle of Wight county in 1700. In it he refers to his wife Ruth, and to his two children as son Thomas and daughter Isabella.

Second. William Newman, aged 35 years, arrived in 1622, in the ship "Furtherance" (Vol. 7, William and Mary Quarterly, page 218), and settled in Isle of Wight county, where, on Aug. 26, 1643, he was granted a patent for 550 acres of land, situated "Northerly towards the Sunken marsh, Easterly upon a swamp, Southerly towards the lower Chippokes Creek." (See William and Mary College Quarterly, Vol. 9, page 144.)

In 1648, Sept. 25, George Codd confessed a judgment in favor of William Newman for 500 lbs. of tobacco, with costs, &c., York county, Virginia.

In 1658 "William Newman, as security for Gyles Thurloe, confesseth judgement to Capt. Gyles Brent for eighteen hundred pounds of sweet-scented tobacco and caske, which is ordered to be paid, with costs, &c.," York county, Virginia.

In 1662 William Newman served as a juror at an inquest over the body of a woman "accidentally shot by the glance of a ball intended for a wild beast." Whether he was William Sr. or William Jr., son of Robert, who was living in York county in 1698, or what relation existed between the two, the writer is not informed. (See William and Mary College Quarterly, Vol. 4, page 250.)

[The will of William Newman, Sr., dated Jan. 20, 1669, was proven in York county court, July 25, 1670, leaving his wife Priscilla executrix; from the will we infer he left no

issue, his wife having been a widow at their marriage, with
an only daughter Joan, who married Lawrence of Compton-
Chamberlin, in Wiltshire, England.

Third. *John Newman*, aged 24 years, emigrated to Virginia
in 1635 in the ship "Globe," and is believed to be the same
John for whose transportation Capt. William Pearce was
granted 50 acres of land the same year. (See presently.)

Fourth. *Thomas Newman*, the brother of John, came to Virginia
in 1635 in the ship "Plaine Joan," aged 15 years. (See later.)

First.   John Newman, as we have seen, emigrated to Virginia in 1635, and settled in James City county, where on
Apr. 1, 1644, Henry Thompson assigned to him one hundred
and fifty acres of land, situated upon "Smith's Fort Creek,
joining the lands of John Buckmaster, which was patented to
the said Buckmaster, which patent was renewed to the said
John Newman" in 1644; here he appears to have resided for
about seven years, as between 1652 and 1677 he had acquired
in the Northern Neck by letters patent, grant, and deeds,
about 4000 acres of land, situated on both sides of Moratico
Creek, in the present counties of Lancaster and Richmond.
He resided near Tarplay's Point, then known as Moratico or
Newman's Neck.   He married, probably, a daughter of Paul
Woodbridge (about 1655), in the then Rappahannock county.
Issue: three children of whom we have record.   His wife
died before 1677, as she is not referred to in the will of her
husband, who died during that year.   His will proven at
Tappahannock court house, Rappahannock county, shows
him to have been a man of wealth, and refers to his children
in the following order:

1. Alexander, "my oldest son," barely of age in 1677.
2. Samuel, a minor in 1677.
3. John, a minor in 1677.

SECOND GENERATION.

First.   Alexander Newman, 1st of John and his wife, *nee*
Woodbridge, born about 1656, the same as "Captain Alex-

ander " of the Richmond county records, married Elizabeth
————, who was, probably, a kinswoman of the Brocken-
broughs. He was a member of the House of Burgesses in
1694, from Richmond county, and but for his death at the
early age of 42, would probably have achieved much distinction. His will, proven in 1698, in Richmond county, is lost
with will book 1, but the records that have been preserved
show that he left his property to his cousin, Thomas Newman,
and to William Dunn ; that he was a wealthy man of much
local prominence ; and that he inherited his father's passion
for acquiring land. He left no issue.

Second. Samuel Newman, 2d of John and his wife, *nee*
Woodbridge, born about 1658, married ———— ————, received his portion of his father's estate in tobacco, the money
of those days. In 1687 he was granted 559 acres of land in
Henrico county, and in 1690, 292 acres in the same county.
The date of his marriage, the name of his wife, and the dates
of their death are unknown to the writer ; lack of time has
prevented a more thorough investigation of the records as to
him and his family ; it is, however, certain that of his children there were the following sons :

1. Samuel, } (See later.)
2. Jonathan, }

Third. John Newman, the third son and youngest child
of John, the immigrant, and his wife, ————, *nee* Woodbridge, born ————, was a minor in 1679, as shown by a deed
of his brother Alexander Newman to Paul Woodbridge, his
guardian ; is not mentioned in the records of old Rappahannock, Essex or Richmond counties after 1679 ; but the
records of Lancaster county show that the land acquired by
him under the will of his father was disposed of soon after he
attained his majority. He is believed to have settled in
Maryland, and to be the John Newman who was the progenitor of the Maryland branch of the family.*

* For his descendants, see manuscript notes by the Publisher.

THIRD GENERATION.

First.   Samuel Newman, 1st of Samuel, of John, the immigrant, settled in the western portion of Spottsylvania county, and in 1748 he was administrator of the estate of his brother Jonathan, who died a resident of Augusta county. (See liber ———, Augusta county ; also, Liber 1, folios 100 and 220, Shenandoah county, Va.). In August, 1757, Samuel obtained a patent for 210 acres of land in Augusta county ; he appears to have removed to Frederick county, and after the organization of Shenandoah he was a resident of said county. (No further record.)

Second.   Jonathan Newman, 2d of Samuel, of John the immigrant, born in Lower Virginia, settled in Augusta county, where he married, ———, Mary ———. Issue, two children :
  1. John.
  2. Walter.

Jonathan Newman died before Feb. 20, 1748, and after the settlement of his estate by his brother Samuel, his widow, with her two minor children, removed to Frederick county, now Shenandoah, where she married Mr. States, and where she was living in 1779. The records of Shenandoah county do not disclose any further information concerning her or her second husband.

FOURTH GENERATION.

First.   John Newman, 1st of Jonathan and Mary, born in Augusta county ; m. Hannah ———. No further record.

FOURTH GENERATION.

Second.   Walter Newman, 2d of Jonathan and Mary, born in Augusta county, Va. After the death of his father removed, with his mother and uncle Samuel, to what is now Shenandoah county. He was a soldier in Dunmore's war and a large planter. Married Catherine ———. Issue, ten children :

  16

1. John,   (See later.)
2. Jonathan, b. ———— ; was living in 1818. No further [record.
3. Mary,   b. ———— ; married Daniel Moffett, born Jan. 20, 1765, son of John Moffett. She received £100 by the will of her father.
4. Elizabeth, b. ———— ; married Zachariah Hay. Received £100 by the will of her father.
5. Catherine, b. ———— ; married Bernard Peel. Received £100 by the will of her father.
6. Samuel,   (See later.)
7. Ann,   b. ————. Received £100 by the will of her
8. Walter,   (See later.)   [father.
9. Lydia,   b. ———— ; married Benjamin Huff. Received £100 by the will of her father.
10. Margaret, b. ———— ; married Martin Ruffner. Received £100 by the will of her father.

Walter Newman, Sr., died in 1815. (Liber J, folio 391, Woodstock court house, Shenandoah county.) His sons, John and Samuel, were executors of his will. On Jan. 20, 1818, they made final settlement or division of the estate with his ten children, at which date all were living.

FIFTH GENERATION.

First. John Newman, 1st of Walter and Catherine, born in Shenandoah county, Va.; a member of the Virginia Senate for four years; married Mary ————. Issue, eight children:

1. Joseph M. In 1836, the date of their father's will, Joseph and George were students of medicine at Orange Court House.
2. George.
3. Walter.
4. Catherine. Married Williams, a resident of Orange
5. Frances.   [county.

6. Sarah Ann.
7. Phoebe Ann.
8. John S.

John Newman died Aug., 1839. His will, bearing date Nov. 7, 1836, proven Aug. 12, 1839, is recorded in Liber V, folio 45, Woodstock court house, Shenandoah county. His wife Mary was executrix; brother Samuel and sister Ann witnesses to the will.

Sixth. Samuel Newman, 3d son and 6th child of Walter and Catherine, born March 2, 1779; married, Jan. 2, 1806, Mary Moffett, born Feb. 9, 1782, daughter of the Rev. Anderson Moffett. Issue, seven children. (From family record.)

1. Catherine,   b. Oct. 20, 1806. (See later.)
2. John,   b. Sept. 25, 1808; m. Ethalinda Tilden, Apr. 30, 1839; d. June 29, 1869.
3. Anderson,   b. Nov. 5, 1810; m. Rebecca Dyer, Apr. 14, 1835; died Mar. 29, 1900.
4. Elizabeth,   b. Jan. 3, 1813; m. John Moffett, Jan. 24, 1844; died June 11, 1845.
5. Margaret,   b. Mar. 17, 1815; m. Corydon K. Moore, Jan. 26, 1841; died Feb. 25, 1895.
6. Walter,   b. Apr. 6, 1817; m. Caroline H. Rice, Dec. 6, 1842; died Feb. 15, 1899.
7. Barbara Ann, b. July 14, 1819. No further record.

Samuel Newman died Aug., 1869. His will bearing date Dec. 26, 1833, proven Aug. 13, 1869, is recorded in liber 14, folio 50, at Woodstock court house, Shenandoah county; he left his wife Mary and six children surviving, the wife receiving her legal portion, the remainder of the estate divided equally between the children.

SIXTH GENERATION.

First. Catherine Newman, 1st of Samuel and Mary, *nee*

Moffett, born Oct. 20, 1806. She married 1829, Jacob Sommers, born June 29, 1799. Three children:

1. Samuel Matthews, b. Dec. 27, 1829.
2. George Anderson, b. Jan. 23, 1832.
3. Mary Regina, b. May 27, 1834.

SEVENTH GENERATION.

Third. Mary Regina Sommers, 3d of Jacob and Catherine, *nee* Newman, born May 27, 1834, married Oct. 25, 1856, Samuel T. Walker, of Shenandoah county. Two children:

1. Luther Sommers, b. Aug. 6, 1857.
2. Robert Jacob, b. Aug. 9, 1859.

Samuel T. Walker, Colonel of the 10th Virginia Regiment, C. S. A., was killed in battle at Chancellorsville, May 3, 1863.

EIGHTH GENERATION.

First. Luther Sommers Walker, 1st of Col. Samuel T. and Mary Regina, *nee* Sommers, born in Shenandoah county, Aug. 5, 1857; married Oct. 21, 1884, Annie Howard Haas. Two children:

1. Arline, b. Mar. 29, 1887.
2. Luther Sommers, b. Nov. 21, 1888.

Mr. Luther S. Walker resides on his farm about two miles from Woodstock; for a number of years he has been clerk of the courts for Shenandoah county, and we are indebted to him for much valuable information concerning his family.

SIXTH GENERATION.

Sixth. Walter, 6th child and 3d son of Samuel and Mary, *nee* Moffett, born April 16, 1817; married Dec. 6, 1842, Caroline H. Rice; died Feb. 15, 1899, leaving among other children a son John W., born Apr. 15, 1845.

SEVENTH GENERATION.

John W. Newman, second child of Walter and Caroline H., *nee* Rice, born April 15, 1845; m. Elizabeth S. Murphy, of Jefferson county, West Virginia, Dec. 4, 1869. Nine children:

1. Fannie,   b. Feb. 22, 1871; m. T. A. Miller, son of
            Phineas, Dec. 29, 1900.
2. William,   b. Feb. 9, 1873; m. Constance F. Henkel,
3. Carrie,   b. June 7, 1875.   [Oct. 11, 1900.
4. Robert,   b. Oct. 5, 1876.
5. Samuel,   b. June 24, 1879.
6. Asa,   b. Dec. 14, 1881.
7. Mary,   b. Dec. 6, 1884.
8. Walter,   b. Aug. 8, 1886.
9. Essie,   b. July 21, 1889.

FIFTH GENERATION.

Eighth. Walter Newman, 4th son and 8th child of Walter and Catherine, born in Shenandoah county; m. 1822, ———. Four children:

1. Benjamin P., b. Jan. 24, 1823.
2. Sarah,   b.
3. Ann R.,   b.
4. Henrietta C., b.

Walter Newman died 1868. His will, dated June 8, 1847, was proven March 9, 1868. (Liber 13, folio 170, Woodstock court house, Shenandoah county.) In it reference is made to his wife as living, but she is not named. His son Benjamin P. is named as executor, and empowered to manage the farm and care for the family.

SIXTH GENERATION.

First. Benjamin P. Newman, son of Walter and ———,

his wife, born Jan. 24, 1823; married May 6, 1851, Elizabeth Hickerman. Three children:

1. Walter Hickerman, b. July 17, 1852; m. Sally Bird Stephenson, June 9, 1890.
2. Edgar Douglass, b. Mar. 26, 1854; m. Mary O. Walton, Dec. 20, 1877.
3. Caroline Mary, b. July 25, 1862; m. Mark B. Wunder, Oct. 18, 1883.

II. THOMAS NEWMAN.

Thomas Newman, born in England about 1620, emigrated to Virginia in the ship "Plaine Joan" in 1635, aged 15 years; probably settled with his brother John in James City county, Virginia, and moved with him to the Northern Neck. His name, however, does not appear upon any record until 1677, when he made a deed to his son Thomas, conveying one-half of his real and personal property to the latter, who was about to be married. This deed, of record at Tappahannock, Virginia, is attested by Philip Pendleton. The immigrant Thomas probably married a daughter of Henry Burdett, Sr., whose will, proven in 1695, in Richmond county, is now lost with Will Book 1; but the remaining records prove that he was executor of, and a devisee under the will. He died intestate, about the beginning of the year 1700, and his personal estate was appraised at 16,577 pounds of tobacco. He probably had daughters; the wives of Avery Naylor, John McMelion (McMillan?), and Frances, wife of John Wilson, may have been among these. He certainly had but one son, Thomas, born probably before 1656, and after the removal of his father to what is now Richmond county.

SECOND GENERATION.

Thomas Newman, Jr., only son of Thomas the immigrant, born in Virginia, is frequently mentioned in the records of Richmond county, and by will and descent acquired nearly all the Newman property in the Northern Neck. He conveyed Moratico to John Tarplay in 1700, and the deed shows that he lived in Littenbourne (Littenbourne parish), probably on the place given him by his father, and recites that the lands conveyed were given him by Capt. Alexander Newman, in his last will and testament. As, at the time of the latter's death, there were three Thomas Newmans in Richmond county, to-wit : the immigrant, his son and grandson, Tarplay instituted an inquiry, in 1711, to ascertain who was the Thomas to whom Capt. Alexander Newman devised Moratico. This inquiry is of record at Warsaw and contains the testimony of Capt. Wm. Woodbridge, Wm. Fitzherbert, Dominick Benneham, Mrs. Winnifred Griffin, and George Glasscock. The first testified that he had often heard Capt. Newman say that "if he died without issue he would give the plantation where he then lived to Thomas Newman, because it should not go out of the name of Newman," and that he was "that Thomas Newman who was reputed to have married the daughter of Mr. Elias Wilson, deceased." Fitzherbert testified similarly, but changed the Captain's language so as to make him declare that he would give the land to Thomas "to bear up the name of Newman," and identified him as "the son of Thomas Newman, who lived across Rappahannock Creek." He died between 1704 and 1707, and left issue :

1. Alexander, born 1678.
2. George, ⎱ evidently twins, born 1681, as both were minors
3. John, ⎰   in 1701 and of age in 1702.
4. Thomas, a minor in 1707.

THIRD GENERATION.

First. Alexander Newman, 1st of Thomas, Jr., bought a large tract of land in 1699, in Lancaster county, formerly owned by John Newman, the immigrant, and by him devised to his son John; upon this he built a stone mill which is still standing; so says the clerk of the county Court. Alexander appears to have resided in Lancaster until about 1735, when, as "Alexander Newman, of St. Mark's Parish," he leased a tract of land in Orange county, on the south side of the Rapidan, of Alexander Spottswood, "for three lives, himself and his sons, Thomas and James." There is of record at Warsaw a deed, dated 1737, from "Alexander Newman of Orange County, Planter," to Landon Carter, conveying the tract of land devised by Henry Burdett, the elder, to Thomas Newman, and the court order showing the acknowledgment of the deed recites that Alexander was the heir at law of Thomas. Upon this tract Carter built his famous home, Sabine Hall; at the time of the sale it seems to have been adversely held by Jane Thomas. Possibly the suit of Alexander Newman *vs.* Humphrey Thomas, abated by the latter's death in 1732, concerned this land.

Alexander Newman was a member of the grand jury of Orange county in 1737, and is mentioned in several suits there, the last as late as 1760. He undoubtedly lived in what is now Culpeper county, and probably died soon after 1760. Between 1740 and 1750 he was engaged in a law suit in Richmond county with his wife Penelope, from whom he had separated. She obtained, finally, a judgment against him for maintenance and support; and Elias Wilson, evidently a kinsman, acknowledged himself surety for the payment of the money. The records disclose the names of three of his sons, viz :

1. Elias.
2. Thomas.
3. James, all probably born between 1705 and 1715.

FOURTH GENERATION.

First. Elias Newman, 1st of Alexander, died in Essex county; his will, of record at Tappahannock, Virginia, was proven in 1750, and names his wife Ann and the following children :

1. Thomas, the oldest child, a minor in 1748, of age in 1752.

2. Elias, d. in 1759; unmarried.   His will proven at
3. Reuben.   [Tappahannock court house.
4. James.
5. Alexander.
6. Mary Ann.
7. William.
8. George, born 1747.   (See his pension application.)

FIFTH GENERATION.

First.   Thomas Newman, 1st of Elias and Ann, settled in
Prince William county, where he was a planter, and died in
1777.   His will is lost, but the remaining records show that
his wife's name was Elizabeth and that he had at least
two sons :

1. Thomas, b. ———.
2. Richard, b. ———.

SIXTH GENERATION.

First.   Thomas Newman, 1st of Thomas and Elizabeth,
of Prince William county, acquired a large estate.   Among
other lands, he disposed of 3,000 acres in Tennessee by his
will, which was proven April 2, 1821.   He married Nellie
Jett, daughter of William, of Prince William county.   Nine
children are named in his will :

1. Elias.
2. Thomas Jett.
3. William Jett.   (See later.)
4. Elizabeth, wife of ——— Hereford.
5. Mary, wife of ——— Spindel.
6. Sarah, wife of James Brown, of Frederick county.
7. Catherine Newton, unmarried.   (See later.)
8. Peggy.
9. Eleanor.

[He appointed his brother Richard, and sons Elias, Thomas,

and William, executors of his will, which is attested by one Edward Newman, whose relationship is not given.]

SEVENTH GENERATION.

Third. William Jett Newman, 3d of Thomas and Nellie, *nee* Jett, was born in Prince William county, where he died in 1824. His will, proven at Manassas, Sept. 6, 1824, mentions wife Mary and a son not named, and is witnessed by Thomas J., Thomas E. and Mortimer J. Newman. The two latter were probably his nephews.

Seventh. Catharine Newton Newman, 7th of Thomas and Nellie, *nee* Jett, died 1855. Her will, proven at Manassas Aug. 6, 1855, mentions her brother-in-law, Christopher Cushing, and his wife Eleanor, nephews Crawford, Henry, Charles L. and Thomas N. Cushing, and nieces Herleby J. Newman and Margaret Ann Benson.

SIXTH GENERATION.

Second. Richard Newman, 2d of Thomas and Elizabeth, of Prince William county, married Delilah Lane about 1787. He lived near the line of Fauquier in Prince William county, and was probably the father of Horace, Sheriff of Fauquier county in 1824. No further record.

FIFTH GENERATION.

Third. Reuben Newman, 3d of Elias and Ann, disappears from the records of Essex county about 1765, and is believed to have settled in Prince William county, with his brother Thomas and cousin John, of Richmond. Owing to a partial loss of the records of Prince William county nothing further is known of him.

Fourth. James Newman, 4th of Elias and Ann, settled in Orange county about 1765, where he was an exceedingly prosperous planter. He is spoken of in the records as "of Bloomfield and Burlington." He married Veranda Noel,

of Essex county, and died in Orange county in 1816, where
his will was proven the same year. Issue, six children :

1. Thomas, b. ——.
2. Reuben, b. ——.
3. Ann, b. ——; m. Geo. Newman, before 1780.
4. Mary, b. ——; m. Edmund Henshaw, in 1780.
5. Patty, b. ——; m. John Henshaw, of Madison.
6. Veranda, b. ——; m. John Henshaw, of Orange.

SIXTH GENERATION.

First. Thomas Newman, 1st of James and Veranda, *nee*
Noel, m. 1799, Lucy, sister of Governor James and Judge
Pendleton Barbour. Issue, four children :

1. James Barbour, b. 1800.
2. Lucetta, b. ——.
3. Veranda, b. ——.
4. Wilhelmina, b. ——.

The will of Thomas Newman, recorded at Orange Court
House, was proven Jan. 23, 1854.

SEVENTH GENERATION.

First. James Barbour Newman, only son of Thomas and
Lucy, *nee* Barbour, lived to the advanced age of over one
hundred years, and died at Burlington, Orange county, Va.
He married Sallie Battaile Fitzhugh, of King George county.
Issue, seven children :

1. Julia, b. ——; m. J. H. Goss, of Georgia.
2. Laura, b. ——; m. her cousin, John Welch,
   [of Madison county, Va.
3. Rosa, b. ——; died unmarried.
4. Thomas Henry, b. ——; was killed in the Civil War.
5. James Barbour, b. ——.
6. Reuben Conway, b. ——.
7. Fitzhugh, b. ——.

EIGHTH GENERATION.

Fifth. James Barbour Newman, 2d son and 5th child of James B. and Sallie B., *nee* Fitzhugh, born in Orange county; married Tabitha Gordon, daughter of William, of Fredericksburg, Va. Two children:

1. Alice, b. ——.
2. Lilly, b. ——; m. —— Thornton, of Fredericksburg.

Sixth. Reuben Conway Newman, 3d son and 6th child of James B. and Sallie B., *nee* Fitzhugh, born in Orange; m. Eleanor Taylor, of Orange. Issue, seven children:

1. Robert.
2. Conway.
3. Rosa, b. ——; m. James Edward Flewellen, of Texas.
4. Nellie.
5. Laura.
6. Eugenia.
7. Elsie.

Seventh. Fitzhugh Newman, 7th and youngest child of James B. and Sallie B., *nee* Fitzhugh, born in Orange county; married Miss Paul, of Washington state. No issue:

SEVENTH GENERATION.

Second. Lucetta Newman, 2d of Thomas and Lucy, *nee* Barbour, born ———; m. James Madison Macon, nephew of President Madison. Six children:

1. Thomas Newman Macon, b. ———; died unmarried.
2. Conwayella Macon, b. ———; m. John Knox, of Richmond, Va. Four children: John C., Lucetta, Madison, and Conway.
3. Edgar Barbour Macon, b. ———; m. Virginia Caison, of Princess Anne Co., Va. Six children: William, Sallie, Barbour, Nathaniel, Henry, and Bessie.

4. Sarah F. Macon, b. ———; m. Thomas Hill, of Culpeper. Two children: A. P. and Carrie B. M.
5. Reuben Conway Macon, b. ———; m. Emma Riley, of Winchester, Va. Seven children: Clifton, Conway, Latimer, Riley, Emma, Kate, and Evelyn.
6. James Madison Macon, b. ———; m. Miss Bridge, of New Orleans. Three children: Conwayella, Edward Adams, and James Madison.

Third. Veranda Newman, 3d of Thomas and Lucy, *nee* Barbour, born ———; m. Nathaniel Welch, of Madison county, Va. Six children:

1. Thomas Newman, who married Lucy Dew. No issue. He was State Senator from Caroline county and Judge of the County Court. Lives in Caroline county.
2. James Barbour, married Ann, sister of Col. A. C. Gibson, of Culpeper. Living at Apopka, Fla.
3. John, married his cousin Laura Newman. Issue: Sallie, who married William S. Powan, of Orange.
4. Lucy, married her cousin Reuben Newman.
5. Elizabeth, died single.
6. Wilhelmina, married Dr. Graves. Issue: Ella.

Fourth. Wilhelmina Newman, 4th and youngest child of Thomas and Lucy, *nee* Barbour, b. ———. (No further record.)

Sixth Generation.

Second. Reuben Newman, 2d of James and Veranda, *nee* Noel, born ———; m. about 1800, Phoebe Butler, of Fredericksburg; resided in Orange county, and was possessed of large means. His will, proven at Orange Court House, Oct. 24, 1842, names his six children:

1. James,   b. ———.
2. Reuben,   b. ———.
3. Thomas Noel, b. ———.

4. John Francis, b. ——.
5. Ellen,   b. —— ; m. Dr. James A. Reid.
6. Phillippa,   b. —— ; died single.

SEVENTH GENERATION.

First. James Newman, 1st of Reuben and Phoebe, *nee* Butler, born —— ; married Mary Scott, of Orange county, where he lived and died. Issue, nine children :

1. Wilson Scott,   b. ——.
2. Richard Henry,   b. —— ; died unmarried.
3. James Stanley,   b. ——.
4. Charles Sheridan, b. ——.
5. John Herbert,   b. —— ; killed in battle in Civil War.
6. Reuben Manning,   b. ——.
7. Fanny Butler,   b. —— ; m. Philip D. Barbour, of Ky.
8. Sarah Jane,   b. —— ; unmarried.
9. Mary Elizabeth,   b. ——.

EIGHTH GENERATION.

First. Wilson Scott Newman, 1st of James and Mary, *nee* Scott, born —— ; married Mary Lou White, ——, of Lexington, Va. He was a lawyer and was killed in battle, 1864. Two children :

1. Mary White, b. —— ; died young.
2. Lily,   b. —— ; m. 1885, Phil. T. Henshaw, of Ky.

Third. James Stanley Newman, 3d of James and Mary, *nee* Scott, born —— ; now a professor in Clemson College, S. C.; married Elberta Lewis, of Georgia. Five children :

1. Clifford Lewis,   b. ——.
2. Wilson Herbert,   b. ——.
3. Charles Carter,   b. ——.
4. Alba,   b. —— ; m. Pierre Bealer, of Georgia.
5. Mary Stanley,   b. —— ; m. Ernest Walker, of Iowa.

NINTH GENERATION.

First. Clifford Lewis Newman, 1st of James Stanley and Elberta, *nee* Lewis, born —— ; has been twice married. 1st, to Fanny Stanley, of Arkansas: one child, a son, Stanley, born ——. 2d, to Nellie Gales, of Arkansas: no issue.

EIGHTH GENERATION.

Fourth. Charles Sheridan Newman, 4th of James and Mary, *nee* Scott, born —— ; a merchant of Knoxville, Tenn.; married Kate Hazen, of that city. Four children :

1. Charles Sheridan, b. ——.
2. Wm. Hazen,   b. ——.
3. James Stanley, b. ——.
4. Mary,   b. ——.

Sixth. Reuben Manning Newman, 6th of James and Mary, *nee* Scott, born —— ; residence, Hilton, Orange county, Va.; married Kate Randolph Taylor. Eight children :

1. Herbert Stanley,   b. ——.
2. James Sheridan,   b. ——.
3. Mary Randolph,   b. ——; m. Benton Haxall Cameron, [of Richmond, Va.
4. Elizabeth Tilghman, b. ——.
5. Fannie Barbour,   b. ——; m. Charles Graham Thom-[as, of Buckingham county, Va.
6. Sarah Taylor,   b. ——.
7. Page Waller, (dau.), b. ——.
8. Kathleen Howard,   b. ——.

SEVENTH GENERATION.

Second. Reuben Newman, 2d of Reuben and Phoebe, *nee* Butler, born —— ; m. Lucy Welch, his cousin. He died in Orange county, where his will was proven Nov. 22, 1872. Three children :

1. Nathaniel Welch, b. ——.

2. Bettie Beckham, b. ——; m. C. J. Stovin.
3. Lucy Florence,   b. ——; m. Joseph Wert, of New York.

EIGHTH GENERATION.

First.   Nathaniel Welch Newman, 1st of Reuben and Lucy, *nee* Welch, born ——; married, ——, Nannie Wert, of New York.   Six children:

1. Fanny,   b. ——; m. G. A. Beck.
2. Lucy,   b. ——; m. Lewis Williams, of Orange.
3. Maggie,   b. ——; m. Ernest Wood.
4. Cora,   b. ——; m. A. V. Houseworth, of Orange.
5. Reuben,   b. —— (a minor).
6. Nellie Reid, b. ——.

SEVENTH GENERATION.

Third.   Thomas Noel Newman, 3d of Reuben and Phoebe, *nee* Butler, born ——; m. Mary Blakey.   Three children:

1. Ella,   b. ——; died unmarried.
2. Ida,   b. ——; m. Dr. E. W. Row.
3. Lena May, b. ——; m. ——— Effinger, of the valley
                                    [of Virginia.

Fourth.   John Francis Newman, 4th of Reuben and Phoebe, *nee* Butler, born ——; was twice married: 1st, to Eliza Sims. Two children:

1. John Williams, b. ——.
2. Eliza,   b. ——; m. Crawford Simms.

He married, 2d, Ann Blakey.   Three children:

3. James Blakey, b. ——.
4. Nannie,   b. ——; m. William J. Walker.
5. Mary Lester,   b. ——; m. James B. Kite.

EIGHTH GENERATION.

First.   John Williams Newman, 1st of John Francis, by his first wife, Eliza Sims, born ——; married, first, Mary Barbour, of Ky. Four children :

1. Philip,   b. ——.
2. William,   b. ——.
3. Frankie,   b. —— (a daughter).
4. Reuben Sheridan, b. —— (a daughter).

He married, second, ——, Lula Gabble. Three children :

1. Naddine, b. ——.
2. Winnie, b. ——.
3. —— (an infant).

Third. James Blakey Newman, 3d child of John Francis, and 1st by his second wife, Ann Blakey, b. ——; m. ——, Hattie Jones, of Missouri. Four children :

1. John,   b. ——.
2. Lucile, b. ——.
3. Nannie, b. ——.
4. Kate,   b. ——.

Sixth Generation.

Fourth. Mary Newman, 4th of James and Veranda, *nee* Noel, born ——; married, ——, 1780, Edmund Henshaw. Two children :

1. Virginia, b. ——; m. Thomas Scott. No issue.
2. Mary,   b. ——.

Seventh Generation.

Second. Mary Henshaw, 2d of Edmund and Mary, *nee* Newman, born ——; married —— Porter. Three children :

1. Courtney, b. ——.
2. Martha,   b. ——.
3. Virginia, b. ——.

17

EIGHTH GENERATION.

First. Courtney Porter, 1st of —— Porter and Mary, *nee* Henshaw, born —— ; m. Peter Cobbs. Four children :

1. Thomas, b. ——.
2. Lucetta, b. ——.
3. Jemima, b. ——.
4. Ann,   b. ——.

Second. Martha Porter, 2d of —— Porter and Mary, *nee* Henshaw, born —— ; married Dr. James L. Jones. Five children :

1. Wm. Russell,   b. —— ; Residence, Richmond, Va.
2. Thomas Scott,   b. ——.
3. Gillie,   b. ——.
4. Edmonia,   b. ——.
5. Mattie Gertrude, b. ——.

Third. Virginia Porter, 3d of —— Porter and Mary, *nee* Henshaw, born —— ; m. Thomas Henshaw. Four children :

1. Scott,   b. ——.
2. Edmund, b. ——.
3. Mary,   b. ——.
4. Martha, b. ——.

SIXTH GENERATION.

Sixth. Veranda Newman, 6th of James and Veranda, *nee* Noel, born —— ; married, ——, John Henshaw, of Orange county, Va. Four children :

1. James, b. ——.
2. John, b. ——.
3. Betsy, b. ——.
4. Sally, b. ——.

SEVENTH GENERATION.

First. James Henshaw, 1st of John and Veranda, *nee*

Newman, was twice married : 1st, to Miss Walker, of Madison county, Va. One child, a daughter, Mary. 2d, to Miss Herndon, of Ky. One child, a daughter, Lucy.

EIGHTH GENERATION.

First. Mary Henshaw, daughter of James, born —— ; married Benjamin Trigg, of Ky.

Second. Lucy Henshaw, daughter of James by the second wife, Miss Herndon, b. —— ; m. —— Holloway. One child, Phillippa.

NINTH GENERATION.

First. Phillippa Holloway, only child of —— Holloway and Lucy, *nee* Henshaw, born —— ; m. John Payton Cowherd. Two children : Caroline and Henrietta.

SEVENTH GENERATION.

Second. John Henshaw, 2d of John and Veranda, *nee* Newman, born —— ; married, ——, Sallie Cowherd.

Third. Betsy Henshaw, 3d of John and Veranda, *nee* Newman, born —— ; married Benjamin Walker. Five children :

1. William, b. —— ; m. Miss Spottswood.
2. Mary, b. —— ; m. Mr. Dunn.
3. Lucy, b. —— ; m. Mr. Sanford.
4. Ann, b. —— ; m. Mr. Timberlake.
5. Eliza, b. —— ; m. John Rowe.

Fourth. Sally Henshaw, 4th of John and Veranda, *nee* Newman, born —— ; married, ——, Frank Cowherd.

FIFTH GENERATION.

Fifth. Alexander Newman, 5th of Elias and Ann, born in Essex county ; removed to Prince William county. Like his brother Reuben, from the partial loss of the records of Prince William, nothing further is known of him.

Sixth. Mary Ann Newman, 6th of Elias and Ann, born in Essex county; referred to in the will of her father. No further record.

Seventh. William Newman, 6th son and 7th child of Elias and Ann, born in Essex county; settled in Orange, with his brother James; married, probably in Culpeper county, Nancy Finney. He lived to the ripe old age of one hundred years, and died in Orange county, 1743, where his will was proven that year. Fourteen children:

1. Abner,	b. ———.	[bell Co., Va.
2. Patsey,	b. ———;	m. Benjamin Porter, of Camp-
3. Frances,	b. ———;	m. ——— Gilbert; died before
4. William,	b. ———.	[1842.
5. Benjamin,	b. ———.	
6. Thomas,	b. ———.	
7. Charles,	b. ———.	
8. Reuben,	b. ———.	
9. Robert,	b. ———.	
10. Fontaine,	b. ———.	[Tennessee.
11. Sarah Bell,	b. ———;	m. Joseph Gee, and settled in
12. Malinda,	b. ———;	m. Joseph Rogers.
13. Polly,	b. ———;	m. Elias Faulconer.
14. Maria,	b. ———;	m. Newman Faulconer, and [moved to Ky.

SIXTH GENERATION.

First. Abner Newman, 1st of William and Nancy, *nee* Finney, born in Orange county; settled in Brunswick county; married ———. Issue, among other children, a daughter Ann, who was the second wife of George Newman. No issue. Abner died in 1842.

Fourth. William Newman, 2d son and 4th child of William and Nancy, *nee* Finney, born in Orange county, where he died. His will was proven Oct. 26, 1857. Nine children:

1. George,   b. ———— ; died at the age of 19 years.
2. Willie Anna,   b. ———— ; m. W. S. Peyton.
3. Jane,   b. ———— ; m. John Bradley.
4. Sarah Martha,   b. ———— ; m. John S. Peyton.
5. Maria,   b. ———— ; m. 1st, John Brady; 2d, ————.
6. John R.,   b. ———— ; m. Margaret Rogers.
7. Betsy,   b. ———— ; m. Garrett Atkins.
8. James Quintus, b. ———— ; m. Mary ————.
9. Wilhemina,.   b. ———— ; m. William McCormick.

No further record of descendants.

Fifth. Benjamin Newman, 5th of William and Nancy, *nee* Finney, born in Orange county ; married Bessie Clayton, and settled in Barren county, Kentucky.   Three children :

1. James Scott, b. ————.
2. William,   b. ————.
3. Tazewell,   b. ————.

Sixth. Thomas Newman, 6th of William and Nancy, *nee* Finney, born in Orange county ; married Jane Hackney. No children.   Died 1847 ; will proven June 25, 1847, at Orange Court House.

Seventh. Charles Newman, 7th of William and Nancy, *nee* Finney, born in Orange county ; married Catherine Chiles. Issue, a son, who was killed in the Civil War.

Eighth. Reuben Newman, 8th of William and Nancy, *nee* Finney, born in Orange county ; married Nancy Hackney. No issue.

Ninth. Robert Newman, 9th of William and Nancy, *nee* Finney, born in Orange county ; married Lavinia Carpenter. Four children :

1. William Thomas, b. ————.
2. Robert,   b. ————.   [Louisa, Va.
3. Sarah,   b. ———— ; m. Fred Grubbs ; resides at
4. Martha,   b. ———— ; died unmarried.

SEVENTH GENERATION.

First. William Thomas Newman, 1st of Robert and Lavinia, *nee* Carpenter, born ———; married ———; settled at Atlanta, Georgia. Issue: a son.

1. Charles L., b. ———. No further record.

SIXTH GENERATION.

Tenth. Fontaine Newman, 10th child and youngest son of William and Nancy, *nee* Finney, born in Orange county; died unmarried.

FIFTH GENERATION.

Eighth. George Newman, youngest child of Elias and Ann, settled in Orange county with his brothers James and William; was a soldier in the war of the Revolution; served as private in the first troop, Lee's Legion, and was present at the battle of Yorktown. He was pensioned Dec. 24, 1832. Died in Orange county, where his will was proven June 26, 1837. He married his niece, Ann Newman, daughter of his brother James. Four children:

1. George, b. ———.
2. Elias, b. ———.
3. James, b. ———. [further record.
4. Elizabeth, b. ———; m. Col. Edward Winslow. No

SIXTH GENERATION.

First. George Newman, 1st of George and Ann, born in Orange county, was twice married, 1st to Miss Tupman; three children; 2d, to Nancy Newman, d. of Abner; no issue.

1. Thomas, b. ———; killed in the civil war.
2. George, b. ———; killed in a railroad accident.
3. James F., b. ———.

SEVENTH GENERATION.

Third. James F. Newman, 3d of George by his first wife,

————, *nee* Tupman, born in Orange county, married the widow Winslow. Three children :

1. Henry Clay, b. ————.
2. Sarah,   b. ————.
3. A daughter, b. ————; married ———— Swan.

James F. Newman resides near Orange, Va.

SIXTH GENERATION.

Second. Elias, 2d of George and Ann, born in Orange county, died unmarried.

Third. James, 3d of George and Ann, born in Orange county, died unmarried.

FOURTH GENERATION.

Second. Thomas Newman, 2d of Alexander of Orange, born ————; married before 1740, Elizabeth, daughter of William Morton of Orange, an ancestor of Gen. J. E. B. Stuart. The will of William Morton and the records of Orange tend to show that Thomas Newman had moved from Orange county before 1747. He died after 1766. Three children :

1. Alexander, b. Oct. 11, 1740.
2. Reuben,   b. ————.
3. Abner,   b. ————.

FIFTH GENERATION.

First. Alexander Newman, 1st of Thomas, of Orange, and Elizabeth, *nee* Morton, born in Orange county, where he died about 1788 ; married Frances, daughter of Andrew and Jane (Morton) Bourne, who was a first cousin on his mother's side. Eight children :

1. George,   b. May 20, 1766.
2. Reuben,   b. 1767.
3. Andrew,   b. 1770.
4. Alexander, b. ————.

5. Thomas, b. Aug. 15, 1775.
6. Jane,   b. ———.
7. John,   b. 1782.
8. James,   b. ———.

SIXTH GENERATION.

First. George Newman, 1st of Alexander and Frances, *nee* Bourne, born May 20, 1766, married Mary Bourne, in Culpeper county in 1790. Died in Culpeper county, where his will was proven in 1802. Issue, one child, a daughter Frances.

SEVENTH GENERATION.

Frances Newman, only child of George and Mary, *nee* Bourne, born Sept. 25, 1796, in Culpeper county, Virginia, where she married Nov. 10, 1815, Willis Roberts; settled in Kentucky, and died in Owen county, that state, May 2, 1830, leaving issue, eight children :

1. George A.,   b. Aug. 8, 1816.
2. Mary,   b. Jan. 22, 1818.
3. John G.,   b. Nov. 1, 1819.
4. Sarah,   b. Aug. 31, 1821.
5. William B.,   b. July 25, 1823.
6. Martha Ellen, b. Mar. 6, 1825.
7. Frances Ann, b. Oct. 20, 1826 ; died Aug. 2, 1842.
8. Gabriel,   b. Oct. 20, 1828.

SIXTH GENERATION.

Second. Reuben Newman, 2d of Alexander and Frances, *nee* Bourne, born in 1767, married about 1800, Katherine Ott, of Hagerstown, Washington county, Md. He lived at Woodstock, Harrisonburg and Staunton, and finally moved to Ohio about 1840, where he died. Eleven children :

1. Elizabeth, b. about 1801 ; married ——— Hisey ; settled
2. Jacob,   b. Mar. 9, 1803, at Woodstock.   [in Ohio.
3. John,   b. about 1804. No record.
4. William,   b. about 1806.

5. Margaret,   b. in 1808 ; m. William Henry
                        Wirt, a cousin of William
                        Wirt, and moved to Indiana.
6. Reuben,   b. about 1810. No record.
7. Katherine,   b. about 1812 ; married ————
                        Kendall, and moved to
                        Ohio.
8. Peyton,   b. about 1813. No record.
9. Oliver Hazard Perry, b. 1815. No record.
10. Howard,   b. about 1817. No record.
11. George,   b. ————. No record.

SEVENTH GENERATION.

Second. Jacob Newman, 2d child and eldest son of Reuben
and Catherine, *nee* Ott, born at Woodstock, Virginia, March
9, 1803 ; married Sept. 21, 1824, Caroline Harrison Austin,
in Albermarle county, Va.; moved to Knoxville, Tenn., in
1836, where he died April 4, 1868. Seven children :

1. Tazewell W., b. Mar. 27, 1827, at Harrisonburg, Va.
2. William,   b. Aug. 18, 1829, at Harrisonburg, Va.
3. James W.,   b. Feb. 8, 1832, at Staunton, Va.
4. Adaline P., b. Sept. 2, 1833 ; m. Dr. John F. Gillespie,
                           [of Summer county, Tenn.
5. Henry A.,   b. Mar. 29, 1835, at Staunton, Va.
6. Oliver H. P., b. May 27, 1837, at Knoxville, Tenn.
7. Howard W.,   b. July 16, 1840, at Knoxville, Tenn.

EIGHTH GENERATION.

First. Tazewell W. Newman, 1st of Jacob and Caroline H.,
nee Austin, born March 27, 1827, graduated in law at the
University of Tennessee in the class of 1841 ; was a soldier in
the Mexican war; served as 1st Lieutenant in a Knoxville
(Tenn.) Company ; was elected to the State Senate in 1860, of
which body he was chosen Speaker ; served as Colonel of the
17th Tennessee Regiment (Confederate) ; was detailed to raise
a regiment in Middle Tennessee during Bragg's Tullahoma

campaign, a portion of which was afterwards known as New-man's Battalion ; was made a Brigadier-General in 1865 ; died in 1867, from wounds received at Chickamauga. He resided at Winchester, Tenn., where on March 11, 1851, he married Sarah Buchanan. Two children :

1. Nannie,   b. ———— ; m. ———— King.
2. Tazewell W., b. ————.

Residence of both, Clarksville, Texas.

Second. William Newman, 2d of Jacob and Caroline H., *nee* Austin, born Aug. 18, 1829 ; a contractor and builder ; served in the Mexican war ; was adjutant of his brother Taze-well's regiment in the civil war, and was several times badly wounded. Died in Atlanta, Ga., in 1889. He married at Winchester, Tenn., Aug. 18, 1853, Julia Logan. Three children :

1. William B., b. ———.
2. Wallace,   b. ————.
3. Jennie,   b. ———— ; married ————.

All three reside at Atlanta, Ga.

Third. James W. Newman, 3d of Jacob and Caroline H., *nee* Austin, born Feb. 8, 1832 ; graduated in law at the University of Tennessee in the class of 1850 ; was a delegate to the Charleston Convention of 1860 ; served on the staff of General Zollicoffer in Civil War ; afterwards was captain of artillery ; located at Fayetteville, Tenn., after the war, and formed a partnership with Governor A. S. Marks and A. S. Colyar ; attained distinction in his profession ; was a delegate to the conventions that nominated Tilden and Cleveland (first nomination); died Dec. 25, 1885 ; married on Jan. 23, 1856, Susan Margaret Horne, of Knoxville, Tenn. Six children :

1. Tazewell W., b. Dec. 29, 1856.
2. George H.,   b. Dec. 12, 1858.
3. Jacob,   b. Oct. 29, 1860.

4. William,   b. Dec. 30, 1866.
5. Margaret Armstrong, b. Nov. 21, 1869; m. N. F. Han-
6. Caroline,   b. ———, 1871.   [cock.

NINTH GENERATION.

First. Tazewell W. Newman, 1st of James W. and Susan M., *nee* Horne, born Dec. 29, 1856; married Elizabeth Bruce in 1882. Four children. Residence, Tullahoma, Tenn. Is a teacher of music.

Second. George H. Newman, 2d of James W. and Susan M., *nee* Horne, born Dec. 12, 1858; a lawyer; an alumnus of the Lexington (Tenn.) Law School; was special Indian agent in the State of Washington, 1894–8; married June 30, 1897, Pauline Anderson. Two children:

1. Oliver Perry, b. Nov. 22, 1899.
2. ———, an infant.

Residence, Fayetteville, Tenn.

Third. Jacob Newman, 3d of James W. and Susan M., *nee* Horne, born Oct. 29, 1860; is a wholesale merchant, Knoxville, Tenn.; unmarried.

Fourth. William Newman, 4th of James W. and Susan M., *nee* Horne, born Dec. 30, 1866; graduated at West Point, class of 1892; now captain in 1st U. S. Infantry; served 18 months in Cuba; served in the Philippines; married, Oct. 27, 1897, Jane Holman, of Fayetteville, Tenn. No issue.

EIGHTH GENERATION.

Fifth. Henry A. Newman, 5th of Jacob and Caroline H., *nee* Austin, born May 29, 1835; graduated in law; residence, Huntsville, Mo., where he married, Aug. 28, 1856, Sarah Frances Austin, his cousin; joined the Confederate army; became major of a Georgia regiment; member of the Missouri Legislature several times, and clerk of the House; appointed State Commissioner of Labor by Gov. Crittenden; Adjutant

of State organization of Confederate Veterans and President
of Board of Trustees of Confederate Home.   Two children :

    1. A son, who lives at Huntsville, Mo.   [ton, Texas.
    2. Callie, married ——— Morris.   They reside near Hous-

Sixth.   Oliver H. P. Newman, 6th of Jacob and Caroline H.,
nee Austin, born May 27, 1837 ; graduated in law at the University of Tennessee in the class of 1856 ; was a private soldier
in his brother Tazewell's regiment, C. S. A.; promoted to
lieutenant ; killed Oct. 21, 1861, at the battle of Rockcastle,
or Wild Cat, Ky.   Never married.

Seventh.   Howard W. Newman, 7th of Jacob and Caroline
H., *nee* Austin, born July 16, 1840 ; was a captain in the 1st
Tennessee regiment (Confederate); married, Jan. 17, 1867,
Margaret Donaldson, at Canton, Ga., where he located ; was
presidential elector for Georgia in 1888.   One child, a son,
Thomas, born ———.   Residence, Atlanta, Ga.

SEVENTH GENERATION.

Fourth.   William Newman, 4th of Reuben and Catherine,
nee Ott, born about 1806 ; married, ———, Catherine Ott ;
moved to Ohio ; left issue :

    1. James W., b. ———.
    2. George Ott, b. ——— ; attorney-at-law.   Residence, Cin-
    3. Charles H., b. ———.   [cinnati, Ohio.
and other children.

EIGHTH GENERATION.

First.   James W. Newman, 1st of William and Catherine,
nee Ott, born ——— ; editor and journalist ; was elected by
the Democrats Secretary of State of Ohio in 1882 ; afterwards
held other important offices.   Lived at Portsmouth, Ohio,
until his death, in 1902.

Third.   Charles H. Newman, 3d of William and Catherine,
nee Ott, born ———, in Ohio and reared there ; ran away

from home and joined the Confederate army; attended Washington College, now Washington and Lee University, after the war; had a difficulty with and killed a fellow-student; was fully exonerated by the courts and by General Robert E. Lee, president of the college; became an Episcopal minister; died unmarried.

SIXTH GENERATION.

Third. Andrew Newman, 3d of Alexander and Frances, *nee* Bourne, born in 1770; was twice married: 1st, to Mary Ann Fennell, of Culpeper county, in 1789; second, to Genette Garner, of Orange county, in 1804. Descendants not traced.

Fourth. Alexander Newman, 4th of Alexander and Frances, *nee* Bourne, born about 1773; married, in 1803, Lucy Sleet, of Orange county. Descendants not traced.

Fifth. Thomas Newman, 5th of Alexander and Frances, *nee* Bourne, born Aug. 15, 1775; married Oct. 25, 1798, Martha Oliver Morris, daughter of George G., of Orange county. Eight children:

1. Sarah,   b. Nov. 20, 1799; m. Apr. 15, 1815, Moses
                  Peregoy; died Jan. —, 1816.
2. Jane,   b. Aug. 22, 1802; m. May —, 1825, John
                  Bourne; died ———, 1865.
3. Alexander,   b. Oct. 5, 1804.
4. George Oliver, b. Mar. 1, 1806.
5. Mary Frances, b. Nov. 10, 1810; m. July 24, ——, James
                  F. Day; died ———.
6. Martha Ann,   b. Feb. 25, 1812; m. Feb. 25, 1836, Alex.
                  G. Tatum; died Jan. 4, 1837.
7. Morris D.,   b. Mar. 1, 1815.
8. Lucetta A.,   b. Apr. 6, 1821; m. Nov. 12, 1846, Silas
                  F. Clare; died ———.

[Martha O. Newman, *nee* Morris, died Sept. 26, 1842. Thomas Newman married, second, on Nov. 2, 1844, Sarah

Freeman. He died on his plantation, near the Rapidan river, in Orange county. His will was proven in 1862.]

SEVENTH GENERATION.

Third. Alexander Newman, eldest son and 3d child of Thomas and Martha O., *nee* Morris, born Oct. 5, 1804 ; married Feb. 22, 1826, Ann M. Burwell; moved to Wheeling, West Virginia, where he was successively State Senator, postmaster, and, in 1848, elected to Congress, but he died before taking his seat, of cholera, while on a visit to Pittsburg, September, 1849. Three children :

1. William Alexander, b. 1827.
2. Thomas,   b. 1829.
3. Roberta,   b. 1831 ; m. William Tate Robinson.

Ann Newman, *nee* Burwell, died May 15, 1836. Alexander Newman married, second, in 1838, Eloisa Tomlinson. Three children :

4. Lewis Steenrod,   b. 1839.
5. George W. Thompson, b. 1841 ; died in 1845.
6. Eloisa Zilla,   b. 1845 ; died 1846.

EIGHTH GENERATION.

First. William Alexander Newman, 1st of Alexander and Ann M., *nee* Burwell, born 1827 ; married, 1848, Sarah Jane Dolonson. Eleven children :

1. Martha Jane,   b. 1849; m. 1869, Dr. R. B. Grimm.
2. Thomas Alexander, b. 1851; died young.
3. James William,   b. 1852.
4. Jesse Lantz,   b. 1854.
5. Mary Ray,   b. 1857; m. 1881, Beverly L. Morgan.
6. Morris Madison,   b. 1859.
7. Alfred Holt,   b. 1862.
8. Kate S.,   b. 1866; m. James Lee West.
9. William Clarence,   b. 1869; died young.

10. Roberta May, b. 1871; m. 1893, George Franklin Glover.
11. Charles Lewis, b. 1873.

NINTH GENERATION.

Third. James William Newman, 3d of William Alexander
and Sarah Jane, *nee* Dolonson, born 1852; by profession a
lawyer; residence, New Martinsville, West Virginia; was
county clerk from 1889 to 1896; married, 1881, Susan B. Hall,
daughter of Leonard and Janet, *nee* McGregor. One child, a
son, William Leonard, born 1883.

Fourth. Jesse Lantz Newman, 3d son and 4th child of William Alexander and Sarah Jane, *nee* Dolonson, born 1854;
residence, Littleton, W. Va.; married, 1881, Belle Anderson.
Six children:

1. Mary Roberta, b. 1882.
2. Nora,   b. 1884.
3. Charles,   b. 1886.
4. James,   b. 1888.
5. Alta May,   b. 1890.
6. Sarah,   b. 1892.

Seventh. Morris Madison Newman, 4th son and 7th child
of William Alexander and Sarah Jane, *nee* Dolonson, born
1859; residence, Reading, Kansas; married, 1897, Della Anderson. One child, a daughter, Claud Miles, born ———.

Eleventh. Charles Lewis Newman, 7th son and youngest
child of William Alexander and Sarah Jane, *nee* Dolonson,
born 1873; residence, Pine Grove, West Virginia; married,
1893, Pearl Harris. One child, a son, William Lee, born ———.

EIGHTH GENERATION.

Second. Thomas Newman, 2d of Alexander and Ann M.,
nee Burwell, born 1829; was twice married: first, to Louisa
Price; second, to ———. He died in 1887; left issue. No
further record.

Fourth. Lewis Steenrod Newman, 4th of Alexander by his second wife, Eloisa, *nee* Tomlinson; residence, Glendale, near Moundsville, West Virginia; has been prominent in politics of his state; received the votes of the Democrats in the Legislature at last election of U. S. Senator; married, 1864, Clementine Pickett. Nine children:

1. Charles Clinton,   b. 1865.
2. Zilla,   b. 1867; m. 1890, J. L. (Little?).
3. Lillie May,   b. 1868; m. 1889, I. B. Wilson; d.
4. Lewis Steenrod,   b. 1871.   [1898.
5. Clementine,   b. 1873; died 1886.
6. Dora Lee,   b. 1876.
7. Edwin Alexander,   b. 1878.
8. William Albert,   b. 1884.
9. Edith,   b. 1886.

NINTH GENERATION.

First. Charles Clinton Newman, 1st of Lewis Steenrod and Clementine, *nee* Pickett, born 1865; graduated in law; married, 1891, Vera Hedges. One child, a son, Walter Hubert, born 1891.

Fourth. Lewis Steenrod Newman, 4th of Lewis Steenrod and Clementine, *nee* Pickett, born 1871; married, in 1900, Catherine Smith. One child, a daughter, Catherine Zilla, born 1900.

SEVENTH GENERATION.

Fourth. George Oliver Newman, 4th of Thomas and Martha O., *nee* Morris, born March 1, 1806; married Rosella Bibb; died Nov. 4, 1854. No further record.

Seventh. Morris D. Newman, 7th of Thomas and Martha O., *nee* Morris, born March 1, 1815; married, Dec. 24, 1825, Mary Ann Tatum; served in both branches of the State Legislature; died in Orange county July 21, 1873. His will, proven at Orange Court House, names his children in the following order:

1. Alexander,   b. ———.
2. George,   b. ———.
3. Thomas,   b. ——— (deceased).
4. Mary Ellen, b. ———; wife of ——— Sudduth.
5. Lucy F.,   b. ———; wife of ——— Sudduth.
6. Isabel,   b. ———; wife of ——— Battaile.
7. A son, Nathaniel, who died before his father, is not named.

SIXTH GENERATION.

Sixth. Jane Newman, born about March, 1781, 6th child
and only daughter of Alexander, of Orange, and Frances, *nee*
Bourne; married, Feb. 22, 1796, Rev. Ambrose Bourne, son
of Francis Bourne (nephew of Andrew Bourne) and his wife
Frances Christopher, grand-daughter of William Morton, of
Orange. They moved to North Carolina. Jane Newman was
the grand-daughter of Andrew Bourne, and of Jane Bourne
and Elizabeth Newman, daughters of William Morton and his
wife Ann, *nee* Motherhead. Lewis Milton Bourne, attorney-
at-law, Asheville, N. C., is a son of Henry Clay Bourne, a son
of Milton Bourne and his wife, *nee* Catherine Wimberly. The
children of Rev. Ambrose Bourne and Jane, *nee* Newman,
were four:

1. Milton,   b. Sept. 16, 1800.
2. Alexander, b. ———.
3. Frances,   b. ———.
4. Jane,   b. ———.

Seventh. John Newman, 7th of Alexander and Frances,
nee Bourne, born ———, 1782; married, first, Feb. 3, 1804,
Sidna Quisenberry, daughter of George and Jane, *nee* Daniel.
Six children:

1. John,   b. 1805 (moved west).
2. Jane,   b. 1807; m. Launcelot Lindsay, and settled
3. Reuben,   b. 1809.   [in Ky.
4. Billingsby, b. 1811; moved to Ky.; married four times.
                                                [No issue.

18

5. Andrew, b. 1814; murdered in early life. Never mar-
6. Susan,   b. 1816; m. Stokely Clark.   [ried.

John Newman married, second, Mrs. Mildred Atkins, *nee* Quisenberry, a sister of his first wife Sidna. Four children :

    7. Eliza,   b. 1820; m. ——— Murphy. Res., Union-
                                               [ville, Va.
    8. Mildred, b. 1822; moved West with her brother John.
    9. George, b. 1825.
  10. Frances, b. 1830; m. Lawrence Faulconer. Residence,
                                    [Hinton, West Virginia.

John Newman married, third, Mildred Waugh; no issue; he died in 1869, in Orange county, where his will was proven the same year.

Jane Daniel, wife of George Quiesenberry and mother of the two Mdms. John Newman, was the daughter of Vivien Daniel, but is omitted in Hayden's list of Vivian's children; unfortunally no direct evidence is of record, but the relationship is asserted by Jane's descendants, and is confirmed by the facts that Vivian Daniel was surety on the bond, given in 1783, by George Quisenberry in Orange county for his intermarriage with Jane Daniel, and that the will of Vivian's brother, John Daniel, made in 1785, and proven in Louisa county, is attested by Vivian Daniel, George Quisenberry, Jane Quisenberry and Margaret Daniel. It is also noted that Jane named her first born Vivian, for her father, and her youngest Elizabeth, for her mother. See "Memorials of the Quisenberry Family," by A. C. Quisenberry.

SEVENTH GENERATION.

Third. Reuben Newman, 3d of John and Sidna, *nee* Quisenberry, born 1809, married ———, Mary Clark, sister of Stokely Clark, who married Susan, sister of Reuben Newman. Mary Clark was a daughter of Henry Towles Clark, of Orange county, and his wife Elizabeth, *nee* Smith, of Culpeper.

Henry Towles Clark was the son of John and Mary, *nee* Towles; daughter of Joseph and Sarah, *nee* Terrill; daughter of Robert Terrill. Joseph Towles was the son of Stokely and Ann his wife, son of Henry, the immigrant, and his wife, Ann Stokely. (Virginia Magazine of History, for July, 1902.) Reuben Newman died at Richmond, Va., in 1875, intestate. Six children:

1. John Wesley,   b. 1832.
2. Joseph Allen,   b. 1834.
3. James Addison, b. July 24, 1836.
4. Henry Towles, b. 1840; died young.
5. Lucy,   b. 1843; m. Mark A. Layton. Res.,
                  [Clifton Forge, Va.
6. Mildred,   b. 1849; m. B. F. Atkins. Residence,
                  [Somerset, Virginia.

EIGHTH GENERATION.

First. John Wesley Newman, 1st of Reuben and Mary, *nee* Clark, born 1832, lives in Staunton, Va.; is a planter; married about 1853, Elizabeth Barger, of Augusta county, Va. One child, a son, Broaddus Barger Newman, born ———; m. about 1880, Miss Kavanaugh, of Staunton, Va.; died, leaving several daughters, who reside with their grandfather Newman, at Staunton, Virginia.

Second. Joseph Allen, 2d of Reuben and Mary, *nee* Clark, born 1834, married in 1858, Belle Peaco, of Augusta county, and died at Staunton, Va., in Jan., 1901. Seven children:

1. John Alexander, b. ———.
2. Susan,   b. ———; married John Lawrence.
3. Ida,   b. ———.
4. Janette,   b. ———; married ———.
5. Lewis,   b. ———.
6. Lynn,   b. ———.
7. Henry Towles, b. ———.

No further record.

Third. James Addison Newman, 3d of Reuben and Mary, *nee* Clark, born July 24, 1836, in Orange county; was first lieutenant in the Montpelier Guards, of Orange, a company of Virginia militia engaged in the John Brown affair; moved to Clarke county, Alabama, soon after; was a contractor and builder; was, with a single exception, the only person in Clarke county to vote against secession; refused a commission in an Alabama command; returned to Virginia and enlisted as a private soldier in Carter's company of artillery; fought in the battles of the Army of Northern Virginia until May 12, 1864, when he was wounded and captured at the "bloody angle" at Spottsylvania; returned to Alabama after the war and engaged in farming; died March 21, 1891. He married, Nov. 10, 1863, Mrs. Elizabeth Coate, *nee* Boroughs, widow of Judge Henley W. Coate, of Alabama. She is the daughter of Thomas Boroughs and his wife, Rebecca Kimbell Morriss, both of North Carolina. Thomas was a son of Bryan Boroughs and his wife, Sally Waddell, both North Carolinians. Bryan was a son of James Boroughs and his wife, ——— Bryan, both Virginians, who moved to North Carolina. James was a son of Zachariah Boroughs, of Virginia. The name Boroughs is frequently misspelled, the most common variant being Burroughs. Rebecca Kimbell Morriss was a daughter of John Morriss and his wife, Elizabeth Lee Armistead; for her descent, see the genealogy of the Armistead family, by President Tyler, in the William and Mary Quarterly. The children of James Addison Newman and Elizabeth (Coate), *nee* Boroughs, were three:

1. William Boroughs, b. May 30, 1866.
2. Thomas Reuben,   b. Apr. 24, 1868.
3. James Bryan,   b. Dec. 19, 1870.

NINTH GENERATION.

First. William Boroughs Newman, 1st of James Addison and Elizabeth, born May 30, 1866; alumnus of Howard College, Ala., class of 1884; of Washington and Lee University, class of 1886; clerk of the Probate Court of Talladega county, Ala.; residence, Talladega Court House; married, December 29, 1887, at Franklin, Texas, Mrs. Sarah Waller (widow of Dr. William F. Waller), *nee* Ellison, born Feb. 7, 1867, eldest daughter of Judge Isaac B. Ellison and his wife, *nee* Elizabeth Price Butler, of Texas. Two children:

1. Mildred, b. Jan. 1, 1890.
2. James Bryan, b. July 10, 1896.

Second. Thomas Reuben Newman, 2d of James Addison and Elizabeth, born April 24, 1868; graduated in medicine; residence, Nashville, Tenn.; married, ———, 1891, Martha Vertrees, daughter of Dr. W. M. and his wife, *nee* Martha Ford, of Nashville. Four children:

1. James Addison, b. 1892.
2. Charles Ford, b. 1894.
3. Thomas Reuben, b. 1897.
4. Martha, b. 1900.

Third. James Bryan Newman, 3d and youngest child of James Addison and Elizabeth, *nee* Boroughs, born Dec. 19, 1870; graduated in law; residence, Nashville, Tenn.; married, Nov. 19, 1901, at Demopolis, Alabama, Lilah McDaniel, second child of John and his wife, Mary A., *nee* Knox; daughter of Dr. James C. Knox and his 1st wife, Jane Bowie; daughter of Chancellor Alexander Bowie and his wife Susan, *nee* Barnett; son of Major John Bowie, the emigrant to America. See Bowie Genealogy, page 334–5, by Walter W. Bowie.

SEVENTH GENERATION.

Ninth. George Newman, 9th of John and 3d by his second wife, Mildred Atkins, *nee* Quisenberry, born 1825; was twice married: first, to Jane Wiltshire; one child, a son, John, born ———; second, to ———; two sons, William and Charles.

SIXTH GENERATION.

Eighth. James Newman, 8th and youngest child of Alexander and Frances, *nee* Bourne, born about 1784; is not mentioned in the will of his brother George, 1802, and is believed to have died before his majority; unmarried. In 1798 "James, son of Fannie, of Orange," was apprenticed to learn carpenter's trade, in Orange county.

FIFTH GENERATION.

Second. Reuben Newman, 2d of Thomas, of Orange, and Elizabeth, *nee* Morton, and grandson of Alexander, born in Orange county, about 1742; died 1825, unmarried. From his will, dated Aug. 20, 1819, proven Aug. 27, 1825, recorded in Liber 6, folio 271, at Orange Court House, we infer he was what the world calls successful in business, as he left a large estate to Henry Hill, alias Henry Newman, and his wife.

Henry Hill, alias Newman, settled in the South, perhaps Mississippi, where he left a family of children. No further record.

Third. Abner Newman, 3d of Thomas, of Orange, and Elizabeth, *nee* Morton, and grandson of Alexander, born in Orange county in 1756; married Hester Mauzy, daughter of Henry and Ann, *nee* Withers, of Fauquier county, son of John and Hester, *nee* Foote, of Stafford county; son of Henry, Sr., the emigrant, and his wife, Miss Conger, daughter of Dr. Conger, of England. Henry Mauzy, Sr., a French Huguenot, fled from France in 1685; upon the revocation of the Edict of Nantes, escaped to England, where he married, and where his son Henry was born, about 1690; emigrated to Virginia between the year 1697 and 1700; settled in Stafford county, where he at once acquired about fifteen hundred acres of land. (See Mauzy Records, by Wm. F. Boogher.) Abner Newman lived in Culpeper, Fauquier and Shenandoah counties. He was pensioned as a private soldier April 9, 1824, as a resident of Shenandoah county, aged 68 years. (See report of Secretary of War of June, 1834, Pension Establishment of the U. S. for the State of Virginia, page 98.) Abner was sheriff for Shenandoah county. He appears to have removed from Fauquier about 1788, as in this year he records a deed of sale for all his lands in the county. Of the children of Abner Newman and Hester, *nee* Mauzy, but little is known; it is believed, however, that with others, William, who married Miss Tucker, in 1804, in Culpeper county; Alexander, who married Peggie Douglass, in 1806, in Rockingham county, and Abner, who married Eliza Cornaga, in 1824, in Culpeper county, were his sons. The dates of his death and that of his wife and children are unknown to the writer. After 1824 he probably removed to Rockingham county with his son Alexander, where he spent the remainder of his life; but owing to the partial destruction of the records of this county during the Civil War, no further mention has been found of him or his children.

FOURTH GENERATION.

Third. James Newman, 3d and youngest child of Alexander, of Orange, son of Thomas, Jr., son of Thomas the emigrant, born between 1705 and 1715; married ———; is believed to have had at least three sons and a daughter:

1. Thomas, b. ———.
2. Robert, b. ———.
3. James, b. ———.
4. Elizabeth, b. ———.

FIFTH GENERATION.

First. Thomas Newman, 1st of James, 3d of Alexander, settled perhaps in Berkeley county, Va., as in 1778 he recorded a deed at Martinsburg conveying certain lands to Elizabeth Newman, who was either his mother or sister. He was executor of his brother Robert's will, proven Sept. 27, 1819, in Hardy county, now West Virginia.

Second. Robert Newman, 2d of James, 3d of Alexander, of Orange, born ——— ; married, 1789, Elizabeth Latham, in Culpeper county. In January, 1816, he appears to have been in Alleghany county, Maryland. On Sept. 27, 1819, his will was proven in Hardy county. It was dated March 18, 1813, and is recorded in Liber 2 of Wills, folio 59. He left his wife Elizabeth all estate during her widowhood. His brother Thomas was executor and brother James one of the witnesses. From the sales of his personal estate, recorded in Liber 2, folio 305, he appears to have had two sons, Gadsby and Edgar, the latter a minor in 1820, and a daughter Nancy, also a minor.

Sixth Generation.

Gadsby Newman, son of Robert and Elizabeth, *nee* Latham, born in Culpeper county; settled with his parents in Hardy county. On Sept. 3, 1824, he married Elizabeth Reed; died early in life. His estate was settled May 15, 1833, Liber 6, folio —, Hardy county records. No further record.

Second. Edgar Newman, 2d of Robert and Elizabeth, *nee* Latham, was living in Hardy county in 1833, as his name appears as a purchaser at the sale of his brother's personal estate. No further record.

Fifth Generation.

Third. James Newman, 3d of James, 3d of Alexander, of Orange, born ——— ; married, ———, 1789, Mary Early, in Culpeper county; was living in Hardy county in 1813, where he witnessed the will of his brother Robert. Whether he was the same James who, with his wife Nancy, made a deed to lands in Culpeper in 1805 is not known.

Third Generation.

Second. George Newman, 2d of Thomas, Jr., son of Thomas the immigrant, born ——— ; married Elizabeth ——— ; died in Richmond county, Va., in 1734. His will was proven at

Warsaw in 1734. Issue: one child, a daughter, Patience, born ———; married before 1733, John Ford. No further record.

Third. John Newman, 3d son of Thomas, Jr., and twin brother of George, married Eliza (probably) Burdett. The will of Henry Burdett, Jr., at Warsaw, proven in 1724, leaves his property to John Newman and his wife Eliza, Thomas Thornton and his wife Susanna, and Humphrey Thomas and his wife Jane; the relationship is not stated. John Newman died in 1759, intestate. Issue, three children:

1. George, b. ——— (a minor in 1733).
2. John, b. ———.
3. Thomas, b. ———.

FOURTH GENERATION.

First. George Newman, 1st of John and Eliza, *nee* Burdett, of Richmond county, where he was born ———; married ———. Five children:

1. George, b. ———.
2. Patty, b. ———.
3. Milley, b. ———; m. ——— Crewdson.
4. Jenny, b. ———.
5. Nancy, b. ———.

George Newman died in Richmond county, Va., where his will was proven in 1784.

FIFTH GENERATION.

First. George Newman, 1st of George, of Richmond county, born ———; married Alice ———. Three children: Joseph, Samuel, and grand-daughter Amelia, daughter of son George, are mentioned in his will, proven in Richmond county, Aug. 2, 1830. Of his four sisters nothing further is known.

FOURTH GENERATION.

Second. John Newman, 2d of John and Eliza, *nee* Burdett,

of Richmond county, where he was born ———— ; married
Elizabeth Deane, daughter of John, of Richmond county;
moved to Prince William county about 1760.   Owing to the
partial destruction of the records of Prince William county
during the Civil War, no satisfactory information of his
descendants has been obtained.

Third.   Thomas Newman, 3d of John and Eliza, *nee* Burdett, of Richmond county, where he was born ———— ; is believed to have moved to York county, where he was clerk
of the courts and deputy sheriff after the Revolution.   He is
mentioned in the will of his brother George.

––––––––––

The Newman Genealogy is based upon facts in the possession of Mr. William B. Newman, of Talladega, Alabama,
taken from family and various county records, liber and folio,
as stated ; also upon researches made by the compiler at his
request.   Mr. Newman intends preparing a genealogy of the
descendants of John and Thomas Newman, Englishmen, and
this sketch is inserted by his permission.

He will welcome any corrections, as well as new matter, and
is especially anxious that dates be given, where possible, with
as much biographical matter as can be had from the records,
family Bibles, and other credible sources of information.

HISTORICAL AND GENEALOGICAL NOTES OF HUGH THOMAS, OF WESTMORELAND CO., VA.

Hugh Thomas, of Westmoreland county, Va., was born about 1663–4 in Charles county, Maryland. His father Hugh immigrated to the province of Maryland in the spring of 1661, as will appear from a demand made on the Lord Proprietor for lands by *Robert Slye*, June 18, 1661, for transporting the said Hugh Thomas. Liber 4, folio 555, Land office of Maryland.

April 19, 1666, Hugh Thomas, Sr., had assigned and patented to him 600 acres of land, called Rich Hill, on the west side of the Wicomico river, in Charles county, Md. See rent roll for said county, liber 1, folio 37, Land office, Md.; and on June 20, 1675, a patent for 83 acres, called Thomas's Addition to Rich Hill; April 14, 1681, 100 acres, called Fortune.

In Nov., 1681, Hugh Thomas was a member of the grand jury for Charles county, liber 1–8, folio 174.

About 1662–3 he married Ann ―――― in Charles county; issue, three sons of whom we have record; Hugh born about 1663; John born 1664–5; and James about 1666.

On Nov. 13, 1684, Hugh Thomas, Sr., sold his Rich Hill plantation to John Harrison, Gentleman, of Charles county; consideration, 13,000 lbs. of Merchantable tobacco, his wife Ann joining in this deed, liber L, No. 1, folio 53, Charles county record. At this date his son John is possessed by deed of gift from his father of the 100 acres called Fortune; See Rent roll No. 2, folio 328 for said county.

Hugh Thomas died in 1688 in Charles county. See letters Testamentary, Provincial, Annapolis, Md.

His son, Hugh, Jr., the subject of this notice, was born as above stated, about 1663, and settled early in life in Cople Parish, Westmoreland county, Va., where he married Ann ――――, and where he died in July, 1718, leaving his widow

Ann and two minor sons, Hugh and Daniel surviving. His will is dated Nov. 6, 1717; proven July 30, 1718; wife Ann, executrix, filed her inventory Sept. 8, 1718. In Sept., 1719, Mrs. Ann Thomas died intestate, as on Sept. 30, 1719, a commission was appointed to appraise her estate with her brother-in-law, John Thomas, as administrator. He reported the amount of appraisement to the court Dec. 16, 1719, and was appointed guardian of his two nephews, Hugh and Daniel, as per the will of their father.

THIRD GENERATION.

First. Hugh Thomas, 1st of Hugh, Gentleman, of Westmoreland county, Va., and Ann his wife, was born about 1705, in Cople Parish, where he married about 1730–5, Mary Carr, daughter of William. See will of William Carr, liber 3, folio 125, proven 1702, Westmoreland county record. Referring to his two infant children, Joseph and Mary, also a deed of gift of 100 acres of land by Joseph Carr for love and affection to his sister Mary, now wife of Hugh Thomas, dated June 12, 1735. See also deed to Hugh and Daniel Thomas for love and affection from their uncle James, dated June 30, 1735, in which they are called his nephews.

In 1744 Hugh Thomas and Mary, his wife, deeded the 100 acres received by gift from Joseph Carr to Daniel Tibbs; consideration, 9,000 lbs. of Merchantable tobacco, and 8 £ of Va. money. Mary Thomas, *nee* Carr, appears to have died about 1745–50, as her name does not occur in any deeds after 1744. Her husband, Hugh Thomas No. 3, remained a resident freeholder in Westmoreland county until 1764, this being the date of his last deed of record in that county. After this he settled with his uncle John and brother Daniel in Prince William county, where he is believed to have died; but owing to the partial destruction of the records of Prince William, there being neither will nor intestate to be found, the date of his death and the names of his children have not been ascertained.

Second. Daniel Thomas, 2d and youngest child of Hugh, Jr., and Ann, his wife, of Westmoreland county, born about 1706–7, married, in Westmoreland county, his first cousin, Catherine Thomas, daughter of his uncle James. See will of James Thomas.

March 11, 1728, he and his brother Hugh secured a warrant for 300 acres of land in Stafford county, and Nov. 16, 1731, for 667 acres in Prince William. These lands were subsequently divided between the brothers by order of court.

All their lands were, subsequent to 1742, in Fairfax county. As evidence that Daniel had settled in that county, it is shown by the records that as a free-holder he voted in 1744 for Capt. Lawrence Washington and Capt. Lewis Ellzey for the House of Burgesses. He continued to reside in this county up to 1757, his name appearing to that date as a successful plaintiff in a number of suits at law.

Early in 1757 he filed a suit in equity against his uncle John and wife Elizabeth; but when the suit was called in the autumn of the same year, the attorney for the defense reported both defendants as dead.

On March 12, 1757, Daniel Thomas sold to William Bayly, of Fairfax county, 333½ acres of land, his half of the 667 granted Nov. 16, 1731, to him and his brother Hugh. Liber A, folio 149, Fairfax county record.

April 15, 1763, account book of Fairfax county: An agreement between Daniel Thomas and William Bayly. This is the last entry of said Daniel Thomas in Fairfax county. He is believed to have removed to Prince William county, where again the loss of records prevents positive information of him or his descendants. The will of his wife's father, James, proven in 1742 in Westmoreland county, makes positive reference to his grandson, William Thomas, the son of his daughter Catherine. This William appears later to have figured in Prince William and Orange counties.

SECOND GENERATION.

Second. John Thomas, 2d of Hugh of Charles county, Md., and Ann, his wife, born about 1664–5, was a planter. He received by deeds of gift from his father 100 acres of land called Fortune, in Charles county, Md., where he doubtless married his first wife ——.

After the death of his parents in Md., and prior to 1717, he settled in Westmoreland county, Va., where he probably married Elizabeth, daughter of Nicholas Spencer, about 1718, as her brother John Spencer records a deed of gift for love and affection in 1718 to 50 acres of land with house and orchard, etc., to John Thomas and wife Elizabeth. It appears from the records that after settling up the estate of his brother Hugh as administrator *de bonis non*, and that of his widow Ann in 1719, he removed to that part of Stafford county, which after 1730 was Prince William, and after 1742 to Fairfax county, with his two wards, Hugh and Daniel Thomas, nephews, and sons of his brother Hugh. There he was the owner of several tracts of land. The last mention of him is in 1755 in the case of the suit by his nephew Daniel at Fairfax Court House previously referred to.

Third. James Thomas, 3d of Hugh, of Charles county, Md., and Ann, his wife, born about 1666–7 ; settled early in life in Westmoreland county, Va., where, after 1700, he married Sarah ——. From 1728 until his death in 1742 he was surveyor for Lord Fairfax and for the county of Westmoreland. He was possessed of a large landed estate : Sept. 17, 1705, a northern Neck deed for 729 acres in Richmond county ; March 8, 1727, 1,728 acres in Stafford county ; Oct. 30, 1728, 1,450 acres in Stafford county ; Aug. 6, 1731, 1,504 acres in Prince William county. June 20, 1735, he records a deed of gift to his two nephews, Hugh and Daniel Thomas, on the Yeocomac river, in the parish of Cople, county of Westmoreland. He died November, 1742 ; his will, bearing date Feb. 10, 1742, was proven Dec. 1, 1742. In which he names his children in the following order: Sons—James, George, John; daughters—Winnifred Thomas, Elizabeth Thomas; his grandson William Thomas, the son of his daughter Catherine, wife of Daniel Thomas; daughter Hannah Thomas, daughter Sarah Jennings, to whom he leaves his lands, etc., and appoints his son John executor and residuary legatee, he to provide for his mother Sarah during the remainder of her life.

Third Generation.

First. James Thomas, 1st of James and Sarah, born in Westmoreland county, died in 1743. His estate personal was appraised at £12 11 shillings and 6 pence; settled in open court 1743. (See Court Docket, Westmoreland county.) In this account neither wife nor children are referred to.

Second. George Thomas, son of James and Sarah, born in Westmoreland county; married Eleanor ———; died in Prince William county January, 1781. His will, bearing date Jan. 1st, 1781, was proven Feb. 5, 1781. In it reference is made to three sisters: Elizabeth Latheram, Ann Winnifred, and Nancy Thomas, to whom he left legacies. To his wife Eleanor he bequeathed the bulk of his estate and appointed her executrix. (Liber G, folio 107, Prince William record.) The inventory of his estate was reported to the court at £13,985 10 shillings sterling money. From the verbiage of his will no information can be gathered as to his children.

Third. John Thomas, son of James, of Cople Parish, Westmoreland county, where he was born, received, by the will of his father, a large tract of land in Prince William county, known as the Sugar Lands. He also purchased several tracts, one from John Foster and wife in Prince William county; consideration £650 Va. money. (Liber Z, folio 166.)

After 1742, the date of the formation of Fairfax county from Prince William, he became a freeholder of Fairfax county. On March 27, 1750, he recorded a deed for several negroes in favor of his mother Sarah ; consideration, £60 Virginia money. (Liber C, folio 6.) This is the last entry we find in Fairfax county of either John Thomas or his mother.

ADDENDUM.—Hugh Thomas, of Frederick county, Md., from whom descended Governor Francis Thomas, deceased, was in no wise, as has been claimed, a relative of Hugh Thomas, gentleman, of Westmoreland county, Va.

Governor Francis Thomas, deceased, was a descendant of a Hugh Thomas who was born in Pennsylvania, and who about 1733 settled in Prince George (later Frederick) county, Md.

The descendants of Hugh Thomas, of Frederick county, Md., will be treated in a similar volume devoted to Maryland.

BIRTH AND DEATH RECORDS FROM THE TOMB-STONES OF THE OLD STONE CHURCH GRAVE YARD IN AUGUSTA COUNTY, VIRGINIA.

Allison, Sarah, born 1760 ; died Jan. 2, 1791.

Allen, Mary, wife of John, born Jan. 1, 1778 ; died May 6, 1819.

Bell, Joseph, born 1774 ; died March, 1823.

Bell, Margaret, wife of James, born Dec. 25, 1785 ; died Feb. 27, 1856.

Bell, Sarah, wife of James, born 1788 ; died Dec. 18, 1806.

Bell, Joseph, born May, 1746 ; died Sept. 13, 1833.

Bell, Major William, born 1744 ; died Aug. 22, 1833.

Bell, Margaret, wife of William, born Feb. 22, 1759 ; died June 20, 1844.

Bourland, James, born Feb. 8, 1780 ; died June 29, 1861.

Bourland, Mary, born Sept. 10, 1791 ; died July 28, 1828.

Beard, Joseph, born June 4, 1778 ; died Jan. 16, 1856.

Crawford, Mrs. wife of Robert, born 1722 ; died Sept. 3, 1807.

Crawford, Major John, born 1763 ; died Dec. 17, 1846.

Crawford, Rebecca, wife of John, born 1769 ; died Dec. 6, 1851.

Crawford, Harriett, wife of John, born 1800 ; died Nov. 29, 1843.

Crawford, Elizabeth, born Dec. 13, 1775 ; died March 24, 1847.

Crawford, Elizabeth, born Sept. 1, 1795 ; died April 2, 1822.

Crawford, George, born 1775 ; died Dec. 17, 1824.

Crawford, Mrs. Jane, born 1751 ; died Sept. 13, 1834.

Crawford, James, born 1777 ; died Feb. 12, 1831.

Crawford, Mary, born Oct. 27, 1795 ; died Jan. 23, 1834.

Crawford, Alexander, born 1791 ; died Nov. 24, 1826.

Crawford, Capt. Samuel, born 1786 ; died Feb. 13, 1846.

Crawford, Sarah, born 1767 ; died 1846.

Clinedinst, Michael, born 1773 ; died Feb. 24, 1848.

Curry, Samuel, born April 13, 1770 ; died July 15, 1845.

Craig, Jane, born 1744 ; died June 11, 1811.

Craig, William, born 1750 ; died Sept. 8, 1829.

Craig, James, born April 17, 1781 ; died March 27, 1863.

19

Craig, Martha, born May 31, 1794; died Nov., 1851.

Craig, Susan, wife of James, born 1796; died May 15, 1821.

Givens, John, born May, 1740; died 1812.

Givens, Jane, born Sept. 14, 1750; died Nov. 13, 1812.

Givens, Letitia, born May 10, 1790; died June 25, 1811.

Gamble, John, born 1760; died January, 1831.

Gamble, Rebecca, born 1767; died May 18, 1832.

Gamble, Elizabeth, born 1788; died June 30, 1861.

Gamble, Philander, born October, 1800; died April 18, 1856.

Harnsberger, Samuel, born 1790; died Oct. 30, 1851.

Harnsberger, Annie C., born Feb. 12, 1797; died April 13, 1860.

Harnsberger, Rebecca, born May 30, 1794; died March 21, 1852.

Henton, Sarah, born 1800; died 1849.

Hufing, Andrew, born 1797; died Sept. 30, 1836.

Huston, Jane, wife of N. H. Huston, born May 21, 1797; died
    Dec. 17, 1854.

Hyde, Mary, wife of Joseph, born Nov. 17, 1797; died March,
    1838.

Kerr, James, born 1800; died 1867.

Kenny, James, born July 2, 1729; died Nov. 7, 1864.

Marvin, Ann, wife of J. Marvin, born 1783; died May 10, 1823.

Montgomery, Wm. Ellis, born Sept. 1, 1796; died Jan. 9, 1853.

Nelson, Alexander, born 1749; died Jan. 9, 1834.

Nelson, Nancy, wife of Alexander, born 1763; died 1829.

Nelson, James, born 1794; died March 11, 1850.

Nelson, Alexander, born Oct. 25, 1798; died Oct. 23, 1850.

Poague, Major William, born March 18, 1781; died Sept. 23,
    1855.

Reid, L., born 1769; died Oct. 28, 1845.

Reid, Benjamin T., born 1798; died July 25, 1859.

Robertson, Alexander, born 1750; died April 22, 1801.

Robertson, Jane, born 1751; died Nov. 25, 1823.

Robertson, Sarah, born 1755; died Sept. 4, 1785.

Robertson, Alexander, born Mar. 1, 1744; died Nov. 25, 1816.

Robertson, Elizabeth, born Oct., 1751; died Feb. 6, 1825.

Robertson, Letitia R., born Jan. 12, 1792; died Aug. 8, 1836.

Rhodes, Mildred, wife of William, born 1795; died Sept. 18, 1833.

Stover, Jacob, born Jan. 23, 1777; died March 12, 1851.

Stover, Margaret, wife of Jacob, born June 14, 1799; died July 15, 1854.

Snapp, Robert, born June 24, 1796; died July 1, 1865.

Speece, Rev. Conrad, pastor of Stone Church for 22 years, born Nov. 21, 1776; died Feb. 15, 1836.

Tate, John A., born 1796; died Nov. 12, 1827.

Van Lear, Nancy, born 1770; died July 9, 1853 (wife of Jacob).

Van Lear, Jacob, born 1773; died Feb. 28, 1845.

Walker, John, born 1770; died April 7, 1836.

Wayt, Susan, wife of John, born 1768; died April 2, 1836.

Wilson, Rev. Wm., second pastor of Stone Church, born Aug. 1, 1751; died Dec. 1, 1835.

Young, Thomas, born 1749; died 1758.

HEBRON CHURCH YARD, BEVERLY MANOR, AUGUSTA COUNTY, VA.

Bell, Francis, born 1770; died Jan., 1851.

Bell, Sarah, wife of Francis, born Jan. 1, 1776; died Dec. 19, 1852.

Bell, Rebecca, wife of Samuel, born Feb. 6, 1779; died July 31, 1855.

Bell, Samuel, born 1759; died May 15, 1838.

Bell, Mary, born Oct. 31, 1751; died Feb. 7, 1794.

Bell, George, born 1787; died March 18, 1852.

Bell, James, born Sept. 13, 1790; died Mar. 27, 1847.

Bell, Rebecca, wife of James, born Jan. 13, 1798; died Apr. 9, 1880.

ROSE CEMETERY, STAUNTON, VA.

Craig, William, born 1789; died May 17, 1869.

Supplied by Miss Minnie F. Mickley, of Washington, D. C., author of the Mickley Genealogy.

HISTORICAL AND GENEALOGICAL NOTES OF WILLIAM CRAIG, OF AUGUSTA COUNTY, VIRGINIA, AND HIS DESCENDANTS.

According to a brief memoir of his family left by William Craig, of Mt. Meridian, Va., grandson and namesake of the immigrant, William Craig and Jean his wife, landed in America from the north of Ireland in the year 1721–22 with three sons, Robert, James and John.   He first settled in Pennsylvania in what is now either Lancaster or Chester county, and thence removed with his family to Augusta county, Va.

The date of his removal is not definitely known.   Robert, the eldest son, seems to have been the first of the family to leave Pennsylvania.   His name appears in Captain John Smith's company of militia in Augusta in the year 1742. (See January number, 1901, Virginia Magazine of History & Biography.)   The baptismal register of the Rev. John Craig, now in the library of Gen. John E. Roller, of Harrisonburg, Va., shows that John, son of Robert Craig, was baptized March 15, 1741, so that it may be fairly inferred that he removed to Augusta in the summer or fall of 1740.   He will be mentioned again in the course of this sketch.

William Craig, the immigrant, and the rest of his family, are believed to have removed from Pennsylvania to Virginia in the year 1744.   This is inferred from the fact that Sarah, daughter of James, second son of William, was born, according to Bible record, Feb. 1, 1743, and baptized by the Rev. John Craig, Oct. 21, 1744.   It would seem that her baptism would have occurred at an earlier period had her father been in Augusta much prior to this date.   In addition to this, James Craig did not take title to lands until Feb. 10, 1745, when Wm. Thompson conveyed to him 305 acres of land "lying in Augusta county, Va., on the northwest side of Middle River near Shenandoe."   This deed is recorded in liber 1, page 30, of the Augusta county land records.

From these facts the inference may be drawn that Wm. Craig, his wife Jean, and his two sons, James and John, removed from their home in Pennsylvania to Augusta county, Va., in the spring or summer of 1744.

The land records at Richmond, Orange and Staunton, do not show any conveyances to Wm. Craig, yet by his will dated Feb. 21, 1756, and recorded at Staunton, Nov. 26, 1759, he devises two-fifths of his landed estate to his "dearly beloved wife Janet (diminutive for Jean), to do with as she chooses," and one-fifth of the remainder to each of his sons, Robert, James and John. Evidently his lands had been acquired by purchase and his deeds were not recorded, which was quite a common practice in the early settlement of the Valley.

But little is known of his life beyond the fact that he was a Scotch-Irish Covenanter Presbyterian. The tradition among his descendants is that he and his family aided in building the old Stone Church in Augusta, and for generations his posterity have been among the most devoted adherents of that historic congregation. He was born between the years 1685 and 1690, judging from the date of James's birth, which was in 1714–15. His wife Jean (or Janet) was evidently still living in 1759, but nothing is known of her further history nor of the date of her death. She was, beyond question, of the same race from which he sprung, and was doubtless a worthy helpmate of the man who was among the pioneer Scotch emigrants to America.

As to the children of William and Janet, his wife, and their descendants, full information is not in the possession of the writer, but enough is known to form the basis of future research.

1. The history of ROBERT and his descendants is almost entirely unknown to the other branches descending from William and Janet Craig. It was long believed that he had removed from Augusta county to the Holston river country about the year 1765, when a large number of persons went

from Augusta to that section.   There are many Craigs in that portion of Virginia, among whom Robert is a common baptismal name, and Craig county is named for a member of this family.   But the will of a Robert Craig, who died in 1788, has recently been discovered at Staunton, and the description of his lands indicates that he lived in the same general neighborhood where John and James resided.   He names his sons John and Robert, and daughters Ann and Rebecca.   The will indicates that there were other sons and daughters, but he does not name them.

It is now believed that this Robert was the eldest son of William the immigrant, but nothing is definitely known of his descendants.   There are Craigs living in various counties of West Virginia who trace their ancestry to Augusta county in an uncertain way, and it is highly probable that this branch are descendants of Robert, eldest son of William the immigrant.

2. JAMES, second son of William and Janet, was born in the latter part of 1714, or in 1715, probably the latter year, in the north of Ireland, and came as a mere boy with his parents to America in 1721-2.   His Bible is now in the possession of the family of the late Rev. Dr. J. N. Craig, of Atlanta, Ga.   The family record states that James Craig died Feb. 7, 1791, in his 76th year, and according to family tradition his death resulted from an accident at his mill on South river.   He married Mary Laird, who died Feb. 20, 1785, in her 70th year.   Her family were also among the pioneer settlers of Augusta.

As previously stated, James Craig acquired his first lands on Middle river, opposite the present village of Mount Meridian, and there he probably resided for some years.   At a later period he removed to a tract of land on South river which he had acquired, and resided there until his death.   A portion of this tract is now owned by Charles S. Patterson, his great-grandson, who lives where his ancestor died.

James Craig led a busy life among his pioneer Scotch-Irish neighbors. He built, at an early date, the flouring and saw-mill on South river, in which he finally met with the accident that caused his death. Some of his account books have been preserved, and the entries therein indicate that none of the business sagacity of his race was lacking in him. He acquired a large landed estate, by patent and purchase, lying in the forks of Middle and North rivers, on South river, and between Middle river and the last named stream.

He appears, from the courts-martial record now in the office of the Hustings court clerk of Staunton, to have been a private militiaman in Captain John Givens' company of militia dur-ing the entire period of the Revolutionary War. But he was far beyond military age when the Revolution began, and is not believed to have seen active service to any extent, if at all. His sons and daughters were given the best educations obtain-able in Augusta at that period, and his memory is preserved among his great-grandchildren who still survive as a man of strong convictions as to the right or wrong of things and uncompromising in his opinions when formed with reference to any subject.

His children were :

1. *Sarah*, born Feb. 1, 1743, probably in Pennsylvania. Married, first, to Mr. Thorpe, of Augusta, and second to James Ely, having one son by each marriage. She removed to Ken-tucky shortly after her second marriage and settled in Lincoln county. Some of her descendants live in the vicinity of Frankfort, among them being Dr. James Ely, a prominent physician of that place.

A daughter of Jas. Ely and Sarah Craig, his wife, named Chloe, married her cousin, Harry Cowan, and had two sons, one of whom was named John. He was a graduate of Centre College, a lawyer by profession, a member of the Kentucky legislature, colonel of the 19th Kentucky volunteers (Union) in the Civil War, and was distinguished for gallantry. His first wife was Carrie Anderson, granddaughter of Governor

Owsley, of Kentucky, and his second wife was Mrs. Davis; both dead; no issue.

The youngest son of Harry Cowan and Chloe Ely, his wife, is Dr. George Cowan, of Danville, Ky. He married, first, his cousin, Letitia Craig, who died young, leaving one son, Dr. Harry J. Cowan, of Danville, Ky., who was one of the finest surgeons and physicians of his state. He died in 1900, at the untimely age of 38, universally regretted by all who knew his worth as a man and skill in his chosen profession.

2. *James*, born July 23, 1745; married Jean Stuart, of Augusta. His will was probated June 22, 1807, at Staunton, and in it he names his wife, Jean, and the following children: John, James, Samuel, George, William, Elijah, Robert, Sarah, Betsy, Agnes, Jane and Mary, wife of John McGill. This James Craig, along with his brother William, inherited that portion of their father's estate which lay between the forks of Middle and North Rivers. He lived on the northwest side of the former stream, a short distance below Mount Meridian. Comparatively little is known at this time of his descendants, but most of them are believed to have gone west.

John, the eldest son, died in 1840 near Weyer's Cave, Augusta county, Va. If he left issue they are unknown to the writer.

Samuel, the third son of James, resided for many years at Craigville, in the western part of Augusta, and his descendants are still in that vicinity.

William, his fifth son, is believed to have married in Augusta, Elizabeth Mills, in 1804, and to have removed to Kentucky, where his descendants are probably to be found.

Elijah, the sixth son, removed to Richmond Virginia, and his descendants reside in that city and Manchester, Virginia.

Sarah married John C. Hamilton, of Christian's Creek, and the will of Jean Craig, *nee* Stuart, wife of this second James, which was probated in Augusta county, Va., January 27, 1817, refers to her daughter, Nancy Hamilton. This daughter is not specifically named in the will of her father, and it is probable that one of the daughters bore a double name, which was not mentioned by him in his will. Andrew Hamilton, of Christian's Creek, married this Nancy Craig, who was, beyond question, the daughter of James and Jean Stuart Craig. These Hamiltons were brothers and grandsons of the Rev. John Craig, the Pioneer Presbyterian minister of Augusta.

3. *Samuel*, born June 26, 1746, removed to Kentucky in 1778 or 1779, and acquired a large tract of land in the Hanging Fork of Dicks River, in Lincoln county. The name of his wife is not known to the writer. He had, among other children, a son named Samuel, who married Miss Gaines, daughter of Richard Gaines, of Lincoln county, Va., and a daughter who married a Masterson. Samuel Craig and his wife, Miss Gaines, had a large family of children, among them being Dr. John Craig, the most celebrated physician of his day in central Kentucky, and Richard Gaines Craig, a captain in the Mexican War. Samuel Craig, Sr., died Sept. 25, 1795.

4. *John*, born Nov. 21, 1747, and died on his 25th birthday, Nov. 21, 1772; unmarried.

5. *George*, was born Jan. 4, 1749, and died Nov. 26, 1801. He married, Dec. 16, 1790, Elizabeth Evans, of Augusta, who died April 29, 1801. George inherited the home place of his father on South River, directly opposite the railroad station known as Harriston, on the Norfolk & Western Railroad. The children of George Craig and Elizabeth Evans, his wife, who reached maturity were:

(*a*) James, who married a Miss Crawford, of Augusta, and removed to Missouri early in the nineteenth century. Three of his sons served as soldiers in the Confederate Army.

(*b*) Mary, married John A. Patterson, of Augusta, who was long a member of the county court of that county under the old system. Among their children are Messrs. Chas. S. Patterson, who married Miss Hopkins, of Rockingham, and resides at the old homestead of James Craig, Sr.; James A. Patterson, who married Miss Poague, sister of Mrs. Gen. James

A. Walker; and Benjamin G. Patterson, deceased, of Harrisonburg, Va., who served as a captain of cavalry in the Confederate Army, and as a member of the Virginia House of Delegates.

(c) Margaret, who married Samuel Patterson and lived a long and honored life in Augusta. Among her children were the late Samuel Patterson, of Fisherville, John A. Patterson, who resides in New Hope, Va., and Wm. Patterson, who was one of the most successful and prosperous business men of Augusta.

(d) George, youngest child of George Craig and Elizabeth Evans, his wife, was born April 29, 1801, at the old homestead of James Craig, senior, and died in Pocahontas county, West Virginia, Oct. 9, 1846. He married, in 1824, Matilda Guthrie, and had issue as follows:

(1) Margaret Ann, married Robert I. Crawford, and lived for many years in Louisville, Ky., where she died March 19, 1892, leaving issue as follows: George M., Newton G., Hugh Brown Craig, and Rev. Alexander W. Crawford.

(2) Caroline Elizabeth, married Mr. John W. Warwick, of Pocahontas county, West Virginia. Issue.

(3) John Newton Craig, a Presbyterian minister and Doctor of Divinity, chaplain in the Confederate army, and for many years secretary of the home mission work of the Southern Presbyterian Church. He spent the last years of his life in Atlanta, Ga., and died suddenly in the month of October, 1900, while addressing the Virginia Synod at Newport News, Va., in reference to the work under his charge. He married Miss Lydia Brevard Harris, of Cabarrus county, N. C. Her great-grandfather was Col. Robert Harris, a signer of the Mecklenburg Declaration of Independence, who lost an arm at Guilford Court House. Issue, who live in Atlanta, Ga.

(4) Hugh Brown Craig was born in 1837, and graduated from Washington College in 1858. He served as adjutant of Edgar's 26th Virginia Battalion in the Civil War. His command was placed on Gen. Lee's extreme right at the

battle of Cold Harbor, June 3, 1864. In the assault made that day upon Gen. Lee, this portion of his line was temporarily broken and Adjutant Craig was killed with the battalion colors in his hand while rallying the men, the color guard having all been killed or wounded. He is buried at old Tinkling Spring Church, in Augusta.

6. *William*, was born Jan. 8, 1750, and died Sept. 8, 1829. He married, in 1778, Jean Anderson, daughter of John Anderson, who was among the first settlers of Augusta and a member of the first county court upon the organization of that county in 1745. John Anderson was also one of the first elders of the old Stone Church. Jean was born in 1744, and was baptized April 29th of that year by the Rev. John Craig, and died June 9, 1811. This William Craig, who preserved the record of his family mentioned previously, was a man of much solid worth and great integrity of character. He did not seek public position, although well qualified by education to take a leading part in the affairs of his county. He inherited one-half of his father's estate, which lay between the junction of Middle and North rivers, and his home was on the former stream, directly opposite the present village of Mount Meridian. A portion of his estate has been owned in more recent years by the late Robert S. Harnsberger. The records of the courts-martial of Augusta, previously referred to, show that William Craig served during the War of the Revolution as a private militiaman from 1778 to 1781, in the company of Captain John Givens, who lived on Middle river immediately adjoining his home. This company saw active service during the Revolution, especially in the year 1781, when it was marched to lower Virginia, and was in the battle of Jamestown. The courts-martial record referred to also shows that Captain Givens' company was ordered to rendezvous September 20, 1781, under Lieutenant-Colonel Samuel Vance, of Augusta. Palmer's Calendar of Virginia State Papers, volume 1, page 514, shows that Colonel Vance (incorrectly spelled Varn) was, on October 1, 1781, encamped four miles

below Williamsburg, in lower Virginia. This command was then on its way to Yorktown, in the siege of which it participated.

George and James, Jr., brothers of William, were also soldiers in the same company, and it is fair to assume that all of them, being of military age, saw full service in the company to which they belonged.

Jean Anderson, the wife of William Craig, was the widow Allen when she married him, her first husband, Lieutenant Hugh Allen, having been killed in the Indian battle of Point Pleasant in 1774. By her first marriage she had three sons, John, William and Hugh Allen, who removed to Kentucky in 1784 with their kinspeople, the Trimbles and others, and their descendants are numerous in that State to this day.

The children of William Craig and Jean Anderson were (four):

(1) Jean, born April 17, 1779, and died June 6, 1850. She married, June 25, 1799, James Patterson, of South River, born Sept. 18, 1772, and died Dec. 29, 1845. Issue, ten children, as follows:

Anne, born March 28, 1800; died in infancy; Nancy, born Nov. 7, 1802; Jean, born March 15, 1805; William, born July 3, 1807; Martha Allen, born Dec. 26, 1809; Margaret, born April 14, 1812; James, born July 11, 1814; John, born Jan. 12, 1816; Mary, born August 20, 1819; and Samuel, born August 18, 1821. The descendants of James and Jean Craig Patterson are numerous in Augusta and Rockingham counties, Virginia, while some are to be found in the West.

(2) James, born April 17, 1781; died March 27, 1863; married, first, his cousin, Susan Bell, daughter of Major Wm. Bell, of Augusta. One child of this marriage reached maturity, the late Jos. Davis Craig, of Mount Meridian, who was a member of the county court of Augusta under the old system, and later a member of the Virginia House of Delegates. His wife was Elizabeth Walker, daughter of Alexander Walker,

of Mt. Meridian, and sister of Gen. James A. Walker, commander of the Stonewall Brigade during the Civil War. Two sons were born to Jos. D. and Elizabeth Walker Craig, his wife; James Alexander, who married Susan Kemper Butler and represented Rockbridge county for several consecutive terms in the Virginia House of Delegates, and Wm. Bell, who married a Miss Brownlee and died without issue.

James Craig married, second, Sept. 29, 1825, Martha Burton, born May 31, 1794, and died Jan. 1, 1851. She was the daughter of May Burton, Jr., of Orange county, Va., captain in the war of the Revolution, lay reader of old Orange Episcopal Church for many years, and member of the county court of Orange, and high sheriff of the county in 1810–12. May Burton, Jr., married Sarah Head, daughter of Benjamin Head, of Orange, who was likewise a captain in the Revolution. The following children were born to James and Martha (Burton) Craig:

1. May Burton, born Oct. 7, 1826; died in Los Angeles, Cal., in 1901. Married, first, Martha Jane McCue, Oct. 25, 1848, daughter of Col. Franklin McCue, of Augusta county, Va. Issue, Franklin McCue, born Jan. 24, 1856; died July 17, 1856. He married, second, Susan Smith Lewis, daughter of Major W. H. Lewis, born June 19, 1837. Issue as follows:

(*a*) Martha May, born Dec. 16, 1860; married Robert Craig Borthwick, Aug. 16, 1882; died Oct. 19, 1885.

(*b*) Margaret Lewis, born July 18, 1862; married March 24, 1897, Charles H. Fisk.

(*c*) Elizabeth Lewis, born Jan. 1, 1865; died Sept. 8, 1865.

(*d*) Bessie Bell, born July 26, 1866; married Feb. 27, 1886, O. L. Boring.

(*e*) Virginia Estill, born July 6, 1869; married Nov. 11, 1896, Allen A. Irish.

(*f*) Lee, born Sept. 14, 1871; married June 24, 1896, Fannie Neal.

(*g*) William Lewis, born May 5, 1873.

(*h*) James Burton, born Nov. 18, 1875.

(*i*) A son or daughter, name unknown.

2. Benjamin James, married Elizabeth McChesney, of Rockbridge county, Va. Issue, five children, as follows:

(*a*) George McChesney, married Miss Johnson, of Florida, and resides near Waynesboro, Va. (1902), and has issue.

(*b*) Martha Burton, married, 1901, Mr. Moffett, of Shenandoah county, Va.

(*c*) James, married Miss Loth, of Waynesboro, Va., 1900, and resides at that place.

(*d*) Evelyn, married Rev. Alexander F. Laird, Presbyterian minister, and now resides in Mississippi (1902).

(*e*) William Brown, unmarried (1902).

3. Susan Martha, born Nov. 25, 1830; died March 6, 1872; married Sept. 25, 1854, Edward Stevens Kemper, of Cross Keys, Rockingham county, Va., born Jan. 18, 1829; died Dec. 26, 1882. She was a woman of rare excellence of character; a christened child of the old Stone church of Augusta when Rev. Conrad Speece was its pastor; a devoted member of the Presbyterian church from her youth; and left to her children a memory of all that is to be reverenced in the name of mother. Her husband was for many years a prominent business man and farmer in Rockingham county; one of the pioneers in the organization of Mutual Fire Insurance companies in the state of Virginia, and county surveyor of Rockingham county. She sleeps in the cemetery at Cross Keys, Virginia, and he at Harrisonburg, Virginia. Issue:

(*a*) James Rodham, born June 10, 1855; married, Feb. 27, 1878, Laura Cordelia Coiner, of Rockingham county, Virginia.

He is a prominent farmer, residing (1902) at Fishersville, Augusta county, Virginia; also organized the Virginia Long Distance Telephone Company, of Virginia, the pioneer corporation of its kind in the State, and was its first president. Issue: Ethel May, born Jan. 26, 1880; Grace, born Dec. 28, 1882.

(*b*) Martha Ann, born Aug. 19, 1857; died Dec. 23, 1857.

(*c*) Charles Edward, born June 5, 1859; married, Dec. 17,

1885, Mary Allen Crawford, of Augusta county, Virginia, born Jan. 8, 1866. He was educated at private schools and academies; graduated from Washington and Lee University, Lexington, Virginia, in the law class of 1882; practiced law in Staunton, Virginia, for ten years; was appointed Assistant Supervising-Architect by Secretary Carlisle in 1893; was made chief executive officer of the Supervising-Architect's office of the Treasury Department Jan. 1, 1895; represented his department on the U. S. Boards of Management for the Expositions held at Atlanta, Georgia (1895), Nashville, Tenn. (1897), and Omaha, Neb. (1898); is a member of the National Society, Sons of the American Revolution, the Virginia Historical Society, of Richmond, Va., and the National Geographical Society, of Washington, D. C. Issue: Edward Crawford, born Oct. 1, 1886; William Holbrook, born Jan. 12, 1889.

(*d*) William Whitfield, born July 23, 1863; died Feb. 25, 1865.

(*e*) Arthur Lee, born Jan. 14, 1866; married, Oct. 6, 1887, Laura Bell Hooke; is an active business man, residing (1902) in Wytheville, Va. Issue: Audrey Lee, born Aug. 15, 1888; Bertha Hooke, born Nov. 25, 1889; died Sept. 23, 1893; Arthur Walker, born Oct. 23, 1891; Harvey Ribble, born June 29, 1893; Laura Marie, born March 13, 1897.

(*f*) Aubrey Craig, born Jan. 23, 1868: died May 30, 1884.

4. Sarah Jane Cornelia, married Dr. Joseph B. Webb, of Cross Keys, Rockingham county, Va., member of the Virginia House of Delegates and State Senate. Issue: James Warfield, died in infancy; Fleta Hope, died young; Iota Joy, married Thomas P. Yager, of Madison county, Va., who now resides at Cross Keys, Virginia.

James Craig, like his father, had no fondness for public life, although in politics he was an uncompromising Whig. He served for many years as an elder of the Old Stone Church, which is situated about seven miles from his residence. His beautiful estate lay directly in the forks of Middle and North rivers, and his home was always the seat of gracious hospitality. He lived a long and honored life, and died with the regret of all who knew him, especially the poor, to whom he had always given freely of the bounty with which the Lord had blessed him. He is buried in the old cemetery of the Old Stone Church with the two women who called him husband.

(3) Sarah, daughter of William and Jean (Anderson) Craig, born March 13, 1783, and died Nov. 30, 1849. She married James G. Laird, her cousin, who was born Nov. 1, 1781, and died July 28, 1857. They are both buried in the cemetery at Cross Keys, Virginia.

James G. Laird was the son of David Laird and Margaret Craig, who is believed to have been the daughter of Robert Craig. She was baptized April 7, 1745, by the Rev. John Craig. If this assumption is correct, the descendants of James G. Laird and Sarah Craig, his wife, are doubly descended from Wm. Craig, the immigrant, and Jean, his wife. David Laird was a captain of one of the first companies of regulars organized in Augusta for service in the Revolution. He was a captain of militia in 1777, and was also at Point Pleasant as a lieutenant in 1774. The relationship between the Mount Meridian Craigs and James, who married Sarah Craig, has always been recognized by the two families, but the degree of kinship is not now known.

James G. and Sarah Craig Laird had two children, both daughters : Sarah, who married Mr. Thurmond, and died in Harrisonburg some years ago, and Margaret, who married Mr. Andrew Irick.

James G. Laird lived and died about two and one-half miles from Keezletown, near the foot of Laird's Knob, which takes its name from his family.

(4) Margaret, daughter of William and Jean (Anderson) Craig, born Dec. 25, 1785, and died Feb. 27, 1856, was the last wife of James Bell, of Augusta, who descended from one of the old pioneer families of that county. He was for many years the senior presiding justice of the Augusta county court,

and one of the most active and enterprising men in that section. He was born in 1772 and died in 1856, and is buried along with his wife in the old cemetery of the old Stone Church. Their children were: John J., who married and died without issue; David S., who married Miss McCue, and had issue; J. Wayt, who married, first, Sarah, daughter of Col. James Crawford, of Augusta, and had issue; and second, her sister Eliza, who died without issue; Henderson M., of Staunton, a lawyer and member of the Virginia House of Delegates, married Miss Kinney and had issue; Jane, who married Mr. Arbuckle, of Greenbrier county, Va.; Elizabeth, who married Chesley Kinney, of Staunton, and had issue; Margaret, who married Frank M. Young, of Staunton, and had issue. David S. Bell, son of James and Margaret, was with his father, a member of the old county court of Augusta. Issue.

7. *Mary*, daughter of James and Mary Laird Craig, was born May 10, 1752, and died Jan. 16, 1778. She married William Anderson, of Augusta, who is believed to have been the son of John, father of Jean, who married William Craig, brother of Mary. James Craig, the elder, in his will, probated at Staunton in 1791, refers to the heirs of his daughter Mary, but does not name them. William Anderson was a captain in the War of the Revolution and removed to Kentucky in 1784, where his descendants are doubtless to be found.

8. *Agnes*, youngest child of James and Mary Laird Craig, was born in Augusta, April 10, 1754. She married James Anderson, brother of Jean and William referred to, and removed to South Carolina, settling in what is now Anderson county. James Anderson served as a captain in the Revolution, and the following children were born to them: Robert, removed to Mississippi and died there; George, who went to Missouri and afterwards to Texas, leaving seven sons and two daughters; James, who was accidentally killed in Alabama, leaving a family; Dr. William Anderson, who lived and died at the old Anderson homestead in South Carolina in 1853,

20

aged 63 years; Mary, who married James Watson, leaving issue; Sarah, married Wm. Orr, of South Carolina, and left issue; Anne, married James Orr, of South Carolina, and left issue; Jane, married Mr. McKensie, and upon the death of her husband removed to Mississippi, issue; Ann married John James Mathews, both dead, no issue living; Elizabeth, the youngest child of James and Agnes Craig Anderson, married Saxon Anderson, not related to her. They removed to Alabama and have issue living in that state.

Captain James Anderson was baptized by the Rev. John Craig at the old Stone Church in Augusta, March 6, 1748, and died in South Carolina, Sept. 9, 1813. His wife Agnes died in the same state in 1841–42, aged about 88 years. She is buried in the family graveyard on the estate of Dr. Wm. Anderson. Her husband is buried in the old Carmel Church graveyard. The descendants of Agnes Craig and James Anderson are numerous throughout the South, and are highly respectable.

3. JOHN, youngest son of William Craig, the immigrant, was probably born in 1717 or 1718, and came to America with his parents as a mere child. He resided in the same neighborhood with his brothers, Robert and James, until 1775, when he removed to Kentucky.

The journal of the Virginia Convention of 1776 contains a petition from him stating that he had removed from Augusta county, Va., to the western country in the previous year with a drove of cattle, intending to settle there. He located in Lincoln county, Ky., and died there in 1862, describing himself in his will as being very old and infirm. The name of his wife is not known, but she is believed to have been either an Allen or an Anderson. The baptismal register of the Rev. John Craig previously referred to shows that William Craig, son of John, was baptized Aug. 10, 1746, and James, son of John, was baptized Jan. 24, 1748. He had other children than these, but their names do not appear upon the register in question, which only covers the period between 1740 and

1749. William is said to have been the eldest son, and was the magistrate of that name who sat in the first court ever held in Kentucky at Harrodsburg, in the year 1781. He is believed by his relatives to have been killed in a duel near Danville in the year 1788. James, the second son, is described in a decision of the court of appeals of Kentucky as having been an efficient soldier and a capable and energetic officer, but whether this service was rendered during the Revolution or in the Indian wars following is unknown.

Mary, daughter of John, married Col. John Cowan, one of the most intelligent of the early pioneers of Kentucky.

John, the youngest son of John, was born in Augusta in 1756. He married there Elizabeth Beard, daughter of Edward Beard, whose wife was a descendant of William Bell, the progenitor of the Stone Church Bells of Augusta. John did not remove to Kentucky with his father and older brothers, but remained in Augusta until 1790. One of his daughters married Mr. Welch. His son William was born in Augusta in 1786, and was a student at the old Liberty Hall Academy at Lexington, Va., in 1804–6, a student at Transylvania University in 1808–10, and studied medicine in Philadelphia in 1810–12; he was a surgeon in the War of 1812 in the regular army, a member of the legislature of Kentucky in 1814–15, an elder in the Presbyterian Church, president of the Danville branch of the bank of Kentucky, a large farmer and a fine physician. One of his daughters married Hon. Thomas M. Green, of Danville, Ky., author of *Historic Families of Kentucky*, etc., and a son is the Rev. Dr. Willis Green Craig, now President of the McCormick Theological Seminary of Chicago.

CHARLES E. KEMPER.

Washington, D. C., July 26, 1900.

NOTE.—James Craig, second son of William, the immigrant (see page 294), was a member of the County Court of Augusta county, Virginia, appointed by Lord Dunmore, then Governor of Virginia, December 6, 1774, which said court was adjourned as of that date from Staunton, Virginia, to Fort Dunmore—now Pittsburg, Pennsylvania—(See Annals of Carnegie Museum, Vol. I, No. 4, 1902). It does not appear from the minutes of the court holden at Fort Dunmore that James Craig ever sat as a member at that place. Again, on January 17, 1776 (Order Book 16, of Augusta county, Virginia, page 30), and on March 19, 1776 (same book, page 128), he was named in the Commissions of Peace and Oyer and Terminer, and on February 17, 1778, he declined, for reasons best known to himself, to qualify.

HISTORICAL AND GENEALOGICAL NOTES OF JOHN ANDERSON AND HIS DESCENDANTS, OF AUGUSTA COUNTY, VIRGINIA.

Seven or eight heads of families who bore the name of Anderson were among the earliest settlers of Augusta county, Virginia. Whether related to each other in any degree is not definitely known, but four of them, whose Christian names were John, George, William and James, settled in the Stone Church neighborhood and are believed to have been brothers. The other Andersons referred to settled on Borden's grant, in what is now Rockbridge county, and are not believed to have been related to those who located on or near Middle river, in Augusta county.

The Anderson who is the subject of this sketch was named John. The Christian name of his wife was Jean, but her surname is unknown. In the year 1738 William Beverly, by deed dated June 5th, conveyed to John Anderson 748 acres of land, which is believed to have been his home farm upon which he lived and died. This land is located on Middle river, at the crossing of that stream by the Valley turnpike and the Valley railroad, and that portion of his estate where he resided is now the property of Andrew Bowling, Esq.

John Anderson was of Scotch-Irish descent, and so, doubtless, was his wife. He probably came to Virginia from Pennsylvania with the first wave of Scotch-Irish immigration which followed in the wake of John Lewis, the pioneer settler of Augusta county. Few of the details of his life are known. In 1742 he was a soldier in Captain John Smith's company of militia in Augusta county, and in 1756 his name appears as a soldier in Captain Christian's company of militia. When Augusta county was created in 1745 he was appointed one of the first magistrates who composed the county court. In 1772 John Poague conveyed 27 acres of land upon which the old Stone Church stands to the Rev. John Craig and the

session of that church. In this deed John Anderson is named
next after Parson Craig, from which it may be fairly inferred
that he was one of the first elders of that congregation. This
inference is strengthened by the fact that Captain James Allen,
his son-in-law, is also named as a member of the session, and
three or four names intervene between him and John Anderson. James Allen is known to have been one of the elders
of this church as early as 1746, and the fact that his father-
in-law precedes him in the deed referred to makes it almost
certain that John Anderson was not only the senior elder
of the church at that time, but one of the first elders originally
elected. His will was made in 1787 and probated at Staunton,
Va., in 1789. His wife was then living, but the date of her
death is unknown. His children, as named in the will, were
as follows: 1st, Robert; 2d, James; 3d, Andrew; 4th, William ; 5th, Margaret, and 6th, Jean.

I. MARGARET is believed to have been the eldest child
of John and Jean Anderson. She was evidently born prior
to 1740, because no record of her baptism occurs in the
register of Rev. John Craig, pastor of the old Stone Church,
which record is now in the library of General John E. Roller,
of Harrisonburg, Va. Besides, her eldest child, Jean, who
married Captain James Trimble, was born in the year 1756,
which would indicate that Margaret Anderson was born at
some time during the period between 1735–40. She married,
as stated, James Allen, son of William Allen, who was among
the earliest settlers in Augusta. James Allen was a captain
of militia in 1756, and also participated in the battle of Point
Pleasant. He died in 1810, 94 years of age, having been an
elder of Augusta Stone Church for 64 years. Their children
were :

1. *Jean*, wife of James Trimble, a captain of rifle rangers
during the war of the Revolution. He removed with his
family to Kentucky in 1784 and resided there until 1804,
when he died upon the eve of his contemplated removal to
Hillsboro, Ohio. Issue: Allen, born in Augusta county, Va.,

Nov. 24, 1783, and died in Highland county, Ohio, Feb. 3, 1870. Allen Trimble was clerk of the courts and recorder of Highland county in 1809–16. In the war of 1812 he commanded a mounted regiment under General William Henry Harrison and rendered efficient service. He was a member of the Ohio House of Representatives in 1816, State Senator in 1817, and Speaker of that body, holding the position until Jan. 7, 1822, when he became Acting Governor, and served to the end of that year. In 1826 he was elected Governor, and re-elected in 1828. His brother, William A. Trimble, was born in Woodford county, Ky., April 4, 1786, and removed with his family to Ohio. He graduated at Transylvania University, and then returned to Ohio and spent some time in the office of his brother Allen. At the outbreak of the War of 1812 he was chosen major in the Ohio volunteers; was at Hull's surrender and liberated on parole. He was afterwards exchanged and commissioned major in the 26th regiment. In the defense of Fort Erie he acted with signal gallantry, and received a severe wound, which was the cause of his death years afterwards. He remained in the army until 1819, with the rank of brevet lieutenant-colonel, and was then elected to the United States Senate; took his seat in December, 1819, and gave promise of much future usefulness. He died, however, Dec. 13, 1821, aged 35 years, being probably the youngest man ever elected to the United States Senate. Captain James Trimble and Jean, his wife, had other children, but the writer is not acquainted with their history.

2. *Ann*, wife of Col. William Poague; and their children were: Allen, John, William, Jean, Mary, James, Thomas, and Hugh. The writer has but little information concerning the children of William and Ann (Allen) Poague, but Thomas was a lawyer of distinction in southwest Virginia, and during the Civil War was colonel of the 50th Virginia regiment when he was killed in battle on Black Water in February, 1863.

3. *Elizabeth*, married the Rev. John McCue, pastor of Tinkling Spring church. They had issue as follows: James A.,

John, and Franklin, long prominent citizens of Augusta; Dr. William McCue, of Lexington, Va., and Cyrus, a lawyer, who died young; the daughters were Mrs. Matthews, Mrs. Porterfield, Mrs. Barry, Mrs. Miller, and Mrs. McDowell, wife of General Joseph Jefferson McDowell, of Hillsboro, Ohio.

4. *Rebecca*, who married Major John Crawford. Issue: Elizabeth, wife of Captain William Ingles; Sallie, wife of John Hyde; Margaret, first wife of Cyrus Hyde; James, who married Cynthia McClung, of Greenbrier county; John, who married Harriet McClung, of Greenbrier; George W., died unmarried; Ann, second wife of Franklin McCue; Mary, wife of Dr. Edward G. Moorman; and Rebecca, wife of Stuart McClung, of Greenbrier.

5. *Margaret*, who married Major William Bell, of Augusta. Issue: Elizabeth Allen, wife of Joseph D. Keyser, of Allegheny county, Va.; Susan, first wife of James Craig, of Mount Meridian, Augusta county, Va.; Mary, wife of Addison Hyde; Margaret Allen, who married first John Crawford, and he dying childless she married, second, Colonel James Crawford; Nancy, wife of Zachariah McChesney; Sarah, second wife of John Wayt, Jr.; Rebecca, wife of Benjamin T. Reid; Julia, wife of Alexander W. Arbuckle, of Greenbrier county, Va.; Jane, wife of Rev. John A. Van Leer, of Augusta county, Va. The only son of William Bell and Margaret, his wife, was William Joseph Davies Bell, who married Lucy Shipp, of Orange county, Va. Nearly all these children of William Bell and Margaret, his wife, left issue, but it would be impossible to enumerate them within the limits of this sketch.

6. *Mary*, who married Colonel Nicholas Lewis, and removed to Kentucky. If there was issue of this couple, their descendants are unknown to the writer.

7. *Nancy*, who married Captain Samuel Frame, of Augusta, whose children were John, Thomas, and Nancy.

8. *Sarah*, first wife of James Bell, and mother of the late Colonel William A. Bell, of Augusta county.

9. *William*, married Susan Bell, of Kentucky, and removed

to that State in 1783, and settled at Lexington. He was the
father of six children. His eldest daughter was the wife
of Matthew Jouett, the distinguished Kentucky artist, and her
oldest daughter married Richard Menifee, the celebrated
Kentucky orator. Another daughter was the wife of Dr.
Alexander Mitchell, of Frankfort, Ky., and one of her daughters married Oliver Frazer, the artist. One of Captain William Allen's sons was Colonel William H. Allen, formerly
of Augusta, and another was Colonel James Allen, of Missouri.

10. *James*, who married Elizabeth Tate. Issue: William,
who married a Miss Poague; John, who married, first, Polly
Crawford, and second, Ann Barry, widow of Dr. William
McCue, and, removing to Michigan, was the founder of Ann
Arbor, so named for his wife; Mary, who married Captain
John Welsh; Margaret, second wife of Major William Poague,
of Augusta; Nancy, wife of Charles Lewis; Sarah, who married George Mayse, of Bath county; and James T., who married Miss Maynard, of Michigan.

The descendants of Captain James Allen and Margaret
Anderson, his wife, are very numerous, and they are scattered
all over the west and southwest. Many of them still remain
in the Shenandoah Valley, and the posterity of this worthy
couple have been noted for their intelligence and devotion to
right principles in all the avocations of life. Much of the
foregoing information was derived from Mr. Joseph A. Waddell's invaluable work, The Annals of Augusta County, Virginia, to whom due acknowledgment is hereby made.

II. JOHN. The Rev. John Craig's record of baptisms previously referred to shows that on October 19, 1740, John, the
son of John Anderson, was baptized at the old Stone Church,
but no mention is made of him in his father's will, and no
tradition concerning him is known to the writer. Therefore,
it is believed that he died unmarried, probably in infancy.

III. ROBERT, who was baptized November 15, 1741, by the
Rev. John Craig at the old Stone Church. He married Ann
Thompson, of Augusta, November 4, 1765, and removed to

South Carolina a few years prior to the Revolution and settled in the western portion of the state near Pendleton. He first located on Long Cane Creek, in what is now Abbeville county, but after the massacre in the neighborhood of Fort Ninety-six he removed to the Waxhaws, now Lancaster county, South Carolina, and after quiet was restored about Fort Ninety-six returned to that neighborhood, finally making his permanent home near Pendleton, as above stated. He served with distinction as a Colonel in the war of the Revolution under his friend and neighbor, General Andrew Pickens, and after the Revolution was made general of the State Militia. His children were:

1. *Anne*, who married Dr. William Hunter. Issue: Dr. John, who married Kittie Calhoun and removed to Selma, Alabama; William, who married a Miss Clayton; Ann, who married John Smith; Mary, who married Rev. David Humphreys; Andrew, who married, but the name of his wife is unknown.

2. *Lydia*, who married Samuel Maverick. Issue: (1) Elizabeth, married Mr. Weyman. This couple had three children, a son named Joseph, and a daughter who married a Mr. Thompson, of Memphis, Tenn. Joseph Weyman married Emily Maxwell, of Pendleton, South Carolina, and their son Samuel now resides in New York City. (2) Lydia, who married William Van Wyck, of New York. Issue: Samuel Maverick, who married Miss Margaret Broyles and had two sons. He was a surgeon in the Civil War and was killed in battle in Tennessee. Zemah, married a gentleman of New York, name unknown, and died leaving two daughters. William, married a Miss Battle, daughter of President Battle, of the University of North Carolina. Augustus, of New York City, for years a judge of one of the superior courts of New York; in 1898 the Democratic candidate for Governor of New York, but was defeated by Theodore Roosevelt, now President of the United States, by 18,000 majority, in one of the largest votes ever polled in the state. Robert Anderson,

Democratic Mayor of New York, and the first Mayor of the greater city. Lydia, who married Mr. Holt, of North Carolina, son of ex-governor Holt of that state. (3) The third child of Lydia Anderson and Samuel Maverick was named Augustus. He removed to Texas and became one of the largest land and cattle owners in the world.

3. *Elizabeth*, third child of General Robert Anderson, married General Robert Maxwell of the Revolution. Issue: John, married Elizabeth Earle; Robert, married Mary Earle; Anne, married Dr. Andrew Moore. Elizabeth (Anderson) Maxwell married, second, a Mr. Caruth, and had by him a daughter named Louisa, who married General James Gillam, of Greenwood, South Carolina.

4. *Robert*, fourth child of General Anderson, married Maria Thomas, of Nassau, New Providence Island. They had ten children: Robert, married Mary Pickens, granddaughter of General Andrew Pickens; Edward; Edmund, who was a Presbyterian preacher; Thomas; John; Julius; William Henry. The three daughters were, Ann, who married Joseph Harris; Caroline, who married Dr. Leroy Halsey, a Presbyterian minister of prominence, and at the time of his death a professor in the McCormick Theological Seminary of Chicago; and Martha, who married Samuel Pickens, grandson of General Andrew Pickens, of the Revolution.

IV. JEAN, fourth child of John Anderson and Jean, his wife, was baptized April 29, 1744, by the Rev. John Craig, at the old Stone Church, in Augusta county, Va. She married, first, Lieutenant Hugh Allen, of Augusta, Nov. 6, 1765, by whom she had three sons, John, William and Hugh, all of whom emigrated to Kentucky, and a daughter whose Christian name is unknown to the writer. Jean Anderson Allen married, second, in 1778, William Craig, of Augusta county, Va., brother of Agnes, who married Captain James Anderson. (For the descendants of William Craig and Jean Anderson, his wife, see sketch of the Craigs.)

V. JAMES, born in Augusta; was baptized in the old Stone

Church March 6, 1748. He married, December 10, 1771, Agnes, daughter of James and Mary (Laird) Craig. It is stated by his descendants that he removed to South Carolina a few years previous to the Revolutionary War and settled, first, near Rock Mills, in what was then Pendleton District, but which is now known as Anderson county, so called for his brother, General Robert Anderson, previously mentioned in this sketch. After residing a few years at Rock Mills, James Anderson removed to the head waters of Rocky river, on Beaver Dam creek, and his plantation is now owned by Richard H. Anderson, his grandson. James Anderson served as a captain in the Revolutionary army and died September 9, 1813. He is buried in the old Carmel Church graveyard, not far from Pendleton, South Carolina. Agnes Craig, his wife, was born April 10, 1754, and died in 1838. The children of James Anderson and Agnes, his wife, were as follows:

1. *Mary*, who was born in Virginia. She married James Watson, and their children were: James, married three times, names of his wives unknown; Samuel, married Harriet Jones; Robert, died unmarried; Cynthia, married Mr. Bennett; Mary, married Mr. Oliver; Eliza, married Mr. Berry; Sarah Ann, married John Couch; Andrew, never married.

2. *Robert*, who removed to Mississippi when a young man, married there, and was the father of three children, one son and two daughters; Christian names unknown.

3. *Sarah*, married William Orr, who removed to Jackson county, Ga., and afterwards to Talladega, Ala. Issue, six children, as follows: Sarah Ann, married James Montgomery; Anson, married Mary Ann Thompson; James Laird, married Elmira McLester; Craig, married Cynthia Montgomery; Columbus, married Elizabeth McAllister; Caroline, married Hugh Montgomery. Nothing is known by the writer as to the issue of the foregoing children of Sarah Anderson and William Orr.

4. *Jane*, married Mr. McKensie. Issue: William; Robert; Jane; a daughter, name unknown. After the death of her

husband Mrs. McKensie removed to Mississippi with her family, and nothing further is known of her descendants.

5. *James*, removed to northern Alabama where he married a Miss Kinkaid. He was accidentally shot and killed while duck hunting on the Tennessee River. It is known that he left two sons, the eldest of whom was named William.

6. *Nancy*, married John Matthews and removed to Jackson county, Ga. Issue: Elizabeth Caroline, married Mr. Mullins; Sarah Ann, never married; John James, married twice, sisters, named Trayler. John James Matthews served in the Confederate army as colonel of a regiment.

7. *George*, removed to Benton county, Mo. He was fond of adventure and enjoyed the life of a frontiersman. He married in Missouri, but the name of his wife is unknown, and in 1849 removed to Texas and settled near Henderson. He was the father of eleven sons and one daughter, the latter of whom he named Missouri Ann, for his adopted state and his favorite sister. Nothing further is known of his descendants, but they are probably numerous in the state of Texas.

8. *Ann*, who married James Orr, of South Carolina, and after residing there several years subsequent to their marriage, finally removed to Jackson county, Ga. They had five children, as follows: Adolphus James, married Martha Fannin; Gustavus John, married Eliza Caroline Anderson; Caroline Agnes, married Madison Mitchell; Augustus, died in infancy; Sarah Ann, never married. Of these children, some are worthy of note. The oldest son was a Methodist minister, and the second a most successful educator and professor in Emory College at Oxford, Ga., for a number of years, and president of a female college at Covington, Ga., and afterwards a professor in Oglethorpe University, of Atlanta, Ga. He founded the public school system of the state of Georgia, and was State Supt. of public schools of that state for sixteen years. He died Dec. 11, 1887.

9. *William*, who will be mentioned later in this sketch.

10. *Elizabeth*, married Saxon Anderson, who was not re-

lated to her. They removed from South Carolina to Marietta, Ga., and afterwards to Talladega, Ala. Issue: Augustus, died in infancy; Mary Elizabeth, not married; George Washington, died in infancy; Eliza Caroline, married Frank Carter; Margaret Taliaferro, married Mr. Wills; David Laird, married, name of wife unknown; James Laird, married Augusta V. Anderson.

11. *Margaret*, died in infancy.

William Anderson, 9th child of James and Agnes Craig Anderson, mentioned above, was born in South Carolina, June 9, 1790, and died in that state May 12, 1853. He was married to Miss Mary McEldowny Hunter, Sept. 16, 1824. She was born May 25, 1802, and died June 1, 1884. They are buried in the family graveyard on the homestead of his father, Captain James Anderson. Issue:

1. Eliza Caroline, born in Pendleton District, now Anderson county, S. C., July 10, 1825, and was married to her cousin, Gustavus John Orr, Dec. 30, 1847. He was born in Anderson county, S. C., August 9, 1819, and died in Atlanta, Ga., Dec. 11, 1887. Issue: (1) William Anderson, born in Anderson county, S. C., Dec. 31, 1848, and died in Newton county, Ga., May 25, 1849. (2) Edgar Harold, born Sept. 25, 1850; married Martha Reynolds, of Atlanta, Ga., Feb. 5, 1885. She was born Feb. 10, 1858. Their children were: Martha Reynolds, born Jan. 10, 1887; Nellie Orr, born Oct. 31, 1889; Edward Harold, Jr., born Dec. 31, 1892; Mary Gertrude, born Nov. 9, 1899. (3) Alice Gertrude, born Feb. 28, 1853; died July 11, 1854. (4) Mary Eliza, born May 1, 1855; died Dec. 21, 1900. (5) Anna Gustavia, born Nov. 2, 1856; died July 12, 1858. (6) James Harrison, born June 26, 1858; died Jan. 20, 1859. (7) Gustavus John, Jr., born Jan. 12, 1860; married Minnie Felda Pou, of Auburn, Ala., May 6, 1886. She was born August 24, 1867. Issue: Gustavus John, born Oct. 5, 1887; Samuel Joseph, born Sept. 25, 1892. (8) Jessie Olivia, born March 29, 1862; married July 16, 1889, Howard Linton Bass, born Dec. 27,

1860. Issue: Anne Frank, born Oct. 23, 1890; Gustavus John, born July 16, 1895; Howard Linton, born July 18, 1897. (9) Cornelia Agnes, born July 17, 1864. (10) Angus Elgin, born June 19, 1867.

2. Sarah Cornelia, second child of William Anderson, was born May 5, 1827, and married the Rev. John McLees, Jan. 1, 1850. He was a Presbyterian minister, and was born March 5, 1812, and died June 6, 1882. Issue: (1) William Anderson, born Sept. 29, 1850; married Caroline Adele De Vose, of Edgefield, S. C., Jan. 17, 1878. She was born March 24, 1853. Their children were: John De Vose, born Jan. 24, 1879; James Maxcie, born Feb. 23, 1881; Edith Sheppard, born March 31, 1883; William Anderson, born Feb. 21, 1885; Sarah Louise, born Oct. 12, 1887; George Leslie, born Oct. 25, 1890; died Oct. 23, 1892. (2) Mary Hunter, born Nov. 16, 1851; not married. (3) Anna Lucia, born Nov. 3, 1853; died June 26, 1855. (4) John Logan, born May 24, 1855; married Annia Leah Cornelson, Feb. 2, 1892. She was born Feb. 21, 1873. Issue: Anna Louise, born Nov. 10, 1892; Cornelia Anderson, born Sept. 9, 1894; George Cornelson, born Dec. 10, 1896; John Logan, born Oct. 5, 1899. (5) James Thornwell, born May 23, 1859. (6) Robert Andrew, born Feb. 25, 1861. (7) Howard Maxwell, born Jan. 15, 1863. (8) Richard Gustavus, born Dec. 4, 1864. Of these sons of the Rev. John McLees and his wife, two, John Logan and Richard Gustavus, are Presbyterian ministers. The other sons are successful farmers residing near Greenwood, S. C.

3. Richard Harrison, third child of Dr. William Anderson, was born Feb. 25, 1829; married August 12, 1856, Josephine Elvira McCann, born August 12, 1837. Issue: (1) Ida Narcissa, born July 18, 1858; married Dec. 4, 1877, John Dixon Smith. Their children were: Harrison Gustavus, born Feb. 4, 1879, married Feb. 6, 1901, Leila Inez Boggs; Jerome Dixon, born March 22, 1881; Julius Edgar, born Aug. 14, 1883, died Aug. 15, 1883; Plumer De Witt, born August 20, 1884; Clyde Nicholdson, born Dec. 26, 1886; Lloyd Hunter,

born June 12, 1889, died in July, 1890; John Adger, born May 29, 1891; Minnie Lee, born Feb. 23, 1894; Selma Josephine, born July 12, 1896. (2) Hampton Gustavus, born August 20, 1861. (3) Julius Harrison, born Feb. 5, 1865. Married Mary Simpson Norris, Nov. 15, 1892. Issue: Louis Harrison, born March 4, 1894; Susan Simpson, born Sept. 15, 1897. (4) Mary Josephine, born Sept. 41, 1869; married Dr. Marion Augustus Thompson, Jan. 9, 1901. (5) William De Witt, born September 29, 1872.

4. Mary Julia, 4th child of Dr. William Anderson, was born March 19, 1831; married Rev. Robert H. Reid, of Orrville, S. C., Nov. 25, 1851. Issue: Ella Louise, born July 4, 1853; married Rev. Robert P. Smith, Nov. 28, 1876. He was born March 24, 1852. Their children were: Mabel Clare, born March 30, 1878; Bernard Reid, born July 6, 1881; Albert Dixon, born August 9, 1883, died May 14, 1884; Mary Julia, born June 30, 1885; Roy Hamilton, born May 26, 1888, and died Sept. 26, 1889.

5. Ann Elizabeth, 5th child of Dr. William Anderson, was born Dec. 22, 1832; married John Robert Tarrant, Oct. 28, 1856. He died March 27, 1891. Issue: (1) William Anderson, born August 4, 1857; died Sept. 30, 1873. (2) Mary Augusta, born Feb. 27, 1859; married George Barksdale, Dec. 21, 1876. Their children were: Claude Bruce, born July 2, 1879, died in June, 1892; Guy Tarrant, born August 12, 1880, died April, 1883; George Roydon, born August 27, 1882; John Hugh, born Sept. 25, 1885; Clara Gladys, born June 25, 1890; Carl, born April 29, 1892; Cecil Bruce, born Jan. 10, 1894. (3) Clara Cornelia, born Dec. 27, 1860; married Joel Smith Bailey, Oct. 25, 1882, who died Sept. 6, 1900. Issue: Joel Smith, born Aug. 12, 1882; Willie Tarrant, born June 6, 1886; Ossamus Bowen, born Nov. 22, 1887; May Maxwell, born May 4, 1889; Clarence Bernard, born July 25, 1894; James Robert, born June 1, 1896, died Sept. 10, 1899. (4) Lucia Linwood, born Nov. 25, 1862; died June 26, 1899; married Dr. James Bryan Hughey, Jan. 7, 1885. Issue:

Robert Duncan, born Nov. 26, 1885; Florence Burkhead, born Dec. 22, 1886; Annie Laurie, born June 17, 1888; Lucia Tarrant, born Aug. 13, 1889; Mary Hunter, born Aug. 26, 1891; Joseph Wilmot, born April 26, 1894; James Bryan, born Aug. 1, 1897, died Oct. 13, 1898. (5) John Robert, Jr., born Jan. 10, 1865; married May 22, 1884, Ida V. Reynolds. Issue: Bennie Clyde, born Dec. 22, 1884; Anna Linwood, born March 6, 1886; Guy Matthews, born Sept. 13, 1888; Blanche Garlington, born April 18, 1890; Leland Reynolds, born Nov. 14, 1892; Robert Hunter, born Dec. 22, 1894; Jessie Virginia, born Oct. 30, 1897; Sybil Hudson, born May 5, 1900; Arthur Anderson, born Jan. 24, 1902. (6) Eugene Hunter, born March 24, 1870; married, July 19, 1892, Mrs. Mary Ida Parks. Issue: Eugene Hunter, born June 16, 1894, died Dec. 17, 1897; Mary Elizabeth, born June 13, 1896; George Barksdale, born Oct. 26, 1898; Clara Augusta, born July 14, 1900; Ruby McBride, born Feb. 5, 1902. (7) Jessie Olivia, born July 16, 1872; died August 31, 1876.

6. William, sixth child of Dr. William Anderson, was born July 7, 1835, and died Nov. 2, 1835:

7. Olivia Louise, seventh child of Dr. William Anderson, was born Feb. 9, 1837. Married Oct. 13, 1858, Rev. Jesse De Witt Burkhead, D. D. He was born Aug. 10, 1833, in Iredell county, N. C. He was a graduate of Davidson College, N. C., took his theological course at Columbia Seminary in South Carolina, and at Free Church College in Edinburg, Scotland. He was a Presbyterian minister of distinction, and died in Montgomery, Ala., April 18, 1892. Issue: (1) Mary Florence, born Nov. 28, 1859. Married in Huntsville, Ala., Sept. 16, 1878, to Malcolm Joseph Gilchrist, and died March 15, 1881. Issue: Jessie Olivia, born Oct. 1, 1879, and married Jan. 29, 1902. Name of husband not given. (2) William De Witt, born June 16, 1861. Married in Montgomery, Ala., June 27, 1890, Annie Laurie Bell. Issue: Jessie De Witt, born July 5, 1893; Ella Louise, born Jan. 22, 1897. William De Witt Burkhead is a Presbyterian minister and is

located (1902) at Mount Meridian, Virginia, as pastor of Mount Horeb Church. (3) Rockwell Giles, born June 28, 1863; died Oct. 23, 1899, unmarried. (4) Arthur Anderson, born Nov. 11, 1866; died Feb. 26, 1884, unmarried.

8. Arrabella Hunter, eighth child of Dr. William Anderson, was born Sept. 3, 1838; died Oct. 7, 1901, unmarried.

9. Rebecca Jane, ninth child of Dr. William Anderson, was born June 23, 1840; died Dec. 30, 1842.

10. Augusta Virginia, tenth child of Dr. William Anderson, was born Jan. 12, 1842, and died Dec. 17, 1898. She was married to her cousin, James Laird Anderson, Dec. 17, 1873. He was born May 2, 1837. Issue: (1) Mary Hunter, born Oct. 30, 1874; died July 30, 1886. (2) William Saxon, born June 14, 1876; married April 10, 1901, Ruby Rowland. Issue: Hugh Rowland, born Feb. 27, 1902. (3) Augusta Virginia, born March 3, 1878; married George M. Douglass, Dec. 16, 1897. Issue: Mary Hunter, born Oct. 23, 1898; Irene, born Nov. 10, 1900. (4) John Heflin, born July 28, 1880. (5) Eliza Caroline, born March 3, 1882.

11. William Henry, eleventh child of Dr. William Anderson, was born Dec. 23, 1843; married Nov. 12, 1862, Clarissa Ann Duckworth, of Anderson county, S. C. She died in 1869. No issue.

Dr. William Anderson was a man of the highest character and fine attainments, a member of the legislature of South Carolina before the Civil War, an eminent physician, and one of the largest land owners in his section.

VI. ANDREW, sixth child of John Anderson and Jean, his wife, was born in Augusta county, Va., about 1750. His will was admitted to probate in the county court of Augusta in 1823. He was twice married, the name of his first wife being unknown to the writer. By this marriage he had the following children:

1. *Dr. George Anderson*, of Montgomery county, Va., born Sept. 4, 1779; died Sept. 22, 1818; married Mary Douglass, daughter of Benjamin Douglass, of Bath county, Va. No issue.

21

2. *Mrs. Brown*, of Kentucky.

3. *Betsy*, first wife of Major William Poague.

The second wife of Andrew Anderson was Martha, daughter of Patrick Crawford, of Augusta, and her children were :

1. *John*, born April 19, 1789 ; died in Montgomery county, Va., March 16, 1821.   He married Elizabeth Fitzhugh Douglass, granddaughter of Benjamin Douglass, and had three children : (1) Mary D., born July 31, 1816 ; married Dr. John Smith, of Russell county, Va.   (2) George W., born April 23, 1818.   (3) Eldred R., born June 3, 1820.

2. *James*, who married Caroline Douglass, sister of John's wife, and had (1) John, (2) Eliza, (3) James, and (4) William, who removed to Tennessee.

3. *Robert*, who married Nancy Dean, of Greenbrier county, W. Va., and had one son, William D., who married Miss Ingles.

4. *William*, who died in New Orleans.

5. *Nancy*, wife of William Crawford, of Augusta.

6. *Sallie*, wife of Jacob Ruff.

Andrew Anderson served as an ensign, lieutenant, and captain in the War of the Revolution, and in 1794 was the colonel in command of the militia of Augusta county, Va. He served for many consecutive years as a member of the House of Delegates from that county.

VII. WILLIAM, seventh child of John Anderson and Jean, his wife, was born about the year 1752.   He served as captain in the War of the Revolution.   His wife was Mary, daughter of James and Mary (Laird) Craig, born May 10, 1752, and died Jan. 16, 1778.   If there was issue born of this marriage they are unknown to the writer.   In 1784 Captain Anderson removed to Kentucky and nothing is known of his descendants.

The writer has endeavored to give as complete a list as possible of John Anderson's descendants in the foregoing paper, but necessarily there are many omissions in some of the lines of descent. For much kindly assistance in the preparation of this article, the writer is indebted to Mrs. Eliza C. Orr, of Atlanta, Ga., and Mrs. Olivia Louise Burkhead, of Huntsville, Ala., granddaughters of Captain James Anderson; also to Miss Harriet Maxwell, of Pendleton, S. C., and Rev. B. Palmer Reid, of Reidsville, S. C.

CHARLES E. KEMPERS.

Washington, D. C., November 18, 1902.

TRANSCRIPT OF THE HUGH DAVIS BIBLE OF DAVIS COUNTY, NORTH CAROLINA.

This record is here inserted that the student of history may readily separate the North Carolina family from that of Spottsylvania county, Va., which follows, their children being cotemporary :

TRANSCRIPT.

Hugh Davis married, ——, Ann ——.   Children :

1. Mary,   b. April 14, 1731.
2. Bridget,   b. Dec. —, 1732.
3. Mirick,   b. Feb. 15, 1734–5.
4. Sarah,   b. July 2, 1740.
5. Lydia,   b. Feb. 19, 1742–3.
6. Hugh,   b. ——, 1748.
7. Joseph (Rev.), b. Nov. 19, 1751.

Mirick Davis, born 1734–5 ; son of Hugh and Ann, his wife ; married Margaret ——.   Children :

1. Hannah, b. May 10, 1761.
2. Bridget, b. Oct. 29, 1763.
3. Mirick, b. Mar. 1, 1765.
4. Gabriel, b. Sept. 10, 1767.
5. Abner, b. Aug. 27, 1773.
6. Hugh, b. June 16, 1778.
7. William, b. Nov. 11, 1780.
8. Mary, b. June 18, 1788.

Hugh Davis, born 1748 ; son of Hugh and Ann ; married —— McCrary.   Children :

1. Susan, b. Dec. 15, 1755.
2. Abner, b. Sept. 17, 1763.
3. Lydia, b. Feb. 9, 1771.
4. John, b. ——, 1772.

Mirick Davis, Jr., born 1765 ; son of Mirick and Margaret ; married Rachel Yountz, 1783, daughter of Rudolph Yountz. Children :

1. Mahaly,   b. Dec. 9, 1783.
2. Mirick,   b. Feb. 9, 1786.
3. Elizabeth, b. Dec. 15, 1788.
4. Susannah, b. Mar. 11, 1791. ⎫ Twins.
5. Rachel,   b. Mar. 11, 1791. ⎭
6. John,   b. July 12, 1794.
7. Lydia,   b. July 24, 1797.
8. Joel,   b. July —, 1800.
9. Fanny,   b. ———; married ——— McCrary.

Rachel Davis, Sr., died in North Carolina in 1881, aged 96 years.

Gabriel Davis, son of Mirick, Sr., and Margaret, born Sept. 10, 1767 ; married, 1792, Nancy (Ann), born June 16, 1774. Children :

1. Mirick, b. Mar. 8, 1793.
2. Abner, b. Mar. 6, 1795.
3. Hugh,   b. Sept. 12, 1797.
4. James, b. Jan. 8, 1800.
5. Gabriel, b. Apr. 23, 1802.

William Davis, son of Mirick, Sr., and Margaret, born Nov. 11, 1780; married ———, 1800, Sarah ———. Sarah, a daughter, born Nov. 23, 1800.

DAVIS FAMILY NOTES. (Revolutionary.)

Affidavit of Hugh Davis, in 1837, then a resident of Nelson county, Kentucky ; states his age at 80 years; that he was born in Prince William county, Va., and that Capt. Jesse Davis, of Prince William county, was his brother-in-law and

first cousin ; that Presley Davis, who was killed at the battle
of Long Island, was a brother of Capt. Jesse Davis ; that John
Davis, who died in the hospital of smallpox, was another
brother; that Capt. Jesse Davis was married to Nancy Milton
(Melton), of Prince William county, about the beginning
of the war, and further, that William M. Davis, of Frankfort,
Kentucky, and Mr. P. Davis, of Washington county, Ky., and
Mrs. Nancy Reynolds, of said county, were the children
of Capt. Jesse Davis and Nancy Milton, his wife.   The military service of Capt. Jesse Davis is given in the following
order : Served as a soldier from Jan. 1, 1777, to Jan. 6, 1778 ;
as a lieutenant from Jan., 1778, to Oct., 1778, and twenty
days in Oct. as captain.   Died Feb., 1782.

Another affidavit in this set of papers states that Elijah
Davis, of Nelson county, Ky., was a son of Jefferson Davis,
who was a soldier in the Continental Line, Revolutionary
army.

Col. William Davis, of Virginia, received Land Warrant
Certificate, No. 597, for 500 acres, May 7, 1797.   (Pub.)

TRANSCRIPT FROM THE DAVIS FAMILY BIBLE OF
SPOTTSYLVANIA COUNTY, VA., WITH DECLAR-
ATION OF REVOLUTIONARY WAR SERVICE
OF THOMAS DAVIS.

The first date intelligible is 1738 ; which is believed to be
the date of marriage of the parents whose names are obliterated
by time.   Their children were :

James Davis, b. March 5, 1741.
Benjamin,   b. Jan. 10, 1743.
Elizabeth,   b. Feb. 22, 1745.
Snead,   b. May   16, 1748.
William,   b. Aug. 26, 1750.

Mary,   b. May   24, 1753.
Felix,   b. Apr. 27, 1755.
Charles, b. Oct. 22, 1758.
Thomas,   b. Nov. 30, 1761.

Thomas Davis married May 1, 1783, Susannah Heath, in Spottsylvania Co., Va., where she was born Feb. 26, 1765; their children were:

Elizabeth Davis, b. Oct.   16, 1784, { in Spottsylvania Co.,
Mary,   b. Dec.   22, 1786, {   Virginia.
Fielding,   b. May   9, 1789, in Woodford Co., Ky.
Larkin,   b. Sept. 27, 1791.
Thomas,   b. Feb.   3, 1794; died Oct.,   1794.
Thomas,   b. Aug.   26, 1795; died May,   1817.
William,   b. Apr.   7, 1798; died Dec.,   1798.
John,   b. June   9, 1800; died Aug. 9, 1800.
Susannah,   b. Aug.   13, 1801.
James,   b. Apr.   17, 1804.
Diannah,   b. June   17, 1806.
Benjamin,   b. March   1, 1809; died Sept. 6, 1828.
Sallie Stephens, b. Apr.   26, 1811.

The last eleven were all born in Woodford county, Ky.

DECLARATION OF THOMAS DAVIS OF WOODFORD COUNTY, KY.

I was born in Spottsylvania county, Va., in 1761. I enlisted April 25, 1779, for 18 months in the war of the Revolution.

I served under Capt. Alexander Parker in Col. Richard Parker's regiment.

I served also for two months as a sub-alternate for my brother Benjamin in a company of militia commanded by

Capt. William Mills (James Cunningham, first lieutenant), and marched to Williamsburg, where I served until discharged.

The day after my return home I was drafted, and served two months in the state, I marched to Yorktown and was present at the surrender of Lord Cornwallis.

My total service was 18 months, for which I received $60.

This declaration is supported by an affidavit of John McGrady, of Woodford county, who served in the same regiment with Thomas Davis.

Thomas Davis was pensioned in Woodford county, Ky., August 18, 1818, in the 57th year of his age. (Pub.)

TRANSCRIPT FROM THE CUSTIS (THOMPKINS) BIBLE.

Now (1902) in the possession of Mrs. Edmonia Bayly, of Staunton, Va., wife of Capt. E. W. Bayly, deceased, late of Staunton, formerly of Accomac county, Virginia.

John Custis and Anne Kendall were married by Rev. John Holebrooke on Monday, 5th of March, 1732.

John Custis, son of said John and Anne, was born July 7, 1734.

Mary Brown Custis, born Jan. 9, 1736.

Peggy Custis, born July 16, 1738.

John Custis departed this life Dec. 27, 1738.

Hannah Custis, born 25th July, 1740; died Aug. 31st following.

John Custis, born April 10, 1743.

Hannah Custis, born 19th May, 1745; died Jan. 27, 1751.

Col. John Custis, died Dec. 1, 1746, aged 40 years.

John Custis (2d of that name, and third son of the above John Custis, deceased), died Aug. 24, 1747.

John Thompkins and Anne Custis were married Feb. 25, 1747, by Rev. Mr. Barlow.

John Custis Thompkins, son of John and Anne Thompkins, was born 27th Nov., 1748, and died 16th Dec. following.

William, second son, was born 16th Sept., 1750, and died the 24th instant.

John Thompkins, 3d son of John Thompkins and Anne his wife, was born the 20th of Nov., 1751.

Bennet Thompkins, 4th son of John Thompkins and Anne his wife, was born Jan. 22, 1755.

John Thompkins, Sr., was born 19th June, 1718, and died Aug. 21, 1757.

SMITH FAMILY OF AUGUSTA AND ROCKINGHAM COUNTIES, VIRGINIA.

Capt. John Smith, born 1698, in England, settled with his parents in Province of Ulster, Ireland; is said to have been an officer of the British army (?), and married, in 1719, Margaret ———; immigrated to America about 1730, with his wife and children; settled, 1st, in Chester Co., Pa., about 1740; removed, with the McDowells and others, to what is now Augusta county, Virginia, then Orange, and on June 26, 1740, proved the importation of himself, his wife Margaret,. their sons Abraham, Henry, Daniel, John and Joseph, from the colony of Penna. (See Orange County Land Records.) In 1738 Augusta county was taken from Orange, the first court being held in Staunton Dec. 9, 1745, prior to which time all the legal business of Augusta county was transacted at Orange Court House. June 26, 1742, John Smith qualified at Orange Court House as captain of the militia for Augusta county.

As a protection against the inroads of the Indians, he had several rude forts, or block-houses, constructed in the Valley, one of which was in the county of Botetourt, on the James river, where Pattonsburg was subsequently located. This fort became the scene of memorable events.

Capt. John Smith, with seventeen men, held a fort, called Fort Vause—variously written Vass, Voss, and Vaus—which was located on the head-waters of the Roanoke river, about ten miles from where Christiansburg now stands. This fort was invested by three hundred French and Indians, and, after a brave resistance for three days, the garrison agreed to surrender the fort, upon a stipulation allowing them to return to their homes. Astonished and mortified at finding so few men in the fort, the enemy disregarded the terms of surrender and held the survivors—now only nine or ten in number—as prisoners. Two of Capt. Smith's sons were with him: John, who was wounded during the siege, and killed by an Indian after the surrender. The prisoners were taken down the Ohio and Mississippi rivers to New Orleans, and on the way down the other young Smith (Joseph), who had survived the disaster at the fort, died. Only five of the prisoners lived to reach New Orleans. Capt. Smith and two others were then sent to France, and he alone returned to America, after an absence of two years. " When the treaty was signed at the fort, Captain Smith was so cautious as to secure the paper by ripping open the lining of his coat and sewing it between, which defeated the most diligent search for it. On arriving at Paris, Capt. Smith produced the agreement, and, upon exhibiting it to the proper authorities, was promptly released, and with his two companions was sent to London, where he received quite an ovation, a street being named in his honor. He there told of the immense territory of the Southwestern country."

Mr. Waddell, in the Virginia Magazine of History and Biography, says:

" Capt. John Smith commanded a company in the disastrous Sandy Creek expedition, sent out on Feb. 18, 1756, and it would seem that after his return he was stationed at Fort Vause; also, that while Capt. Smith was detained as a prisoner and absent two years, *his pay during that time, and also that of his son, Lieut. John Smith, Jr., up to the time he was killed at Fort Vause, on June 25, 1756, was provided for by an Act of Assembly, passed by the House of Burgesses.—Hening's Virginia Statutes.*"

As a further proof of the accounts given by Mr. Waddell, and Benj. H. Smith, the Editor of the Virginia Magazine of History and Biography, adds: " A register of the persons who have been either wounded, killed, or taken prisoner by the enemy in Augusta county, as also such as have made their escape;" and among many other names and dates are found the following: " June 25th, 1756, at Fort Vause, Capt. John Smith, prisoner returned 1758, Lieut. John Smith (Jr.), killed, Joseph Smith, prisoner, died on the way to New Orleans."

"After his return to this country, probably in impaired health, he seems to have taken no active part in Military affairs.

"He survived until the Revolutionary War began, and this, his military spirit having revived, he applied for a Commission and was refused on account of his advanced age, then 78 years, which greatly offended him. He died shortly after this at Smithlands, the residence of his son Daniel, two miles north of Harrisonburg, Virginia.

"His sons, Abraham, Henry, and Daniel, were also prominent in the French and Indian Wars; his son-in-law, Hugh Reece Bowen, was killed at the battle of Kings Mountain, near the close of the fight, as a Lieut. of Campbell's Regiment of Riflemen, Virginia Militia, on Oct. 7, 1780, and left many highly respectable descendants in southwestern Virginia, namely, Tazewell, Wythe, and Montgomery counties."

Capt. Smith was one of the first Vestry Members for the parish of Augusta; their first Meeting was held April 5, 1747, at which date John Smith, John Buchanan, James Patton, John Madison and others, took the oath appointed by act of Parliament as such. His name appears as being present at all meetings from 1747 to Nov. 23, 1756; at this meeting John Matthews, Jr., was chosen Vestryman in place of Capt. John Smith, who had been captured at Fort Vause on Nov. 20, 1758, there being a vacancy, Col. (formerly Capt.) John Smith having returned to Virginia, was chosen Vestryman, which position he held until May 25, 1760. The military record of Capt. John Smith is well known, he having received from his colony, grants of land for his service as early as 1754. (See records.) His military record is too well known to require any further notice in this paper.

On March 30, 1745, John Smith, Gentleman, had patented to him 400 acres of land in the great survey on Mossy Creek, and 400 acres on Spring Creek; from this time on for many years the records of Augusta show that he and his sons handled many thousand acres of the best lands in the Shenandoah Valley. He died 1776. His wife Margaret Smith died ———. They had six children, namely :

1. Abraham, b. 1722, in Ireland. (See later.)
2. Daniel,   b. 1724, in Ireland. (See later.)
3. Henry,   b. 1727 ; m. Amy ———.   [1756.
4. John, Jr., b. 1730 ; was killed at Fort Vause, June 25,
5. Joseph,   b. 1734, in Chester Co., Pa. Was taken pris-
                  oner at Fort Vause; d. on way to New
                  Orleans, 1756.
6. Margaret, b. 1741 ; m. Hugh Reece Bowen, who was a
                  Lieut. in Campbell's regiment of Rifle-
                  men, Va. Militia, was killed at the battle
                  of Kings Mountain, Oct. 7, 1780, leaving
                  his widow and children surviving. Of
                  his descendants, no further record.

SECOND GENERATION.

First. Abraham Smith, eldest child of Capt. John the emigrant and Margaret Smith, born in Ulster Province, Ireland, 1722, was Capt. during the French and Indian Wars from Sept. 11, 1756, to April 19, 1760. In 1778, one of the 1st Justices for Rockingham Co., and County Lieut. He is frequently referred to in the preceding pages of the work in connection with French and Indian war records of his county. Married Sarah Caldwell, of Augusta county, resided near North Mountain in Rockingham county, Va., on a large land estate called " Egypt," where he died. Two children :

1. John,   b. Dec. 16, 1755.
2. Henry, b. 1758.

THIRD GENERATION.

First. John Smith, born Dec. 16, 1755, son of Abraham and Sarah (Caldwell) Smith, was a soldier in the Revolutionary Army, distinguished himself at the Battle of Point Pleasant as ensign in the company commanded by his uncle Daniel.

He inherited his father's plantation at foot of North Mountain. He married on Sept. 14, 1775, Mary Jane Hart, daughter of Silas, 1st Sheriff of Rockingham county. Eleven children:

1. Abraham, Jr., b. Feb. 22, 1778; d. Apr. 22, 1778.
2. Joseph,   b. June 27, 1785; d. May 14, 1863.
3. Silas Hart,   b. Jan. 8, 1787; d. Sept. 15, 1842.
4. Nancy,   b. Feb. 19, 1783; d. Aug. 25, 1854.
5. Margaret,   b. June 10, 1776; d. Sept. 13, 1862.
6. Abraham,   b. Jan. 8, 1781; d. Feb. 20, 1852.
7. Sarah,   b. Dec. 7, 1788.
8. Jane,   b. Aug. 27, 1790; d. July 30, 1836.
9. William,   b. Apr. 1, 1792.
10. Lucinda,   b. Aug. 24, 1793.
11. Annis,   b. March 11, 1795.

FOURTH GENERATION.

First. Abraham Smith, Jr., born 1781; son of John and Mary Jane (Hart) Smith; was three times married, 1st to Julia Lyle. Three children:

1. Margaret Lyle, b. ——.
2. Mary,   b. ——; m. Ezra Walker. No issue.
3. Joseph,   b. ——; m. Fannie Faucett. One child, a daughter Josephine, born ——.

Second marriage of Abraham Smith to Martha McDowell Reed, of Lexington, Va. Two children:

1. Juliet,   b. ——.
2. Magdaline, b. ——.

Third marriage of Abraham Smith to Charolette Gambill, of Rockingham Co. Three children:

1. Jennie,   b. ——; m. Alex. McNutt Hamilton.
2. Jouette,   b. ——; d. unmarried.
3. Mary Walker, b. ——; d. unmarried.

FIFTH GENERATION.

First. Margaret Lyle Smith, 1st of Abraham and Mary Jane (Hart) Smith, born ——— ; m. Robert S. Brooke, as his 2d wife, she being 1st cousin to his 1st wife. Six children :

1. John Brooke,   b. ——— ; m. ———, Ann Carter, of Berkley.
2. Martha Brooke,   b. ——— ; m. ———, Walter Chermside, of England, brother of Gen. Sir Herbert Chermside, of the British army. Four children : 1. Margary; 2. Mable; 3. Juliet; 4. Herbert.
3. Juliet Brooke,   b. ——— ; unmarried.
4. Mary Brooke,   b. ——— ; m. ———, John W. Bocock.
5. Frank Brooke,   b. ———.
6. Berkeley Brooke, b. ———.

Fourth. Juliet Smith, 4th of Abraham, and 1st by his 2d wife Martha (McDowell) Smith, born ——— ; m. C. C. Strayer. Two children : Henry and Ernest.

Fifth. Magdaline Smith, 5th of Abraham, and 2d by his 2d wife Martha (McDowell) Smith, b. ——— ; m. Isaac Coffman. Four children :

1. Samuel,   b. ———.
2. Frank,   b. ———.
3. Juliet,   b. ———.
4. Herbert, b. ———.

FOURTH GENERATION.

Second. Joseph Smith, 2d of John and Mary Jane (Hart) Smith, son of Abraham, born June 27, 1785; resided at Folly Mills, Augusta Co.; was twice married, first to Elizabeth B. Muse, 1810, born 1790, died in child-birth Nov. 17, 1810. Left a daughter, Elizabeth, born 1810; m. Robert S. Brooke as his first wife. Three children :

1. Virginia Brooke, b. ——— ; m. D. B. B. Donaghe.

2. Margaret Brooke, b. ——; m. Thomas P. Eskridge.
3. Elizabeth Brooke, b. ——; m. James C. Cochran.

Second marriage of Joseph Smith to Ann Price, born Dec. 10, 1784. She died Aug. 24, 1849. No issue.

THIRD GENERATION.

First. Henry Smith, 2d and youngest child of Abraham and Sarah (Caldwell) Smith, born on the plantation called "Egypt;" m. Margaret Cravens, daughter of Robert and sister to Elizabeth, wife of Benjamin Smith, son of Daniel and Margaret (Davis) Smith. Three children;

1. Benjamin, b. ——; settled in Kentucky. No record.
2. William, b. ——; settled in Georgia. No record.
3. Abraham b. ——.

FOURTH GENERATION.

Third. Abraham Smith, son of Henry and Sarah (Caldwell) Smith, born ——; m. Mary Scott, born 1795, died 1837. Issue, one child, a daughter, Martha, born ——.

FIFTH GENERATION.

Martha Smith, daughter of Abraham and Mary (Scott) Smith, born ——; m. Yelverton Shands. Five children:

1. Frank, b. ——.
2. Yelverton, b. ——.
3. Sally, b. ——.
4. Mary, b. ——.
5. William, b. ——.

SIXTH GENERATION.

William Shands, 5th of Telverton and Martha (Smith) Shands, born ——; m. Annie Smith, a cousin, and daughter of Judge John Wms. Green Smith and sister to Mrs. J. Fred Effinger.

SECOND GENERATION.

Daniel Smith, 2d of Capt. John and Margaret Smith, born in Ireland in 1724, came to America with his parents aged about six years; finally settled in Augusta county, where he married Jane Harrison about 1751, born 1735, daughter of Daniel Harrison, and sister of Col. Benjamin Harrison, of Augusta county (see Harrison family.)

March 10, 1751, he purchased a tract of land on the head of Linsville Creek, adjoining the land of his father-in-law, where he built his residence later known as "Smithland," a magnificent estate in Augusta county, now Rockingham. His is said to have been the first brick house built in the Valley; situated two miles north of Harrisonburg, Va. Smithland, the estate on which he lived and died, was patented Aug. 20, 1741, by Daniel Harrison, his father-in-law. (Deed book 1, Augusta county records.)

In 1757 Col. Daniel Smith was one of the Justices for Augusta county; was Capt. of a company under Gen. Lewis in the battle of Point Pleasant; he was a member of the Courtmartial for West Augusta district from the beginning of the French wars until Oct., 1777; on Sept. 20, 1781, he was commissioned, in the Revolutionary army, as Deputy Purveyor, Southern Department. As the Presiding Justice of Rockingham county, he signed the court records for the last time on Sept. 24, 1781, and left immediately for Yorktown, where he joined four of his sons, viz.: John, Daniel, Joseph, and Robert, who were in the Revolutionary army. After the return of the troops from the siege of Yorktown, Daniel Smith, then designated Colonel, summoned those from Rockingham, for a review to celebrate the victory; the last act of which was the "running salute." As the troops began firing, his horse became frightened, sprang aside, spraining his rider's back and throwing him; from which injury he died in a few days.

In 1778 Rockingham county was formed from Augusta; the plantations of Col. Daniel Smith being in the new county;

22

338   GLEANINGS OF VIRGINIA HISTORY.

He was commissioned by the Governor one of the first Justices, the first court being organized April 27, 1778, which convened in his house until suitable buildings could be constructed. He is said to have been the wealthiest man of his day in the county; he was a member of the convention in 1775. He died in 1781, his will proven Nov. 26th of this year, his wife, Jane (Harrison) Smith, qualified as executrix, giving bonds of £50,000; was probably buried in the old Dayton graveyard near Smithsland, where some of the early members of the family are interred; his widow, Jane (Harrison) Smith, died 1796; their children were twelve:

1. John Smith,   b. Nov. 30, 1752.
2. Daniel Smith,   b. June 25, 1754.
3. Joseph Smith,   b. Feb. 9, 1756.
4. Robert Smith,   b. Nov. 28, 1757; died unmarried.
5. Margaret Smith, b. Oct. 27, 1759. No record.
6. Benjamin Smith, b. May 25, 1761.
7. Ann Smith,   b. Sept. 6, 1763. No record.
8. Jane H. Smith,   b. July 19, 1765; m. Smith Lofland.
                    [No record.
9. Sarah Smith,   b. Oct. 13, 1767. No record.
10. Abraham Smith, b. July 23, 1770; died unmarried.
11. William Smith, b. Aug. 20, 1775.
12. James Smith,   b. March 6, 1779.

From the family Bible in possession of James Smith, of St.
[Paul, Minn.

THIRD GENERATION.

First. John Smith, Jr., son of Daniel and Jane (Harrison) Smith, born Nov. 30, 1752, in Augusta county; was commissioned March 14, 1776, ensign in the 4th Virginia Regiment; August, 1776, 2d lieutenant; Feb. 21, 1777, 1st lieutenant; resigned May 26, 1778. He was again commissioned 1st lieutenant Sept. 12, 1778, and was present at the surrender of Yorktown, Oct. 19, 1781. Married, ——, 1776, Margaret Davis. Issue, two children of whom we have record:

1. Margaret Reed, b. April 23, 1777.
2. Daniel,   b. March 12, 1779.

FOURTH GENERATION.

First. Margaret Reed Smith, 1st of John and Margaret (Davis) Smith, born 1777; married, 1797, Alexander Herring, of Rockingham county, Va.   Ten children :

1. John Smith Herring, b. in 1798 ; was a distinguished lawyer and a member of the Virginia State Senate ; never married ; died in Ohio.
2. Eliza Herring, b. 1800 ; died unmarried.
3. Martha Davis Herring, b. 1802 ; married Col. Geo. H. Chrisman.
4. Wm. Herring, b. 1804; settled in Ohio; died unmarried.
5. Alexander, b. 1806; graduated in law; settled in Ohio; died unmarried.
6. Daniel Smith Herring, b. 1808 ; graduated from West Point ; died in Florida during the Seminole War ; unmarried.
7. Margaret Davis Herring, b. 1810 ; never married ; died October, 1902.
8. Stephenson Herring, b. 1812 ; died on the Mississippi river, unmarried.
9. Rebecca Herring, b. 1814 ; died in childhood.
10. Ann Harrison Herring, b. 1816 ; m. 1st, Judge Madison McAfee, of Miss.; 2d, Wm. G. Richardson, of Kentucky.   No issue.

[For Richardson family, see Richardsons and their Kin, by W. F. Boogher.]

Second.   Daniel Smith, 2d of John and Margaret (Davis) Smith, born 1779 ; at the age of 21 years came into possession of his interest in his grandfather's estate, inherited through his father; studied law under Judge Bushrod Washington ; began the practice of his profession at his old home in Harri-

sonburg; was a member of both houses of the Virginia Legislature; first a member of the House of Delegates in 1805;
passed his life on his estate known as "Waverly," where he
generously dispensed his hospitality; was Judge of the Circuit
and Supreme Courts for over forty years; his portrait can be
seen in the Court House at Harrisonburg, Va., the only one
the county officials will permit in the building; married,
June 10, 1809, Frances Strother Duff, b. Feb. 11, 1792, d. Oct.
4, 1849.   Seven children:

1. Margaret Davis Smith,   b. Apr. 4, 1810.
2. Elizabeth Strother Smith, b. Mar. 16, 1814.
3. Lucius Quintus Smith,   b. 1816; d. 1847, in Dayton,
4. Frances Evelyn Smith,   b. 1819.   [Ohio, unmarried.
5. Marie Antoinette Smith,   b. Sept. 18, 1827.
6. John Williams Green,   b. Sept. 17, 1829.
7. Daniel Smith, Jr.,   b. Apr. 10, 1835; d. 1860, un-
                                                  [married.
Daniel Smith, Sr., died Nov. 8, 1850.

FIFTH GENERATION.

First.   Margaret Davis Smith, 1st of Judge Daniel and
Frances S. (Duff) Smith, was twice married: 1st, to John
Craig, in 1834.   Issue, one child, a son, Robert Craig, who
died 1889, unmarried.   2d marriage to M. H. Effinger, in
1845.   One child, J. Fred Effinger, born May 13, 1846.

Margaret Effinger, *nee* Craig, *nee* Smith, was remarkable
for her many qualities.   Early in life she became the center
of a brilliant and cultured company, which gathered in her
father's hospitable home "Waverly;" and during her long
life, was at all times, considered one of the most brilliant and
fascinating women of the state, a strong and accurate mind,
combined with great kindness of heart, dignity and character.

SIXTH GENERATION.

J. Fred. Effinger, born May 13, 1846, only child of M. H.
Effinger and Margaret Davis Smith, *nee* Craig, widow, mar-

ried Nov. 27, 1886, Frances Strother Smith (his cousin), born March 17, 1861; daughter of Judge John Wms. Green Smith. Five children:

1. J. Fred. Effinger, Jr., b. Aug. 4, 1887 ; died in 1888.
2. Margaret Smith, b. Jan. 1, 1889 ; died in 1889.
3. Robert Craig, b. May 24, 1890.
4. Frances Smith, b. April 4, 1892.
5. Katherine Taylor, b. Aug. 16, 1896.

FIFTH GENERATION.

Second. Elizabeth Strother Smith 2d, of Judge Daniel and Frances S. (Duff), born 1814; married Judge Christopher Columbus Scott, of Arkansas, Aug. 2, 1832; he was born in Halifax county, Va., April 22, 1807, and died Jan. 13, 1859, leaving his widow surviving; issue, nine children:

1. Daniel, b. June 4, 1833 ; died May 20, 1857,
2. Frank T., b. 1835. [unmarried.
3. Mary Frances, b. June 14, 1837.
4. Christopher C., Jr., b. 1839.
5. Elizabeth, b. 1841.
6. Robert, b. 1844 ; died Aug., 1848.
7. Catherine, b. 1846 ; died 1864, unmarried.
8. Julia, b. 1848.
9. Nellie, b. 1852.

SIXTH GENERATION.

Second. Frank T. Scott, born 1835, 2d of Judge Christopher and Elizabeth S. (Smith) Scott, married ——, 1869, L. McMahon. Five children: Francis T., Jane, Christopher C., Francis T., and Mary Scott.

Third. Mary Frances Scott, born June 14, 1847, 3d of Judge Christopher C. and Elizabeth S. (Smith) Scott, married July 18, 1854, John W. Tobin, residence, New Orleans. Seven children:

1. Mary H., b. Feb. 4, 1856 ; died in 1859.
2. Daniel G., b. Feb. 25, 1858 ; died in 1859.
3. Mary, b. Nov. 16, 1859 ; m. Chas. P. McCann. Four children : Kate, b. 1882 ; Fannie Tobin, b. 1883 ; David C., 1884 ; Chas., 1887.
4. Fanny (called Jack) (girl), b. July 10, 1863 ; married Capt. T. H. Underwood, U. S. Army ; one child, a son, Tobin, born 1897.
5. Maude, b. July 30, 1867 ; married Leon G. Gibert ; one child, a son, Gustavus, born 1893.
6. Ellen Tobin, b. July 24, 1869 ; m. A. S. J. White ; two children : Maude, b. 1898 ; Ellen, b. 1899.
7. John Francis, b. June 17, 1871.

Fourth. Christopher C. Scott, Jr., born 1839 ; married ——, Jane Toney. Three children :

1. Elizabeth, b. ——; m. Bleeker Luce, of Fort Smith, Ark.
2. Birdie, b. ——; m. ——, Dr. Sharpe, of St. Louis.
3. Nellie, b. ——, 1883.

Fifth. Elizabeth Scott, born 1841; married Levi Gailliard ; died 1866. Issue, two children :

1. Scott, b. ———. No record.
2. Lillie, b. ——; m. ———.

SEVENTH GENERATION.

Second. Lillie Gailliard, born ——— ; married, ———, Charles Urquhart. Residence, New Orleans. Three children :

1. Elise (or Alice), b. 1892.
2. Lillian, b. 1894.
3. Wilkins, b. 1897.

SIXTH GENERATION.

Eighth. Julia Scott, 8th of Judge Christopher and Elizabeth S. (Smith) Scott, born 1846–8 ; married J. W. Carhart. Two children :

1. Whitefield, b. 1876.
2. Lucia,   b. ——; died in infancy.

Ninth.   Nellie Scott, youngest child of Judge Christopher and Elizabeth S. (Smith) Scott, born 1852; married, ——, Dr. A. A. Tufts.   One child, a daughter, Maude Shippen, born 1873; died 1876.

FIFTH GENERATION.

Fourth.   Frances Evelyn Smith, 4th of Judge Daniel and Frances S. (Duff) Smith, born 1819; married July 2d, 1839, Andrew Plunkett Beirne.   Two children:

1. Mary Frances,   b. June 15, 1840.
2. Andrew Plunkett, Jr., b. April 6, 1842.

SIXTH GENERATION.

First.   Mary Frances Beirne, 1st of Andrew Plunkett and Frances E. (Smith) Beirne, born June 15, 1840; married July 9, 1861, John Marshall Kinney.   Four children:

1. Nettie,   b. April 12, 1863; m. Edward Harman.
2. Cabell,   b. April 3, 1866; m. ——, Annette Trowbridge, in 1892.
3. Evelyn,   b. Aug. 12, 1872; m. John A. Renalhan.
4. Beirne Kinney, b. April 17, 1875.

Second.   Andrew Plunkett Beirne, Jr., 2d of Andrew, Sr., and Frances E. (Smith) Beirne, born April 6, 1842.   He was a naval cadet at Annapolis at the breaking out of the Civil War; he resigned and joined the Confederate navy in May, 1861, and served until captured at Mobile, in 1865; married, Dec. 19, 1867, Elizabeth Caperton.   Six children:

1. Lewis Caperton, b. Oct. 1, 1868; m. Rhoda Beatty, 1902.
                         (See Beatty Family Records, by
                         the Pub.)
2. Elizabeth,   b. Oct. 20, 1870.
3. Mary Plunkett, b. Dec. 17, 1872.

4. Andrew Plunkett, b. Sept. 14, 1874.
5. Frances,   b. Nov. 25, 1876.
6. Alice Beulah,   b. Aug. 21, 1880.

Fifth. Marie Antoinette Smith, 5th of Judge Daniel and Frances S. (Duff) Smith, born Sept. 18, 1827; married, April 29, 1847, William Henry Tams,* at "Waverley," Rockingham county, Va., the home of her father, born Dec. 8, 1824, at Fayetteville, North Carolina, died at Rawley Springs, Va., Aug. 2, 1873. She died Feb. 1, 1902. Ten children:

1. Mary Purviance,   b. July 14, 1848; d. June 10, 1849.
2. Fannie Smith,   b. May 28, 1850.
3. William Purviance, b. March 11, 1852.
4. Maggie,   b. July 18, 1854; d. June 4, 1856.
5. Marie Antoinette,   b. July 8, 1856.
6. Mary Carolina,   b. Aug. 2, 1858; d. June 25, 1875.
7. Rosalie Beirne,   b. March 21, 1860.
8. Briscoe Donaghe,   b. Feb. 28, 1862; d. Jan. 14, 1889,
                                      [unmarried.
9. Florence Brownlow, b. Sept. 22, 1864; d. July 14, 1865.
10. Weightman Hanson, b. Aug. 20, 1867; m. Alice Beamer.

SIXTH GENERATION.

Third. William Purviance Tams, 3d of Wm. Henry and Marie Antoinette (Smith) Tams, born Mar. 11, 1852, in Rockingham county, Va. In 1853 his parents settled at Staunton, V.; here he received his early training. In 1873 he grad-

---

* William Tams, born March 13, 1794, was a native of Burslen, England; immigrated to America in 1820; settled in North Carolina, where he married, in 1824, Mary Brownlow Purviance, of Fayetteville, a granddaughter of Col. Wm. Purviance, of Huguenot descent, who settled in North Carolina in 1763; was appointed colonel of militia for New Hanover county 1775–6, page 365, "Revolutionary History of the State, by J. S. Jones." His only living child, William Henry Tams, born 1824, at Fayetteville, North Carolina, was a Master of Arts of Princeton College before he reached his nineteenth year; and, after graduating in law at the University of Virginia, settled in Rockingham county, Va., where he married Marie Antoinette, daughter of the distinguished jurist Judge Daniel Smith.

uated from the Virginia Military Institute with distinction. After teaching military tactics and chemistry for one session, he returned to Staunton, and shortly thereafter entered the service of the Augusta National Bank, becoming its cashier in 1880, which position he still occupies. He has been active in municipal affairs, and is at present chairman of the city council. He married, Nov. 17, 1880, Sue Lewis Frazier, born May 19, 1859, daughter of the late Hon. William and Susan Massie Lewis Frazier, of Staunton, Va.   Two children :

1. William Frazier,   b. March 17, 1882. ⎱ Both of whom
2. William Purviance, b. May 19, 1883. ⎰
        are graduates of the Virginia Polytechnic Institute.

Seventh. Rosalie Beirne Tams, 7th of Wm. Henry and Marie Antoinette (Smith) Tams, born March 21, 1860 ; married, Dec. 9, 1880, Conway McNeece Whittle, son of Commodore William C. Whittle.   Three children :

1. William Tams Whittle, b. ———; died in infancy.
2. Rosalie Beirne,   b. ———.
3. Mary Conway,   b. ———; died in infancy.

FIFTH GENERATION.

Sixth.   John Williams Green Smith, 6th of Judge Daniel and Frances Strother (Duff) Smith, born Sept. 17, 1829; was twice married, 1st to Catherine M. Taylor, of Jefferson county, Ky., Nov. 30, 1853.   Five children :

1. Marie Antoinette, b. Nov. 28, 1855 ; d. Oct. 9, 1868.
2. Annie Taylor,   b. Sept. 29, 1857.
3. Frances Strother, b. March 17, 1861.
4. Catherine Taylor, b. Jan. 10, 1864.
5. Lucius Green,   b. Nov. 3, 1871.

Catherine Taylor Smith died Jan. 18, 1873.   The 2d marriage of John Williams Green Smith was on March 13, 1875, to Sarah McKeldon.   One child, a son, Herbert McKeldon, born April 10, 1876.

SIXTH GENERATION.

Second. Ann Taylor Smith, 2d of John Williams Green and Catherine (Taylor) Smith, born Sept. 29, 1857; was twice married: 1st, to William Shands, March 4, 1878; he died Oct. 12, 1880, leaving one child, a son, William, born May 5, 1879; 2d marriage of Ann Taylor Shands, to Walter Newman Peale, Feb. 4, 1891. He died Feb. 6, 1894. No children.

Third. Frances Strother Smith, 3d of John Williams Green and Catherine (Taylor) Smith, born March 17, 1861; married Nov. 27, 1886, J. Fred. Effinger, her cousin. Four children. (See Effinger record.)

Fourth. Catherine Taylor Smith, 4th of John Williams Green and Catherine (Taylor) Smith, born Jan. 10, 1864; married Feb. 27, 1889, Benjamin Gause Gregg. Three children:

1. Benjamin Gause, b. Nov. 21, 1889.
2. Lucius Smith,   b. May 11, 1892.
3. Jessie Chestnut, b. Aug. 22, 1896.

Fifth. Lucius Green Smith, 5th of John Williams Green and Catherine (Taylor) Smith, born Nov. 3, 1871; married, June 30, 1896, Jessie Bright Dent. Their son, Garrard Dent Smith, born June 27, 1897. Jessie Bright Dent was the daughter of Marshall Mortimer Dent, of Morgantown, West Virginia, son of Dr. Marmaduke and Sarah (Price) Dent, daughter of Wm. Price, of Kingwood, West Virginia. Dr. Marmaduke Dent was the son of Capt. John Dent and Margaret Evans, daughter of Col. John Evans and Ann Martin, of Loudoun county, Va. Capt. John Dent * was born 1755,

---

* Capt. John Dent enlisted from Monongalia county, Va., April, 1777, as a private soldier, for three years, under Capt. Davis Scott, of the 13th Virginia Regiment, commanded by Col. John Gibson; marched to Fort Pitt, then to Fort Kittanning, where he remained two months. In the fall of 1777, as sergeant, with twelve men, marched to a point near Wheeling, where they built a fort. In the spring of 1778 was appointed lieutenant of Capt. Jacobus Sullivan's company, under Gen. McIntosh; marched to Beaver Creek, where they built a fort. In

in Maryland (?), and is a direct descendant of William and Elizabeth (Foulk) Dent, the immigrant. (See notes of the Dent Family by the publisher.)

Sixth. Herbert McKelden Smith, 6th and only child of John Williams Green, by his second wife, Sarah (McKeldon) Smith, born April 10, 1876; married, Feb. 1, 1898, Ida Morgan Glover. No children.

THIRD GENERATION.

Second. Daniel Smith, Jr., 2d of Colonel Daniel Smith and Jane Harrison Smith, born June 25, 1754; commanded a company at the battle of Point Pleasant, after his captain had been wounded. Of him nothing further is known.

Sixth. Benjamin Smith, 6th of Colonel Daniel and Jane (Harrison) Smith, born in Augusta county, Va., May 25, 1761; married about 1782–3, Elizabeth Cravens, born 1762, daughter of Robert. (See Cravens Family.) He was a lieutenant in the Revolutionary army and present at the surrender of Yorktown; was the owner of a fine estate near Harrisonburg, about two miles from his father's place, "Smithland," and about the same distance in the opposite direction from

the fall of 1778 marched to Tuscaroah river, where they built Fort Lawrence. February, 1779, marched to Fort Pitt, where he commanded seventy-five men to harrass the Indians. In the winter of 1779–80 he returned to Fort McIntosh, where he was in command, by order of Col. Gibson, of a cavalry company in pursuit of deserters, where he remained until November, 1780, when he resigned. On Aug. 28, 1832, he filed his declaration for a pension, stating his age at seventy-seven years; his service as ensign two months and twenty-nine days; as lieutenant, one year and nine months. He married, June, 1780, Margaret Evans, and died Sept. 20, 1840. In 1845 his widow Margaret filed her claim for a pension for the services of her husband; with which declaration was filed a copy of their family Bible, stating her marriage to Capt. John Dent as June, 1780, and the date of his death as Sept. 20, 1840. The names and births of their twelve children recorded in the following order: Elizabeth, b. Dec. 26, 1781; John S., b. Jan. 24, 1783; George, b. Nov. 18, 1784 (d. at New Orleans July, 1805); Dudley S., b. March 1, 1787; Ann, b. May 23, 1789; Nimrod, b. June 18, 1792; Margaret Higgs, b. April 1, 1794; Enoch, b. May 21, 1796; James, b. Aug. 15, 1799; Marmaduke, b. May 25, 1801; Nancy, b. April 3, 1803; Evans, b. Feb. 28, 1808.

Judge Daniel Smith's estate, known as "Waverley." His home was known as the Old Stone House. Wishing to free his slaves, in September, 1810, he removed with his family to Ohio, and settled near where the town of Lancaster now is. He was a man of high integrity, strong character and religious conviction. He died August 18, 1812, his wife surviving; she died Feb. 22, 1837, aged 75 years. Both were buried in the old Methodist churchyard. Their house at Lancaster was destroyed by fire in 1859, with all family records, hence the deficiency of dates, etc. Nine children:

1. John,   b. 1783.
2. Ann, or Nancy,   b. 1784.
3. Robert,   b. 1785.
4. Daniel,   b. ———.
5. Margaret,   b. 1792.
6. Elizabeth,   b. 1795.
7. Benjamin Harrison, b. 1797.
8. James Harrison,   b. 1798.
9. Jane Harrison,   b. ———; died young.

FOURTH GENERATION.

First. John Smith, 1st of Benjamin and Elizabeth (Cravens) Smith, born 1783, in Rockingham county, Va.; married, ———, 1809, Adamena Carthae, of Rockingham county; lived in Charleston, W. Va., later in Lancaster, Ohio; served in the commissary department in the War of 1812; died from an accident in 1827. His wife Adamena was born July 28, 1783; a member of one of the oldest families of the valley of Virginia; is said to have been a woman of remarkable beauty, devoted Christian, and universally beloved; she died in Charleston, W. Va., June 16, 1848. Issue, four children:

1. Charles, b. 1810; was elected to Virginia State Senate in 1834; died in Vicksburg, Miss., before taking his seat.
2. Mary Smith, b. 1811; married, in 1834, Geo. Hudson; died 1837, leaving a daughter, Mary, born 1835, died 1848.

3. Elizabeth Frances Smith, b. 1819.
4. John Benjamin Smith, b. June 22, 1822, in Charleston,
[W. Va.

FIFTH GENERATION.

Third. Elizabeth Frances Smith, 3d of John and Adamena (Carthae) Smith, born in 1819; married, ——, William Noyes. Four children:

1. Adelbert, b. ——; m. ——. Res., W. Va.
2. Charles, b. ——; m. ——. Res., W. Va.
3. Wright, b. ——; m. ——. Res., W. Va.
4. John Smith, b. ——; m. Mary McKay, an aunt of Mrs. Roger M. Smith, of Jefferson Co., Kentucky. Res., Louisville, Ky.

Fourth. John Benjamin Smith, 4th of John and Adamena (Carthae) Smith, born June 22, 1822; he passed part of his early life with his grandmother, Elizabeth Cravens Smith, at Lancaster, Ohio; returned to Charleston, W. Va., where he engaged in commercial life. In 1854 he moved permanently with his family to Louisville, where he represented the Kanawha Salt Company, and rapidly rose in prominence, becoming a merchant and financier of marked ability. In 1857 he retired from active business, later engaged in banking, and was the founder of the bank of Commerce of Louisville, of which he was President for many years; was vestryman of Christ Church for twenty-seven years, of which the Rev. Dr. James Cregg (?), who performed his marriage ceremony in Va., was rector. He was a man of simple taste, gentleness and refined manners. He married July 18, 1844, Caroline Amelia Welsh, born Feb. 16, 1827; d. of Levi Welsh and Catherine G. Slaughter. He died April 20, 1887, in Louisville, Ky. Had issue, five children:

1. Levi Welsh, b. ——, 1845; died 1848.
2. Mary Cornelia, b. Feb. 9, 1848.
3. Kate Welsh, b. Sept. 13, 1850.

4. Amelia,   b. 1852; died young.
5. Roger Morris, b. Mar. 20, 1858.

SIXTH GENERATION.

Second. Mary Cornelia Smith, 2d of John Benjamin and
Caroline Amelia (Welsh) Smith, born 1848; married June 14,
1871, H. D. Newcomb, of Louisville, Ky. He died Aug. 10,
1874. Two children:

1. Warren Smith,   b. Aug. 10, 1872; d. Jan. 16, 1895,
                       in Louisville, during his senior
                       year at Harvard College.
2. H. Dalton Newcomb, b. Nov. 24, 1873; graduated at
                       Yale, 1896.

The second marriage of Mary Cornelia Smith Newcomb,
May —, 1878, to Richard Tenbroeck; one child, a son,
Richard, born Sept. 13, 1879. Richard Tenbroeck, Sr., died
Aug. 1, 1892.

Fifth. Roger Morris Smith, 5th of John Benjamin and Caroline Amelia (Welsh) Smith, born March 20, 1858; was educated at the University of Virginia, sessions 1876–7–8, returning to Kentucky he became interested in the Provision and
Pork Packing business of Hamilton Bros. & Co., of Louisville,
Ky., in which firm he remained for several years; retiring
from mercantile life, located on a farm in Jefferson county,
where for twenty years he has been engaged in the breeding
of thoroughbred horses and cattle. He married June 8, 1881,
Jane McKay Hamilton, born Aug. 21, 1860; daughter of
Samuel S. Hamilton, of Maryland, and Elizabeth McKay, of
Louisville, Ky. One child, a daughter, Elizabeth Hamilton
Smith, born June 6, 1883. Residence, St. Matthew's, Jeffer-
son county, Ky.

FOURTH GENERATION.

Second. Ann or Nancy, 2d of Benjamin and Elizabeth
(Cravens) Smith, born 1784, in Rockingham county, Va.,

where she married in 1800 Major Joseph Brown. Seven children : (See Brown Family).

1. Benjamin S.,   b. ———.
2. Thomas,   b. ———; m. Lucy Hollister. No issue.
3. Mary Brown,   b. ———; m. —— Pyle. No issue.
4. Eliza,   b. ———; m. Mr. Knowlton.
5. Ophelia,   b. Oct. 17, 1816.
6. Ellen,   b. ——— ; m. Dr. Jno. Russell, of Mt. Vernon, Ohio, where she died in 1879, leaving many descendants, who now reside in California.
7. Adelaide,   b. ———; m. —— Orr. Their children all died young.

FIFTH GENERATION.

First. Benjamin S. Brown, 1st of Major Joseph and Ann (Smith) Brown, born ———; married Catherine Thomas. Four children :

1. Joseph,   b. ———.
2. Jesse Burgess, b. ———.
3. Richard,   b. ———.
4. Catherine,   b. ——— ; m. John James.

FOURTH GENERATION.

Fourth. Eliza Brown, 4th of Major Joseph and Ann (Smith) Brown, born ———; married ——— Knowlton. Two children :

1. Benjamin, b. ———.
2. Julia,   b. ———.

Fifth. Ophelia Brown, 5th of Major Joseph and Ann (Smith) Brown, born October 17, 1816, at Mount Vernon, Ohio, where she married, March 20, 1839, Worthy Paul Meacham, born April 24, 1802, in Southwick, Hampton Co., Mass. He died in Ohio, May 17, 1853. She died July 8, 1883, in Ross Valley, California. Three children :

1. Benjamina Catherine, b. March 15, 1841.
2. Anna Roxalina,   b. Jan. 31, 1844.
3. Adelaide Ellen,   b. June 19, 1846.

FIFTH GENERATION.

First. Benjamina Catherine Meacham, 1st of Worthy Paul
and Ophelia (Brown) Meacham, born at Mount Vernon, Ohio,
March 15, 1841; married, in San Francisco, April 3, 1866,
William Harney.   One child, a daughter, *Annie Ralston,* born
Jan. 25, 1867.   Benjamina Catherine died in San Francisco,
Nov. 26, 1882.

SIXTH GENERATION.

First. Annie Ralston Harney, only child of William and
Benjamina C. (Meacham) Harney, born Jan. 25, 1867; mar-
ried, Dec. 8, 1885, at Fern Hill, Ross Valley, California, Evan
Cyfeiliog Evans, an Englishman.   Three sons:

1. Evan Cyfeiliog, b. Sept. 21, 1886.
2. Henry L.,   b. March 3, 1888.
3. Arthor C.,   b. Dec. 8, 1890.   Res., England.

FIFTH GENERATION.

Second. Anna Roxalina Meacham, 2d of Worthy Paul and
Ophelia (Brown) Meacham, born at Mount Vernon, Ohio,
Jan. 31, 1844; married, July 11, 1867, at San Francisco, Cal.,
Albert Dibblee, born at White Plains, New York, Feb. 18, 1821,
died at Ross Valley, Cal., Dec. 6, 1895.   Four children:

1. Albert James,   b. Feb. 25, 1870.
2. Anita Lavina,   b. Feb. 8, 1871.
3. Harrison,   b. April 30, 1874.
4. Benjamin Harrison, b. July 8, 1876; graduated from
                              [Harvard, class 1899.

SIXTH GENERATION.

First. Albert James Dibblee, 1st of Albert and Anna Roxalina (Meacham) Dibblee, born Feb. 25, 1870; graduated in

law from Harvard, 1893; is a member of the bar at San Francisco; married, April 21, 1899, Ethel Rogers, of Columbus, Ohio.

Third. Harrison Dibblee, 2d of Albert and Anna Roxalina (Meacham) Dibblee, born April 30, 1874; a graduate of Harvard, class of 1896; is engaged in mining; married, Jan. 11, 1899, Adelia Halliday Davidson, at San Rafael, Cal.

FIFTH GENERATION.

Third. Adelaide Ellen, 3d of Worthy Paul and Ophelia (Brown) Meacham, born June 19, 1846; married, March 1, 1866, A. D. Elwell. One child, Frank Elwell, born Nov. 27, 1866. A. D. Elwell died Dec. 3, 1874.

The second marriage of Adelaide Ellen Elwell, Dec. 8, 1876, to Dr. Henry W. Boone, of South Carolina. She died Oct. 12, 1881, at Shanghai, China.

SIXTH GENERATION.

First. Frank Elwell, only child of A. D. and Adelaide Ellen (Meacham) Elwell, born November, 1866; married ———. Four children:

1. Frank,   b. ———.
2. George,   b. ———.
3. Adelaide,   b. ———.
4. Burnadine, b. ———.

FOURTH GENERATION.

Third. Robert Smith, 3d of Benjamin and Elizabeth (Cravens) Smith, born 1785; settled in Ohio with his parents in 1810; married, 1834, Phoebe Searle, of Providence, R. I., born in 1810. He died Feb. 21, 1870; she died Feb. 22, 1884. Five children:

1. Elizabeth Cravens, b. April 5, 1835; died age 23 years, unmarried.
2. Daniel, b. 1837; m. Dilly Hunter. No record.

23

3. Geo. Creed, b. 1839; died young, unmarried.
4. James, b. 1841; m. Rebecca McLeary. Two children:
    1. Wm. C., b. ——.   2. Robt. McLeary, b. ——.
5. Fanny, b. Dec. 8, 1844; m. June 2, 1870, Samuel Rutter.
    Two children: 1. Robt. Smith, b. Mar. 14, 1871.
    2. Elizabeth, b. August, 1875.

FOURTH GENERATION.

Fourth. Daniel Smith, 4th of Benjamin and Elizabeth (Cravens) Smith, born in Rockingham county, Va., about 1787.

He was a man of fine mind, remarkably bright and witty. He studied medicine, and practiced in Lancaster and Charleston during his early life. He was known as "General Smith," which title was conferred for services in the war of 1812–1814, being a Surgeon-General.

He served under General William Henry Harrison, also under Commodore Perry at the battle of Lake Erie; was a member of the Ohio Legislature Sessions of 1817–18; a delegate from Kanawha county, Va., to the general assembly, during the sessions 1828–29–37–38–41–44.

He was a man of enormous size, weighing over 300 lbs. He married late in life Mrs. Nancy Harriman, of W. Va. No issue; died at Charleston, West Virginia, 1854.

FOURTH GENERATION.

Fifth. Margaret Smith, 5th of Benjamin and Elizabeth (Cravens) Smith, born 1792; married ——, 1811, John Creed. She died Sept. 11, 1823. Issue, six children:

1. Mary,   b. 1812; died in infancy, 1813.
2. George,   b. 1814.
3. Mary (2),   b. 1816.
4. Elizabeth,   b. Oct. 1, 1818.
5. Margaret Davis, b. 1820.
6. Jane Harrison, b. 1822.

FIFTH GENERATION.

Second. George Creed, 2d of John and Margaret (Smith)

Creed, born at Lancaster, Ohio, in 1814; married Oct. 25, 1836, Elizabeth A. Clement, and died Aug. 29, 1845. Elizabeth, his widow, died May 7, 1889. Four children:

1. George, b. July 19, 1836.
2. Mary Livering, b. Jan. 17, 1840.
3. John Marshall, b. April 30, 1842.
4. Charles Hopkins, b. May 20, 1844.

SIXTH GENERATION.

First. George Creed, son of George and Elizabeth (Clement) Creed, born at Lancaster, Ohio, July 19, 1838; married Dec. 6, 1864, Alice Peters. Four children:

1. Mary Low, b. Sept., 1865; died Dec., 1865.
2. Frank Peters, b. Sept. 2, 1867.
3. Ann Peters, b. Nov. 15, 1871.
4. Fanny, b. Jan. 5, 1875.

SEVENTH GENERATION.

Second. Frank Peters Creed, son of George and Alice (Peters) Creed, born Sept. 2, 1867; married March, 1894, Ida Mitchell. Four children: Frederick, b. 1894; Garrett, b. 1896; Ann Maria, b. July 19, 1898, and Cornelia, b. Oct., 1899.

Third. Ann Peters Creed, daughter of George and Alice (Peters) Creed, born Nov. 15, 1871; married March, 1895, Dr. W. H. Silbaugh. Two children: George Creed, b. 1896, and Harold, b. 1898.

Fourth. Fanny Creed, daughter of George and Alice (Peters) Creed, born Jan. 5, 1875; married March, 1897, Charles W. Griffith. One child, a son, Paul Winters, born Oct., 1897.

SIXTH GENERATION.

Second. Mary Livering Creed, 2d of George and Elizabeth (Clement) Creed, married 1858, Frederick F. Low. One

child, a daughter, Flora, born Dec. 4, 1858, at Maysville,
California.

Third. John Marshall Creed, 3d of George and Elizabeth
(Clement) Creed, born April 30, 1842; married 1872, Mary
Sullivan. Six children:

1. Joseph,   b. Nov. 1, 1872, at San Francisco, Cal.
2. George Dominick, b. Aug. 11, 1874.
3. Ellen Elizabeth,   b. Oct. 30, 1876.
4. Mary Agnes,   b. Jan. 22, 1878; died Dec. 31, 1878.
5. Elizabeth Ann,   b. July 5, 1879.
6. Charles B.,   b. Mar. 11, 1881.

Fourth. Charles Hopkins Creed, 4th of George and Elizabeth (Clement) Creed, born May 20, 1844; married ——,
Louise Withoff. Nine children:

1. Celia Withoff,   b. Oct. 29, 1868, at Lancaster, Ohio.
2. Mary Low,   b. June 10, 1870.
3. Elizabeth Clement, b. Jan. 27, 1873.
4. Anna Withoff,   b. Oct. 22, 1874.
5. Flora Low,   b. Sept. 22, 1876.
6. Louise Withoff,   b. Oct. 15, 1878.
7. George,   b. Aug. 13, 1880; died Feb. 14, 1883.
8. Jennie Collette,   b. Sept. 26, 1882.
9. Charles Henry,   b. April 4, 1885.

Residence near Lancaster, Ohio.

FIFTH GENERATION.

Third. Mary Creed (2), 3d of John and Margaret Smith
Creed, born at Lancaster, Ohio; married ——, William A.
Ritchie. Seven children:

1. Creed Ritchie, b. ——; m. ——; died 1877, left
                          three children.
2. Henry Ritchie, b. ——; killed in the Civil war.
3. Alexander,   b. ——; killed in the Civil war.
4. Catherine,   b. (see later).

5. Margaret, b. ——; m. ——, William Walbridge. No
6. James, b. ——. [issue.
7. Wm. A., b. ——; unmarried.

SIXTH GENERATION.

Fourth. Catherine Ritchie, 4th of William A. and Mary (Creed) Ritchie, born ——; married, ——, Charles Simpkins, of San Francisco, Cal. Two children:

1. Alice, b. ——; m. Robert Lewis Coleman. Two children: 1. Robt., Jr., b. ——. 2. Caroline, b. ——.
2. Henry Ritchie, b. ——; unmarried.

Sixth. James Ritchie, 6th of William A. and Mary (Creed) Ritchie, born ——; married, ——, Phoebe Boerstler. Two children:

1. Elizabeth, b. ——.
2. Margaret, b. ——.

FIFTH GENERATION.

Fourth. Elizabeth Creed, 4th of John and Margaret (Smith) Creed, born Oct. 1, 1818; married Darius Tallmadge as his 2d wife. No issue. Mr. Tallmadge died ——; his widow Elizabeth resides at Trenton, N. J.

Fifth. Margaret Davis Creed, 5th of John and Margaret (Smith) Creed, born 1820; married Major Andrew Parks, attorney-at-law, of Charleston, West Virginia, where they both died, he in 1864 and his wife Margaret in 1866. Four children:

1. Creed Parks, b. ——; was killed during the Civil War.
2. Bushrod Washington, b. ——; m. ——; died 1875.
3. Harriot Washington, b. ——; m. ——, T. W. Tallmadge, of Washington, D. C., as his 2d wife, June 26, 1867. Two children: 1. Flora Harriot, b. Oct. 1, 1868; d. Feb., 1900. 2. Andrew Parks, b. Jan. 16, 1870; electrical engineer and contractor, Washington, D. C.

4. Andrew Parks, b. ———; m. ———. Residence, West
   Virginia.

Sixth. Jane Harrison Creed, 6th of John and Margaret
(Smith) Creed, born 1822; married, ———, John C. Fall,
of California. She died 1859. Two children:

1. Kate Fall, b. ———; died in infancy.
2. Sallie Fall, b. ———; m. Commodore Rogers, of the
   U. S. Navy. Residence, Washington, D. C. Issue,
   one child, a son, Ralph Fall Rogers, born ———.

FOURTH GENERATION.

Sixth. Elizabeth Smith, 6th of Benjamin and Elizabeth
(Cravens) Smith, born 1795; m. ———, 1826, Hugh McElroy;
died Sept. 4, 1827; her only child dying in infancy.

Seventh. Benjamin Harrison Smith, 7th of Benjamin and
Elizabeth (Cravens) Smith, born Oct. 31, 1797. He was a
noted lawyer for over 60 years and a large land owner in
western Virginia. In 1833 was elected a delegate to the Virginia State Senate; was twice re-elected. In 1849 was appointed by President Taylor U. S. States attorney for the
western district of Virginia, remaining in office during the
term of Taylor and Fillmore. In 1852 was elected a member
of the Constitutional Convention of Virginia, and in 1862 a
member of the convention which formed the state of West
Virginia. He was again appointed district attorney by President Lincoln, and continued in office for five years, when he
resigned. He married, Dec. 19, 1826, Roxalana Noyes, daughter of Isaac Noyes, of Charleston. Three children:

1. Cynthia Elizabeth, b. Oct. 22, 1827.
2. Isaac Noyes,   b. April 6, 1831.
3. Roxalana Emeline, b. May 13, 1841.

Benjamin H. Smith died in Charleston, W. Va., Dec. 10,
1887. His widow, Roxalana (Noyes) Smith, died Feb. 10,
1859.

FIFTH GENERATION.

First. Cynthia Elizabeth Smith, 1st of Benjamin Harrison and Roxalana (Noyes) Smith, born Oct. 22, 1827 ; married, ————, Fred F. Brooks.   Two children :

1. Lilly Rand Brooks, b. 1852; m. 1874, Wm. Burlingham. Three children : 1. Frederick Harrison, b. Jan. 18, 1877.   2. William, b. Oct. 15, 1879.   3. Prentis, b. Oct. 14, 1881.
2. Morris Oden Brooks, b. 1862 ; unmarried.

FIFTH GENERATION.

Second. Isaac Noyes Smith, 2d of Benjamin Harrison and Roxalana (Noyes) Smith, born April 6, 1831. In his early youth was a pupil in the Charleston Academy ; at the age of sixteen years entered Washington College, now Washington and Lee University, graduating with the degree of Bachelor of Arts ; studied law under his father, and afterwards attended the law school of Judge John W. Brockenbrough.

In 1852 was licensed to practice law, in which he was eminently successful. In 1859 and 1860 he represented the county of Kanawha in the legislature of Virginia. During the Civil War he served as major of the 22d Virginia Regiment C. S. A.

He was a man of extensive information and breadth of thought, including not only the graver things of business, but the nobler affairs of life—love of humanity, devotion to family and friends—unobtrusive, but zealous in good works. His life was moulded by three principles : love of God, charity for his fellowman, and respect of self; and it is not eulogistic to say that, gauged by these standards, his life was complete. He married, Nov. 29, 1860, Caroline Shrewsbury Quarrier, born Oct. 23, 1839.   Seven children :

1. Benjamin Harrison, b. Mar. 20, 1862 ; d. May 18, 1887.
2. Alexander Quarrier, b. Mar. 24, 1864.
3. Harrison Brooks,   b. Sept. 7, 1866.

4. Elsie Quarrier,   b. April 4, 1869.
5. Isaac Noyes,   b. Dec. 21, 1876.
6. Christopher Tompkins, b. Feb. 16, 1879.
7. Winston Shrewsbury,   b. Dec. 23, 1880; d. Oct. 10, 1882.

SIXTH GENERATION.

Second.   Alexander Quarrier Smith, 2d of Isaac Noyes and
Caroline S. (Quarrier) Smith, born March 24, 1864; married
June 2, 1891, Ethelind Parker Appleton, born June 28, 1867.
Three children :

1. Benjamin Harrison, b. July 16, 1893.
2. Elsie Quarrier,   b. March 25, 1898.
3. Everard Appleton, b. April 1, 1900.

Third.   Harrison Brooks Smith, 3d of Isaac Noyes and
Caroline S. (Quarrier) Smith, born Sept. 7, 1866; married
May 12, 1896, Katherine Dana Bowne, born June 8, 1872.
Two children :

1. Harrison Bowne, b. March 2, 1898.
2. Helen Dana,   b. March 2, 1900.

Fourth.   Elsie Quarrier Smith, 4th of Isaac Noyes and Caroline S. (Quarrier) Smith, born April 4, 1869; married Nov.
29, 1892, Frederick M. Staunton, born May 17, 1866.   One
child, Caroline Quarrier, born May 6, 1894.

Fifth.   Isaac Noyes Smith, 5th of Isaac Noyes and Caroline S. (Quarrier) Smith, born Dec. 21, 1876; married Oct.
25, 1890, Elizabeth Adelaide Dana, born Oct. 24, 1876.

FIFTH GENERATION.

Third.   Roxalana Emeline Smith, 3d of Benjamin Harrison and Roxalana (Noyes) Smith, born May 13, 1841;
married ——, Col. Amos Balfour Jones.   One child, a daughter, Lena, born 1865; was twice married: 1st, to Wm. B.
Dixon.   Issue, one child, William Boulton Dixon.   2d marriage to D. L. Laine.   (No further record.)

FOURTH GENERATION.

Eighth. James Harrison Smith, 8th of Benjamin and Elizabeth (Cravens) Smith, born 1798–9; married Nov. —, 1828, Elizabeth Standeland White, daughter of Rev. Wm. White, of Philadelphia; was a successful merchant, and died Aug. 9, 1830, at Lancaster, Ohio. One child, a daughter, Elizabeth Tacy, born Aug. 3d, 1829; married Dec. 10, 1850, Wm. Latta. He died Nov. 13, 1874. Six children:

1. John Latta,   b. ————.
2. James,   b. ————; died unmarried, age 24 years.
3. William,   b. ————.
4. Catherine,   b. ————.
5. Elizabeth,   b. ————.
6. Morton Brasee, b. Sept. 11, 1868; d. July 16, 1896. No [further record.

FIFTH GENERATION.

First. John Latta, 1st of William and Elizabeth T. (Smith) Latta, married Mary E. Smith, 1885. One child, Harrison Smith Latta, born 1886.

Third. William Latta, 3d of William and Elizabeth T. (Smith) Latta, born ————; married 1st, Sarah Bennett. One child, son, James, born Dec. 1, 1880; 2d marriage of William Latta to Ellen M. Stewart; one child, a daughter, Alice, born July 8, 1888.

Fourth. Catherine Latta, 4th of William and Elizabeth T. (Smith) Latta, born ————; married 1st, ————, S. G. Griswold. One child, a son, Latta Griswold, born 1876. The second marriage of Catherine Latta Griswold to Horace S. Wade. Now resides at Orange, New Jersey.

Latta Griswold, student at Princeton Seminary.

Fifth. Elizabeth Latta, 5th of William and Elizabeth T. (Smith) Latta, born ————; married, ————, Dr. L. H. Laidley, of St. Louis, Mo. Three children:

1. Latta Laidley,   b. ———— ; died in infancy.
2. Paul Laidley,   b. in 1882.
3. Edward Laidley, b. in 1886.

THIRD GENERATION.

Eleventh. William Smith, 11th of Col. Daniel and Jane (Harrison) Smith, born Aug. 20, 1775; m. ————, Diana McDonough, born Sept. 19, 1776. Five children:

1. Edward H., b. July 1, 1799.
2. Jane H.,   b. Dec. 18, 1800.
3. James,   b. July 7, 1802; d. unmarried, Oct. 18, 1827.
4. Mary,   b. 1804.
5. William,   b. 1806.

William Smith, Sr., died Oct. 6, 1806. His widow Diana died Jan. 22, 1842.

FOURTH GENERATION.

First. Edward H. Smith, 1st of William and Diana (McDonough) Smith, born July 1, 1799; m. ————, Julia Harrison. No record of children. He died 1852. She died 1883.

Second. Jane H., 2d of William and Diana (McDonough) Smith, born Dec. 18, 1800; m. Dr. Michael Harris. Three children:

1. McDonough, b. ————.
2. James,   b. ————.
3. Crampton,   b. ————.   No further record.

Fourth. Mary Smith, 4th of William and Diana (McDonough) Smith, born 1804; m. ————, Col. Wm. B. Yancy. Seven children:

1. Diana S.,   b. ————.
2. William B.,   b. ————.
3. Edward S.,   b. ————.
4. Thomas Layton, b. ————.
5. Charles Albert, b. ————.

6. Mary Frances, b. ——; died unmarried.
7. Margaret Jane, b. ——.

FIFTH GENERATION.

First. Diana S. Yancy, 1st of Col. Wm. B. and Mary (Smith) Yancy, born ——; m. Geo. O. Conrad. Six children:

1. Thomas William, b. ——; m. 1st, Minnie Palmer; 2d, Lucy Jeffries.
2. Edward Smith, b. ——; m. Jennie Irick.
3. Mary Lynn, b. ——; unmarried.
4. Fannie Kyle, b. ——; m. Dr. T. Oliver Jones.
5. Margaret Elizabeth, b. ——; m. 1st, Jno. L. Logan; 2d, Talfourd N. Hass.
6. Geo. Newton, b. ——; m. Emily Pasco.

Second. William B. Yancy, 2d of Col. Wm. B. and Mary (Smith) Yancy, born ——; m. Julia Winsboro. Eight children:

1. William L., b. ——; m. Mary Gibbons.
2. Thomas, b. ——; m. Mollie Mauzy.
3. Stuart, b. ——.
4. Emma, b. ——; m. Chas. Gibbons.
5. Nettie, b. ——; m. Whitfield Mauzy.
6. Albert, b. ——; m. Birdie Shipp.
7. Julia, b. ——.
8. Frank, b. ——.

Third. Edward S. Yancy, 3d of Col. Wm. B. and Mary (Smith) Yancy, b. ——; m. Fanny Mauzy. Three children:

1. Charles, b. ——.
2. Joseph, b. ——.
3. Maggie, b. ——.

Fourth. Thomas Layton, 4th of Col. Wm. B. and Mary (Smith) Yancy, born ——; m. Margaret Newman. Two children:

1. William,   b. ———; m. Sallie Yancy.
2. Mary Rebecca, b. ———; m. Geo. Sipe.

Fifth. Charles Albert Yancy, 5th of Col. Wm. B. and Mary (Smith) Yancy, born ———; m. Julia Morrison. Four children:

1. Lottie,   b. ———.
2. Lulu,   b. ———.
3. Burbridge, b. ———; m. Minnie Reid.
4. Nannie,   b. ———.

Seventh. Margaret Jane Yancy, 7th of Col. Wm. B. and Mary (Smith) Yancy, born ———; m. Joseph Mauzy. Nine children:

1. Thomas,   b. ———; m. Byrd Roller.
2. Minnie,   b. ———.
3. Fannie,   b. ———; m. Prentiss Weaver. Issue, —
4. Layton,   b. ———.   [children.
5. Diana Lynn, b. ———.
6. Charles,   b. ———.
7. Virginia,   b. ———.
8. Harry,   b. ———.
9. Margaret,   b. ———.

[For the early Mauzy family, see records by the publisher hereof.]

THIRD GENERATION.

Thirteenth. James Smith, 13th of Col. Daniel and Jane (Harrison) Smith, born March 6, 1779; m. ———, 1804, Rebecca Emmett, of Augusta county, Va. In 1807, having conscientious scruples on the question of slavery, he moved to Ohio; settled at Mount Vernon; was clerk of the county court for twenty years. In religion was a member of the Christian Church, in which he was an ardent worker, filling the pulpit as well as attending to his secular duties; was the author of several books on the Trinity. He died while returning from court at Madison, Ohio, being thrown from his horse. Seven children:

1. Jane Harrison, b. 1805.
2. Diana, b. 1808. (No record.)
3. Benjamin F., b. 1811.
4. James, b. 1815.
5. Vespasian, b. 1818.
6. Adeline T., b. 1821.
7. Henrietta Clay, b. 1824.

FOURTH GENERATION.

First. Jane Harrison Smith, 1st of James and Rebecca (Emmett) Smith, born in Rockingham county, Va., Nov. 18, 1805; married Col. Charles Sagar, Sept. 25, 1823, at Mount Vernon, Ohio. Seven children:

1. Elizabeth Rebecca Jackson, b. Oct. 18, 1824; d. in Oakland, Ohio, Nov. 21, 1854; unmarried.
2. Jane Caroline, b. Jan. 19, 1827; d. in Lebanon, Ills., March 19, 1866; unmarried.
3. Diana Eliza, b. Oct. 16, 1829; d. June 22, 1898, in Lebanon, Ills.; unmarried.
4. Marcus Smith, b. Dec. 26, 1831. (See later.)
5. Charles Henry, b. in Lancaster, Ohio, Nov. 5, 1838.
6. Frances Henrietta, b. in Oakland, Ohio, Aug. 22, 1844.
7. Irene, twin sister of Frances H., died at Oakland, Ohio, Feb. 6, 1856.

FIFTH GENERATION.

Fourth. Marcus Smith Sagar, 4th of Col. Charles and Jane Harrison (Smith) Sagar, born Dec. 26, 1831; married Eleanor McMaster, Dec. 31, 1858. Three children:

1. Emma, b. ——; died in infancy.
2. Henry, b. ——; m. ——. No issue. [Chicago.
3. Adolph, b. ——; unmarried; resides with his mother in

Marcus Smith Sagar died March 30, 1897, in Chicago.

Fifth. Charles Henry Sagar, 5th of Col. Charles and Jane Harrison (Smith) Sagar, born Nov. 5, 1838; married, March 3, 1859, Amelia W. Starkel. Five children:

1. Charles Emil,   b. Jan. 15, 1860.
2. Frances S.,   b. ——— ; died in infancy.
3. Edgar Grant,   b. Oct. 30, 1864.
4. James Richard, b. Oct. 5, 1871.
5. Jesse B.,   b. ——— ; unmarried.

SIXTH GENERATION.

First. Charles Emil Sagar, 1st of Charles H. and Amelia W. (Starkel) Sagar, born at Washington C. H., Ohio, Jan. 15, 1860; married in Lebanon, Ills., Sept. 21, 1881, Addie V. Moore. Three children:

1. A daughter,   b. ——— ; died Dec. 11, 1882.
2. Charles LeRoy,   b. March 6, 1884.
3. Chauncey Moore, b. July 20, 1890.

Third. Edgar Grant Sagar, 3d of Charles H. and Amelia W. (Starkel) Sagar, born Oct. 30, 1864, in Lebanon, Ills.; married Oct. 16, 1889, Sarah Louise Gleishbrin, of Belleville, Ills. Three children:

1. Martha May,   b. Nov. 9, 1890.
2. Helen Luella, b. Sept. 5, 1894.
3. Edgar Charles, b. Jan. 8, 1898.

Fourth. James Richard Sagar, 4th of Charles H. and Amelia W. (Starkel) Sagar, born in Lebanon, Ills., Oct. 5, 1871. Is a Presbyterian minister. Res., Hardine, Ills., married Feb. 21, 1893, Bertha A. Smith, in St. Louis, Missouri. Five children:

1. Dorothy Bess,   b. Nov. 7, 1893.
2. Mildred Mae,   b. July 5, 1895; died ———.
3. Elsie Louise,   b. July 27, 1896.
4. James Donald,   b. July 22, 1898.
5. Alice Marguerite, b. Sept. 2, 1899.

FIFTH GENERATION.

Sixth. Frances Henrietta Sagar (twin sister of Irene), daughter of Col. Charles and Jane Harrison (Smith) Sagar, born Aug. 22, 1844; married Nov. 19, 1861, John H. Eckert. Three children:

1. Iona May,   b. ———.
2. Harry,   b. ———; died in infancy.
3. Frances A., b. ———.

SIXTH GENERATION.

First. Iona May Eckert, 1st of John H. and Frances H. (Sagar) Eckert, married George Nunnelly. One child, a daughter, Ethel. Iona May (Eckert) Nunnelly, died Dec., 1894.

Third. Frances A. Eckert, 3d of John H. and Frances H. (Sagar) Eckert, born ———; m. ———, Henry James. One child died in infancy. Mrs. Frances Sagar Eckert, widow, residence, Arkansas City, Kansas, resides with her daughter, Frances James.

FOURTH GENERATION.

Third. Benjamin F. Smith, 3d of James and Rebecca (Emmet) Smith, born at Mount Vernon, Ohio, 1811; was Auditor of Knox county, Ohio; and four years a member of the State Legislature. In 1857 moved to Minnesota, was Mayor of Mankato, and served as Senator from that district; was grand commander of Knight Templars of his State; Col. of the 8th Minnesota regiment, and appointed to the command of Fort Snelling during the Indian war. He married 1830, Julia Stilly. Thirteen children:

1. Rebecca, b. Feb. 2, 1831; died Aug. 26, 1849.
2. James Monroe, b. Dec. 31, 1832; died Mar. 17, 1836.
3. John Stilly, b. Apr. 7, 1834. (See later.)
4. Diana Jane, b. Jan. 23, 1836.
5. Sarah, b. July 31, 1837.
6. Mary Henrietta, b. Mar. 4, 1839.

7. Eliza Ann, b. Aug. 13, 1840.
8. Emmet Thompson, b. Apr. 17, 1842 ; d. June 22, 1843.
9. Dorcas Virginia, b. June 19, 1844 ; d. Apr. 17, 1848.
10. Benjamin Finney, b. Oct. 30, 1845 ; d. Apr. 18, 1847.
11. Adrienne Antoinette, b. Mar. 6, 1847.   (No record.)
12. Julia Adaline, b. Oct. 21, 1848 ; d. May 10, 1877.
13. Henry Warden Burr, b. Aug. 15, 1850.

FIFTH GENERATION.

Third. John Stilly Smith, 3d of Benjamin F. and Julia (Stilly) Smith, born April 7, 1834 ; m. ——, Mary Dayton. Three children :

1. Benjamin Dayton, b. ——; m. ——; has children. No further record.
2. Minnie Louise,   b. ——; died 1886.
3. Ada Lena,   b. —— ; m. ——, Harvey Williams; has children.   No further record.

Fourth. Diana Jane Smith, 4th of Benjamin F. and Julia (Stilly) Smith, born Jan. 23, 1836 ; m. Andrew C. Dunn. Seven children :

1. Mary Tillinghast, b. ——; m. Francis A. Molyneaux.
2. Gertrude,   b. ——; died in infancy.
3. Ellen,   b. ——; died in infancy.
4. Edward Gano,   b. ——; died in infancy.
5. Alice Hope,   b. ——; m. William H. Hodgman.
6. Ethel,   b. ——; died in infancy.
7. Andrew Paul,   b. ——.

Fifth. Sarah Smith, 5th of Benjamin F. and Julia (Stilly) Smith, born July 31, 1837; m. Nahum Bixby. Three children :

1. Julia, b. ——; m. Evans, now the widow Evans.
2. Jesse, b. ——; died ——.
3. James, b. ——; died ——.

Sixth. Mary Henrietta Smith, 6th of Benjamin F. and Julia (Stilly) Smith, born March 4, 1839; m. ———, Geo. Parrot. Three children :

1. Ruth, b. ———.
2. Winnie, b. ———.
3. Bernice, b. ———; died ———.

Seventh Eliza Ann Smith, 7th of Benjamin F. and Julia (Stilly) Smith, born Aug. 13, 1840; m. C. Brown. Two children :

1. Gertrude, b. ——— ; m. ———, Eugene Chamberlain. Has children.
2. Effie, b. ——— ; m. ———, Willie Chamberlain. Has children.

Thirteenth. Henry Warden Burr Smith, 13th of Benjamin F. and Julia (Stilly) Smith, born Aug. 15, 1850; m. ———, Miss Ralph. Five children :

1. Ralph, b. ———.
2. Roy, b. ———.
3. Walter, b. ———.
4. Bessie, b. ———.
5. Hazel, b. ———.

FOURTH GENERATION.

Fourth. James Smith, 4th of James and Rebecca (Emmett) Smith, born at Mount Vernon, Ohio, 1815, where he practiced law for some years, and was identified in the municipal affairs of the town ; he moved to St. Paul, Minnesota, in 1857, and has been one of the leading lawyers of the state, one of the founders of the city of Duluth, and was instrumental in the building of the St. Paul and Duluth railroad, of which he was President, Counsel, and Director for many years ; a member of both Houses of the Legislature for seven terms, and is now the oldest living representative of our family ; m. in 1848, at Mount Vernon, Ohio, Elizabeth L. Morton. Five children :

24

1. Elizabeth,   b. ——— ; d. in infancy.
2. Henrietta C.,   b. 1851.
3. Ella Augusta, b. 1852.
4. James Morton, b. 1854 ; m. ———, Elizabeth L. Mor-
                      ton, in Mount Vernon, Ohio.
5. Alice Morton, b. 1858.

James Smith, Sr., died Nov. 22, 1882.

Fifth. Vespasian Smith, 5th of James and Rebecca (Emmett) Smith, born at Mount Vernon, Ohio, Oct. 21, 1818. He graduated from the medical college of Cleveland, Ohio, practiced medicine in his native town, moved to Superior City, Wisconsin, in 1857, settled at Duluth, Minnesota, in 1870, with which city he was identified from its infancy, was one of the first Mayors, and foremost in all public enterprises ; he was the second Collector of Customs for the Port of Duluth, which position he held for nine years. Married 1846, Charlotte Neely, of Penna., born 1824. Four children :

1. Charles Emmett, b. 1847 ; died 1869.
2. Louise Eleanor, b. 1848.
3. Frank Branden, b. 1852.
4. Wm. Neely,   b. 1863 ; died 1896.

Dr. Vespasian Smith died Oct. 9, 1897.
Charlotte (Neely) Smith, his widow, died 1899.

FIFTH GENERATION.

Second. Louise Eleanor Smith, 2d of Dr. Vespasian and Charlotte E. (Neely) Smith, born 1848 ; m. 1871, Dr. McCormick. Two children :

1. William Smith, b. 1874.
2. Clinton Pristely, b. 1875.

Third. Frank Branden Smith, 3d of Dr. Vespasian and Charlotte E. (Neely) Smith, born 1852 ; m. Isabel F. Eysten, 1878. She died 1894, leaving three children :

1. Vespasian,   b. 1881 ; died 1898.
2. Pauline,   b. 1883.
3. Margaret Eysten, b. 1894.

FOURTH GENERATION.

Sixth. Adeline T. Smith, 6th of James and Rebecca (Emmett) Smith, born in Mount Vernon, Ohio, July 31, 1821 ; m. Rev. A. A. Davis, June 25, 1850, at Oakland, Ohio. Six children :

1. Adeline Augusta, b. July 29, 1851, at Frederickstown, Ohio; died Oct. 29, 1851.
2. Frederick Schiller, b. Aug. 19, 1852, at Mount Vernon, Ohio ; died December, 1852.
3. Elizabeth Rebecca, b. Oct. 13, 1853, at Sunbury, Ohio.
4. James William Smith, b. Oct. 9, 1855, at Sunbury.
5. Edward Douglass, b. June 9, 1858, at Sunbury ; died Sept. 22, 1862.
6. Fairman Hewlett, b. May 24, 1860, at Sunbury ; died Nov. 29, 1860.

FIFTH GENERATION.

Third. Elizabeth Rebecca Davis, 3d of the Rev. A. A. Davis and Adeline T. (Smith) Davis, born Oct. 13, 1853 ; m. Dec. 8, 1881, at Sunbury, Ohio, Theodore Moore. Two children :

1. Forest Benson, b. Oct. 22, 1882.
2. Ernest Smith, b. May 24, 1884.

Fourth. James William Smith Davis, 4th of the Rev. A. A. Davis and Adeline T. (Smith) Davis, born Oct. 9, 1855 ; m. Oct. 15, 1882, Addie L. Payne, of Cardington, Ohio, where they reside.

FOURTH GENERATION.

Seventh. Henrietta Clay Smith, 7th of James and Rebecca (Emmett) Smith, born 1824; m. Charles Lybrand ——, 1846.

One child, a daughter, Charlesette, born 1847.   Henrietta
Clay Lybrand died 1847.

FIFTH GENERATION.

First.   Charlesette Lybrand, 1st of Charles and Henrietta
Clay (Smith) Lybrand, born 1847 ; m. William Swartz, Nov.
27, 1867.   Six children :

1. Mary Ella,   b. Aug. 26, 1868.
2. Addie Elizabeth,   b. Mar. 13, 1871.
3. Daisy,   b. Dec. 5, 1873.
4. Henry Ferdinand,   b. Sept. 9, 1875.
5. James Benjamin,   b. July 26, 1877.
6. Geo. Charles Lybrand, b. May 27, 1879.

Charlesette Swartz died June, 1880.

The Smith, Harrison and Cravens family records were
courteously supplied by Mr. William P. Tams, of Staunton,
Virginia, and Mr. Roger Morris Smith, of St. Matthew's, Jefferson county, Kentucky.   These gentlemen have spent much
time and thought in the study of their family history.

For any errors in the mechanical construction of the paper
the publisher is responsible.   In several instances where dates
are omitted from the records, there were doubts as to the order
of birth of various members of the families.   The publisher
hopes his arrangement of them will be found satisfactory, and
will welcome any corrections, additional data, or historical
data.

HARRISON FAMILY OF AUGUSTA AND ROCKING-INGHAM COUNTIES, VA.

Thomas Harrison, the founder of this family, on March 15, 1744, obtained from Lieut.-Gov. William Gooch a grant for 258 acres of land in Orange county, later Augusta county, situated at the head spring of the east fork of Cook's Creek. Of his early life, or the date of his death or that of his wife, nothing definitely is known; it is claimed by some of his descendants that he belonged to the James River Harrisons; of this, however, we find no proof; some writers claim that he was an immigrant direct to Chester county, Penna., then to Orange county, Va., about 1743.

The publisher is of the opinion that Thomas Harrison descended from one of the early Maryland immigrants, some of whom are known to have settled in Virginia, in what was then Stafford county, about 1700; after 1730 Prince William county, which at this date embraced the counties of Fairfax, Loudoun and Fauquier; this territory being the natural route to Augusta county, where about 1743–4 he removed and settled on Cook's Creek. After 1690 the names of several branches of the Harrison family disappear from the Maryland records, and later are found in Virginia, but owing to the destruction of the early records of Stafford, and many of those of Prince William counties, it is doubtful if satisfactory record proof can be obtained. Of the children of Thomas Harrison we have no record, except that of Daniel.

SECOND GENERATION.

Daniel Harrison, son of Thomas and Jane (Delahage) Harrison, born in 1700 (perhaps Charles county, Md.); was twice married: 1st, to Margaret Cravens, a sister of Robert. Seven children:

1. Robert,   b. 1725.
2. Daniel, Jr., b. 1727.   No record.

3. Jesse,   b. 1729. No record.   [record.
4. Mary,   b. 1733 ; m. Wm. Cavanaugh. No further
5. Jane,   b. 1735 ; m. Daniel Smith, Sr. See record.
6. Abigal,   b. 1731 ; m. Jeremiah Reagan. No record.
7. Benjamin, b. 1741.

Margaret (Cravens) Harrison died in 1753.

The second marriage of Daniel Harrison to Sarah Stephenson, widow of William, in 1760, whose will was proven May 16, 1759. As in 1761 Sarah Harrison joined her husband (Daniel) in making deeds to some of his lands. Daniel Harrison, Sr., died July 10, 1770.

THIRD GENERATION.

First. Robert Harrison, 1st of Daniel and Margaret (Cravens) Harrison, born 1725 ; died unmarried in 1761 ; his will bearing date May 4, 1761, was proven at Augusta county Court Aug. 18, 1761. In this will reference is made to his father Daniel Harrison ; his brother Jesse ; Ann, the daughter of brother Jesse, under 18 years of age ; his brother Daniel, Jr.; to Daniel Smith, the husband of his sister, Jane, born 1735 ; to Daniel Smith's son, Robert Smith ; his brother, Benjamin Harrison; his sisters, Mary and Abigal Harrison. Appointed his brother-in-law, Daniel Smith, and Jesse Harrison, executors. Silas Hart, Hugh Hamilton, William Minter and William Gregg, witnesses.

Seventh. Benjamin Harrison, 7th of Daniel and Margaret (Cravens) Harrison, born 1741 ; died 1819 ; married Mary McClure, born 1745, died 1815, daughter of John. One child, a son, Peachy, of whom we have record, born April 6, 1777 ; graduated in medicine ; became a distinguished physician ; was an active Christian, and characterized throughout life by public spirit, integrity and benevolence ; married, Feb. 29, 1804, Mary Stuart, born Sept. 12, 1783, daughter of John and Frances (Burnsides) Stuart, daughter of John and Mary Burnsides. Mary (Stuart) Harrison died Sept. 19, 1857, aged 74 years. Had issue eight children :

1. Edward Tiffin, b. Aug. 20, 1805 ; d. June 21, 1828.
2. Gessner, b. June 26, 1807. (See later.)
3. Frances Moore, b. Feb. 23, 1809 ; d. July 10, 1810.
4. An infant, b. Feb. 28, 1815 ; d. young.
5. Mary Jane, b. Nov. 5, 1816 ; d. Dec. 17, 1889.
6. Margaret Frances, b. April 24, 1818. (See later.)
7. Caroline Elizabeth, b. May 22, 1822 ; d. Sept. 5, 1890. (No further record.)
8. Peachy Rush Harrison, b. Jan. 4, 1825.

FOURTH GENERATION.

Second. Gessner Harrison, 2d of Peachy and Mary (Stuart) Harrison, born June 26, 1807. In 1825 entered the University of Virginia. Took the degrees of medicine and ancient languages in July, 1828. On Aug. 10, 1828, was appointed professor in the school of ancient languages, which position he held until his death, on April 7, 1862. He married, Dec. 15, 1830, Eliza Lewis Carter, daughter of Professor George Tucker, of the University of Virginia. Ten children :

1. Maria Carter,	b. Nov. 14, 1831.	
2. Mary Stuart,	b. Feb. 10, 1834.	
3. George Tucker,	b. July 23, 1835.	
4. Edward Tiffin,	b. Sept. 9, 1837.	
5. Peachy Gessner,	b. Dec. 24, 1839.	
6. Charles Carter,	b. May 10, 1842 ; d. Feb., 1882.	
7. Henry William,	b. Sept. 15, 1844.	[No record.
8. Eleanor Rosalie,	b. July 16, 1847.	
9. Robt. Lewis,	b. March 2, 1850. No record.	
10. Francis Washington,	b. Feb. 15, 1852 ; d. young.	

FIFTH GENERATION.

First. Maria Carter Harrison, 1st of Gessner and Eliza Lewis (Carter) Harrison, born Nov. 14, 1831 ; d. Oct. 21,

1857; m. Nov. 14, 1849, Rev. John A. Broddus. Three children :

1. Eliza Sommerville, b. ———.
2. Ann Harrison,   b. ———.
3. Maria Louisa,   b. ———.

Second. Mary Stuart Harrison, 2d of Gessner and Eliza Lewis (Carter) Harrison, born Feb. 10, 1834; m. July 31, 1853, Prof. Francis H. Smith, of the University of Virginia. Twelve children.

SIXTH GENERATION.

First. Eliza Lewis Carter Smith, 1st of Frances H. and Mary Stuart (Harrison), born ———; m. William W. Walker, of Westmoreland county; died Sept. 2, 1880.

Second. Eleanor Annabel Smith, 2d of Frances H. and Mary Stuart (Harrison), born ———; was twice married : 1st, to Fielding Miles, of Blacksburg, Va. Issue, a daughter, Elise Miles. Second marriage to Professor Kent, of the University of Virginia. One child, a daughter, Eleanor Kent, born ———.

Third. Francis Albert Smith, born ———; died in infancy.

Fourth. Maria Smith, born ———; died in infancy.

Fifth. Lelia Maria Smith, 5th of Frances H. and Mary Stuart (Harrison) Smith, born ———; married Lucien Cocke, of Roanoke, Va. Four children :

1. Frances,   b. ———.
2. Mary Stuart, b. ———.
3. Lucien,   b. ———.
4. Janie,   b. ———; d. April 5, 1899.

Sixth. Gessner Harrison Smith, 6th of Frances H. and Mary Stuart (Harrison) Smith, born ———; graduated in law; settled at Kansas City, Mo., where he practiced his profession, and died Feb. 18, 1892.

Seventh. Summerfield Smith, born ———; died in infancy.

Eighth. Geo. Tucker Smith, 8th of Frances H. and Mary Stuart (Harrison) Smith, graduated in medicine, is a surgeon in U. S. Navy.

Ninth. Mary Stuart Smith, born ———; died Oct. 15, 1900. No further record.

Tenth. Rosalie Smith, 10th of Frances H. and Mary Stuart (Harrison) Smith, m. Dr. J. Carrington Harrison. One child, a son, Francis Henry.

Eleventh. Courtnay Smith, died in infancy.

Twelfth. Duncan Smith, 12th and youngest child of Francis H. and Mary Stuart (Harrison), born ———. Art student, New York City.

FIFTH GENERATION.

Third. Geo. Tucker Harrison, 3d of Gessner and Eliza Lewis (Carter) Harrison, born July 23, 1835, graduated at the University of Virginia, studied Civil Engineering, was a surgeon in the Confederate army throughout the war; resides in New York, where he is well known as a physician; m. Lelia Bell. Three children:

1. Gessner, b. ———. Physician in New York City.
2. Lelia Bell, b. ———.
3. Elizabeth, b. ———.

SIXTH GENERATION.

Third. Elizabeth Harrison, 3d of Geo. Tucker and Lelia (Bell) Harrison, born ———; married Wm. E. Echols, Prof. of Mathematics, University of Va. Two children:

1. Lilly,   b. ———.
2. Marion Patton, b. ———.

FIFTH GENERATION.

Fourth. Edward Tiffin Harrison, 4th of Gessner and Eliza Lewis (Carter) Harrison, born Sept. 9, 1837; d. Dec. 2, 1873. (No further record.)

Fifth. Peachy Gessner Harrison, 5th of Gessner and Eliza Lewis (Carter) Harrison, born Dec. 24, 1839; m. ——, Julia Riddick. Four children :

1. Edward,   b. ——, at Richmond.
2. Gessner,   b. ——, at Richmond.
3. Lewis,   b. ——, at Richmond; a student at the
                                      [University of Virginia.
4. Julia Peachy, b. ——, at Richmond. Res., Richmond, Va.

Seventh. Henry William Harrison, 7th of Gessner and Eliza Lewis (Carter) Harrison, born Sept. 15, 1844; graduated in medicine, is a practicing physician in Roanoke, Va. No record.

Eighth. Eleanor Rosalie Harrison, 8th of Gessner and Eliza Louisa (Carter) Harrison, born July 16, 1847; m. ——, Wm. Mynn Thornton (Prof. of applied mathematics in the University of Virginia). Six children :

1. John,   b. ——. Medical student in the
2. Eliza Carter,   b. ——.   [University of Va.
3. Eleanor Rosalie,   b. ——.
4. Janet,   b. ——.
5. William Mynn, Jr.,   b. ——.
6. Charles Edward,   b. ——.

FOURTH GENERATION.

Sixth. Margaret Frances Harrison, 6th of Peachy and Mary (Stuart) Harrison, born April 24, 1818; m. Wm. F. Stephens; died June 13, 1858. No further record.

Eighth. Peachy Rush Harrison, 8th of Peachy and Mary (Stuart) Harrison, born Jan. 4, 1825; entered the University of Virginia on October 1, 1841 ; graduated in medicine, July 4, 1846 ; attended Clinical lectures in Philadelphia, and commenced the practice of medicine in Harrisonburg, Virginia, as his father's partner in the spring of 1848 ; married June 6, 1848, Mary Frances Rodes, born Jan. 14, 1828 ; daughter of William, of Albemarle.   Two children :

1. Mary Lynn, b. May 5, 1850.
2. Lucy May, b. April 2, 1852.

CRAVENS FAMILY OF AUGUSTA COUNTY, VA.

Of Robert Cravens, whose family have intermarried with that of the Smith and Harrison families of Augusta and Rockingham counties, Virginia, but little is known.   He is believed to have first immigrated into Orange county, with the Smiths and McDowells, about 1740.   He married Mary Harrison, a sister of Daniel.   He was a large planter, and for his day a man of wealth in lands, etc.   He was the brother of Margaret Cravens, wife of Daniel Harrison, of Augusta county.   (See Harrison family.)   He died in Augusta county in 1762, where his will, bearing date Oct. 2, 1761, was proven May 18, 1762, in which are mentioned the following legatees :

1st.   His wife Mary (Harrison) Cravens.
2d.   His son John Cravens.
3d.   His son William.
4th.   His daughter Margaret (Cravens) Harrison.
5th.   His daughter Agnes.
6th.   His daughter Margaret (Cravens) Smith.
7th.   His son Robert.
8th.   His daughter Elizabeth (Cravens) Smith.
9th.   His two grandsons, Robert and John Cravens.
10th.   His granddaughter Mary (Cravens) Black, wife of Robt.

SECOND GENERATION.

First. John Cravens, the son of Robert and Mary, born
———; m. the widow Dyer, relic of William. He died July,
1778, leaving a family of children. No further record.

Second. William Cravens, son of Robert and Mary, born
———; was a soldier in the French and Indian wars, and is
frequently referred to in the preceding pages of this work;
married Jane ———. No further record.

Third. Margaret Cravens, daughter of Robert and Mary,
born ———; m. her cousin Zebulon Harrison.

Fourth. Agnes Cravens, daughter of Robert and Mary,
born ———; m. Samuel Hemphill.

Fifth. Maggie Cravens, daughter of Robert and Mary,
born ———; m. Henry Smith, son of Abraham, son of Capt.
John. (See Smith record.)

Sixth. Robert Cravens, Jr., son of Robert and Mary, born
———; m. Hester ———; died April 27, 1784.

Seventh. Elizabeth Cravens, daughter of Robert and Mary,
born ———; m. ———, Benjamin Smith, son of Daniel and
Jane (Harrison) Smith. (See Smith record.)

BROWN FAMILY OF AUGUSTA AND BATH COUNTIES, VIRGINIA.

John Brown, born Feb. 15, 1743, O. S., in Ireland; probably of Scotch-Irish parentage, immigrated from Dublin to
America about 1760; doubtless through the influence of Capt.
John Smith, McDowell and others, who had twenty years
previously settled in the upper valley of Virginia. He married Mary Donnelly about 1778, who was born in America of

NOTE.—No effort has been made by the publisher to trace the descendants
of the children of Robert Cravens and his wife Mary (Harrison) Cravens.

Irish parentage in 1761, and settled in the Warm Spring Valley on the Cowpasture River, a branch of the James, called by the Indians Wallahatoolah. His tract of land containing 400 ácres was known as Flowing Spring, named from a series of springs which flowed at irregular intervals, gushing out of the earth in such an unusual manner as to attract the attention of Thomas Jefferson and other writers on Virginia.

During the Revolution John Brown enlisted a company of militia soldiers in Augusta county from the neighborhood in which he lived, of which he was captain, and Robt. Thompson, lieutenant, Col. Sampson Matthews, commander; his company marched to Richmond, thence to Petersburg and Amelia county, where they saw active service; was in the engagement with the British at the battle of Hot Water, and again at the battle of Green Spring (Jamestown), in which Major Brown (then Capt.) was taken prisoner July 6, 1781.

Upon the organization of Bath county, Aug. 26, 1791, Major Brown was commissioned one of the first justices for the county, which position he continued to hold until his death; was also Capt. of militia for the county, occupying various positions of trust, as Sheriff and Treasurer for Bath county, and later was Major in command of the 2d Battalion of Bath county militia; April 12, 1796, was elected a member of the General Assembly of the state of Virginia, and again in 1802–3–4. Lieut. Robt. Thompson, Jan. 8, 1833, in his declaration for a pension says: he was commissioned Lieut. of Virginia militia of Augusta county, and served as such under Capt. John Brown; that he was in the battle of Hot Water and at Jamestown; that they marched to Richmond, Petersburg, Amelia county, etc., under command of Col. Sampson Matthew, and was with Gen. Campbell, Wayne and Morgan.

Mary (Donnelly) Brown, wife of Capt. John, died about April, 1815, as a deed bearing date April 1st, of this year, was signed by her, but not acknowledged. Major Brown died Feb. 6, 1830, his will bearing date Nov. 6, 1824, with codicil dated March 17, 1828; was proven June term of Court, 1830;

recorded in Liber 4, folio 39, will book of Bath county, Va. To his two daughters, Peggy (Brown) Wallace and Rosannah (Brown) Morgan, he devised all lands on the east side of Cowpasture River, etc., to be divided equally between them, each to pay their brother Joseph Brown $250.00; to his grandson N. I. Brown Morgan, a negro boy; to his grandson John Brown Wallace, a negro boy; the residue of his estate, real and personal, to his son John Brown; he to pay his brother Joseph $500.00; and directed his body to be buried by the side of his deceased wife. Appointed John Brown, Gerard Morgan and Joseph Wallace, executors. Witnesses: Matthew Wallace, Charles Harnsell and William Benson.

The codicil makes his granddaughter, Mary Ann Blackburn Brown, a beneficiary.

TRANSCRIPT FROM THE BROWN FAMILY BIBLE.

John Brown, born Feb. 15, 1743, O. S.
Died Feb. 6, 1830, at 11 o'clock p. m.
Mary Brown, wife of above, died July 7, 1824, in the 63d year of her age.

Five children :

1. Charles Brown, born April 6, 1779; died Aug. 16, 1780.
2. Joseph Brown, born Dec. 2, 1780; married Nancy Smith, July 20, 1802. He died June 10, 1829.
3. Peggy (Margaret) Brown, born April 1, 1784; married Joseph Wallace, Nov. 16, 1808. She died March 29, 1828.
4. John Brown, born Tuesday, May 8, 1787; married, 1st, Sept. 15, 1818, Adelaide Kyle; 2d, May 16, 1850, ———, at the age of 63, his wife's age 30. He died Sept. 2, 1861.
5. Rosannah Brown, born on Friday, April 17, 1789; married June 21, 1810, Gerard Morgan.

EARLY MARRIAGES, ORANGE COUNTY, VA.

Barnett, William, to Elizabeth Carrer, 1771.
Barber, Thomas, to Mary Thomas, 1771–74.
Hawkins, Moses, to Susan Strother, Mar. 3, 1770.
Herndon, Zachariah, to Mary Scott, 1771.
Johnson, William, to Ann Barnett, Feb. 10, 1770.
Sisson, ———, to Millie Braham, 1771–74.
Taylor, Zachriah, to Alice Chew, 1771.
Terrell, Zachriah, to Millie Walker, 1771.
———, George, to Catherine Spencer, 1771–74.

[From the fly-leaf of a memorandum book, Orange Court House. Where names or dates are omitted, the record is defaced by time.—Pub.]

FROM THE MARRIAGE BONDS OF ORANGE COURT HOUSE.

Hawkins, John, to Mary Gaines, widow, Apr. 28, 1780.
Helm, William, to Matilda Taliaferro, May 31, 1784.
Head, Benjamin, to Margaret Carr, Aug. 21, 1784.
Head, John, to Nancy Sanford, Nov. 26, 1787.
Head, Tavenah, to Janney Pluncket, daughter of Jesse, Dec. 20, 1798.
Hawkins, Benjamin, to Sallie Scott, Mar. 1, 1799.
Hawkins, James, to Betty Coleman, Sept. 3, 1799.
Head, George Marshall, to Millie Rucker, Nov. 10, 1799.
Hawkins, James, to Elizabeth Keeton, daughter of John, Nov. 11, 1799.
Hanks, Rodny, son of Reuben and Elizabeth, to Alice Chandler, March 26, 1803.
Hawkins, Moses, to Joyce Quisenberry, Apr. 23, 1804.

MARRIAGES SOLEMNIZED IN ALBEMARLE COUNTY, VIRGINIA, BY THE REV. JOHN GIBSON, FROM 1800 TO 1846.

John Gibson was born 1759, in Culpeper county, Virginia, son of Peter, where he resided until 1782. He was reared on the plantation of his father with only the limited opportunities of the Log Cabin School House for an education, and these but for three months in the year.

September 30, 1778, at the age of nineteen, he enlisted as a private soldier in the Culpeper county militia, or minute-men, under Capt. Francis Miller, with whom he marched from Culpeper to Orange, thence to Spottsylvania, thence to Essex county, and later to Mobinhills, below Richmond, at which place his command was stationed four weeks with troops from all parts of Virginia. Subsequently they marched to Williamsburg, where he remained till the end of the service for which he enlisted.

In 1779 he again enlisted for three months, as a substitute for his father, Peter, under Capt. James Smith; was at Williamsburg, Norfolk and Jamestown. In April of that year he was honorably discharged.

In 1781 John Gibson was drafted, on his own account, by Capt. Fisher Rice, under whom he marched from Culpeper to Louisa county. He served until discharged, returning to his home in Culpeper. In 1782 he removed with his parents to Albemarle county, where he married and reared a large family, living in the same neighborhood for sixty-eight years.

In early life Mr. Gibson made a profession of religion, and joined the Methodist Episcopal Church. In 1793 he was licensed by the Quarterly Conference of said Church as a local minister, and as such performed many marriages in the community in which he lived. He kept a record of these marriages from 1800 to 1846. On Aug. 3, 1846, he filed the same in the United States Pension Office with his application for a pension, from which application the foregoing facts have been taken, together with the following list of marriages:

Austin, Samuel and Elizabeth Johnson, Sept. 9, 1801.
Austin, Renelder and Mahala K. Wats, February 11, 1830.
Austin, Henry and Henrietta Dickerson, January 26, 1830.
Ansel, Robert and Harriet Boswell, May 14, 1835.
Allen, Orville and Sarah Ann Davis, December 18, 1844.
Archer, James W. and Nancy Roberts, May 10, 1846.

Bush, Aaron and Mary Meadows, November 11, 1804.
Bingham, Wyat and Rebecca Bingham, July 23, 1812.
Breading, James and Rachel Gibbins, April 9, 1816.
Bingham, John and Mary Harshbarger, August 22, 1816.
Burns, James and Elizabeth Knight, April 28, 1818.
Brickham, Blewford and Elizabeth Catterton, Dec. 17, 1822.
Brown, Bernis and Patsey M. Garrison, December 22, 1822.
Brown, Clifton and Sally Brown, January 30, 1823.
Brown, Garland and Patsey Ballard, September 23, 1824.
Breading, Ephraim and Jenny Haney, October 15, 1824.
Bingham, George and Priscilla Ross, June 8, 1824.
Bedders, Fielding and Hannah Mohler, Aug. 20, 1824.
Brown, George S. and Amanda Brown, November 18, 1830.
Burkhead, Francis and Emily Wood, January 24, 1832.
Burton, Aylett and Patsey Williams, January 1, 1833.
Baker, Noah and Susan Going, September 19, 1833.
Brian, James and Elizabeth Freek, October 1, 1834.
Blackwell, William B. and Mary Elizabeth Sims, September 10, 1835.
Bruce, Louden B. and Lina Shiflett, April 20, 1837.
Bryan, Robert and Lurania Jollett, January 16, 1839.
Baughker, Asa and Eliza Rucker, March 4, 1842.
Breading, Harrison and Lucretia Morris, September 19, 1843.

Conley, David and Catharine Wyant, March 10, 1804.
Collier, Martin and Fanny Marshall, January 30, 1817.
Coleman, William and Nancy Dowel, June 11, 1818.

25

Carthra, Charles and Elizabeth Brown, October 6, 1818.
Connel, Timothy and Nancy Wyant, March 7, 1822.
Cretshall, Godfrey and Sally Wood, December 21, 1824.
Crawford, Obadiah and Anna Wyant, June 16, 1825.
Catterton, Michael and Lucy Mills, May 22, 1826.
Connell, John and Tilda Morris, August 6, 1829.
Crawford, Wade and Elizabeth Morris, Nov. 17, 1829.
Collier, Chapman and Charlotte Morris, Jan. 26, 1830.
Connell, Zachariah and Drucilla Morris, Feb. 6, 1834.
Collier, Caswell and Elizabeth Haney, April 27, 1837.
Coatney, John and Nancy Smith, Feb. 4, 1838.
Currier, James and Louisa Shiplett, Dec. 19, 1839.
Collier, George and Susan Shiplett, Jan. 21, 1842.
Cave, Hiram and Madison Shiplett, June 5, 1844.

Duke, William and Linny Gibbs, January 2, 1803.
Dowel, Major and Frankey Jones, Nov. 15, 1804.
Dowel, Major and Elizabeth Martin, April 28, 1807.
Davis, Thompson and Nancy McClary, May 12, 1808.
Davis, John and Sally Davis, Jan. 4, 1809.
Dowel, William and Sally Picket, Jan. 18, 1810.
Douglas, George and Rhoda Bingham, April 3, 1810.
Dean, George and Mary Rindle, Feb. 18, 1811.
Davis, Lewis and Susana Sandridge, Feb. 15, 1814.
Davis, Lewis and Dosha Ham, May 17, 1814.
Dowel, John and Emily Walton, Nov. 11, 1814.
Dickenson, John and Ann Brown, Jan. 17, 1815.
Davis, Robin and Lucy Shiplett, March 16, 1815.
Dossey, John and Nancy Marshall, Dec. 10, 1816.
Dunn, James and Betsey Collins, Nov. 12, 1818.
Dunn, John and Elizabeth Johnson, Nov. 8, 1822.
Dossey, Richard and Milly Howard, Jan. 15, 1824.
Dunnavan, William and Fanny Knight, March 15, 1825.
Davis, Isaac and Martha Langford, Nov. 26, 1829.
Durrett, Thomas G. and Frances Sims, Sept. 30, 1830.
Dickinson, Nimrod and Elizabeth Robinson, Dec. 16, 1830.

Dickerson, William and Ellen Lane, Jan. 25, 1831.

Dowel, Madison and Elizabeth Huckstep, October 10, 1831.

Dunn, James and Elizabeth Gentry, July 10, 1834.

Dowel, Fountain and Lucy Ann Bingham, Jan. 19, 1837.

Dunn, James and Carolina Salmon, Sept. 19, 1839.

Davis, Smith and Mary Snow, Jan. 17, 1840.

Davis, John C. and Agnes Jane Robert, Jan. 12, 1843.

Davis, William F. and Ardena Wyant, Dec. 31, 1844.

Davis, Elijah and Barbrana Shiplett, April 23, 1846.

Estes, Elisha and Maria Bingham, August 24, 1815.

Ellis, Thomas and Mary Ballard, April 5, 1821.

Early, James and Milly Thompson, Dec. 11, 1828.

Elliott, Parrott and Amanda A. Cattleton, Oct. 5, 1843.

Elliott, Marshall and Malinda Shiplett, April 9, 1846.

Frazier, John and Lucy Shiplett, January 20, 1811.

Fishel, Robert and Nancy Walton, Jan. 6, 1831.

Frazier, Livingston and Delithia Rosanber, Aug. 19, 1834.

Frazier, John H. and Mary I. Morris, April 5, 1836.

Frazier, James and Sarah I. Rucker, Dec. 23, 1838.

Frazier, Michael and Virinda Shiplett, July 4, 1844.

Grimes, David and Sallie Sexton, January 12, 1801.

Gentry, John and Patsey Hicks, Nov. 25, 1804.

Gentry, George and Elizabeth Dunn, Nov. 1, 1808.

Gibson, Pater and Fanny Estes, Dec. 24, 1809.

Gaines, John and Anna Gaines, Jan. 11, 1810.

Gentry, Christopher and Sally Dunn, Aug. 2, 1810.

Gaines, Thomas and Louise Evans, Jan. 17, 1811.

Garrison, Volly and Sarah Dowel, Aug. 29, 1816.

Gaines, Henderson and Malinda Gaines, Jan. 4, 1820.

Gardener, Wilson and Milly Ballard, Sept. 21, 1820.

Gardner, Garland T. and Mary Garrison, Oct. 17, 1822.

Gentry, Fountain and Ann Knight, Feb. 9, 1823.

Greenning, Isaac and Polly Stone, Dec. 23, 1824.

Garten, James A. and Nelly Sullivan, Dec. 18, 1828.

Garrison, Yelly and Nancy Perce, Dec. 31, 1828.

Greening, Nehemiah and Elizabeth Keyseer, Nov. 22, 1830.

Garrison, Ralph and Frances Marshall, Dec. 22, 1831.

Goings, Henderson and Agnes Goings, Jan. 19, 1831.

Garrison, Robert and Sarah Dunn, Aug. 23, 1831.

Gentry, Austin and Jane F. Nailor, Jan. 3, 1833.

Garrison, William and Nancy Sullivan, Jan. 17, 1833.

Going, Levi and Frances Going, Sept. 19, 1833.

Gardner, Brightbury B. and Lucinda Wood, Nov. 7, 1833.

Gardener, James and Mary Wood, October 25, 1835.

Gear, Nathaniel and Sarah Lamb, March 23, 1836.

Goring, Charles and Matilda Middlebrooks, July 30, 1835.

Garrison, Ryland and Rhody Keatin, Dec. 22, 1836.

Graham, William, Esq., and Lucinda P. Eddens, April 14,

Gentry, John and Caroline Douglas, Dec. 5, 1840.   [1840.

Garrison, John and Delila Monday, Dec. 22, 1842.

Gibson, Leroy and Elizabeth Goodall, Sept. 24, 1842.

Goodall, James and Pyrna Gibson, Sept. 22, 1842.

Garrison, Austin and Sarah Jane Taylor, Dec. 20, 1842.

Gentry, James and Luthana Sandridge, Nov. 6, 1845.

Hicks, Joel and Elizabeth Davis, Nov. 30, 1800.

Harvey, Richard and Dolly Gentry, January 3, 1805.

Hall, Nathan and Julia Ham, May 5, 1805.

Herndon, Edward and Polly Mayab, Nov. 6, 1806.

Herring, Willis and Elizabeth Roch, Nov. 16, 1806.

Harvey, Anthony and Polly Bingham, Feb. 25, 1808.

Ham, Joseph and Elizabeth McCawly, August 15, 1811.

Hall, John and Annie Wilkinson, January 1, 1818.

Harris, Lansy and Dosha Ann Bailey, August 9, 1821.

Haney, James and Aggie Lamb, March 4, 1824.

Howard, Richard and Elizabeth Pettet, Nov. 2, 1824.

Hoffman, William and Fanny Mitchell, July 22, 1828.

Haws, John and Elizabeth Offal, Jan. 28, 1830.

Hoye, Isaac and Mildred Hamble, March 15, 1831.

Huckstep, William G. and Frances Ann White, Oct. 9, 1831.

Hall, Lewis and Elizabeth Seamans, May 20, 1831.
Howard, Eli and Ann Marshall, May 22, 1834.
Hall, Samuel and Elizabeth Dowel, Oct. 2, 1834.
Hupp, Jacob and Matilda Lawson, March 25, 1837.
Hall, Wootson and Sarah Wilkinson, Oct. 30, 1838.
Hall, Richard M. and Lurania Powell, March 3, 1839.
Ham, Robert and Mary Douglas, March 27, 1843.
Hall, Richard and Sarah Gwin, July 20, 1846.

Johnson, Martin and Polly McClary, Nov. 8, 1805.
Jarrell, Willis and Malinda Herring, June 4, 1829.
Jones, Isaac and Rebecca Vier, Dec. 24, 1829.
Jackson, William E. and Susan Jane Gentry, Dec. 21, 1830.
Jackson, Stephen and Dosha Gowen, Feb. 3, 1831.
Jarrell, James and Kiziah Hufman, April 16, 1838.
Jear, Thomas and Nancy I. Lamb, Oct. 16, 1845.

Keating, James and Elizabeth Dowel, Jan. 18, 1812.
Keaton, Nathan and Jane Keaton, May 29, 1828.
Keaton, James and Sarah McCawley, Oct. 27, 1829.
Knight, William B. and Polly Morris, Dec. 28, 1830.
King, Sabrat and Jerusha Herring, Oct. 15, 1835.
Keaton, Lively and Sophia Shiplett, Jan. 5, 1838.
Keaton, James and Betsey Powel, Jan. 19, 1842.

Lawson, John and Eve Hornest, Feb. 14, 1803.
Lamb, John and Lucy Knight, Nov. 8, 1820.
Lain, Thedunk (Theodore) W. and Dorcas McCud, Aug. 8, 1821.
Lune, Aaron W. and Frances Dickerson, Jan. 26, 1831.
Langford, Garrett and Jane Sandridge, Dec. 6, 1832.
Lawson, Moses and Rebecca Goodall, Dec. 29, 1833.
Lamb, Henry and Elizabeth Catterton, Jan. 2, 1834.
Lawson, Alfred and Frances Wyant, Aug. 10, 1834.
Lawson, Joseph and Selina Snow, Feb. 17, 1835.
Lamb, Johnson and Nancy Varant, April 25, 1837.
Long, James and Sarah Beasley, May 9, 1839.
Lamb, James and Isabella Craig, April 14, 1839.

Lankford, Warner and Frances Fisher Walton, July 16, 1840.
Long, John and Rebecca Long, Nov. 9, 1843.
Lawson, Theopholis and Carolina Herring, April 14, 1844.
Long, Laton and Rebecca Jane Gibson, Dec. 4, 1845.

Morris, Elisha and Sally Davis, Oct. 16, 1804.
Morris, John and Nancy Shiplett, Oct. 25, 1804.
Meadows, John and Elizabeth Wyant, March 6, 1806.
Morris, David and Polly Morris, March 30, 1809.
Meadows, James and Mary Wyant, June 22, 1809.
Mason, Reuben and Maria Mason, Sept. 18, 1812.
Maupine, John and Rosana Maupine, Nov. 12, 1812.
Morris, Davis and Nancy Shiplett, May 14, 1813.
Mason, Matthew and Fanny Marshall, January 13, 1814.
Marshall, James and Fanny Roberson, Oct. 20, 1815.
Maiden, William and Sally Gardner, April 9, 1816.
Morris, Simpson and Juda Shiplett, Aug. 26, 1818.
Morris, Blewford and Mary Dunnivan, Dec. 25, 1818.
Marshall, Eppa and Nancy Dunn, Jan. 11, 1821.
Marshall, Wiley and Sally Dossey, Jan. 6, 1824.
Milliway, Isaac and Judith Milliway, Jan. 12, 1825.
Marshall, Henry and Dolly Shiplett, Oct. 5, 1825.
Marshall, Greensville and Frances Marr, Jan. 1, 1828.
Marshall, Wilson and Sophia Beddows, Jan. 6, 1828.
Martin, George and Elizabeth Burkett, May 4, 1826.
Mason, Enoch and Frances Payne, Jan. 5, 1832.
Morris, Absalom and Nancy Knight, Feb. 16, 1832.
Mooney, Thornton and Elizabeth Sullivan, Feb. 23, 1832.
Maupine, David and Virginia Mills, April 5, 1832.
Mooney, John and Vienna Sullivan, Aug. 16, 1832.
Mallory, Nathan and Cally Harris, Nov. 6, 1832.
Mallory, Alfred M. and Nancy Williams, Feb. 26, 1834.
Marshall, Thornton and Polly Shiplett, Feb. 27, 1834.
Morris, Tabner and Eliza Shiplett, Dec. 25, 1835.
Mason, Thompson and Harriet Cave, Jan. 21, 1836.
Maupin, John D. and Narcissa Davis, March 3, 1836.

Moyers, Michael P. and Susan Melone, March 8, 1836.

Morriss, Garrett and Sarah Baughker, April 17, 1836.

Marshall, Tavener and Airy Gibson, Sept. 6, 1836.

Melton, James C. and Martha Pretchett, Nov. 8, 1836.

Marshall, Fountain and Judith Gardner, Dec. 22, 1836.

Marshall, Ansel and Elizabeth Lamb, Jan. 5, 1837.

Morris, Gordon and Margaret Douglas, March 23, 1837.

Marshall, William and Mary Ann Shackelford, May 4, 1837.

Maupine, Pleasant and Sarah Catterton, Aug. 31, 1837.

Marshall, William and Malinda Lawson, Jan. 18, 1838.

Malloy, John B. and Elizabeth Roberts, March 8, 1838.

Marshall, Winston and Jane Norford, July 26, 1838.

Morris, Lively and Kiziah Frazier, Nov. 27, 1838.

Morris, Garrett and Martha Malloy, Jan. 24, 1839.

Maiden, James and Mary Ann Wyant, Aug. 6, 1840.

Morris, Joseph and Polly Shiplett, Oct. 1, 1840.

Morris, Revily and Delila Morris, April 15, 1842.

Mallory, Elihu and Nancy Collier, Nov. 15, 1842.

Morris, William and Sally Shiplett, Sept. 25, 1843.

Morris, Riley and Harriet Morris, Nov. 7, 1843.

Morris, Henry and Lucy Shiplett, Jan. 16, 1844.

Morris, Harrison and Caty Morris, Dec. 19, 1844.

Morris, Luis and Elvanda Morris, Dec. 19, 1844.

Mills, David W. and Sarah E. Richards, Feb. 20, 1845.

Monday, Meredith and Mahuldy Hall, April 20, 1845.

May, Edmond and Elvina Snow, Oct. 22, 1845.

Morris, Pleasant and Susan Frances Frazier, Dec. 4, 1845.

McCawley, Peter and Agnes Garrison, Jan. 8, 1807.

McCollister, Jacob and Jeane Maiden, June 8, 1809.

McDaniel, Amsted and Julia McCawley, March 20, 1815.

McDaniel, Ellis and Nancy Shiplett, June 3, 1819.

McClary, John and Jane Davis, March 25, 1823.

McDaniel, John and Patsey Snow, April 28, 1825.

McClary, Isaac and Amanda Davis, Dec. 10, 1829.

McCawley, Thomas and Polly Keating, June 15, 1830.

McClary, George and Betsey Walton, Feb. 16, 1831.

McDaniel, Reuben E. and Sally Dunn, Dec. 20, 1836.
McCallister, Benjamin and Frances H. Dickerson, Feb. 29, 1839.
McGee, Angus and Polly Shorb, Oct. 30, 1842.

Nailor, John and Elizabeth Wells, Dec. 4, 1806.
Norris, Caleb and Harlena Harris, Dec. 22, 1837.
Norris, William and Mary Gibson, Jan. 24, 1839.
Norris, Jurrile and Virindy Morris, March 18, 1842.

Olava, Ealy and Martha Rhodes, Oct. 6, 1836.

Pense, John and Polly Smith, Jan. 11, 1807.
Powell, James and Betsey Powell, Oct. 31, 1816.
Powell, Robert and Nancy Shiplett, March 31, 1829.
Powel, Simon and Clarissa Lamb, August 30, 1832.
Powell, Yancey and Elizabeth Ann Beadle, Oct. 24, 1833.
Powell, Sinclair and Delilah Frazier, Dec. 31, 1834.
Parrott, William H. and Mary Wilcox, Jan. 29, 1834.
Parrott, William and Nancy F. Thompson, Feb. 21, 1835.
Patterson, John and Harriett Shiplett, Sept. 29, 1839.

Rucker, Javis (or Jarvis) and Milly Grayson, June 10, 1810.
Roach, Jacob and Elizabeth Haney, Sept. 13, 1810.
Roberts, Curtis and Sally Chewning, March 17, 1814.
Rife, Henry and Milly Bingham, June 6, 1816.
Rucker, Dewet and Nelly Rucker, Feb. 27, 1817.
Rippito, William and Rachel Stone, Dec. 21, 1823.
Runkle, William and Elizabeth Powell, Feb. 6, 1827.
Runkle, George and Frances Powell, Feb. 7, 1828.
Roberts, John H. and Mary White, Dec. 30, 1830.
Robert, John and Lucy Lamb, Jan. 6, 1833.
Randolph, Richard and Phoebe Huffman, June 2, 1833.
Rapp, John and Frances Ann Elizabeth Walton, March 11,
    1834.
Roach, Mickelberry and Angelina Rucker, Jan. 31, 1839.
Robert, Durrett and Amanda Lamb, Feb. 4, 1842.

Riddle, James and Frances Riddle, May 25, 1843.
Riddle, William and Nelly Riddle, May 25, 1843.

Sullivan, Richardson and Polly Marshall, Nov. 15, 1900.
Sandridge, Reuben and Jestin Keaton, Oct. 9, 1804.
Shiplet, Thomas and Susanah Wyant, Feb. 11, 1807.
Shiplet, Overton and Sallie Herring, Jan. 20, 1809.
Sampson, William and Sally Sampson, Sept. 26, 1810.
Snow, Lewis and Polly Dunn, Jan. 3, 1811.
Shiplet, Edward and Joice Herring, March 7, 1811.
Shiplet, Thomas and Lucy Ham, Sept. 19, 1811.
Shiplet, Nathaniel and Betsey Proctor, Jan. 7, 1812.
Shiplet, Stephen and Joanna McDaniel, Jan. 11, 1816.
Shiplet, Michael and Minnie Shiplet, Feb. 10, 1817.
Snow, Henry and Polly Snow, May 27, 1818.
Sandridge, Stephen and Mira P. Gardener, March 22, 1821.
Shiplet, Micajah and Lotty Shiplet, Aug. 29, 1821.
Shiplet, Preston and Martha A. Thacker, Dec. 19, 1821.
Stone, Henry and Polly Michael, Jan. 9, 1823.
Sullivan, Jeremiah and Frances Collins, Jan. 1, 1824.
Shiplet, John and Polly Shiplet, Aug. 25, 1824.
Shiplet, Gaitwood and Lucinda Snow, April 14, 1825.
Shiplet, Burrel and Patience Shorb, Feb. 28, 1827.
Stevens, William and Lucy White, Aug. 22, 1827.
Sandridge, Nicholas and Elizabeth Sandridge, May 1, 1828.
Sullivan, Sinclair and Frances Luck, Aug. 7, 1828.
Shiplet, Benson and Teana Shiplet, Nov. 6, 1828.
Shiplet, Washington and Sally Morris, March 2, 1830.
Sullivan, David and Polly Seamans, Dec. 23, 1830.
Sandridge, William and Elizabeth Garrison, Jan. 6, 1831.
Sandridge, Joel and Frances Sandridge, Nov. 24, 1831.
Shiplet, Brightbuar and Tempy Shiplet, Jan. 25, 1831.
Sims, Blewford and Mildred Austin, Feb. 2, 1831.
Shiplet, Valentine and Jane Shiplet, Sept. 4, 1832.
Sandridge, Nathan and Jane H. Gardener, Jan. 3, 1833.
Shiplet, Lewis and Eliza Keaton, Jan. 30, 1834.

Shiflet, Fielding and Mary Shiflet, Nov. 6, 1834.
Sandridge, Benjamin and Salina Ellett, Nov. 20, 1834.
Shiplet, Burton and Nancy Frazier, Dec. 1, 1834.
Shiplet, Kinnel and Mary Ann Lawson, March 22, 1835.
Smith, Thomas and Elizabeth Harris, June 5, 1835.
Shurmond, George W. and Eliza Catterton, Oct. 13, 1885.
Sandridge, Michael and Nancy Talor, Nov. 17, 1835.
Shiplett, Davis and Julia Morris, March 24, 1836.
Shiplett, William and Polly J. Shiplett, April 13, 1836.
Snow, Obadiah and Nancy Watson, April 17, 1836.
Shiplett, Ahaz and Jenny Shiplett, April 21, 1836.
Shiplett, Nelson and Carry Davis, May 23, 1836.
Sandridge, Austin and Sarah Sandridge, Aug. 18, 1836.
Sandridge, Joel and Susan Wood, Sept. 28, 1836.
Shiplett, John and Elizabeth Shiplett, March 16, 1837.
Smith, Dobert and Nancy Lamb, May 14, 1837.
Sandridge, Nathan and Parmelia Garrison, Aug. 29, 1837.
Shiflet, Henderson and Milly Shiflet, Dec. 22, 1837.
Shiplett, Wiley and Margaret Shiplet, Jan. 3, 1838.
Shiflett, Solomon and Frances Collier, October 18, 1838.
Stephens, Livingston N. and Sarah Parrott, Nov. 28, 1838.
Sandridge, Pleasant and Charlotte Wilkinson, Dec. 6, 1838.
Shiplett, Asa and Jane Shiplet, Dec. 10, 1838.
Shearman, Thomas and Ann E. Early, Dec. 13, 1838.
Shiplett, Smith and Sarah Shiplett, Dec. 23, 1838.
Shiplett, Forril and Catharine Morris, Jan. 15, 1839.
Shiflet, Harry and Caroline Bateman, June 16, 1840.
Shiplett, Jackson and Harriet Bateman, June 16, 1840.
Shiplett, Stephen C. and Mary M. Collier, Oct. 28, 1840.
Shiplett, Solomon and Winney Shiflet, Jan. 21, 1842.
Shiplett, Hardin and Theodosia Ham, May 19, 1842.
Shiplett, Nicholas and Nancy Lawson, Jan. 11, 1843.
Shiplett, Morton and Rosalania Shiplett, June 5, 1843.
Shiplet, Sampson and Claussa Shiplet, Dec. 28, 1843.
Shiplett, Henry and Eliza Morris, Jan. 25, 1844.
Shiplet, Haston and Liddy Shiplett, March 30, 1845.

Tyre, Alexander and Franky Gaines, April 22, 1813.
Turk, Archibald and Jane Maupin, Oct. 14, 1813.
Thompson, William and Mary Ballard, Sept. 4, 1816.
Tyre, Garrett and Margaret Barnett, Aug. 11, 1829.
Thacker, John and Jane Shorb, Nov. 19, 1829.
Thorp, Peter and Elizabeth Middlebrook, July 31, 1830.
Thomason, Thomas and Catherine Smith, Feb. 15, 1830.
Tate, Noah and Jency Goings, Oct. 25, 1831.
Taylor, John W. and Johanna H. Taylor, March 12, 1835.
Thrift, George and Eliza Early, Feb. 14, 1838.
Turner, Robert and Peachey Morris, Dec. 27, 1838.

Via, Clifton and Judy Sandridge, Feb. 8, 1816.
Vier, John A. and Mary Maupin, March 13, 1832.
Via, Hiram and Harriet A. Nalor, March 10, 1836.
Via, Thomas M. and Nancy J. Dunn, Dec. 20, 1836.

Ward, John and Jenny Seamans, March 6, 1801.
Warran, James and Sally Rucker, Feb. 21, 1808.
Wells, William and Polly Howard, Dec. 15, 1808.
Wood, Levi and Susanah Esters, Oct. 20, 1811.
Wood, John and Sally Jones, Jan. 13, 1814.
Walton, Jesse and Nancy Gentry, May 9, 1816.
Wood, James and Rebecca Marshall, Dec. 23, 1817.
Wayland, Jeremiah and Mary Ramsay, Jan. 14, 1819.
Ward, Samuel and Mildred Norris, Feb. 8, 1820.
Ward, John and Sarah Ward, Oct. 2, 1822.
Wood, Achillis and Polly S. Via, Nov. 28, 1824.
Walton, Warring and Lucinda Sandridge, Oct. 21, 1825.
Wyant, David and Elizabeth Lawson, Dec. 5, 1826.
Wyant, Pater and Polly Frazier, March 11, 1829.
White, Garott and Dicey Gentry, March 19, 1829.
Whitehead, William and Malinda Cox, Feb. 20, 1830.
Wood, Willis and Emily Walton, March 1, 1830.
Wilerson, Nicholas and Nancy Luck, Nov. 15, 1832.
Wood, Ezekiel and Patsey Thomas, March 14, 1833.

Wolfe, George and Ellen Ferguson, April 14, 1833.
Walton, Ison W. and Ann Dickerson, Aug. 11, 1835.
Wood, Zachariah and Mary Ann Wood, Dec. 22, 1835.
Watson, Benjamin and Eliza Hughes, Sept. 8, 1836.
Watson, John and Macy Lamb, Sept. 19, 1837.
Wyant, Frederick and Elizabeth Barnes, April 1, 1838.
Wood, Nimrod I. and Dosha A. Maden, Aug. 19, 1842.

"Please note: Pages 397 and 398 were old advertisements which we eliminated."

INDEX.

(399)

26

27

28

Owen, John, 227
Owsley, Governor, 296
Owsley, William, 220

Page, John, 25
Paines, George, 8
Palmer, Job, 227
Palmer, Minnie, 363
Pangle, Henry, 178
Parker, Richard, 131
Parks, Andrew, 357, 358
Parks, Bushrod Washington, 357
Parks, Creed, 357
Parks, Harriot Washington, 357
Parks, Margaret Davis, 357
Parks, Mary Ida, 320
Parris, Thomas, 8
Parrot, Bernice, 369
Parrot, George, 369
Parrot, Mary Henrietta, 369
Parrot, Ruth, 369
Parrot, Winnie, 369
Pasco, Emily, 363
Patterson, Anne, 300
Patterson, Benjamin G., 298
Patterson, Charles S., 294, 297
Patterson, James, 300
Patterson, Jean, 300
Patterson, John, 300
Patterson, John A., 297, 298
Patterson, Margaret, 298, 300
Patterson, Martha Allen, 300
Patterson, Mary, 297, 300
Patterson, Nancy, 300
Patterson, Samuel, 298, 300
Patterson, William, 298, 300
Patton, James, 332
Paul, Miss, 252
Payne, Addie L., 371
Pay-roll for a detachment of 3d Virginia

Regiment 1776 (names not indexed), 176, 177
Pay-roll of officers of the Virginia continental line 1782, 1783 (names not indexed but arranged in alphabetical order), 134–170
Pay-roll of regiment from Northern Neck of Va. and Md., commanded by Col. Theodoric Bland for Nov. and Dec., 1777 (names not indexed), 185–215
Peachy, William, 127
Peaco, Belle, 275
Peale, Ann Taylor, 346
Peale, Walter Newman, 346
Pearce, William, 239
Peel, Bernard, 242
Peel, Catherine, 242
Pendleton, Edmund, 25
Pendleton, James, 133
Pendleton, Philip, 246
Percy, Sir George, 5
Peregoy, Moses, 269
Peregoy, Sarah, 269
Perry, 397
Perry, Commodore, 354
Peters, Alice, 355
Peters, Richard, 127, 232, 233
Pettis, 397
Peyton, Francis, 217
Peyton, John S., 261
Peyton, Sarah Martha, 261
Peyton, Valentine, 116, 117, 118, 119, 120, 133
Peyton, W. S., 261
Peyton, Willie Anna, 261
Phelon, P., 231
Philips, Ann, 220
Philips, Jeremiah, 178
Pickens, Andrew, 313, 314

438

INDEX.

Webb, Fleta Hope, 303
Webb, Iota Joy, 303
Webb, James Warfield, 303
Webb, Joseph B., 303
Webb, Sarah Jane Cornelia, 303
Weeden, George, 129
Weems, 397
Welch, Ann, 253
Welch, Elizabeth, 219, 253
Welch, George, 227
Welch, James Barbour, 253
Welch, John, 251, 253
Welch, Lucy, 253, 255
Welch, Laura, 251, 252
Welch, Mr., 307
Welch, Nathaniel, 253
Welch, Sallie, 253
Welch, Thomas Newman, 253
Welch, Veranda, 253
Welch, Wilhelmina, 251
Welsh, Caroline Amelia, 349
Welsh, Catherine G., 349
Welsh, John, 312
Welsh, Levi, 349
Welsh, Mary, 312
Wert, Joseph, 256
Wert, Lucy Florence, 256
Wert, Nannie, 256
West, Francis, 6
West, George, 216, 217, 219, 221
West, James Lee, 270
West, John, 6
West, Kate S., 270
West Point, garrison at, 1784, 229–231
West, Thomas, Lord de la Warr, 5
Westmoreland county, soldiers of the French and Indian war (names not indexed), 102
Weyman, Elizabeth, 313
Weyman, Emily, 313

Weyman, Joseph, 313
Weyman, Mr., 313
Weyman, Samuel, 313
Whaley, James, 218
Wheeler, Benj., 227
Whitcomb, Major, 175
White, 397
White, A. S. J., 342
White, Elizabeth Standeland, 361
White, Ellen, 342
White, Isaac, 227
White, Joel, 218, 219
White, Mary Lou, 254
White, Maude, 342
White, Sim, 227
White, William, 361
Whittle, Conway McNeece, 345
Whittle, Mary Conway, 345
Whittle, Rosalie Beirne, 345
Whittle, William C., 345
Whittle, William Tams, 345
Wigg, William, 227
Wiggington, Spence, 219
Wilcocks, Charles, 180
Wilcocks, Letitia, 180
Wilcocks, William, 227
Wilcox, Eleanor, 221
Wildman, Joseph, 218
Wilkie, William, 227
Willett, 397
Williams, Ada Lena, 368
Williams, Catherine, 242
Williams, Ephraim, 16
Williams, Harvey, 368
Williams, James, 227
Williams, John, 218
Williams, Lewis, 256
Williams, Lucy, 256
Williams, Thomas, 218
Wills, Margaret Taliaferro, 317

29

ERRATA.

Munroe, last line page 7, should be Monroe.
McCome, 21st line page 41, should be McCone.
Loudon, 3d head line page 88, should be Loudoun.
Zachriah, 33d line page 179, should be Zachariah.
Earling, 4th line page 217, should be Farling.
Russeell, 23d line page 218, should be Russell.
Respess, 14th and 25th line, page 219, should be Respass.
Conard, 22d line page 220, should be Conrad.
Quiesenberry, 14th line page 274, should be Quisenberry.
Conger, 24th and 25th line page 278, should be Conyer.
Notes of William Craig (head line), page 291, should be Birth and Death
Record from Tombstones.
Conard, 18th line page 302, should be Conrad.
Arrabella, 5th line page 321, should be Arabella.
Kempers, 7th line page 323, should be Kemper.
And, beginning 29th line page 331, should not appear.
Elverton, 27th line page 336, should be Yelverton.
Emmet, 20th line page 367, should be Emmett.
Emmet, 2d line page 368, should be Emmett.
Pristely, 29th line page 370, should be Priestly.
Frances, 11th, 14th, 22d and 29th line page 376, should be Francis.
Frances, 3d and 8th line page 377, should be Francis.
Conger, page 406, should be Conyer.

In all cases where official records are printed, the original spelling is given.